CREW CHIEF

W9-BZF-569

CREW CHIEF

by

Jesse T. McLeod

Daring Books
Canton • Ohio

Published by Daring Books
Box 20050, Canton, Ohio 44701

∞

Library of Congress Cataloging-in-Publication Data

McLeod, Jesse T., 1947-
    Crew chief / by Jesse T. McLeod.
      p.   cm.
    Includes bibliographical references.
    ISBN 0-938936-78-6 : $16.95
    1. Vietnamese Conflict, 1961-1975--Personal narratives,
American. 2. Tet Offensive, 1968. 3. McLeod, Jesse T.,
1947- . I. Title.
DS559.5.M42 1988
959.704'38--dc19   88-25711
                                                       CIP

Printed in the United States of America

Dedication

To Molly and Galen. May this book in some small way help you to understand why I'm so emotional and sometimes cry without explanation.

Contents

Acknowledgments

The author is grateful to the following persons for their help: Deborah McLeod, who gave me the courage to start what ended up taking seven years to finish, Dave Keck, who planted the seed for the book in a hayfield and kept encouraging me through the years (Dave also helped with editing and provided me with the sourcebook I needed by Shelby L. Stanton titled *Vietnam Order of Battle*.) Paul Streater and Rupert Sparks, Jr. helped me most with R&R. Doctor Alan Bachman put me in touch with Major Richison and others of the Ohio Army Aviation Reserves such as Mr. Guest and Mr. Lindsay, and others too numerous to mention. Thanks also to Joan McLeod who did the final editing before it was sent to the publisher, and to all my family and friends who kept encouraging me to keep writing.

My special thanks go to Judy McLeod, without whose patience and many typings, I could never have finished. I am also greatly indebted to Dr. Richard Pinkerton of California State University, who was instrumental in helping me to get the book published. Finally, these acknowledgments would be incomplete without crediting Jesus Christ, whose divine protection not only kept me alive in Vietnam, but also enabled me to recall many of the events and conversations that took place so many years ago.

Introduction

I fell out of bed one night in the midst of a nightmare. My wife asked the obvious question, "Were you dreaming?"

"Yes."

"Would you like to tell me about it?"

"I don't remember what it was about."

That was what came out of my mouth. Oh, how I wanted to pour out my heart, to share my memories, to release what was locked within me, yet, I could not. To talk about Nam, the real Nam, the Nam of pain and suffering and fear was, for me, an impossibility. Sure, I could tell of an occasional funny experience or of the long hours of boredom, but not the stuff nightmares are made of.

Not long after that, I was at a luncheon meeting where one man seated at my table seemed to be doing all the talking. "Why can't these guys from Vietnam just forget about it and get on with their lives? Why do so many of them have marriage problems? After all, a lot of those guys have been back for ten years or better, and it's time to quit crying about it.They're just a bunch of cry babies."

I looked up from the table top I'd been staring at and saw the one man in the group (a WW II vet) who knew I was a Vietnam vet. He looked me in the eye and I knew he wanted my approval to speak. I shook my head ever so slightly as if to say, please don't tell him, but he spoke anyway.

He asked the first gentleman, "Have you heard any of their stories? Have you felt their fear or experienced their humiliation at the hands of people like yourself? If you haven't walked in their shoes, then maybe you should keep your big mouth shut."

The thing that bothered me most was, "How were people ever going to understand if no one told them what we went through?" Sure, the vast majority of guys who served in Nam never saw that first minute of combat. There was only a small percentage of us who were exposed to combat almost every day. How do you explain to someone what it was like? The ups, downs, the harassment, the fear, the constant fatigue. These aren't things one tries to explain in a half hour.

After much thought and encouragement by a high school history teacher, I decided to write this book. My goal is to help those who wish to understand us to come a little closer to that end. For me, it has been very painful to remember and write about and I apologize if the content of the stories or language offends anyone. I ask the reader to remember that the average age of the Vietnam Vet was only 19, and many pray like David, "Remember not the sins of my youth and my rebellious ways; according to Your love remember me for You are good, O Lord," Psalm 25:7 NIV. Some of the story is my own, some of it belongs to others I've known, but most all of it has a basis in fact.

I will begin during the 1968 Tet Offensive.

My personal experience was that Tet was a time of the most vicious and most intense fighting during my tour. I didn't like living part of it. You may find parts of it you don't like reading. Yet, these are some of the stories locked in our memories, so I ask you, "Is it worth remembering?" To me, it was necessary.

I have talked with fellow Vietnam veterans who were in companies similar to mine. Some of these men have only good memories of Nam and consider it to have been a "good gig." One former pilot told me he'd never been shot at, let alone taken any hits or been shot down. The one thing that is obvious to me as I speak with other vets is that no two men had the same experience. As I thought about it, I realized that each company had its own rules and those rules changed with a new commander. The constant moving of men from spot to spot and the shifting of personnel from company to company caused a stirring that made it impossible for one vet to say whether or not another's stories were true. For example, I had three different "permanent" pilots and countless spot pilots during the time I flew. The co-pilots changed on a daily basis as did (for the most part) the door gunners. I did have several permanent door gunners on my ship, but none lasted more than thirty to forty days. My point in all of this is that there are combat veterans who didn't experience any trauma and some are questioning those who did. Every person alone knows what he went through, and for some it's impossible to explain or discuss those feelings.

Jesse T. McLeod

1

"Prepare for War! Rouse the warriors! Let all the fighting men draw near and attack." Joel 3:9 NIV

Guard Duty

Jim MacLaughlin enjoyed his job as a crew chief on a UH-1 Huey about as much as he hated pulling guard duty. He took a great deal of pride in his work. As a result, he was well-liked and respected by most of the officers and enlisted men in his company. He always did his best to be as clean as possible and to present himself as a soldier who was proud of his uniform.

He had been "in Country" since May and had been flying since early October. It was January, to be exact, the twenty-ninth of January. The first day of the Vietnamese New Year would start tomorrow. In honor of that event, both sides had declared a thirty-six hour truce which would start at 1800 hours that night.

Pulling guard duty in Jim's company was a fact of life for everyone whose rank wasn't sergeant or higher. On this night, Jim had two more hours before he had to report for guard. Of all the different types of duty he had pulled, guard was second only to KP (Kitchen Police) in terms of undesirability, although, guard wasn't so bad if you were lucky enough to be assigned to interior as opposed to bunker duty. Of all the times he had pulled guard duty, only once had it been interior duty. The rest of the time (about every ten days) he'd been stuck on the bunkers. Interior duty was preferred because one never had to leave his own company area and thus, could sleep in his own bed when not on duty. The responsibility when on interior duty was simply to walk around the company area looking for anything or anyone who wasn't supposed to be there. This walk occurred sometime during the night and usually lasted only two hours. The officer in charge of guard duty hardly ever checked on the interior guards once they started their duty—primarily because he usually couldn't find them. There wasn't any assigned pattern they had to follow. Each man was responsible for waking the next person and was not supposed to leave his post until the replacement had dressed and relieved him.

Bunker duty was a lot different. The bunkers were musty little one-room hollow mounds made out of sandbags. The outside of the bunkers looked like they wouldn't withstand a good, big, healthy wind, let alone an enemy attack. The sandbags were so deteriorated that many had broken open, spilling their contents. Since the bags had been filled with local soil, the bunkers gave the appearance of large gray warts that had died after hemorrhaging from various ulcers and open sores.

Some of the guys called the local soil, "laterite". Jim was sure it was some type of red clay with a high mineral content and just enough small stone to make it hard to shovel. Filling sandbags with it when it was wet required two shovels—one shovel to dig the soil and the other to scrape it off the first. When the bags and their contents dried out, it was like one solid block of concrete. Filling sandbags with it when it was totally dried out required the use of a pick first. But then, one of the first things a soldier learned about sandbags was to never, ever, put sand in them. Sand is simply too easy to shovel and put into bags, plus it doesn't require all the extra work of the locally available soil. It wasn't hard to look at a bunker and tell which part had been built with wet soil and which with dry. When the wet soil in the bags dried, the bags themselves rotted away and a solid block remained.

To enter the bunker, one walked through the open doorway, made an immediate right turn, took three steps, turned left, took three more steps, turned left again, and arrived in one large room. The entranceway had wood pallets for flooring, which had two purposes: first, they kept the guards out of the mud during the rainy season, and secondly, they made it impossible to enter the bunker quietly. Once in the bunker, one had all the comforts of home. The walls were decorated with leaky sandbags, and there was a twenty-five watt bulb in the middle of the six-foot ceiling. Each bunker came equipped with a set of bunk beds and mattresses, with barely enough space between the top and bottom to turn over. The mattresses looked and felt like they were left over from WW II. The floor was dirt and there was the ever present musty smell one would expect from a medieval dungeon. In the wall that faced 'no mans land' was a series of three small openings, through which one could shoot or simply look out.

Jim decided he should quit thinking about the bunkers and start getting ready. He still had a lot to do and only two hours before reporting for guard. One good thing about bunker duty was that it meant getting the next day off and as much as Jim enjoyed flying, he was more than ready for a day off. Being a crew chief with the 187th Assault Helicopter Company had provided him with a lot of different experiences. Some of the things he did, he enjoyed; others he found to be disgusting, nauseating parts of the war. He badly wanted and needed a break, even if for only a day. His body felt tired and his mental alertness had begun to slip noticeably from the long, stressful hours. He had been on more single ship night missions in the last two weeks than during the whole time he'd been flying. Single ship night missions were usually death-defying feats of bravery with a high casualty rate and, consequently, were hated by most guys.

Jim had several misgivings about this cease fire. The first was that if they could stop the fighting for thirty-six hours, why couldn't they stop it forever? His second and primary concern was that everywhere he looked, he saw signs of a massive build-up by the enemy and, almost everyday, his company saw North Vietnamese Army Regulars (NVA), or at least some signs of their existence. American troops were involved in more sustained fighting—something the Viet Cong wouldn't do under any conditions. The NVA alone would stand and fight. Only a month ago, American troops were complaining that the Cong wouldn't fight, they just melted away. Now, almost every day, they were seeing heavy action and were taking some pretty severe losses. The enemy fire directed at Jim's company was a lot more accurate of late, and it seemed that everyday at least one chopper took a hit. A month ago that was unheard of.

The M16 in Jim's bunk had been completely broken down and

cleaned, a job he performed almost every night. When in a hurry, Jim cleaned only the two spots that would inevitably cause jamming: the firing chamber and the trap door spring. If the firing chamber had sand or dirt in it, the bolt wouldn't seize onto the shell and eject the spent cartridge, a situation that had cost more than one GI his life. As Jim reassembled his M16, he made sure each part was spotless and would thus pass the inspection that was always a part of guard duty. Jim put the reassembled rifle in his wall locker, got out the shoe polish and started on his boots. The easiest way to stay out of trouble on guard duty was to be very sure every part of his uniform was perfect before reporting for duty. Jim finished his boots, stripped, put on a towel and his shower thongs, picked up the soap, and headed for the showers. He had just recently started to wear the thongs to the enlisted men's showers. No one had thought it important until one of the guys from maintenance stepped barefoot on a scorpion. He was taken to the hospital screaming with intense pain.

The water was nice and warm as usual in the early afternoon. Jim looked around and saw that some of the other guys going on guard that night were already present. All the showers in Tay Ninh were of the same construction: large black water tanks mounted on overhead platforms, which allowed water to flow by gravity to the shower head below. This arrangement worked fine unless one was unfortunate enough to be taking a shower when the water ran out. Then, not only was there not enough water to finish, but one also got covered with sand and dirt drawn from the nearest river by the transport truck earlier that day. Having finished his shower and brushed his teeth, Jim headed back to the hooch to dress.

Jim's hooch was like all the rest, a building about 16′ by 30′ with a cement floor, wood sides half way up and wire mesh up to the metal roof. Inside was one large room with an aisle through the entire length and doors at either end. On both sides of the aisle, spaced every so often, was a foot locker. Behind each foot locker was an army bunk with green mosquito netting held up by four, three-foot poles. Beside each bunk and, against the wall, was each man's wall locker.

He could smell the sickeningly sweet aroma of pot almost from the moment he entered the hooch. His company was in the process of drawing up battle lines between the pot users and the non-users.

Jim had never been a user but, like most guys, had simply kept his mouth shut and looked the other way. Now, he was falling more and more into the camp of the radical non-users. He'd heard all the arguments from both sides, yet, when he sat back and looked at it, it was only the users who claimed what a great thing it was and how it didn't affect their personalities or performance. Jim didn't agree, for he had witnessed more than one GI who had been a good soldier, proud of himself as reflected in his dress and conduct, until he'd started smoking pot. Once on pot, there seemed to be a gradual change in his conduct and general outlook on life.

In fact, he had seen it enough times that he could draw up a typical transition profile of a user. The almost undetectable change in users started with neglecting little things like haircuts. Progressing into heavier use, it seemed to cause a kind of laziness exhibited by neglect of one's personal appearance and surroundings. Little things, like not sweeping up their area each morning or making their bunks, were usually followed by personal degeneration. Wearing clean clothes became unimportant, hair was left unwashed and often showers were skipped altogether. Eventually, a user became a general slob and his vocabulary dwindled to a handful of words. Their performances on the helicopters were much the same. Jim disliked flying with a pothead, regardless of his job or rank. More often than not, the door gunners didn't clean their guns, and one never knew what a stoned pilot was going to do. Crew chiefs really into pot flew in ships that Jim wouldn't get into for anything. Fortunately, he now had enough time in the company and enough respect that he rarely had to fly in someone else's plane. He knew from observation that some of the potheads didn't change oil filters, pull inspections, grease bearings or do a lot of the things a crew chief was supposed to do. Sloppy maintenance was easy to get away with as long as one took the time to adjust the log book accordingly.

If a crew chief didn't feel like pulling his fifty hours inspection, which took about two hours by himself, and included such things as engine and transmission oil filter inspection and oil changes, he could get away without being caught by turning in his log book as though it had been done. As a result, it was nearly impossible for anyone other than the crew chief, whose ship was parked next door, to know if the inspection had been pulled or not. So Jim knew who around him was and was not pulling inspection. After all, if he spent two nights a week pulling inspections and performing other tasks on his ship, it wasn't too hard to figure out why the guy on his right never did.

It was the crash about a week ago of a chopper in Jim's platoon that had really brought things to a head and started the conflict between the users and non-users. Things had been really slow that day when, suddenly, the next to the last ship in the flight went down. The flight had just dropped off troops and started to climb, when at about one hundred feet, a MAY DAY came over the radio.

"May Day! May Day! This is Chalk Nine going down!"

That was all the pilot had time to get out before the ship crashed. The chopper behind Chalk Nine circled and landed but found no one alive. Since there hadn't been a fire or explosion, the wreckage had been sling loaded back to Tay Ninh.

Late that night, a group of guys collected at the club to discuss it over a beer. During the conversation, the company clerk said he had been ordered to fill out paperwork as though they had been shot down by enemy fire and were, thus, listed as "killed in action". The crew chief on Chalk Ten reported that it looked to him like Chalk Nine's main rotor had quit turning, but he really wasn't sure. The fellows from maintenance thought that made a lot of sense, since one of them (against orders), sneaked out to the wreckage and pulled the transmission and engine oil filters. He claimed the engine filter looked okay, but the transmission's internal filter had so much metal in it, he could hardly get it out to look at it. As the crew chiefs talked about it, no one could remember seeing the crew chief do any recent maintenance. No one in the group disputed the fact that their dead comrade was a lazy pothead. The next day the wreckage was sling-loaded to Saigon. The cause of the crash was supposed to be determined there, but no one heard anymore about it. If it hadn't been for the fact that one of the most well-liked pilots in the company had been killed in that crash, nothing more would have come of it. As it was, that crash was the constant topic of conversation, and a lot of the guys blamed the potheads for his death. Things that were tolerated a few days earlier, no longer were, and a lot of the men were making it tougher on the users.

Pot had a smell all its own, and once Jim walked into his hooch he knew it was in use. Slowly he walked down the aisle looking in each bunk for the perpetrator. There wasn't anyone in the hooch, but Kenny's bunk looked like someone had spent the day in it. Jim figured it must have been Kenny, but whoever had been smoking before he walked in must have walked out the other door only seconds before. Since no one was around, he headed back to his own bunk to finish getting ready for guard.

Jim put on a clean uniform and the boots he had just polished. As he dressed, he began to wonder if he would get stuck with perimeter duty tonight or get to pull interior duty, where he could sleep in his own bed. By now he was ready to go. His watch told him he still had fifteen minutes before time to report. This was a good time to add a few lines to a letter. As he sat down on his foot locker, the platoon's main flunky, Bob Kenny, came in the door with his pet monkey.

Sp/4 Kenny, a short, stocky man with round features, had been a door gunner who hadn't taken very good care of his guns. As a result, he rarely flew and was put on details such as driving water trucks, picking up the platoon's gunners after the flight had landed, and supervising the Vietnamese civilians doing manual labor in the company area.

"Hi, Mac, I see you've got guard tonight."

"Yes, in about fifteen minutes. Put on a record, would you please?"

Kenny put the monkey down, got his record player out and put on The Supremes. Kenny's favorite record started right out with, "I Hear a Symphony". The monkey had climbed unnoticed into the rafters and started squawking. Jim couldn't help but laugh, thinking that Diana Ross wouldn't appreciate that accompaniment. Suddenly, something hit Jim on the left shoulder. He turned his head to look and by reflex his hand went up to brush it off, when the foul smell and sight of monkey shit on his clean uniform hit him.

Jim's face went red with anger!

"Dammit, Kenny, that sorry-ass monkey just threw shit at me. Man, I've told you before, I'm going to kill that son-of-a-bitch and this is the day."

"Mac, don't use your M16. You'll have to clean it again before guard.

Besides, you should be leaving right now."

Jim was so mad he couldn't see straight. He knew Kenny was right. It was time to leave and now he had to change shirts and wash his hands. He hurriedly changed as he told Kenny, "I hate that damned monkey and everybody else in the hooch does too. You'd better get rid of it before it does something to the Captain or one of the pilots."

The monkey sat in the far corner of the rafters screaming with delight. "Mac, twenty years from now you'll think about this and laugh. You'll remember it as part of the good times."

"Kenny, there is nothing about this place that is worth remembering. Especially you and that damn monkey!"

Jim fell into formation just as his name was being called by the Sergeant of the Guard. He was assigned bunker duty, and it wasn't long before the inspection was over. The OD* didn't seem any happier about being on guard than any of the enlisted men. He made sure each man knew what was expected of him and that his weapon was clean. After chow they would be given the code.

Everyone but the officer ate together. So Jim asked around until he found someone from the OD's company. "What's Lieutenant Tetley like?"

"Oh, he's fair enough, doesn't believe in pulling chicken shit on you. Do your job and he won't bother you, screw up and he'll hang ya."

Jim's bunker was at the west end of the flight line. Everything that took off and landed had to fly over his bunker. He was really kind of glad it worked out that way. All he had to do was listen for the gunships to take off and land and he would have a pretty good idea of how the truce was holding up. If the gunships were constantly going in and out, it wasn't going to be a quiet day tomorrow. He wasn't too concerned, though. He had tomorrow off.

There were four men in the bunker with Jim. They cut a deck of cards one guy had brought to determine who had what shift. When Jim pulled the card that gave him the one o'clock shift, he thought the only way for things to get better would be for him to go to bed at once. He'd had a monkey throw shit on him, got stuck on perimeter

---

*O.D. - Officer of the Day - Officer in charge of guard detail.

duty, and then got stuck with the worst time slot possible, one to three in the morning. Jim found a bunk and laid down.

"Hey, man, wake up. It's your shift."

"I'm not on until one o'clock."

"It is one o'clock, get up so I can go to bed."

Jim got out of bed and asked what had been happening.

"Not a thing."

"Phone hasn't rung, no flares, nothing?"

"You got it."

"How about the choppers, they been flying?"

"Yeah, they've been going in and out all night. The guy with the shift before me said it started about ten or ten-thirty, and it's been going on ever since. Why did you ask about the choppers?"

"It's my company and, if there is that much activity, the truce has to be long since over."

Jim picked up the starlight scope and looked out through the darkness in front of his bunker. The ghostly green light that enabled him to see into the darkness showed him that nothing was moving out front. He looked for the orange strip on the claymores'* backs, found each one and felt a lot better at once. He knew the orange strip was put on a claymore's back so the defender could tell where the mines were after dark. Jim had heard more than one grunt** tell about watching an orange strip slowly turn, or look out and see their claymores still there but no orange strip. The VC*** had turned them around so that when the GI blew the claymore, he blew it at himself.

Jim placed his M16 where he could grab it to fire in a hurry, then pulled the blackout curtain before turning on the light to check the M60.**** It checked out okay. So Jim again killed the light and opened

---

*Claymore mine - a mine that is flat, thus being a one directional mine. The front is filled with large steel shot and the back is filled with plastic explosive and used to propel the shot outward in a sixty-degree arc. Strictly antipersonnel and used in defensive positions by American troops. It was connected by a wire to a hand held generator that had to be squeezed to fire the claymore mine.

**Grunt - American infantryman (slang).

***V.C. - Viet Cong.

****M60 - Machinegun used for medium to heavy fire support. Fires a 7.62MM round. Also used as door gun on Hueys (helicopters). Fired six hundred rounds per minute.

the blackout curtain, then turned on the starlight scope and looked around. Nothing, absolutely nothing, was moving, and the orange strips were all still where they should be. Suddenly, he could hear, then see, two gunships coming in. Looking at his watch he saw it was only ten after one. What in the world was he going to do to stay awake 'til three? He played with the starlight scope for awhile, mentally broke down and reassembled the M60, and it was still only one-twenty.

Boredom rapidly set in and he found his head bobbing as he started to fall asleep. He got up and did some jumping-jacks and would continue until three if he had to. It certainly was a lot better than going to jail for six months if he got caught sleeping on his shift. He spent some more time playing with the starlight scope and still it was only one-thirty. An hour and a half to go yet. How in the world was he going to make it 'til three?

The whop, whop, whop of the helicopters taking off helped wake him. He watched the flight take off and counted each ship 'til all ten passed over. There was only one reason the whole flight would be leaving at one-thirty in the morning; some troops somewhere were getting the hell kicked out of them. There was no question about it, the truce had to be over almost before it started. He counted three more choppers taking off and could tell by their sound that they were gunships. Almost immediately, two more ships took off. Jim wondered if the flight was taking both a heavy and a light fire team* with them or if the guns were being sent someplace else.

Boredom. It was without question the worst thing about guard duty. It was one of the few times he really wished he smoked, just so he would have something to do to stay awake.

Suddenly, Jim heard the wood pallets squeak telling him someone was coming in the bunker entrance. He picked up his M16 and pointed it at the entrance, pulled the blackout curtain, put his hand on the light cord, and said, "Halt."

The intruder stopped and his frame was now visible to Jim. He pulled the light cord and could faintly see an American uniform. He wished the lightbulb was more than twenty-five watts. He decided

---

*Heavy fire team - Three or more gunships. Light fire team - Two gunships.

to give the password. After all, the GI was probably getting nervous looking at the business end of his M16.

"Black"—the response came back—"Velvet."

It was right and he sure was glad. "Enter and identify yourself."

In walked a PFC* followed by Lieutenant Tetly. Jim snickered to himself that the gutless lieutenant made his driver walk in first.

"I'm Lieutenant Tetly, the OD. Everything okay?"

"Just fine, Sir."

"Good. We'll stop by later. Let's go, Private."

"Lieutenant, is the truce over?"

"Just about. How did you know?"

"I'm with the helicopter company and the only time we fly night missions is in an emergency. I just watched the whole flight leave. How bad is it?"

"It begins to look like almost everybody but us has been hit. Keep your eyes open."

The two men turned and left. Jim looked at his watch. It was one-forty, another hour and twenty minutes to go. At least he was wide awake. Jim shut off the light, opened the blackout curtain and looked out. Nothing but black. He turned on the starlight scope and looked around, checked the claymores and started praying that Tay Ninh didn't get hit.

The time really dragged on until just after two o'clock when the artillery opened up. Jim walked out the back door long enough to see the shells hitting across camp with three flares scattered above the far perimeter. Jim hurried back to his starlight scope and stayed there. He knew Tay Ninh had been hit. Probably just a probe at first, with the real threat coming later. As the artillery continued to fire, he knew he wouldn't have any trouble staying awake the last hour.

It was two-fifteen when the phone that connects each bunker to the command post rang. "Bunker number forty-three. Specialist MacLaughlin speaking, Sir."

"This is Lieutenant Tetly. Manchu Company's** bunker line is

---

*P.F.C. - Private First Class, third lowest ranking soldier in Army.

**Manchu Company - 4th Batallion, 9th Infantry, part of the 25th Infantry Division.

under severe pressure. I want two men awake until further notice. Understand?"

"Yes, Sir."

The phone went dead and Jim had to decide who to wake up, the man before him or the one after him. For no particular reason, he woke the man after him and told him what was going on. There was still some artillery firing when Jim saw the slicks* come in. He counted nine ships and looked at his watch, two-fifty. Wherever they went, it wasn't far in order to get there and back in only one hour and twenty minutes. The one missing ship didn't overly concern him since it was common to have one sent off by itself. At 0300 hours Jim decided he might as well stay up for another half hour since two people had to be awake. Besides, he found it a lot easier to stay awake with the second man up. The only trouble was this guy smoked and it wasn't long before Jim decided to step outside for some fresh air.

He had been outside only a short time when a jeep stopped on the road parallel to his bunker. The man beside the driver hurriedly jumped out and moved quickly toward Jim. Jim decided to challenge him just in case it was the OD again.

"Halt!" The man stopped moving and Jim spoke again, "Black."

"Velvet. I'm the Sergeant of the Guard. I'm hunting for Specialist MacLaughlin."

"That's me. What's up?"

"We got a call from your CO**. He wants you back ten minutes ago."

"Why?"

"I don't know. Just get your gear and let's go."

Jim and the Sergeant went back in the bunker, told Private Khalid what was happening, picked up his gear and left.

Once back in his company area Jim found Gillett, a tall New Yorker with thinning hair, and asked what had happened that the C.O. had pulled him off guard.

"Mac, all hell has broken loose out there. We've been pulling Manchu out of forward encampments since about one-thirty, and in the

*Slicks - Slickship - Huey helicopters UH-1 used for troop transport and resupply missions.

**C.O. - Commanding Officer, Company Commander, also called "Six" as in Blackhawk "Six."

process we've run out of crew chiefs. If anybody else gets hurt, I'm going to have to fly myself. Get your flight gear and let's go. 925 (pronounced Niner Two Five) is waiting on you."

"Well, so much for days off."

When Jim got to his ship, Blackhawk* 925, he found the rest of the crew there waiting. Mr.** Walker, a tall well-built warrant officer, was the ship's pilot. Mr. Glass, the co-pilot or peter pilot as everyone called them, was already in the right hand seat. Jim thought to himself that was typical of a peter pilot. Climb in and sit down.

A short plump Sp/4, Mike Polaski, had already started untying the main rotor blades. Polaski was an excellent door gunner. He didn't mind helping a crew chief out and always took good care of his guns. If you flew with Polaski, you knew the two M60 door guns weren't going to jam.

Jim put his gear in the ship and checked the logbook. Mr. Walker started to crank the engine and Jim could hear the familiar whine of the turbine as it began to turn. He put the logbook back, put on his chicken plate*** and flight helmet, then turned on his intercom.

"Mr. Walker, you on line?"

"Yeah, Mac, welcome back. We ready to go?"

"The log checks out okay. How thoroughly did you preflight**** this thing?"

"Polaski and I went over it just like you taught me. So if we didn't do it right it's your fault."

Jim laughed and the two men looked each other in the eye. Their faces showed the respect they felt for each other. Mr. Walker gave the thumbs up sign and Jim responded the same way saying, "Okay, let's fly."

Mr. Glass saw Polaski connect his intercom and said, "Climb in Polaski. It's time to go play war."

---

*Blackhawk - Call sign and name of the 187th Assault Helicopter Company.

**Mr. - Proper way to address a Warrant Officer.

***Chicken plate - Bullet proof vest worn by flight crews.

****Preflight - Visual inspection of aircraft before flight.

2

"Beat your plowshares into swords and your pruning hooks into spears: let the weak say, 'I am strong.' " Joel 3:10 KJV

It Begins

As the chopper grabbed sky Jim looked at his watch, 4:15 am. It was going to be a long day. Mr. Walker came over the radio. "Blackhawk Lead, this is Blackhawk 925. Do you copy? Over."

"This is Blackhawk Lead. What's your status, 925?"

"We picked up MacLaughlin, refueled, and are south bound out of Tay Ninh. Where do you want us to join you? Over."

"Pick us up at Cu Chi, 925. Lead, out."

Polaski's familiar nasal twang came over the intercom. "What time did you start guard last night, Mac?"

"One o'clock, and I want to tell you I thought I'd never stay awake. What'd you do last night?"

"Oh, the usual. Played a little golf, went swimming, watched TV, and read the evening paper. What the hell do you think I did? I got drunk and went to bed until a little after one when Gillett got us up. That's what!"

Jim laughed to himself. He liked flying with Polaski. He had a real sense of humor. He remembered the time Polaski had turned on his radio to broadcast outside the ship and shouted across the company frequency, "I'll take a banana cream pie a la mode to go, please."

The Blackhawks had already made several extractions before Jim's ship joined up. So once in the flight they became known as Chalk

Nine. They continued to pull troops out of forward positions to beef up base camps and almost every extraction turned into a hot LZ*. Fortunately, all the hits taken were in noncritical areas. Jim could tell from the radio traffic this was a major offensive. Saigon and Ben Hoa both were having house to house fighting with the American Embassy and the Cholon district being major confrontation points.

The Blackhawks were now on their way to make the last extraction from this outpost. These were always the worst because there weren't any ground troops left for protection and, in this case, they started receiving fire before they'd even gotten on short final approach. The flight was in a staggered right formation to give it more concentrated fire from their door guns. In only seconds they were in and out and the last of the grunts were safely on board. The only trouble was that they weren't out of reach of enemy fire yet. Jim and the other three crew members heard it—it almost always sounded the same: the sharp THUNK of metal hitting metal. Polaski not only heard it, he felt it. His first thought was that he had been stung by a bee. But when he looked down at his left leg, his pants were turning red. He began to feel the warm flow of blood down the side of his leg as he looked down and saw his blood already becoming a part of the dirt that covered the chopper floor. He thought of the phrase, "from dust to dust..." In that same moment a controlled but tearful Polaski keyed his mike. "Mr. Walker, I'm hit! Mac, HELP ME! I got it in the leg!"

"Sit tight, Polaski. I'll be right there." Jim looked for a way to get to his door gunner, but the grunts were in his way. There was a lieutenant seated with his back to Jim. He grabbed the surprised lieutenant by the collar and pulled his body backward and shouted in his ear. "My door gunner's shot, get him up here!" The lieutenant shouted orders, and in only seconds, Polaski was on the ship's floor with a PFC putting direct pressure on the open wound while another applied bandages to his leg. From the moment Polaski had made his plea for help, Walker had been busy.

"Lead, this is Chalk Nine. We're breaking formation for Cu Chi medical; Polaski's been hit, Chalk Nine out."

---

*Hot. L.Z. - Receiving fire from landing zone.

The only sound in reply was the click click of Lead's mike being double keyed in response.

"Mr. Glass, dial Cu Chi Tower. Get clearance for the medical pad, then dial the medical unit and tell them we're in bound with one WIA.*" As he was talking, he broke the ship from formation and increased the ship's airspeed until it was red lined on the airspeed indicator. Jim heard Mr. Glass call Cu Chi Tower and get clearance for the medical pad. While Mr. Glass was changing radio frequencies, Jim came over the intercom.

"Mr. Walker, as many hits as we took, you better keep an eye on your gauges."

"Oh, shit, Mac, we're losing hydraulic pressure!"

"Mr. Walker, if that gauge is correct, you're going to start feeling it in the stick shortly. We'll have to land on the runway instead of the medical pad."

"Well, the gauge is correct. I'm starting to pick up some vibration. Mr. Glass, you work the pitch and R.P.M. I'll take the stick. Mac, get up here and read instruments."

Jim worked his way through the ship and grunts and over Polaski, who smiled at him, as he carefully stepped over his prone body. By the time Jim had positioned himself behind the radio console between the two pilots, the ship was shaking violently from the loss of hydraulic assist on the controls. It was all the two pilots could do to maintain control. Each was required to use both hands on their respective sticks.

"Mac, dial 41.8 Cu Chi Tower on the UHF radio and tell them what happened and ask for a new landing spot."

"Roger." Jim dialed 41.8 and changed his controls to broadcast outside the ship. "Cu Chi Tower, this is Blackhawk 925. Over."

"This is Cu Chi Tower, 925. Over."

"Roger, Cu Chi Tower. We've lost hydraulic assist and have one WIA on board. We will not be able to land at the medical unit as previously requested. Will you give us an alternate landing spot and advise medical unit to have transportation for wounded meet us."

"Roger, 925, I'll advise medical. You can land direct at far end of

---

*W.I.A. - Wounded in Action.

helicopter maintenance area. Please advise your E.T.A.* Over."

Walker came over the intercom, "Two minutes, Mac."

"Roger, Cu Chi. Our ETA is zero two minutes. Over."

"925, be advised winds are steady at zero two knots from the west. Make direct approach and we now have you on visual. Also be advised extreme pressure on east perimeter from Charlie. Cu Chi out."

"Did you get that, Sir?"

"Yea, thanks Mac. How's Polaski?"

With a quick glance backward Jim responded, "He'll make it—if we do."

The two pilots worked together to bring 925 into Cu Chi. Jim read off airspeed, altitude, engine RPM**, and main rotor RPM all the way down. The three men worked together like the team they should be; each did his job and trusted the others without question to do theirs correctly.

Once safely on the ground the grunts helped load Polaski into the ambulance. Jim opened the pilots' doors, slid back the bulletproof plating for pilot protection and spoke. "Mr. Walker, I should be able to fix this thing if there's not too much wrong. Suppose you could get that lieutenant to give us one of his men to take Polaski's place?"

"No. But I can ask." Mr. Walker walked over to where the lieutenant was standing. "Could I speak to you, Lieutenant?"

"Sure. By the way, you did a great job of landing this crate. What's wrong with it, anyway?"

"We lost hydraulics, which makes it a lot like driving a car with the power steering out. Plus, as you noticed, the rotor blades turning causes a terrible vibration."

"I noticed. I thought we were going to bounce out of the ship. What can I do for you, Chief?"

"I need a door gunner. Could you give me one of your men who knows how to use and work on an M60?"

"You're not going to fly that thing like that are you?"

---

*E.T.A. - Estimated time of arrival.

**R.P.M. - Revolutions per minute.

"Oh, no, Sir. My Crew Chief thinks he can fix it without too much trouble."

The lieutenant walked over to where his troops were standing around smoking. "Hey, any of you guys want to fly as a door gunner?"

PFC Green's hand went up in a flash. "I will, Sir."

"Okay, Green. Get your gear and report to that warrant officer."

"Yes, Sir." Green was all smiles. He figured being a door gunner was the easiest job in Vietnam. "Sir, PFC Green. The lieutenant told me to report to you."

Mr. Walker returned Green's salute and told him where to put his gear. Jim was busy inspecting the ship and, as he walked around the left side, Mr. Walker spoke. "Mac, this is PFC Green. He's our gunner 'til we get back to Tay Ninh. Private Green, meet Jim MacLaughlin. He's the crew chief on this ship. If you have any questions ask him. He's one of the best."

"Sir, I'm going to have to crawl under this ship and get up in the hell hole*. I can't find any broken lines out here. Why don't you tell Green what his job is and what's expected of him." With that, Jim lay down on his back and started to crawl under the chopper's belly and up into the hell hole. "Mr. Glass?"

"Yeah, Mac. What do you need?"

"Get my tool box out of the storage compartment and give me a 3/4 inch open end and a crescent wrench, please."

Mr. Glass found the two wrenches and crawled under the ship. He placed them in Jim's visible hand reaching out from the hell hole. "Find the problem, Mac?"

"Yes, Sir. Evidently a bullet just grazed this line, causing a slow leak. You should see this place. It's a mess, and I'm covered with oil." Jim took off the ruptured line, handed it to Mr. Glass and crawled out. "OK, Mr. Glass, here's what I want you to do. Take this line over to the parts tent. Here's my book. I'll open it to the page where this line is shown. Sir, take the book also and you shouldn't have any trouble getting the correct part. Bring me back the new line and enough

---

*Hell Hole - Hole in the bottom of a Huey where the cargo hook sticks out. It is directly under the transmission, very oily and barely large enough for one man to fit in from the waist up.

hydraulic oil to completely refill this thing—please. In the meantime, I'll finish checking out the ship. Okay?"

"Hey, I'm a warrant officer. I don't run errands for enlisted men."

"Look, Mr. Glass, I'd send the new door gunner but he doesn't even know what type of helicopter we're flying. I can't send him after parts. Mr. Walker and I can finish inspecting this thing. You wouldn't know what to look for. Besides, as a warrant officer, you shouldn't have any trouble getting the parts I need, just act like you know exactly what you're doing and nobody will question you. Work it right and you might even get a jeep ride back."

Mr. Glass looked at Walker who was now standing beside Jim. Mr. Walker smiled and waved bye-bye. Mr. Glass slowly shook his head and picked up the part and book and started to leave.

"Hey, Mr. Glass, don't forget the oil and bring me some rags to wipe off with also, please. Mr. Walker, get a Phillips screwdriver and open up that inspection panel in the floor where the bullet hole is, please. I'm going to climb on top and check the rotor head and blades."

The new door gunner stepped forward and said, "Specialist, what do you want me to do?"

"You can start by calling me, Mac, just like everyone else. I'll tell you what, why don't you check out those M60's? All of Polaski's stuff is under his seat on the left side. Green, just one thing to remember while you're going over those guns: if we ever get this thing flying again where we're going, I guarantee you, you'll want 'em to work."

Each man went to work. It didn't take Jim long to determine that everything was okay on top. As he started down the chopper's side, Mr. Walker spoke. "Mac, I got all except two of those screws out, but they just won't come."

"Okay. You put some constant pressure on 'em and let me tap the top of your screwdriver at the same time with a hammer. Sometimes that will break them loose." In this manner the last two screws were removed and then the inspection plate. Jim had really expected to find a control rod with a bullet hole in it. To his amazement, not one thing had been hit except the aircraft's skin. The inspection panel was replaced and the three men sat down. Mr. Walker kept glancing at his watch. Finally, Mac said, "What's the matter, Mr. Walker, you got a hot date this afternoon?"

Walker laughed as he responded, "Why?"

"You can't keep your eyes off your watch."

"Oh, just thinking. Six* is going to be wondering where we are."

"See if you can raise him on the radio. Besides, it'll take me, oh, about a half hour yet after Mr. Glass gets back."

"Yeah, I think I will." Mr. Walker put on his helmet and turned on the radio.

"Mac, I got a question."

"What's that, Green?"

"How do you get away with talking to officers like you do? I mean, you give them orders just like some PFC and they do it. You don't say 'Sir' all the time or anything. They would court martial your butt in a second in the infantry."

Jim laughed and looked to see that Mr. Walker still had his helmet on. "I'll tell you, Green, it's all a matter of timing. Do it at the wrong time and you're in trouble. It's that simple. For example, I'm the guy who knows how to make this thing fly again. If they want it to fly and, if I need help, then they do what I say. Of course a lot of it's in the tone of voice I use. I never use a tone that says I'm the boss. It's always a tone that says you're the boss but I need some help from you. As for saying 'Sir' all the time, well, it just gets in the way. Most all the pilots are pretty good about it. Again, as long as the tone of voice implies 'Sir' they don't really care. Just say it once in a while to show them that you're willing and you'll be okay. Remember, too, that we spend an awful lot of time together. Like Mr. Walker and I. We've been together for ten to twelve hours a day every day for the last couple of months. We're a lot alike and we have a lot of respect for each other. In fact, we've become very good friends. You just have to be very careful with an officer you don't know. Also, I say, 'please.'"

Mr. Walker finished his radio conversation and the three men sat down to eat their C-rations and shoot the bull.

After what seemed like hours, Mr. Glass arrived. He had the part and the oil, but no rags. "Mr. Glass, thanks for getting this stuff."

"No problem, Mac. By the way, Mr. Walker, I stopped by operations. They had word that Charlie had broken through one of the walls."

*Six - Designates a Commander, Company, Division or otherwise.

"Which wall?"

"I don't know. Everyone started getting excited so I left." As the three men looked at each other, it dawned on them what they had been hearing.

Mr. Walker was the first to speak. "Mac, hurry up and get that line on. That small arms fire we've been hearing has to be what this is all about."

Jim crawled under the ship and up into the hell hole. The three remaining men moved to the side of the ship where the firing was coming from and could see rapidly approaching American troops. Mr. Walker shouted at a staff sergeant to find out what was going on. He could hardly believe it when told the place was being overrun and to fall back to the maintenance area drainage ditch.

Instantly, Walker started shouting instructions. "Mac, get out from under the ship! Green, Mr. Glass, get the guns and ammo off the ship!"

They now found themselves on the edge of a major fire fight and in the thick of the retreat. Jim picked up his M16 and all the M60 ammo he could carry. Mr. Walker had already taken one M60 off its mount and wrapped as much M60 ammo around him as he could carry. Mr. Glass had the other M60 and some ammo and Green had his M16 and the rest of the M60 ammo. As the four men retreated, the two pilots took turns firing cover with their M60's. They had been joined by several other GI's but now were being pursued by an even larger number of NVA. They were only about fifty feet from the drainage ditch when it happened; the spine shivering scream of Mr. Glass as he fell to the ground. Jim shoved his weapon and ammo in someone else's hands. An unknown GI picked up Mr. Glass's M60 as Jim bent down. The adrenalin in Jim's body was flowing in abundance, so it was with relative ease that he threw Mr. Glass over his shoulder in a fireman's carry. In this manner, he ran as well as he could the rest of the way to the ditch, with the warm trickle of Mr. Glass's blood running down his back. As the American troops jumped in the ditch, they cleared a field of fire for those already there. The ensuing discharge of lead caused the pursuit to drop off. Jim laid Mr. Glass down in the bottom of the ditch. He didn't have to check for life. He knew Glass was dead. Mr. Walker and Green came over and gave Jim his M16. It was then that Jerry Green saw the blood soaked dead American. Green looked up and, before he knew what was happening, he had thrown up all over himself and Mr. Glass. Mac took him by the arm and turned him away.

"Don't be embarrassed, Green, it happens to a lot of us the first time. We just don't have time for it now. Get that M16 off your shoulder and start firing."

Jim said a quick prayer and looked up, his own eyes moist and one cheek wet. The enemy pursuit stopped soon afterward. The same staff sergeant came by and gave everyone orders. He put Mr. Walker and Jim on one M60 and, about twenty-five feet away, Green and another GI on the other M60. The sergeant got everyone placed and shouted, "Get ready, because the next time they come, it will be a mass suicide charge."

"Mr. Walker, you fire, I'll feed the gun."

"Okay. Oh, shit! Mac, I just peed my pants."

"Hey, don't worry about it. No one will notice. Mr. Walker, we're going to make it."

"Yeah, but if I don't, who wants to be sent home with pee in his pants?"

Both men could now hear the familiar whap, whap, whap of approaching Hueys. Turning to look, they saw two gunships approach just as they banked to make their run on the gathering enemy troops. Jim recognized the boomerangs painted on the noses of the choppers. The Blackhawks had worked with this company before. The first gun run finished, both ships made a sharp bank and came right back in. Both were mini gunships and Jim knew the 6000 rounds per minute that the miniguns fired had to be taking a fierce toll on Charlie. All the American troops in the ditch were cheering. Mr. Walker shouted, "That a boy! Go get 'em." Then, "Mac, they're leaving. Oh, shit. They must be out of fuel or ammo."

Someone shouted, "Here they come!"

Jim looked back down in time to see enemy troops charging at them. Their screams sent shivers down his spine. Bullets were hitting all around them but no one seemed to notice. Every man in the ditch was firing at the human wave charging his way. Both Jim and Mr. Walker were too busy to feel fear; with each totally in control of himself now. All of their thoughts and energies were directed to the task before them. The fire coming from the ditch was taking a terrific toll, but it was the two M60's from Jim's chopper that were holding the line and making the real difference.

(Several years later, Jim visited the battlefields of Gettysburg. As he stood at the high water mark of Pickett's Charge, looking out over the open space those southern boys traversed, his chest swelled with emotion and his eyes broke with the tears of a day gone by. His knees buckled, he sat down and wept as his mind raced back to that ditch and the stand he'd made half a world away. One of the guys he was with at Gettysburg sat down beside him and asked if he was okay. Jim nodded his head yes. He was unable to speak. He shrugged his shoulders, blew his nose and said, "Sometimes it just happens like that.")

The human wave charging their way had been reduced to just a handful of NVA by the time it reached Jim's ditch. Jim ducked a fixed bayonet and a screaming NVA who lunged by his head. As if by instinct, he'd known the action was too close for an M16. His hand reached into his pocket and, in a flash, he held the Army issue switchblade. In that same moment the enemy soldier turned and Jim buried the blade in his chest. Jim prided himself on keeping the heavy blade very sharp—as a result it slid smoothly between the ribs with surprisingly little effort. In the same movement he pulled it out and stabbed again, this time in the guts. He heard Walker scream and turned in time to see an NVA about to thrust his bayonet into Walker. Jim's knife found its mark in the NVA's back as Walker side stepped the pained man's thrust. Jim grabbed the man's hair, yanked his head back and, with his blood drenched knife, slit the NVA's throat. Out rushed a mixture of air and blood that bubbled down his chest. Walker looked at Jim, "Thanks". Jim simply nodded his head. It was over quicker, by far, than it had begun.

American reinforcements were jumping over the ditch in hot pursuit of the few remaining NVA troops. Neither man spoke. Jim wiped his knife and hands as clean as possible. He picked up his M16, grabbed the M60, and climbed out of the ditch without speaking. Medics busied themselves with the wounded as reinforcements continued to arrive. There was nothing left to be done at the ditch so Jim simply turned and walked away. Green, with his guns, found Mr. Walker and the

two men turned and followed Jim. They were all still hyped up from
the events just past and, about one hundred feet from the ditch, Walker
put his arm around Jim's shoulder and gave it a squeeze.

"Mac, you want to fly right seat back to Tay Ninh?"

"Sure. You know I just had a thought. Why didn't they blow our
ship?"

"It probably didn't occur to them or they didn't have time."

The three men put their weapons and ammo down. Mr. Walker
and Jim walked around the chopper—their eyes scanning every inch
of the ship.

"Mr. Walker, they took the time to pull the soundproofing down
and to take the first aid kit out but not to blow it. Why?"

"You think it's booby trapped?"

"Yeah. There has to be something under that soundproofing they
took down."

"Hey, Mac."

Jim looked up to see Green pointing at the front end of the skid.
There, wedged under the curved part of the skid, was a fragmentation grenade. Jim reached down and removed it, being careful not
to allow the handle to spring loose.

"Okay, you two. See if you can find the pin laying around
someplace." After searching and coming up empty handed, Jim decided to take it to a clearing and give it a toss.

"Hey, here it is. You know what they've done? They've pulled the
pin and given it a toss!"

Jim carefully worked the pin back in the hole and bent the end over
slightly. He gave the grenade a toss to Green and looked at Walker.
"I'll still bet there's something under that soundproofing. Probably
another frag."

"Probably. But what if there isn't. What if it's something else? At
least with a frag, if the pin pops, you have a couple of seconds to
pick it up and give it a toss. If it's something else, you're not going
to know what it's going to do or how to handle it."

"Sir, they're not going to be carrying anything special. It's all going to be dual purpose stuff."

"True. Can't you gently feel for something solid under it?"

"Why do you automatically assume me? Green, how long you been in country?"

"Not quite a month. Why?"

"I just thought maybe you might have worked with booby traps before."

"Nope."

"Okay. I'll do it. If nothing else, I can always run like hell." Slowly, and very gently, Jim felt the soundproofing blanket for something solid. Every instinct he had told him something was there. He just hoped it was a frag and only one. As he felt the blanket he prayed. "Lord Jesus, help me please, please help me." There it was! He'd hit something solid. With great care he tried to determine what it was. The all too familiar pling told him all he needed to know. With a frag you had only seconds. With one hand, Jim tore off the blanket and, in one fluid movement, he grabbed the frag and threw it. Jim said another prayer, this time in thanks, that it had blown harmlessly on its way to the nearby clearing.

Jim walked over to where Green and Mr. Walker stood. He sat down on a thirty gallon drum and took a long deep breath. Mr. Walker spoke first, "This is turning into one hell of a day! Mac, you know I've never really believed that story you tell—that you have a guardian angel. I just want you to know. I believe!"

Jim looked him in the eye and, at that moment, the realization of all he had recently been through caused him to lose his composure. Fatigue , stress and emotional strain swept through his body. He bent over and lost muscle control, the convulsions and weeping almost knocked him off the barrel. It was Mr. Walker who stopped Jim's fall and cradled his head to his chest. The two men shut out all time as they wept together and embraced, drained of emotion.

It was a full ten minutes before Jim felt he was in control of himself again. He got some C-rations and sat down for a snack. The pound cake, cheese and crackers tasted good. He ate and then checked the ship for more grenades. He found none. Green had left to get some of his personal gear while Walker put the soundproofing back up. He also mounted the door guns and put the ammo back in the left seat box, since there wouldn't be anyone flying behind the right door anyway. Jim crawled back under the chopper and up into the hell hole.

"Mr. Walker, I just had a thought. Get my flashlight and look in the fuel tank for a frag, will you? If there's one in there, it'll have a rubberband around it instead of a pin in the handle."

"Sure, Mac. What do I do if I see one?"

"Well, say so and I'll get the hell out from under here, for one thing!"

"I don't see anything, there isn't anything in there. Did you hear me, Mac?"

"Yeah, thank you."

By the time Jim had finished putting the line on and filled the hydraulic reservoir, Green was back. Mr. Walker was the first to see him coming, carrying a foot locker over his shoulder and a duffel bag in one hand.

"Green, what are you doing?"

"I packed all my stuff and moved out."

"You what? You can't do that! We just borrowed you for one day. I'm not sure we can keep you that long now that I don't have a peter pilot."

Green's face showed every bit of the disappointment he felt. Laying his stuff down he looked at Walker. "Sir, I thought I was to be a permanent part of your crew."

"Look, Green, you need orders to change companies. We lost a gunner and, to keep from flying back to Tay Ninh just for a gunner, your lieutenant let us borrow you. Now, I've got to go get a co-pilot."

Jim felt really sorry for Green. It was obvious he really wanted to fly.

"Mr. Walker, Gillett told me this morning that the only people he had left to fly were Kenny and himself. So unless you want Kenny as a gunner, we'd better find a way to keep Green."

Mr. Walker looked at Jim with dismay. Jim slowly nodded yes. Walker shrugged his shoulders and said, "Okay, Green, put it in the ship, I'll see what I can do. Mac, we ready to go?"

"Yes, Sir."

"Okay. Let's go get a peter pilot."

Jim untied the main rotor blades and helped Green put on his chicken plate and helmet. He showed him how to work the lip mike and how to turn his radio on and off. Mr. Walker had climbed in and started to crank the engine before Jim had Green strapped into his monkey harness*. Walker had the ship running by the time Jim climbed in the peter pilot's seat and, after putting his helmet on, heard Green say, "Can everybody hear me?"

Walker looked at Jim and laughed. Green came over the intercom, "Gee, Mac, this is neat."

Walker casually reached down and switched his and Jim's radio to private. "Mac, he's like a kid with a new toy."

"Give the guy a break. Remember how excited you were the first time you climbed in one of these things! Besides, it wasn't him who peed his pants back in that ditch." They both laughed.

Walker spoke, "Man, I'd never been so scared in all my life. I couldn't control myself anymore than a bitch in heat."

"Oh, but you did, not your bladder obviously. But you controlled your mind enough to make the rest of your body do what it had to do. You sure made that M60 sing."

"Mac, while we're on the subject, I may never get another chance. Thanks for saving my life. If it wasn't for you and that switchblade, I'd be dead."

They looked at each other and Jim nodded his head. "You're welcome. Although it's not me you should be thanking. But I do appreciate it. You should be thanking Jesus. Without Him we both would be dead, I don't even remember getting the knife out of my pocket." As the two men looked at each other, they knew a special bond had been formed.

Walker turned the radios back to the previous setting and made contact with the tower for clearance to taxi to the runway and leave.

Once airborne and headed for Tay Ninh, Walker contacted "Six" in C and C**. Walker spoke briefly about what had happened and stated they could rejoin the flight after picking up a co-pilot. "Six" said that he would advise Operations so there would be a co-pilot ready.

---

*Monkey Harness - Restrainer straps that went around the waist and over the shoulders and interlocked in the front with a quick release buckle. A long tail (thus the name) comes from the back of the harness and hooks onto a ring or secure part of the ship. This tail allowed movement while still being strapped in.

**C and C - Command craft that is filled with communications gear. Used to direct and coordinate operations from the air.

3

"The trouble he causes recoils on himself; his violence comes down on his own head." Psalms 7:16 NIV

You Do What You Have To Do

No one spoke as they landed at Tay Ninh and taxied as close as possible to operations. Somewhat miffed at not having a co-pilot waiting on them, Mr. Walker headed for operations. Jim helped carry Green's foot locker and duffle bag into the hooch, where Gillett was in the process of cleaning out Polaski's gear. Introductions were made and Gillett told Green that he might as well have Polaski's spot. They were giving Gillett a quick account of what had happened when a Sp/4 came in.

"I'm from Operations. I'm looking for a PFC Green."

"That's me."

"We're going to try to get some orders cut, but we need some information."

"Let me put this stuff away and I'll be right over."

"I'd appreciate it if you make it as quick as possible. Furthermore, don't get too settled in, because I'd be very surprised if we can keep you."

"Okay, I'll be right there."

The Sp/4 left as Green stuffed his duffle bag in the wall locker.

Once this was finished, Jim and Green headed for Operations. As they walked across the company area, they heard someone shout, "MacLaughlin."

Jim turned to see Mr. Halsey headed their way. "Oh, great, here comes trouble! Green, just keep on walking and tell Mr. Walker that Mr. Halsey has me."

"Mac, you . . ."

"Get out of here before he gets you, too!" Jim turned and waited for Mr. Halsey.

"MacLaughlin, where's your hat?"

Jim looked the tall, thin, sunken chested, acne-scarred warrant officer in the eyes and knew it was harrassment time. "In the helicopter, Sir."

"Specialist, you know perfectly well you're supposed to have on a cap. STAND AT ATTENTION when I speak to you, Specialist!" Halsey's voice expressed the hatred he felt. His face was twisted as he made a real effort to look mean. Jim came to attention but couldn't help smiling as he watched Halsey's face, "You find something amusing, MacLaughlin?" Jim just stood there without answering. "Answer me, Specialist!"

"What makes you think I find anything amusing, Sir?"

"Don't get smart with me, Specialist! By the way, don't you salute officers anymore, Specialist?"

"Yes, Sir." Jim brought his right hand up in salute.

"That's better. Now, what is it that you find so funny?"

"I'm not laughing, Sir. I find nothing funny."

"MacLaughlin, you've got oil and dirt and who knows what else all over you! You look like hell, you know that soldier? Your personal appearance is disgusting. How long has it been since you changed fatigues? Your boots need shined, plus you need a haircut."

Jim thought, *so do you, you SOB, right below the chin.* "I put on clean clothes this morning, Sir."

By this time, eight or ten people had gathered at a safe distance. Some were maintenance people, some were platoon sergeants like Gillett, and some were the walking wounded. Halsey walked around Jim checking his uniform. Jim stood at attention wondering, "What's next?"

"Specialist, your back pocket is unbuttoned."

Jim couldn't help but smile. After what he had just been through he really didn't care if it was unbuttoned.

"MacLaughlin, just what is it that you continuously find so funny?"

"Nothing, Sir."

"Soldier, when you stand at attention, you don't smile. So, I'm going to take that smile off your face. Get down and give me fifty."

Jim's smile disappeared alright. In its place was a look of pure hatred. Halsey thought for a moment that he finally had him. All he had to do now was push MacLaughlin just a little more, and he would do something that he could be sent to jail for.

"Don't you find that funny, MacLaughlin?" Jim just stood there and looked Halsey in the eyes. "I'm giving you a direct order, Specialist. Get down and give me fifty."

Jim sat down and started to count, "One, two. . ."

"What the hell do you think you're doing?"

"I'm doing what you told me, Sir, giving you fifty. You didn't say fifty what, so I'm counting to fifty for you."

"You insubordinate, smart-mouthed, little bastard. I'm going to bust your ass to an E-fucking-nothing!"

"On what grounds, Sir? I've done everything you told me to do!"

Halsey knew he was right. MacLaughlin had beat him again. Maybe. In a perfectly calm voice Halsey made one last try. "Okay, MacLaughlin, I want you to do seventy-five pushups and count out loud as you go. If I hear one word otherwise, I'll court martial your ass."

Jim sat there on the ground and looked up at Halsey. Each man showed the hatred he felt for the other. Jim thought about what he had just gone through a short time ago. He tried to stare Halsey down as he wondered why creeps like him lived, while the nice guys like Glass got it. However, Halsey could hold his own and said, "Now, MacLaughlin, not ten minutes from now."

Jim took a deep breath, looked around and saw Gillett standing by the hooch door with a look of disgust on his face. Jim rolled over very slowly and even more slowly started the pushups. "One . . . Two. . ."

Suddenly, Jim heard Walker's voice shouting from across the

company area, "MacLaughlin, what are you doing? The XO* has been waiting on you."

"Sir, Mr. Halsey thought I should do seventy-five pushups first." Walker had walked up to where Halsey was standing and shook his head. "Mr. Halsey, would it be okay if my crew chief went on a mission with me—or should I tell the XO what you're doing is too important to interrupt?" Jim laughed to himself. Man, you could cut the sarcasm with a knife.

Halsey spoke as he walked away, "He's all yours."

Jim stood up, brushed himself off and said, "Thanks. What took you so long?" They laughed together as Walker gave Jim's shoulder a squeeze with his hand.

"Mac, you're just lucky I got here at all. Green waited until I got finished talking with the XO before he told me Halsey had you."

"Mr. Walker, we both know there's no such thing as luck. Jesus Christ, yes; luck, no. By the way, what was the XO's problem?"

"He needs a ship to go pick up some ARVN's (Army of the Republic of Viet Nam) at Chon Thanh and take them to An Loc."

"We're not going back to the flight?"

"Nope."

"Who do we get as a Peter Pilot?"

"Ratcliffe."

Mr. Ratcliff was a short chunky man with a roly poly face. He wasn't one of the best pilots by a long shot, but he was still new in the country and fresh out of flight school. When they got to the ship, Green couldn't wait to ask, "Hey, Mac, what was that officer's problem?"

"Oh, he's a hard nose, Green. He believes in harrassment for the fun of it. Just forget it."

They untied the ship and hovered to the fuel dump. From there, they went to the ammo bunker and re-armed.

Once airborne, Green couldn't contain his curiosity any longer. "Mac, tell me about you and Mr. Halsey."

"Not now, maybe later tonight."

Ratcliff spoke up, "Hey, don't worry about me. I don't like the guy

---

*X.O. - Executive Officer, second in command to Company Commander.

anymore than most of the EMs* do. Besides, I'd like to hear your side of the story. Halsey claims you screwed him."

"Yeah, and he didn't even get a kiss." There was a pause as Jim wondered if he should. "Okay, everybody, it's story time. First you have to understand Halsey. He's the kind of person who never had any responsibility, authority, or respect before in his life. Once he did get a little authority, he couldn't handle it. One look at him and you know he never was involved in any kind of sports; in fact, I wonder how he ever got in the Army, let alone made officer. Once he became an officer, he simply didn't get respect, so, he figured he could order people to give it to him, and, of course, that just doesn't work. Then, to show how mean he is, he started harrassing the EM.

"I didn't have any more trouble with him than anyone else did. Oh, the usual, shine your boots, button your buttons, and get a haircut—until I had to fly with him one day about two months ago. We had a single ship mission that we had to leave on before daylight. It was just getting light when Halsey decided to do some low level flying through the Hobo Woods, of all places! That was right after they'd gone through the Hobo with plows and knocked down trees and everything. Well, of course, I objected to putting it on the deck and said so. Halsey told me not to get smart with him, that he was an officer and would make the decisions on the ship, that I was a stupid enlisted man and my job was to sit behind my M60 with my big mouth shut. Now, understand, I didn't object to flying on the deck. I objected to it because we didn't have enough light, and because we had no idea what was still sticking up, or had been put back up. Basically, I think Halsey is a hot dog without the skill of a hot dog. So, he takes it down. He starts flying so low that I'm looking up at some of the bushes. I figured surely he'd get us all killed, especially when I looked at the airspeed indicator and saw it sitting on 110 knots. We were just about out of it when WAPP! Well, to make a long story short, Halsey had hit a twig that was still standing and busted out the plexiglass bubble covering his foot pedals. In the process, he got his leg cut up. The jerk tried flying without the foot glass but the

*EM - Enlisted man.

wind kept blowing dirt up in his face, so he had to go back to Tay Ninh to get a new bubble. When we landed, he gave everyone strict orders that we were to say we took a hit when we landed at Duc Hoa.

"The maintenance officer took one look at the bubble and knew a bullet hadn't done it. Neither Polaski nor I felt like lying for the guy so when the maintenance officer asked how it happened, I told the truth. This made the Major as mad as a wet hen. He left Polaski and me, swearing he would make Halsey pay for that bubble. The best part was that Halsey had gone to change his pants and clean up his leg. While he was in the shower washing it off, the flight surgeon came in and, of course, asked how it had happened. Halsey told him that we had taken a hit in his foot window, that it had shattered the plexiglass and a piece had cut him. Well, the flight surgeon insisted on treating him and filling out the papers for a purple heart. So Halsey didn't have any choice but to go along, or to tell the truth. By the time he got back to the ship, it was ready to fly and the flight surgeon and maintenance officer were converging on the CO's office at the same time. Man, I have to laugh just thinking about it. There must have been so much smoke in that office it's a wonder the place didn't burn down. To make things even better, neither Polaski nor I told Halsey what we had done to him. He flew the rest of the day so darned happy with himself you would have thought he was the cat that ate the canary.

"When we landed that night there was a jeep waiting for him. Before he got out of the chopper, he asked if we were all going to report it like he told us to. Polaski and I both said, 'right', that's all, just one word, 'right'. He took it just like we wanted him to. Plus, the peter pilot was so busy kissing his ass that if Halsey had turned real quick, he would have broken the dude's nose. The jeep driver took him straight to the CO. I'm not sure what happened there other than he got an Article 15 and fined two hundred dollars, plus he had to pay for the window and labor to replace it—no purple heart and reduced to peter pilot status for thirty days. Which is, of course, the ultimate insult, and he figures it's all my fault. Now, any little chance he has to get even, he takes.

"I think the guy figures I'm stupid enough to do something during one of his little harrassment sessions, that he could use to get me court martialed. Then, he could have the last laugh by sending me to jail."

"Mac, I don't understand why the CO lets him get away with it. It's pretty obvious what he's doing!"

"I don't know, Mr. Ratcliffe, unless the CO figures he treats all the EM that way. Which he does, I just get it more severely. What do you think, Mr. Walker?"

"I think we're about ready to land at Chon Thanh and I need the radios. We'll finish talking about it on the way to An Loc."

It wasn't long until the ship was on the ground at Chon Thanh. Sitting there waiting for them was a South Vietnamese Major and three NVA prisoners. Each of the NVA's were bound; their hands were tied in front with a stick wedged against their backs and between their elbows. Their feet were tied together with a rope running from the stick to the bindings on their feet. Each prisoner had to be partially lifted up and put in the chopper. The Major sat facing the three NVA's who were kneeling on the chopper floor with their backs to the pilots. Jim found it a little unusual that the Major would spend so much time and effort obviously placing each of the three in the chopper and on the floor, exactly in the location he wanted them.

As the chopper took off, Jim looked at the four passengers. The ARVN Major was no bigger than his three prisoners, the biggest of which couldn't have been over five feet tall. In fact, they looked almost identical—short and skinny. The helicopter was high enough that Jim allowed his M60 to drop into the rest position, that way he could watch what was going on. The Major was ranting and raving at the three NVA on the floor. It didn't take a student of psychology to see they were three distinct personalities. The one seated on the far end was a hard nose, whose mere presence kept the other two from telling the Major what he wanted to know. On the other end was your basic follower, who probably didn't know anything anyway. It was the man in the middle who was getting most of the Major's attention. Jim figured he probably was an officer, but not as high ranking as the Hard Nose. He, more than likely, knew what the Major wanted to know but was afraid of Hard Nose. The Major was screaming at the three in Vietnamese, Jim wished he could understand what was being said. The poor guy in the middle looked like he was scared stiff but wasn't going to talk with Hard Nose sitting there. That's when it happened. The Major simply grabbed one end of Hard Nose's stick and gave it a flip. Hard Nose disappeared out the cargo door. Jim was stunned.

"Green, did you see that?"

"Yeah, and I think he's getting ready to do it again to the dude on the other end."

The Major was really putting the pressure on the two remaining NVA and, in fact, was threatening to do the same to each of them if they didn't talk. It was Walker who came over the radio next. "Mac, what are you two talking about back there?"

"That ARVN Major just threw one of his gooks* out the door, and I think Green's right, he's about to do it to this other dude."

"Well, don't let him. We're not barbarians!"

Jim really didn't know what to do, so he shouted, "Hey, Major!"

At the same time the Major grabbed one end of the stick and with little effort, rolled the resisting NVA out the door. He then turned to Jim, "No problem, GI. No problem, all done."

He turned back to the one remaining NVA, smiled and asked a question. The prisoner was terrified and his pants showed the dark spot of a man who had just lost control. It didn't affect his tongue, though, as he began to talk so fast the Major had to slow him down. There was no more hesitation in answering questions when the Major asked.

The rest of the way to An Loc, Jim thought about what had happened. He even shut off all his radios except the inter-ship conversation. It was almost as if he were being mentally ripped in half, one half said so what, especially after what he had been through. Besides, what was the difference? The enemy was the enemy and if he died being thrown out of a helicopter, it wasn't any different than if he got shot. Further, the third dude did sing like a canary, which was, of course, the whole purpose. But his other half told him that what had been done just wasn't right. Jim looked down at his clothes with dried blood all over them and thought of the morning at Cu Chi. Yet, the look of total terror on the two men's faces as they went out the door caused a shiver to go up his spine. How could he condone what

*Gook - Slang for any Southeast Asian person.

had been done. Still, he couldn't bring himself to feel truly sorry for the dead NVA. The fatigue, pressure, stress and general conditions were beginning to get to him. He found himself praying to God that he would get shot—a nice clean wound that wouldn't do any permanent damage but would send him home, and he meant it.

When the chopper landed at An Loc it was met by a jeep. Out stepped an American full bird colonel who wore a Big Red One shoulder patch. He returned the Major's salute and it became quickly evident the two men knew each other. Jim had to snicker at the Mutt and Jeff contrast between the two men: the colonel's six and a half foot, two hundred fifty pound frame really made the Major look like a midget. Walker shut the chopper down and Green let Walker out of his door before the blades had completely quit turning.

"Colonel, my name is Mr. Walker, I'm the pilot. I would like to have charges brought against this man for throwing two NVA prisoners out of my helicopter at 2000 feet."

"Mr. Walker, I don't really give a damn what he did just as long as he got results."

"Colonel, I. . ."

"Mister! I don't have time to worry about two dead NVA. Listen, the truce started at 1800 hours last night and was called off by 0900 this morning. We've been getting the hell kicked out of us since 2300 last night. Just in case you aren't aware of it yet, Mr. Walker, we are in the middle of the biggest battle of the war. They've thrown everything they've got at us, and we're going to be very lucky to hold our base camps. It wouldn't surprise me in the least if we get kicked completely out of the country, lock, stock and barrel. To help prevent that, I need to know some very important information about the enemy troops in this area and I need it now. I don't have time for niceties, and I don't have time for stupid court martials. Do I make myself clear?"

"Yes, Sir." Mr. Walker saluted, turned and met Jim's eyes with his own. Jim saw, 'I tried', just as Walker saw the response, 'I know, and it's okay.'

The flight back south to join the rest of the company was quiet. Jim turned Saigon back on and listened to whatever music was playing. Green daydreamed, Ratcliffe and Walker were busy driving and getting artillery and air strike clearances.

It was almost midnight when the flight finally landed for the night. Jim introduced Green to Kenny and asked him to show Green where to clean and store the guns. He pulled his daily inspection as quickly as he could, filled out the log book, so he could turn in the daily log sheet and headed for the hooch. He had just walked in the door when Gillett yelled at him, "Mac, you had anything to eat lately? The CO has the mess sergeant fixing supper for the flight."

"Man, that sounds good! Come on and eat with me, Gillett, I want to talk to you."

The two men went through the line filling their plates with mashed potatoes, gravy, corn and roast beef. The coffee tasted like burnt acid, but there wasn't any ice for water and, without ice, the water always reminded Jim of recycled piss. The food didn't have much taste but was hot and therefore good, Jim had long ago decided the mess hall food was good if it was hot and bad if it was cold.

A short time later, Green and the rest of the gunners came in. Gillett asked, "What in the world have you guys been doing, spit shining those guns?"

One of the gunners answered, "No, Gillett, the CO ordered the guns left on the ships tonight, so we had to get them out of armament and get Kenny to take us back out. Hey, Gillett, what's going on anyway? We never left the guns on before."

"All I know, fellows, is Charlie has evidently decided to play for real."

After the flight crews finished their meals, most of the men headed for one of two places, the club or the showers. On the way out of the mess hall, Green asked Jim where both were located. "Let's get a shower first while there's still some water." The showers weren't quite full of guys when they arrived. The shouts as the ice water hit bare skin bounced off the shower walls and into the night.

"Hey, Mac, is it always this cold?"

"Only late at night. Just be glad there's still water. When it runs out, the last bit of water is full of sand and grit, and you never know when it's going to hit you." They had just left when the obscenities started.

"That, Green, is what it sounds like when the water has just run out."

Back in the hooch Green spotted Jim's shirt, "Hey, Mac, you going to keep that shirt?"

"Of course I'm going to keep it. It'll wash out and you'll never be able to tell it from any other."

"No, no, I mean why don't you keep it like it is and send it home? You could have it framed and wouldn't even have to stretch the truth to impress all the girls."

Kenny spoke up, "Mac, I'll tell you what I'll do, I'll buy that shirt for ten bucks."

"What for?"

"I know a guy in supply who really goes in big for that kind of stuff. You should see some of the letters he sends home. He's a real Saigon warrior*. He would probably rip your name tag off and sew his on, then send it home with some cock and bull story, I mean really, the thing looks like you've been through hell with it." Kenny held the shirt up to get a good look at it. "I'll tell you what, since the thing is almost totally covered with blood and oil, I'll give twenty bucks top for it."

Jim looked Kenny straight in the eye. "Go to hell, Kenny. I wouldn't sell it to you for a hundred bucks!" With that, he grabbed the shirt from Kenny's hands and stuffed it into his dirty clothes bag.

It was almost one-thirty a.m. when Jim got into bed and pulled his mosquito netting down. Sleep came the instant his head hit the pillow.

Jim's eyes felt it first—then his brain seemed to explode with the blinding light in his face. "Mac, wake up, I need a crew for a single ship night mission. You want it?"

"Yeah, I'll go, but get that flashlight out of my face, please. What time is it?"

"Almost two-thirty. I'll get Green up and drive the two of you to the flight line."

"Two-thirty! Gillett, I've only been in bed an hour."

"I know, Mac. You want me to get someone else?"

"No, I'm awake. I'll go."

Jim could really feel the fatigue; his chest felt heavy and it was

---

*Saigon Warrior - Person who has not seen combat and tells fictionalized combat stories.

almost more than he could manage just to crawl out of bed. Gillett
helped put their gear in the truck and it wasn't long before they were
at the aircraft. Jim was untying the main rotor when the two pilots
arrived. They looked like they came out of the same mold: tall, dark
and skinny. John O'Neal was from Wyoming and Dave Gabrys was
from Colorado.

"Mr. O'Neal, Mr. Gabrys, how did you two get stuck flying
tonight?"

As O'Neal placed his gear in the chopper, he turned to answer Jim.
"We both had yesterday off, so they figured we would be in the best
shape for tonight. Besides, Walker has enough hours that if he flies
tonight he'll be over the hour limit. Is this crate ready to fly, Mac?"

"Yes, Sir, I always preflight before I quit for the night."

"Okay, I'll take your word for it, especially since it's so dark." In
no time at all the ship was airborne and headed east of Tay Ninh.

"Mr. O'Neal, where we going?"

"Mac, we're headed for Xom Bau Dau, Manchu company had a
couple of snipers on Nu Ong* who sniped on more than they could
chew. They're supposed to be headed north on Highway 14 in an effort to stay alive."

"How in the world are we going to spot them at this time of night?"

"They have a radio and a M14 with a starlight scope on it, so they
should be able to contact us, for that matter, they should see us a
long time before we see them."

"How long they been on the run?"

"I'm not real sure. Evidently, they got in trouble about 0100 and
have been trying to get picked up ever since. Let's cut the chatter
now so we can raise 'em on the radio."

Mr. Gabrys had already tuned into their frequency and was listening for their transmission. The wait seemed forever as the single Huey
glided silently east over Highway 13 toward the point where 14 and
13 met. O'Neal looked over to Gabrys who was studying a map and
asked, "How much further 'til we meet up with Highway 14?"

"About four miles, yet."

It was then that they all heard it, very faint, almost a whisper: "This

---

*Nu Ong - An area containing three mountains in a very flat area.

is Frog calling Lizard. Do you read me? Over."

O'Neal spoke at once, "Roger, Frog. This is Blackhawk 925. We're inbound to your location. By the way Frog, Lizard sends his regards, Can you give me your exact location? Over."

Again, in a voice that betrayed his exhaustion, they heard a whisper, "Negative, Lizard, on the Location. Charlie is on this frequency. Can you lock on this frequency if I leave my mike on and find me? Over."

"We can come close. I understand you should be able to see us. Is that correct? Over."

"Affirmative. Over."

"What highway are you now on, Frog? Over."

"Negative, Blackhawk, be prepared to decode. Wait one! Okay, look, Charlie is getting hot again. I've gotta leave this location. I'll leave the mike on, DO NOT, I repeat DO NOT contact me. I see you. I'll call you. Out!"

O'Neal spoke, "He's crazy as hell if he thinks I'm going through that decoding garbage. If he wants a ride he can just tell us where the hell he's at."

"Dave, can you use that radio direction locater? He must be on 13 headed west."

"Yeah, you're probably right! I haven't used a beacon locater since school though." After about two minutes Gabrys spoke, "Okay, I've got him dead ahead. It's a pretty strong signal so we must be close."

"Blackhawk 925, this is Frog, land on the flashlight signal, out!"

"Mr. O'Neal, that wasn't the same man was it?"

"No, but, Dave, they said there were two of them."

"Blackhawk, (huff,huff), this is Frog, (huff, huff). Disregard that transmission (huff, huff). It was Charlie (huff, huff). We have (huff, huff) you on visual (huff). Charlie is about two hundred meters back (huff, huff). You just flew past us (huff). Do you have us? (huff)"

"What direction are we turning, Frog? Over."

"To your (huff, huff) left. Come get me, PLEASE!" (Huff, huff).

"John, we did fly over the signal and it is now behind us. He also got the left turn right, but then he had a 50-50 chance."

"Okay, let's go get him. You two in the backseats awake?"

"Yes, Sir."

"Yes, Sir."

"And, Green, don't fire your M60 until we are on the way out. If Charlie is only two hundred meters back, he's close enough to hear us but not see us. However, the flash of that gun will give them a spot to aim at."

O'Neal came over the radio, "Okay, Frog, we're on our way down. Give us a talk down."

"Roger, you are directly to my north (huff). Now (huff), you're flying by me (huff). You're over the highway and fifty meters (huff) in front (huff). Set it down. I'll come to you. Out."

"Sir, what if it's Charlie?"

"Then cut loose with that M60."

"Green, don't worry about it. If it's Charlie, you'll be dead before you know otherwise."

"Mac, you really know how to encourage a guy."

"I love you too, Green."

"Cut out the chatter back there. Damn, it's dark. I wish I could turn on some lights. I don't even have our navigation lights on. Can anybody see how close the ground is?"

"No, Sir."

"Can anybody see anything?"

There was total silence as every eye searched for some clue to the ship's proximity to earth, tree or, hopefully, highway. Finally, Jim spoke as Mr. O'Neal slowly eased it downward. "Sir, Frog said we were directly over the highway. All you can do is ease on down."

At that point they felt the skids touch down. Instantly, two men jumped on board and Jim could see one raising his arm upward. Jim almost screamed as the adrenalin pumped through his body. "They're on. Let's go!" With that, O'Neal put everything he had into it and the ship jumped upward and away. Jim could see plainly the flashes of enemy fire and hear the all too distinct thunk, thunk as his chopper took hit after hit. It was all he could do to keep from blindly spraying the area, but he knew every fifth round he fired was a tracer. The trail it left would be like saying, here I am, everybody, shoot. In only seconds, they were out of the area and on their way back to Tay Ninh.

"Mr. O'Neal, we took some hits, so keep a close eye on your gauges."

"Got you covered, Mac."

Their two passengers had begun to regain their breath and had taken seats on the bench. One was seated close to Jim. He placed his hand on Jim's shoulder and pulled the crew chief towards him. Looking at the grunt, Jim realized he wanted to say something. Placing his face only inches from the grunt's, he keyed his mike so everyone could hear. The voice was full of emotion and all knew he had to be crying, "Thank you. Thank you for coming to get us. We've been running almost all night trying to stay ahead of them. Every time we thought we had lost them they would turn our direction and we had to start moving again. You guys looked like a chariot from heaven sent to pluck us from death."

Jim shouted back at the man so he could hear, "Who did you shoot? Ho Chi Minh?"

"We got their CO."

With that the conversation ended and both men leaned back to rest. The next voice Jim heard was O'Neal's. "No wonder they spent so much effort pursuing those two. Look, Mac, these gauges read just fine and we're about five minutes out of Tay Ninh. Where do you want me to put it down?"

"Just take it right on in to maintenance and park it. I know it took several hits that will have to be patched."

It was 0433 when Jim took off his boots and shirt and lay down on his bunk. Sleep, as always, came instantly for him, but it didn't last long.

"Mac, wake up, it's 05:15, What time did you get back last night?"

"Gillett, it was four-thirty this morning. That's forty-five minutes sleep I got last night and the night before I was on guard duty. That's only five or six hours sleep in the last forty-eight hours."

"Mac, if I had someone else to fly in your place, I'd set you down, but I just don't. In fact, I've got to send Green to Cu Chi for a flight physical today. Come on, I'll eat breakfast with you and you can tell me about last night."

"Man, that was something else. We picked up these two guys, one was a radio man, the other a sniper. You should have seen this guy's rifle, Gillett. He had an M14 with a starlight scope on it and a silencer on the end that must have stuck out a foot. I don't know how much that thing weighed, but he had to think it was a ton after running up

Highway 13 from Nu Ong and then down 14, 'til we picked them up. Come on. Let's go eat and I'll tell you all about it."

Breakfast was the same as always: eggs done to your choice, toast—sometimes donuts, and the ever present coffee. Whenever the cooks were fixing omelets Jim always had one. His favorite was ham and cheese, but any omelet had flavor, and that was more than he could say for eggs sunny side up or over easy, which usually ended up being over hard. Unlike a lot of guys, he always took his malaria tablet. But then he didn't get the diarrhea like some of the other guys, so he really didn't mind.

The two men were about finished with their meals when Gillett poked Jim with his elbow. Pointing to a guy at the end of the table putting Tabasco sauce on his eggs he said, "Mac, what septic tank do you suppose that guy lived in that taught him to put Tabasco sauce on his eggs?"

"Mexico!" Both men broke into laughter. They looked at each other and laughed that much harder. Before long, they had the whole mess hall looking their direction.

Jim placed his steel pot* with the ice cold shaving water on his bunk between himself and his mirror. He was well lathered and had started to shave when he saw it. There in the rafters was Kenny's monkey directly over Bob Athia's bunk. It didn't dawn on Jim what was happening until he turned around and started laughing at the spectacle above. Bob Athia was a well-built man of about 5'7" and one hundred fifty pounds. An Oklahoma boy with brown hair and eyes, he already had a big dislike for Kenny's monkey.

"Hey, Bob, Kenny's monkey's about to come all over you."

Athia looked up to see the masturbating monkey directly over his bunk. Grabbing a combat boot, he threw it at the monkey and shouted, "I'll kill you, you son of a bitch."

The boot missed but caused the monkey to move just as he ejaculated, spreading semen on Bob's bunk, the floor and Dick Hunter's wall locker. Dick Hunter stood six feet, weighed about one hundred ninety pounds, and like most of the other men in the hooch, he didn't have any love for the monkey. So with the mess on his wall

_____

*Steel Pot - Steel part of a infantryman's combat helmet.

locker that now confronted him, he picked up his M16 and with the actions of a man who meant business, he jammed in a full magazine and pulled back the bolt.

Kenny, who had been watching with Gillett and Jim, jumped on Hunter before he could take aim. Athia's temper was on full boil. He jumped on Kenny and a full scale fight was under way. Gillett started forward to break things up when Jim grabbed his arm and said, "Let 'em fight. It'll do Kenny good. Maybe he'll even decide to get rid of that damn monkey."

Gillett ignored him and moved forward shouting, "Alright, you guys, I'm giving you a direct order: break it up. I mean it. Stop it." The three separated as Gillett shouted, "attent-hut", and came to attention facing Gillett, who started his lecture, "Kenny, Mac thought I should have let them beat the hell out of you and believe me I would have if I was sure that Athia and Hunter would be flyable. You just might have gotten lucky and really hurt one of them, so I had to stop it. However, Kenny YOU WILL get rid of that monkey and YOU WILL clean up the mess he just made! Do you understand me?"

Kenny nodded his head, "Yes".

"Hunter, you know perfectly good and well it's an automatic Article 15 for unauthorized discharging of a weapon in the company area. So you should be glad Kenny stopped you. Okay, let's get finished up in here, you're supposed to be on your ships shortly."

The truck ride to the flight line was filled with conversation and bet-taking on when, if at all, Kenny would get rid of his monkey. One thing about a group of GI's, they were willing to take bets on anything. Once at the ship, Jim started his preflight inspection. It wasn't long before the gunners were dropped off. They usually went to the armament bunker for ammo and smoke grenades before going to their ships. Jim's ship had been fixed and moved out of maintenance and into its revetment. The first thing he checked was the log book to see what maintenance had been done. As he had suspected there was no major damage to the ship, only superficial wounds which required some simple skin patching.

Jim was almost finished with his preflight when Gary Broadnex, his gunner for the day, showed up. Gary was a short, five-foot-five, stubby fellow with a roly poly disposition. Yet his one hundred sixty-five pounds of mostly muscle made him very physical, "Hi, Mac, I heard that new guy has to go get a flight physical today. My ship's in maintenance, so for today, I fly with you."

"I'll tell you, I'm glad to see you. I was afraid I'd get stuck with Kenny or one of our pothead friends."

"How are you betting on Kenny's monkey?"

"Oh, it'll still be there tonight."

It wasn't long before Mr. Walker and Mr. Valadores walked up. Mr. Valadores looked every bit the Spaniard his name indicated. A full faced man of medium height and build, Valadores hoped to be a comedian once out of the service. Everyone enjoyed flying with him because of his great sense of humor.

In another twenty minutes, the flight of ten ships and two gunships was airborne. Their mission for the day was to put troops in position to start a sweep in the direction of fire support base, BURK. BURK would then act as a blocking force, along with troops from the First Infantry Division.

BURK was located alongside a dirt highway surrounded by trees, except where the engineers had cleared them to allow for a good field of fire. No one liked flying in or around trees. They were hard to get over on take off and harder still to find a safe place to land in case of power failure or other emergency.

It was a long, boring flight from Tay Ninh to the drop sight, although no one was in a real hurry to get there. Jim pulled the sun visor down on his helmet and pulled his seat belt tight to take a nap. The boredom and exhaustion was putting him to sleep. He awoke when he heard Valadores say, "Is that our L.Z.?"

Walker's response was only to shake his head in the affirmative. Jim looked out the door and saw they were on long final approach to the hour glass.

It was called the hour glass because, from the air, that's what it looked like. In reality, it was a grass clearing surrounded by trees. Everytime the Blackhawks had landed there they had been shot at and this time wasn't any different. It started with small arms fire as they came in on short final. The bottom right side of the hour glass suddenly looked like a fire works display. Jim could only guess at what it looked like from the ground as all twenty M60's opened up, each firing a tracer every fifth round. Unfortunately, the worst was to come as the ships touched down. Out of the hour glass's neck came fire that Jim couldn't see but Broadnex announced, "We're getting shot at by a bunch of 50's. There are four, no eight of them. That thing must be a dual quad fifty*. As the flight started to lift off, Jim could see fire coming from his side of the bottleneck. It was Valadores who asked the question first, "My Lord, those look like basketballs coming at us! Mac, what is that thing down there?"

"It's got to be an anti-aircraft gun." Jim continued to fire his M60 at the ack-ack gun, hoping to silence it long enough to get past. His voice was full of agitation and emotion as he related to the others what he saw as he looked backward. "Oh, shit, Chalk Seven just took a direct hit from that ack-ack. It just literally blew up."

Jim hadn't finished speaking when the intership radio cracked, "Lead, this is Chalk 10. Chalk 7 just took a direct hit from anti-aircraft fire. He went down out of control and is on the ground in flames now. There appear to be no survivors. Trail, out."

The mike clicked twice. The big question on everyone's mind now was, who was in Chalk Seven? It was a First Platoon ship, so no one on 925 knew who was in it. Of course, it just wasn't right to go on the radio and ask.

"Trail, this is Lead. How many ships did we leave behind? Over."

"Lead, this is Trail. Two by my count. Over."

"Six, this is Lead. Do you copy? Over?"

"Roger, Lead. We're over the L.Z. in C and C. Take the flight back to BURK and pick up troops there and insert them ASAP**. I'll get Saigon and see if we can't get some fixed wing help up here. Six out."

The flight had already turned to head for the dirt road alongside BURK. In no time, troops were on board and headed back to the hour glass. This time, though, there was more prepping of the L.Z. for their landing. The first time in the gunships had made a couple of runs but drawn no fire, which meant, of course, the NVA troops on the ground were well disciplined. So this time the L.Z. was also

---

*Dual Quad 50 - 50 caliber machinegun with eight barrels firing together.

**A.S.A.P. - As soon as possible.

prepped with artillery fire from BURK's 105MM guns.

All the friendly troops were supposed to be on the left, so only those guns on the right side of the ships opened fire as they approached the L.Z. On command, the right side guns opened fire with each person expecting at any second to see the basketball sized tracers start blowing them out of the sky. The ships were on the ground and the troops out and nothing—not even small arms fire. The flight took off and was gone without receiving that first sign of enemy fire.

"Mr. Walker, you know I'm enormously glad we didn't get shot at again, but I don't understand why."

"The only thing I can figure, Mac, is that when they started getting artillery fire on them they packed up and left."

"But, Sir, with those two guns working together they could have blown every one of us out of the sky, then taken the troops on the ground at their leisure."

"Wouldn't you guess that was their plan to begin with, but the guys they had operating the fifty and ack-ack were such poor shots they didn't get the job done. I mean, after all, the 50 only got one ship and the anti-aircraft one, and either one of them alone should have gotten all ten of us. But at the worst, both together should have knocked down seven or eight of us. When that didn't happen, they figured correctly that we would be right back with more troops, and it did only take us about thirty minutes turn around time. You can bet they didn't want to lose those two guns, so they figured since plan A didn't work, use plan B. Pack up and leave."

"Yeah, you're probably right which means two things: one, someone in Saigon told them where, when and with what we were coming, and two, they also knew where the trap was laid and were not about to get caught in it."

"You got it, Mac. We'll put a little red apple on your tree tonight and send you to the head of the class."

"You're so kind."

Valadores broke in, "Hey, you guys, I've had my UHF* on. Six has been talking to Tay Ninh. They're going to let us get fuel this

---

*UHF - Ultra high frequency radio - used for long range communication (mostly Air Force.)

time but that's it. No more fuel except for gunships until they can get the bridges the NVA blew fixed to get a convoy through. And, of course, they'll probably have to have the Air Force fly in fuel first."

Jim reached up and flipped his UHF and VHF* switch on just in time to hear Six calling Lead, "I read you loud and clear, Six. Come on in."

"Roger, Lead. You can only get the flight topped off once at Tay Ninh. I've tried Quan Loi, and Dau Tieng and they're both out of fuel except for gunships. The next closest place is Cu Chi. They said they have a reasonable supply, but with everyplace else running low, Cu Chi won't last long either. I'll keep you advised. Six, out."

It wasn't long until the flight landed at the fuel pumps, refueled and picked up troops.

Jim always thought that, in many ways, the ferrying of troops was one of the worst parts of the war. It was the boredom, hour after hour of the same patch of sky to look at, the same jungle or rice paddy, the same trees and water from eighteen hundred feet was very monotonous. Boredom, long, long hours of boredom combined with the ever present fatigue, made it extremely hard to stay awake.

It took about thirty minutes to get to the L.Z. with American troops on both sides of the hour glass. There wasn't any firing of the ship's M60's. It was a routine landing and take off. Now they had to make the forty-five minute flight to Cu Chi, then up to Tay Ninh to pick up troops and back to the L.Z. Jim figured it would be an easy two hours before they got back to the L.Z. again.

He could hear Lead asking Six what kind of resistance the grunts had met. The response didn't surprise Jim. No contact with the enemy. Of course, the American troops hadn't moved until the second lift had been put in. By that time, the NVA had broken down their big guns and split. By the time our troops got there, they could see by the crushed grass the spot where both guns had been. No other sign of their existence was present: no shells, nothing. The walk to BURK would be just as uneventful. No question about it—the NVA had planned on a very big slaughter. Lack of skill by the guys working

---

*VHF - Very high frequency radio - used for medium range communication.

the fifty and ack-ack had caused a very quick change in plans. Jim realized their plan was good—very, very good. If the NVA had as few as one hundred fifty troops in the area, it would have been easy pickings because there couldn't have been more than fifty or sixty U.S. troops on the ground, depending on how many of the flight crews survived in fighting condition.

The tension seemed to release as Jim leaned back, allowing the fatigue to consume him. Before falling asleep he said, "Thank you, God."

Jim awoke to hear Broadnex and Walker talking. Cu Chi was in sight and before long, the flight had refueled and then relocated on a side road. Jim was glad he hadn't gotten caught sleeping and, also, that there'd been a change in plans, even though he didn't know what or why. The flight was now in Cu Chi sitting on a side road shutting off the engines, which meant they were going to be there for a while.

Almost as quickly as the engines were shut down, the crews broke out the C-rations. The pilots took their C's and walked up to lead ship to discuss the day and get instructions from Six. Jim had tied down the main rotor blade and started to open his C-ration box, when a Chaplain stuck his head in the ship and said, "I've got a jeep over there in the clearing," as he pointed in its direction. "I'll be holding services in three minutes and I'd like to have you men join me." With that, he turned and walked down the line of choppers and made the same invitation to each man he saw.

Jim turned to Broadnex and said, "Come on, let's go."

"Mac, that's sissy stuff. I'm not going over there."

Without responding, Jim gulped his C-ration and walked over to the jeep taking a seat on the ground along with some grunts who had come over and the handful of Blackhawks. There were about a dozen men present. The chaplain started, "In the name of the Father, Son and Holy Ghost. Amen. Men, I've only been in country a few weeks, but in that short time, I've learned these impromptu services are often more meaningful to you than the regular Sunday services I hold. I've also learned those choppers won't wait for me to finish, so I better get the most important part done first. Is there anyone here who hasn't been baptized and would like to do so now?" The chaplain looked quickly around and seeing no response moved on. "Is there anyone here who already knows the Lord Jesus Christ and believes in Him?" This time the response was unanimous as each man raised his hand. "In that case, is there anyone here who would like to receive Holy Communion?"

The response was slower but, again, several hands went up, including Jim's. It would be his first communion since he left the states and he knew he had many sins of which to repent. His first thought was of R & R and all he had done there. The chaplain's voice continued. "Very well, men, all I have is a canteen of water and some C-ration crackers. Under the circumstances, though, I don't think the Lord will mind their use." He then placed the canteen and crackers on the jeep's hood and said, "Let us pray. 'Our Father, who art in heaven. Hallowed be Thy Name. Thy kingdom come, Thy will be done on earth as it is in heaven. Give us this day our daily bread; and forgive us our trespasses as we forgive those who trespass against us and lead us not into temptation, but deliver us from evil. For Thine is the kingdom and the power and the glory. Amen'. Men, our Lord Jesus Christ on the night He was betrayed took bread and when He had given thanks, He broke it and gave it to His disciples saying, 'Take, eat, this is My Body which is given for you, this do in remembrance of Me. After the same manner also, He took the cup, when He had supped and when He had given thanks, He gave it to them saying, 'Drink ye all of it, this cup is the New Testament in My Blood which is shed for you and for many for the remission of sins. This do, as often as you drink it, in remembrance of Me. The Peace of the Lord be with you always. Amen. The table of the Lord is ready.

"Men, those of you who believe in the Lord Jesus Christ as your personal Savior and who truly repent of all your sins, rise and receive the Lord's table."

Jim and most of the men rose and moved forward. The words just spoken rang in his ears, emotion filled his chest and a tear fell from his eye down the side of his face as the chaplain handed him a small piece of stale cracker and said, "Take, eat, this is the Body of Christ given for you." Each man was served and the chaplain picked up the water canteen, passing it to each man as he spoke, "Take, drink the Blood of Christ shed for your sins."

After all the men had been served, he had them take their seats on the grass again and spoke once more, "The Body of our Lord Jesus Christ and His precious Blood strengthen and preserve you in true faith unto everlasting life. Amen." After a short pause, he addressed the group as though giving a sermon. Jim's eyes were full of moisture and the emotion he felt at that moment would haunt him always. He wanted to weep openly but forced back the tears, not wanting to seem unmanly. He had just received the most meaningful communion of his life. It was the chaplain's voice that brought him back from his own deep thoughts. "Men, like me, some of you have only been in country a short time, others are probably about to rotate home." As the chaplain spoke he could look over the men in front of him and see the helicopters parked behind them. The pilots in the first chopper were climbing out and quickly moving back towards their ships. Knowing he now had only seconds before the fly-boys in his group would have to leave, his message now became shorter, "I can never know your trials because, like millions of others, I'll never walk in your shoes." He could see the main rotors being untied, "There will be times when you think Christ has forsaken you. However, take a lesson from the old Jews. They sinned and the Lord punished them but he never forsook them. He always loved them and was always with them just as he will always be with you. That doesn't mean you won't be killed. St. Paul and Peter were killed because they loved Jesus. He will always be with you, even in death, and for that reason, LIVE without fear!"

The all too familiar whine of the chopper engines starting to turn reached their ears. The fly boys all stood at once and started to leave but were stopped and turned around by the chaplain's words. "Men, give me only one second more." He raised his right hand and said, "The Lord bless you and keep you. The Lord make His face to shine upon you. The Lord lift His countenance upon you and give you His peace. Amen."

With his still raised hand he waved them on. To a man, they turned and ran to their respective ships. Watching them go he was reminded of a phrase he had heard before, but couldn't quite bring to mind, something about the flower of American Youth.

Broadnex had already untied the rotor and Walker had started to turn the engine. Jim quickly put his chicken plate on and then his helmet. Having plugged his helmet in he spoke. "What's happening?"

Walker responded, "To make a long story short, there was only one way out of our trap at BURK. Naturally, that's the way the NVA are going. Since we now have to go to Saigon to get fuel, we're simply going to let them go and pull our own troops out. It seems the turn around time will be too great to chance putting in a blocking force."

The flight back to BURK and the Hour Glass was uneventful, giving Jim time to think about the chaplain's words. They picked up the same troops they had dropped off earlier along with the flight crew that had been shot down. The charred remains of the other ship still lay in a broken, ugly heap. The second ship had been chinooked out earlier. What little was left of the four men, who had been burned in the chopper hit by anti-aircraft fire, lay on the ground beside their ship.

"Mr. Walker, did you see those bodies as we took off?"

"Yeah, Mac, I did. Not a nice way to die."

"Sir, where are we dropping these troops?"

"Since the pressure is off at BURK, they're going all the way to Saigon. We're supposed to put them in a polo field the French built. In fact, it's alongside a building used as a French Academy. Evidently the Cholon district of Saigon is catching hell. We heard on the radio that the M.P.'s have finally secured the U.S. Embassy."

The flight down to Saigon seemed to take forever. Jim was overwhelmed as they approached the old French polo field. He had no idea that any such place existed in Vietnam. Old world money and lots of it was very evident. A brick fence surrounded the polo field and a brick two-story building that might have been a barracks or school at one time stood just outside the field. Half round red tile roofing lay broken on the ground beside the building. Grass was growing in the cracks around the old flag pole in what had once been an area where ceremonies were held. The grass on the field had been recently mowed like someone expected to play one day this week. Only the trash on the field told of the departed army that had used its grounds as a camping area.

The flight landed on the edge of the polo field not far from the old barracks. There were still signs of the recent heavy combat that

had taken place in and around the field but the flight didn't draw any
fire. From the polo field they went to the fuel dump to put on fuel.

"Flight, this is Lead. A jeep will approach one of our ships; whoever
the lucky one is that they pull up beside, you're to get four rubber
bags and take them back up to BURK with you."

As Jim put fuel in his chopper, he listened to the radio and hoped
that jeep driver didn't pick his ship. Broadnex's voice told him he
hadn't hoped hard enough. "Oh, shit, why us? Eight choppers sitting here and that bastard has to pick us."

Valadores spoke, "Broadnex, this is just your lucky day. Stop bitch-
ing and go get the bags."

When Jim climbed back on board, there in the cargo area were
four neatly folded black rubber bags. He hated those bags and if he
never saw a black rubber bag again, it would be too soon.

The flight back to the Hour Glass seemed to take forever. It was
the routine of the long flights and the boredom that once again made
it really tough for Jim to stay awake.

Once at the L.Z., Walker hovered their ship over to where the bodies
lay. Two grunts ran over to give assistance as Broadnex and Jim stepped
out of the chopper, each carrying two bags. It was the close-up sight
of the bodies that first made Jim look away. He tried not to look but
the sickly sweet smell violated his nostrils and tightened his throat
almost to the choking point, forcing him to look at the badly charred
body before him. The sight and smell was almost more than he could
stand. He put his handkerchief to his mouth and tried to block out
the smell as the other hand unzipped the bag. The flies were all over
the bodies, like bees on honey. Already swollen considerably, the
bodies looked and smelled worse than words could describe. Jim bent
over and with Broadnex's help, tried to roll the first body on top of
the opened bag. It was as if on cue they both turned and vomited.
Gagging and choking and vomiting, they finished the gruesome task
and zipped up the bag. The second body was just as bad as the first;
both started dry heaving when Broadnex pulled off a large chunk of
cooked flesh and meat in his hand. Unable to pick up the charred
remains, they tried to push the body into position. Finally, the job
was done and with the grunt's help, they were loaded onto the ship.
All four men tried to wash the bitter taste out of their mouths with

ice water from Jim's cooler, to no real avail. They swished it around, gargled and spit, Only the air rushing over their bodies as the ship flew along prevented them from smelling the odor that had attached itself to their clothing.

Jim settled back in his seat for the long flight back to Saigon. It was already starting to get dark, and the total exhaustion that overcame him was more than he cared to resist.

"Mac, you awake? Mac, wake up!"

"I'm awake, Mr. Walker. I'm awake!"

"You were, like shit, MacLaughlin! Now, stay awake, damn it! There are too many other choppers around, plus jets. I don't have to tell you that a phantom's nose wouldn't look at all good sticking out of our cargo door."

"Mr. Walker, do you know how much sleep I've had the last few days? Not more than three hours. I'm beat. Besides, these sixty minute lifts are boring as hell back here. Not to mention the fact I just had the dry heaves."

"MacLaughlin, there are millions of people in the world you could never convince that flying in a helicopter and getting shot at is boring. Get another drink of water and you'll feel better."

"Sir, I could care less what people think and I'm not thirsty."

"Okay, Mac, let's change the subject. I'm supposed to have R & R* next month. You just went. Tell me about it."

Jim figured why not, it'd take his mind off everything, "Okay, it was January 17 through 21. I went to Manila but you could care less. You just figure that if I'm talking, I won't go to sleep."

"That's not true, I really want to hear about it, and if it helps keep you awake, so much the better. Start with picking up your orders."

"Okay, I don't mind telling you about it because I had a great time. In fact, if I can work it out, I'm going back. I picked up my orders from the company clerk that morning, I was all on my own as far as getting there and back, so I hopped a ride on the courier flight down to Cu Chi. At Cu Chi I had to do some processing out of country and get my shots updated. I spent most of the time standing in

---

*R & R - Rest and recreation.

line. You know the Army, hurry up and wait. Since it was night by the time I got done, I stayed with the 116th Flight Platoon. The Hornets had an empty bunk."

4

"I noticed among the young men, a youth who lacked judgment." Proverbs 7:7, N.I.V.

R & R

Yes, Jim thought to himself, it had been quite an experience, but he didn't want to tell Walker the whole story. His mind drifted back to that first day of R & R. He remembered checking in and taking his sheets to the hooch he'd been assigned for the night. He found an empty bed, decided that it looked as flea infested as any of the others available, and unrolled the mattress to lay the sheets down. Someone touched him on the arm and said, "Aren't you Jim MacLaughlin?"

Jim turned and, seeing a slightly familiar face, shook his head and said, "Yes."

The other GI laughed and said, "I'm John Seiko."

Jim was stunned. He hadn't seen John since high school, where they had been classmates almost two years ago. John had grown at least four inches and had lost all his baby fat. In school, John had been at least one hundred pounds overweight.

"Jim, you didn't recognize me!"

"John, I hate to admit it, but I didn't. Man, you have changed!"

"I know! Joining the Army was the best thing that ever happened to me. Look, Jim, you coming or going on R & R?"

"I'm going, how about you?"

"I just got back from Hong Kong and have the day to kill; then tomorrow, I check out of here and head back to the Big Red One over at Di An. Look, let's check in your M16 and ammo and go get a drink."

"John, that sounds great, but I have to check in at reception in about fifteen minutes."

Together, they made Jim's bunk and walked over to check in his ammo and M16. From there they headed to the reception center, where Jim was given a list of do's and don'ts and a departure time for the next day. From there they hopped a ride on a jeep to Saigon. The staff sergeant driving turned out to be a nice guy who took them to a bar and told them to have a good time.

The place was packed with people, and it didn't take long until they decided to leave. Once on the street Jim remembered why he hated Saigon. The place was a pigsty and the people were barbarians. The two GIs hadn't gone fifty feet down the road, when a little boy about six years old, with bare feet, ragged shorts and no shirt approached.

"Hey, GI, you want number one woman?"

"No, kid, we're not interested. Now beat it!"

"Come on, GI, you want layed? Buy my Mama San, she virgin, number one lay, GI. Number one, you like, you like!"

John decided to have a little fun with this kid, so he said, "Hey kid, your mother good looking?"

"Number one, GI, number one, you like."

"You sure she's a virgin, kid?"

"Sure, GI, she virgin, you like, number one, number one!"

"Beat it, kid! We're not interested in your mother. Go on, get out of here!"

John laughed and laughed. "I'll tell you, Jim, this is some country where little kids try to sell you their mother and sisters."

"Yeah, and look at those kids—the streets and the buildings."

"Hey, GI, you no want Mama San? But sister, she pretty."

"She a virgin too, kid?"

"Sure GI, she virgin, number one, you like very much."

"Hey kid, how many kids your Mama San have?"

"Eight, you want sister?"

"No! No! No! Now beat it kid, go on, git!"

Jim pulled on John's arm and pointed down the alley. There, beside a bunch of old crates and boxes, squatted a Vietnamese man with his pants down having a bowel movement and the whole area smelled like it wasn't the first time it had been used as a toilet. Jim wasn't really surprised, though, as there was garbage and trash all over the place and the streets were covered with dirt and sand. From the same alley, an old woman came out of a restaurant with a pail of slop and gave it a sling into the gutter. The street was lined on both sides with bars, restaurants and open-air shops. The shops were filled with varied and sundry goods. Some had meat hanging that was covered with flies, some were filled with black market goods. Everything from guns, ammo and other weapons of war to booze and C-rations was available. As the two men walked by the bars, they were accosted by men and sometimes women. Each tried to sell the age old folly of soldiers in any army: drink and girls—girls on stage, all nude girl reviews, all nude go-go dancers, strip shows, topless waitresses, girls for sale by the ejaculation or by the hour, day or week—girls were definitely available.

As they walked, they were stopped by a very attractive girl in the doorway of a bar, who was pleasant and spoke fairly good English. As she talked, she put her arm around John's waist and began to rub his crotch. As she worked on John, Jim couldn't help but be stunned by her beauty. She was a small woman, of about sixteen, he would guess. Her hair and makeup were perfect and her oriental dress, slit to her hips, showed enough of her petite figure in a provocative sort of way to cause both men to give consideration to the offer she proposed. She had John sold and knew it from her hand, so skillfully manipulating his engorged shaft. In a sexually playful gesture, John began tickling her under the arms and on the tummy. It was this that caused both men to lose interest instantly in her and move on. "My God, Jim, did you see those teeth when she started to laugh?"

"Unfortunately, yes. I have never seen such a disgusting mess in my life. Those teeth were half rotted away with just stubs sticking up and what was left had a sickly black and green color. I thought I was going to gag."

"Jim, you thought you were going to gag, how about me? I could just see myself screwing that broad and me laying a few French kisses on her. I think I'm going to be sick. Come on, this looks like a half way decent place. I'll buy you a beer."

It was a typical small bar, not much space, with only three tables and bar stools running the length of one wall. The table they took was made of wood, but didn't look like it would hold the two beers they ordered. The bamboo walls showed various sized holes and cracks. The floor was dirt and was probably raked out once a week, whether it needed it or not. They ordered only American beer in cans and insisted that they remain unopened before being placed on their table. Time slipped by quickly as the two old friends discussed their high school and Army days.

Very late that night when they left, the kids were still selling their female relatives and the men on every street corner were still selling watches and cigarettes. Both GI's were in a silly, drunken condition and when Jim asked to see a watch hawker's selection, they literally fell over each other laughing. The watch hawker had pulled up both sleeves. Watches covered both arms from his wrists to his elbows. Then he pulled up both pant legs exposing more watches on each leg from the ankles to the knees. From there they caught a taxi back to the base and left the Saigon shanties behind.

(In three years, Jim MacLaughlin would attend his high school class reunion, where the emcee would tell that John Seiko had been killed in action in South Vietnam at some place called Hobo Woods. Jim immediately recognized the date as being only days after they had been together in Saigon. Jim's chest would fill with painful emotion, his head would drop into his hands and on down to the table. Tears would fill his eyes until, finally, overcome with emotion he would weep openly.)

Wake up time for Jim was 0500/hours. He watched for Seiko, but didn't see him. So he decided to try to look him up again when he got back from R & R. When Jim reported in at the reception center, he was told to turn in his bedding and be ready for departure at 1000/hours. He already had his bedding, so he could go straight to the supply hooch, and from there to the mess hall for the predictable Army chow which he knew was as big a mess one place as another. Jim arrived back at the orientation center at 0945/hours with khaki uniform on, suitcase in hand and ready to go. At 1035/hours, an Army sergeant began the briefing by saying they were going to hurry, as they were running late. The sergeant checked everyone's orders and, when finished, told the group they would be met in Manila and given a briefing. From there the sergeant led the group to the finance center where their M.P.C.'s (Military Pay Currency) were exchanged for real American green backs. As each person walked through the finance center door, the sergeant directed him to a waiting bus.

Jim found himself somewhat amused at how tough some tours of duty were in Vietnam. Here there were numerous soldiers doing nothing more each day than driving a bus and directing other people around, but he knew this was nothing new. He had often been told that it took eight or more support people for each combat soldier. Still, he couldn't help but wonder if these Saigon Warriors wouldn't be the ones to tell the biggest war stories back home.

The bus arrived at Tan Son Nhut airport at 1200/hours. The group was led by the same sergeant from the customs area. Going through customs wasn't any real problem. It was a simple matter of opening one's suitcase for inspection and then passing through the turnstile.

Once more they followed that fine old Army tradition, "Hurry up and wait." At 1245/hours, the group finally was ready to board an Air Force DC-6 for Manila. Standing in line, it occurred to Jim there weren't any officers or women in the group of about thirty enlisted men. He decided they probably sent officers in separate groups, but he wondered how women went on R & R.

When Jim got on the plane he was horrified! There weren't any seats! Halfway panic stricken he looked around to see what the others were doing. They, for the most part, were looking around to see what everyone else was doing. One Sp/5 had started unfolding the plane's fold down benches from the walls. Jim's only thought was, "You have got to kidding me!", as he sat down and looked for the seatbelt that wasn't there.

The Sp/5 seated next to him said, "They could have at least told us it was a no frills flight."

Jim laughed and commented, "With the no-expenses barred treatment we have received so far, I'm afraid to see what the stewardesses look like."

He didn't have to be concerned. There weren't any. Somewhat to his surprise, the plane managed to get off the ground. It landed at Clark Air Force Base, Manila, at 1805/hours. As they disembarked, they were led into another customs center and from there to the briefing room.

The staff sergeant entering the room looked like a hundred other young men. He was about twenty-one, tall, thin, with a fair complexion. Despite his squeaky voice, he tried his best to sound like a nail biting drill sergeant. "Good evening, men. My name is Staff Sergeant Pedro. I'll be giving you a lot of information, so listen up. First, each of you must pick one hotel from the list on the blackboard. Write the name of said hotel in the space marked hotel on the white sheet of paper you were given as you entered this room. If you don't know anything about any of the hotels, just pick a name that sounds good and write it down. We are not allowed to give out any more information about the hotels."

Jim looked at the list and wrote down Shoreline Hotel. He wished he knew more about it than just the name. Sergeant Pedro explained what they could and couldn't buy (mostly what couldn't be bought and taken through customs), and where they could not go in Manila, since part of the city had known Communist sympathizers. They were not to wear their uniforms at all, from the time they arrived at the hotel until the morning they dressed to return. If they became ill or needed any other services, such as legal or medical, they were to call the base operator or present themselves to the M.P. at the gate. Sergeant Pedro also stressed the importance of not being arrested by the local officials.

Finally, he had the group finish filling out the required paperwork. "In conclusion, gentlemen, I welcome you to Manila and assure you that there is no reason each of you shouldn't have a very nice visit. To help you enjoy yourselves we have compiled a list of bars that we strongly recommend. You can visit them tonight. At these bars you can buy drinks and female companionship without fear of M.P. disapproval. The girls are checked out on a regular basis by a doctor. We also recommend that you pay in advance for your room for the duration of your stay. That way, if anything happens to your money, you have a place to stay and you can eat here on post. If there are no questions, pick up your suitcases and file outside. You are to get on the bus marked with the name of the hotel you chose. Have a good time men. Move out."

The bus ride to the hotel took about thirty minutes. In no time at all, Jim had checked in and arrived at his room on the tenth floor. He was pleased with the room. It was clean with one large bed, a bath and shower, dresser, desk and chair. In general, this is what he would expect in a nice but older hotel in the states. Jim quickly showered and changed. He wanted to eat and then find a bar. He walked out the hotel door and saw several taxis. One of the drivers approached and asked, "You need a taxi, Sir?"

"Yes, I do."

"Get in, Sir, get in. My name is Joe. Where you want to go?"

"I'm here on R & R . I'd like to get something to eat and drink."

"I know the exact place, sir. And let me add, I would consider it a privilege to be your personal guide and driver while you're here."

Joe started the '58 Ford he used for a taxi and drove off into the night, and Jim started on an adventure that would affect his relationship with women and his future wife more than he could possibly realize.

"Joe, I'm not sure I understand your offer. How much do you want for this service?"

"Nothing, Sir, except the usual taxi fee. You see, it works out good for both of us. You have me for a guide around the city, and I'll take real good care of you—even give you some advice and answer all your questions. You'll want to go various places and I know the best. Besides, you won't have to worry about a taxi. I'll always be there as your personal driver, not taking any other fares while you're here. It's a good deal for me, also; I can count on your using my taxi, so I'll have a fare each day. You simply tell me what time to be at the hotel in the morning and I'll be there waiting."

"Joe, how do you charge? By the mile, day, or hour?"

"By the mile, Sir. Look, business is bad right now and I know how much the average GI travels on R & R. So, I know I'll make more money working for you than by trying to hack it, and you get a good deal in return."

"Okay, Joe, you've got a deal under one condition. Stop calling me, Sir. My name is Jim MacLaughlin. Call me Jim or Mac, or MacLaughlin, but don't call me, Sir. Okay?"

"Okay, okay, Jim. You've made a wise decision. Here we are,

Howard's Bar and Restaurant. I'm sure you can find everything you want in there. When you're ready to leave, I'll be here waiting. You're going to like it here."

Jim got out of the taxi, a little unsure of himself. He had never done anything like this before, but he sure wasn't going to miss his chance now. He just hoped he didn't lose his nerve. Upon entering, he noticed several young girls standing around. As much as he hated it, he knew he blushed when they smiled at him. The maitre'd met him and asked if he would like to go to the bar or the restaurant. Jim chose the restaurant and dined on the best steak, mashed potatoes and peas he'd had since the States.

After dinner, he paid his bill and proceeded to the bar. He was shown to a table where he ordered a whiskey sour. A short, heavy set Philippino man approached the table and sat down. "Hi, my name is Manuel Romulo. You're here on R & R?"

"Yes, I am. My name is Jim. Have a seat, make yourself at home."

"Thank you. Are you interested in a girl, Jim?"

"Sure, you the boss?"

"Yes, I am. Do you have a girl picked out?"

"No, and I have to admit I've never done this before."

"Jim, my good friend, that's no problem."

Manuel slapped his hands and shouted to no one in particular in a language that Jim didn't understand. In a routine that was obviously standard procedure, all the girls who weren't sitting with a man moved to a bench along one wall and sat down. There must have been fifteen girls on that bench. Each was different in many ways. They ranged in age, from what Jim guessed to be about fifteen, to what must have been forty-five or forty-six. Some were just plain ugly, some homely, some plain, some attractive, and some were very, very pretty. There were fat girls, skinny girls, and everything in between. All but a few were dressed in western clothing. Manuel gave Jim several minutes to look the girls over and make a selection. Finally, Jim smiled and looked over at Manuel, who had been in the business long enough to know that this is where he should take the lead.

"Jim, would you like to go up and take a closer look?"

"No, I don't think so."

"Is there one that you would like to have come over? Would you like to talk to her?"

"How about the one with the deck of cards in her hands?"

"An excellent choice, Jim. She is one of my very best girls."

Manuel motioned to the girls and directed the one Jim had picked to his table. The rest of the girls dispersed and Jim watched the slender, young beauty walk to his table. She had a graceful walk and held herself in a manner as if to show that she had grown up in an above average home. She had a light complexion and dark hair and eyes. Her skirt ended well above her knees, revealing two beautiful legs. As she sat down she smiled at Jim. He realized instantly she hadn't shown any teeth. Manuel spoke first.

"Jim, this is Rose. Rose, I'd like you to meet Jim."

Rose looked Jim in the eye and said, "Hi, you're very nice looking."

"Thank you, and may I say, you're the most beautiful Rose I've ever seen." Jim paused for a moment and said, "I know this sounds strange, but could I see your teeth?"

Rose flashed him a very toothy smile and a very puzzled look.

Manuel spoke, "Is everything okay?"

"Yes, just fine, thank you."

"Would you like to use the bed in the back room before you decide?"

Jim shook his head and said, "No, that won't be necessary."

Manuel and Rose exchanged several words in the local dialect. This irritated Jim, but he didn't think it wise to demand they speak English. It was obvious that Manuel was giving Rose instructions, since he was doing most of the talking. She simply responded with one or two words or a nod. Finally, she left and Manuel turned to Jim and said, "Now then, we can talk business. Do you want her for all four nights that you're here, or do you wish to change girls each night? Let me add, there is less cost if you keep her for the duration of your stay."

"I'll keep her for all four nights. How much?"

"Twenty dollars a night, that is eighty dollars for the four."

Jim was shocked and it showed on his face. Manuel saw it and responded at once, "I told you she is one of my very best girls, and she costs accordingly."

"Okay, no problem. When do you want paid?"

"You can do it right now. Would you also like some herbs to smoke?"

"Herbs? You mean pot?"

Manuel held out his hand to take the money Jim was counting and said, "Yes."

Jim's response was a curt, "No!"

"That's perfectly fine. Now if you have any problems with her of any kind, please let me know. If you wish for any reason to change girls at any time, feel free to do so. There won't be any additional cost."

The two men shook hands. Manuel turned and motioned to Rose, who, at some time during the discussion, had taken a seat on the bench. She picked up a small handbag and approached them. Jim, watching her movements in the very short dress, was filled with great anticipation.

"Let me carry your bag, Rose."

She handed him the bag and took his extended arm.

Outside, Jim looked around for Joe and he spotted him getting out of his taxi parked just across the street. Joe hurriedly crossed the street, took the bag from Jim, and led the couple to his taxi.

Once inside the couple made small talk. Jim learned that English is taught in the schools along with their local dialect. That explained why everyone he met spoke English, and why many of the signs were in English, also.

At the hotel they got on the elevator just behind an older Philippino couple who appeared to be in their fifties. As the elevator started its rise, the older couple looked Jim and Rose over closely. The man spoke very curtly to Rose in the local dialect. Her response was one or two short words with her head down looking at the floor. Finally, the elevator stopped at Jim's floor. He took Rose's hand and started out the door. The man shouted at them as they left. Rose turned and responded very sharply. As the elevator doors closed between the two antagonists, the man spit on the floor at Rose's feet. Jim took her arm and led her down the hall.

"I take it he doesn't care much for you, or me—and neither of our professions."

"Oh, he likes yours alright. He still thinks General MacArthur is God's second son. It's me he doesn't approve of."

Jim unlocked the door, put the bag on a chair, closed the curtains and embraced Rose. Their kiss was long and passionate. Jim's hand moved to the top of her dress and pulled on the zipper. Rose wiggled and the dress dropped to the floor leaving her in only her very lacey bra and small bikini panties.

She was very pleased with herself for having spotted him when he first entered Howard's. She had smiled and shuffled her cards as he shyly glanced her way, and watched as he blushed and moved on past. She liked these American boys who blushed. They always turned out to be very kind and gentle. The fact that this one was also very nice looking made it just that much better. It had been a simple thing to make herself scarce until he moved to the bar. Then, to make sure he noticed her again, she had moved by his table shuffling the cards, before Manuel had sat down with him. Once Manuel ordered the girls to the bench for his scrutiny, she'd made sure she got the seat direct-ly in front of him. Thus, the first girl he saw would be her. And, she knew that the shuffling of the cards would subconsciously attract his attention. All she had to do then was to give him her most in-viting smile. If his choice was close, the cards would tip the balance in her favor, and this would also make his description of her to Manuel that much easier.

Sometime later Jim opened his eyes and watched her dry him with a towel before laying down beside him. "You know, Rose, you're beautiful and Manuel was right, you're very good."

"Thank you. I like you, Jim, and I'll try to make you very happy while you're here. We'll make love more than you ever made it in your life."

Jim laughed and said, "That wouldn't be hard to do. I'm a virgin, or rather, I was. Wow, is that an embarrassing thing to admit."

"It doesn't matter. In fact, I'll make you a promise: before you leave Manila, I'll be so implanted in your mind that you'll think of me on your wedding night."

"That, Rose, is some promise. Come on, let's take a bath."

Rose moved off the bed and wrapped a large towel around her. Jim had already started the bath and climbed in when Rose entered. She picked up a wash cloth and a bar of soap. Then she got down on her knees.

"Come on, Rose, get in, it really feels good."

"Later, Jim. First, let me bathe you."

She started scrubbing his back and shoulders and watched his muscles roll under his bronzed skin as she rubbed. She sensed that he possessed a great deal more strength than his stature indicated. He lay back in the tub completely relaxed and allowed her to start on his feet. The pleasure he felt at that moment was indescribable. "Rose, this feels wonderful. How did you ever learn to bathe a man?"

"My mother died when I was thirteen and I assumed her duties, one of which was bathing my father."

Jim looked up at her, "You said her duties. Does that include sleeping with him?"

"Of course not. I assumed only her jobs and responsibilities. Of six children, I was the youngest and only daughter."

"What did you do, run away?"

"Oh, no. My father was fairly rich and I had a good life until he was killed in a car crash when I was almost sixteen. Then, I came to Manila to live with my oldest brother and his family. Once here, I started dating American boys from the base, which my brother didn't like. We got into a real big fight one day, and he kicked me out. I'd already met Manuel a few months earlier through one of the guys I was dating, and he'd extended me an offer to work for him. So, there I was with no money, job, or place to stay and only in Manila about six months. There wasn't a whole lot I could do. Besides, the money's good and I do enjoy my work."

The excitement that had started to stir in Jim disappeared after hearing Rose's story. He simply lay there totally relaxed and touched by her story, while her soft hands finished scrubbing his body. She rinsed him off and helped him rise from the tub and step out. "Jim, I'll take a quick bath and be right out. Okay?"

"Take your time, Rose."

Jim closed the bathroom door behind him as he heard her step into the bath. He put on a shirt and sat down at the desk to look through the pamphlets provided by the hotel. Suddenly, he began to feel very tired and it occurred to him that it must be pretty late. He had left his watch on the bedside table, so he rose and started in its direction, intending to check the time and go straight to bed. He dropped the shirt to the floor and picked up the watch. He was shocked: it said 2:35 a.m.

Jim awoke, and for a moment was disoriented. He moved just slightly

and felt Rose's body beside him. With that touch, he realized where
he was, and why. It was pitch dark so Jim figured it couldn't be time
to get up yet. Reaching for his watch, the luminous dial said 5:05.
He lay there trying to go back to sleep but couldn't. About ten minutes
later he decided it was useless, got up and went to the bathroom.

Jim really didn't know why he was taking a shower, but it sure felt
good. He washed and then just stood there letting the water beat down
on his fatigued body. The pounding water massaged and relaxed him
until, finally, it took an enormous effort to shut it off. He dried slowly and contemplated shaving but the watch said only 5:45, and he
really didn't feel like doing anything but going back to bed.

Awakened by Rose pulling the sheet from his body, he opened his
eyes enough to see that it was daylight. Thinking it couldn't be more
than 6:00 or 6:30, he glanced at his watch and was surprised at the
10:45 reading. He felt Rose enter the bed and glanced down at her
naked body. She bent over and kissed him. Immediately, a shiver went
up his spine. He watched with both surprise and pleasure as Rose
kissed her way up his leg.

Jim again stepped out of the shower. It was already past 12:30. He
had shaved while Rose showered, and it was a good thing. He'd told
Joe to be out front at 12:00. Opening the bathroom door he could
see Rose seated at the dresser fixing her hair. As he dressed, he found
himself thinking what a beauty she was, even the morning after.

"Ready to go get something to eat, Rose?"

"Anytime you are."

Jim rested his hand on her shoulder and directed her through the
door. Then he allowed his hand to slide gently down her back to her
bottom, where he gave her a little pat. What he was really doing was
checking for a bra and panties. The bikinis were there, but no bra.
With the pat, Rose turned her head toward him and each gave a knowing smile.

Jim was glad no one else was in the elevator, especially after last
night's encounter. It also gave him a chance to look Rose's dress over
a little more closely. It was about three inches above her knees and
very clingy. It was a red silk-like fabric with a large yellow floral
print. It had a mandarin collar and buttoned to her waist. Rose had
left the top two buttons undone, and it looked very appealing.

"Well, do you like what you see?"

"I was just admiring your dress. It's very pretty, almost as pretty as what's in it." Rose couldn't help herself as she reached up and gave him a kiss on the cheek. She was beginning to like this American GI. His boyish innocence and charm, the combination of honesty, shyness, and his sexual vitality all began to tear at the invisible wall that usually protected her emotions in these situations.

As they reached the sidewalk, Joe pulled up with his taxi. Rose wasn't surprised when Jim held the door for her and allowed her to enter first.

"Where to, Jim?" Joe asked.

"I don't know! Rose, you pick a place. As long as it's a place with good food, I don't care what kind."

"Joe, take us to the Jade Palace, please."

"Okay, Rose. Well, Jim, did you sleep well last night?"

Jim broke into laughter: long, hard, and deep laughter. When he finally got control of himself he looked at Joe through the center rear view mirror and said, "Somehow, I just don't believe that's what you really wanted to ask."

There was a long silence during which Joe decided he had been put nicely in his place. Jim wasn't going to volunteer any information. So, how was he to report to Manuel?

"Jim, it'll take about an hour and a half at the Jade Palace. Is there something you would like to do after lunch?"

"Yeah, Joe, I'd like to shop for some clothes, maybe a suit."

"Okay, no problem. I know just the place. I'll even give you some free advice: when you find what you like, let Rose deal for a price. Here we are, at the Jade Palace. Have a nice lunch!"

Before he could get out, Rose gently pulled on Jim's arm and said, "I'll need $5.00 for the head waiter."

Jim wondered why, but gave her the five spot and got out. He opened the door to the Jade Palace and followed her in. Rose greeted the head waiter politely, trying not to show her familiarity with him or the place, yet it was obvious she'd been here frequently. Jim smiled to himself as the two haggled in the local dialect. Rose opened her hand, showed the five, and ended the argument.

The head waiter led the two through the main dining room which had a Polynesian decor. After winding their way through the tables they entered a hallway. On each side were four doors, all closed. The head waiter opened the third door on the left and Jim followed Rose in.

After seating them, the head waiter gave each a menu, asked if there was anything they desired and left. Jim looked around. It wasn't much more than an enclosed private booth. The only light was from a single candle placed in the center of the table. The walls were painted with a continuous mural which included the door. The painting was of fishermen, boats, islands and birds. It was really quite good. The tablecloth was scarlet with a velvet texture.

"This is quite a place, Rose."

"Do you like it?"

"So far, although I've never been in a private dining room for two before."

"You'll like it. The food and service are excellent and the privacy allows us to do most anything we wish. The walls are all soundproofed so there won't be any distractions from the people on either side of us. You know, these booths are used by some very important people both in and out of government."

"I'm surprised you could get one for only $5.00."

"Oh, you couldn't during their busy hours—it would cost $20 or $25 during lunch or dinner. As late as it is now, though, he more than likely had a couple of them empty."

"How do you call the waiter?"

"You see that handle on the door? You pull it up and it drops a little green flag. Each door has one at a different height so the waiter can see them all at once. What would you like to eat?"

Jim looked at the menu. "You're obviously familiar with this place, what would you recommend?"

"Well, you said you like all kinds of seafood. Why don't you try the filet of flounder stuffed with crab meat? It's sauteed in butter and is delicious. You get rolls, butter and a tossed salad, with the dressing of your choice, plus tea or coffee."

"I'll take the coffee and French dressing on my salad."

Rose laughed and shook her head slightly. "They have an excellent house dressing. Why don't you try it?"

"No, thanks. I really like French. If they don't have that, then I'll try the house special. What are you going to have?"

"Tea, house special on the salad and I believe I'll take the monkfish."

"Monkfish? I've never heard of monkfish."

"It's a type of saltwater fish. I'll give you some and you can see how you like it."

"Would there be a problem, Rose, if you ordered for the both of us?"

"No, I can do that if you like. In fact, it probably would be easiest that way. Are you ready?"

Jim nodded his head yes and Rose flipped the handle up. In about thirty seconds there was a knock and the handle dropped down. Rose spoke and the door opened. The waiter entered, smiled and took their orders. He didn't speak the first word of English. He placed a pitcher of ice water and two glasses on the table and left closing the door behind him.

"Why won't he speak English?"

"The owner won't let anyone speak English during work. I don't know why."

"Do we have to drop our flag again in order to get our food?"

"No, he should be back shortly with the salads, then he'll be back in about ten minutes with our meals. Once he leaves the meals, you'll have to drop the flag to get him back."

The waiter knocked on their door and waited for Rose to speak. He placed their salads, smiled at them and left. In a few minutes the same procedure was repeated for the main course. Along with the meal the waiter brought pots of coffee and tea.

Jim's meal was excellent. He hadn't eaten crabmeat before, but found it very tasty. Rose's monkfish was absolutely delicious, and he decided to remember monkfish when he got back to the States. During the meal the conversation centered around the usual small talk of weather and food. As both finished eating, Rose slid off her shoes and rested her feet on the bench beside Jim. Jim had refilled both cups. "I hope you didn't mind my waking you this morning."

"No, it was past time to get up, and I had told Joe to pick us up about 12:00. Besides, I loved the way you woke me. You can wake me every morning the same way." Jim placed his hand on Rose's leg and started caressing her calves.

"I'm glad you enjoyed it."

She placed her foot between Jim's legs and with her toes began to massage him.

"Rose, you keep that up and we'll have to go back to the hotel instead of shopping."

"Why would you want to wait 'til then?"

The surprised look on Jim's face asked, "Here? You've got to be kidding?"

Rose smiled seductively and put her feet back on the floor. The next thing Jim knew she was under the table. The emotions that swept over him at that moment were shock, surprise, disbelief, and fear. However, they were soon displaced by great excitement and anticipation. He felt her hands working his zipper.

When they left the restaurant, Joe was seated on a bench just outside. In the taxi, Joe spoke first, "Well, how did you like the Jade Palace?"

"Hey, okay, I really liked that place. The food was excellent, the service just right, I'd certainly recommend it—I can't wait to see where she takes me tonight."

"You still want to do a little shopping?"

"Yes, I do." Jim watched the city slip by as Joe drove. He was amazed at the four lane super highway on which they traveled; for some reason, he hadn't expected Manila to be a city of expressways. Joe stopped the taxi on a small side street. Now this was what Jim thought Manila would look like: the shops were so close together they shared sidewalks. It was obviously an older part of the city, for the store fronts showed the effects of time and age.

They walked a short way down the street and entered a men's clothing store that had large plate glass windows with protective iron bars. Once inside, Jim was really surprised at how small it was. Each wall was stacked to the ceiling with bolts of fabric separated into types of cloth and again into colors, plaids, checks, and stripes. Jim was amazed. He had never seen so many different selections in one place before. The center of the room was only about five feet wide and had two tables, each about three feet wide and five feet long. The room couldn't have been more than thirty feet long, with fourteen or fifteen foot ceilings. As Jim looked around a tall, well built Philippino man of about forty-five approached.

"May I help you, Sir?"

"Yes, you may. I'm interested in having a suit made."

"Well, we can certainly help you in that department. What type of fabric were you interested in?"

"I don't know. I hadn't thought that far."

"Why don't you let me show you some fabrics and we can go from there?"

Jim spent considerable time looking at the fabric. Finally, he decided on a light blue cashmere and asked the shop owner, "How much?"

"Well, Sir, that depends. Do you want a vest? How many pairs of pants? And what type buttons, single or double breasted?"

"Single breasted, vest and one pair of pants."

"Ninety dollars should cover it."

At that point, Rose and the shop owner got into a heated discussion. Jim figured Rose was trying to get him a lower price and that the shop owner wasn't giving much. Finally Rose took Jim by the arm. "Come on, we're leaving. There are other clothing stores."

As they started out the door, the shop owner said, "Okay. I'll go forty-five, but no more."

Rose nodded approvingly, and Jim said, "Deal."

At that point, the owner pulled out a tape and started measuring Jim. As he did so, they discussed fabrics and before Jim left, he'd bought a second suit of a wool blend, with two pair of pants.

When they left, Jim asked Rose if they could just walk and browse for a while. Rose took his arm and they started down the street. By the time Joe found them, Jim had bought an onyx bull for his father, a jade Buddha for his mother, and various charms and trinkets for his sisters. Once back in the taxi, Joe asked, "Where to?" Jim glanced at his watch. "I'm hungry. Rose, pick a restaurant!"

When Jim got out of the taxi he looked at the sign, "The Bay Restaurant." They were seated outside a boardwalk-type area. The brightly lit harbor loomed in front of them. Jim ordered lobster, baked potato, peas and salad. Rose ordered oysters on the half shell with rice and clam chowder. As they ate, Rose explained that this was Manila Bay and Harbor. She gave him the history of the harbor and even told him from where some of the ships had come. Jim was surprised. There was even a rich man's yacht about a half mile out in the harbor, all lit up just like in the movies.

Jim's meal was excellent though Rose had tried unsuccessfully to get him to try an oyster. Every time he looked at one, all he could think of was trying to swallow snot!

The room at the Shoreline Hotel looked mighty good to Rose, who was tired and had done more walking than she cared to think about. After all, they'd walked about four hours and then, after dinner they'd walked around the harbor. Now, all she wanted to do was to go to sleep. However, she was out of luck for Jim felt good and wasn't at all sleepy.

Sometime later Rose awoke and realized Jim wasn't in bed. Looking around the room she could see him sitting in a chair gazing out the window. "Something wrong, Jim?"

"No, I just couldn't sleep. You know, Rose, this is quite a view."

She got up, put on one of Jim's shirts and knelt beside him. By moving her hand along Jim's thigh, she could tell that he, too, had on only a shirt. She had learned a long time ago there was one surefire way to make a man tired, this time sleep came quickly and restfully for both.

Rose woke before Jim and decided she would shower and attend to her toiletries before he awoke. The next thing Jim knew he was dreaming, or so he thought. Opening his eyes, he saw Rose once again waking him with her mouth. He felt good, refreshed and he certainly enjoyed waking up this way.

By 12:30 they were in a little oriental restaurant. Jim's plate of sweet and sour pork was very good. He was glad he hadn't taken more than one of Rose's stuffed mushrooms, though. Unlike the small, crisp, firm mushrooms back in the States, these were a soft mushy variety that Jim did not care for.

After eating, they went back to the tailor's where he made some final alterations. Jim was very pleased with both suits and looked forward to picking them up the next day. From there Jim wanted to visit the American cemetery. Joe asked if he had a relative buried there.

"No, Joe. I just want to see it. Okay?"

Neither Joe nor Rose was happy about the trip to the cemetery as their silence showed. Once there, Rose asked if she could wait in the taxi.

"Have you ever been here before?" Jim asked.

"No."

"Well, maybe the walk would do you both good. After all, if not for these men and thousands like them, you would be speaking Japanese now. In fact, you, Joe, would be driving Jap men around, while Rose would still be Rose. Come on, Rose, the walk will do you good."

They walked through the entrance and followed a path into the midst of many crosses. The military precision was perfect; no matter which way they looked the crosses formed a perfectly straight row. Jim was reminded of a poem he was supposed to have memorized in school. It was something about Flanders Field and row on row, the poppies grow. The quiet beauty was magnificent and he could feel a special presence, something he would never be able to describe.

"Come on, Jim. Let's go."

"No, Rose, I need to stay a while. You know, I can feel their presence. It's strange, I know, but I can feel them. You don't understand, do you?"

She looked him in the eye and shook her head.

"You see, they're my brothers. We're comrades, these men and I bonded together by our country and its love of freedom. It's hard to explain. Most people don't understand what we, these men and I, have in common is mostly boredom. One could describe our jobs as long hours of boredom interrupted by short moments of total terror. At any moment we know that we could join our brothers in a place like this; yet none of us really accepts the fact that we could be killed. It's always the other guy who gets it. Only in very special moments would you find any of us willing to admit that each of us could die." After several minutes of silence Jim looked down at Rose. "Go on back to the taxi, Rose." She gladly left. To her, the place was beautiful but morbid, a place where only old people visited.

Jim walked alone among the rolling hills, the crosses in perfect formation, the trees and bushes placed in equally perfect locations. He came to an oval with a tower at one end. The tower had an alter and was obviously there as a place of worship. The oval was broken into different sections by walls, with the names of the men buried there carved in the stone. It was very impressive, but most impressive of all, were the rooms on the end. Using different colors of stone, various battles were mapped out on each wall. Jim spent a lot of time reading and looking at the maps. It was beginning to get dark when he finally returned to the waiting taxi.

"Joe, tomorrow I want to go to Corregidor."

Joe shook his head slowly. "You don't have time, Jim. You have to pick up your suits tomorrow afternoon and Corregidor is an all day trip. You can't pick up the suits the following day because you have to be at the R & R center by seven in the morning."

"You sure we can't get back in time to get the suits tomorrow night?"

"No way, Jim. I'm sorry."

"Okay, let's go get something to eat." Jim was bitterly disappointed and even considered taking a chance on the suits but decided Joe should know best. After all, he lived here.

Once again, Rose took them to a seafood restaurant, where she ordered shrimp and Jim ordered red snapper. After their orders had been taken, Rose started the conversation. "I'm really glad I had the opportunity to spend these last few days with you. It's been very enjoyable and, in this short time, I've grown to like you very much."

"That's nice of you to say, Rose. I've really enjoyed Manila and the days we've spent together. But most of all, I've liked the nights and you."

"Jim, I love you. I don't want you to leave me. Take me back with you, please."

Jim was shocked. He hadn't expected this and didn't know what to say. He liked Rose, but he didn't want to marry her, however, he certainly didn't want to hurt her feelings.

"Rose, I can't do that! I leave day after tomorrow."

"We could go to the U.S. Embassy tomorrow and make application for marriage. Then, when you get back to the States, you could send for me. I'd make you very happy. I'm an excellent cook. I'd make love to you whenever and however you wanted. All the American men I've known say that American women won't make love except when they're in the mood. According to the Americans I know, that isn't very often. I'll do it every night and even during the day if you want. I'll even wake you in the morning just like I've been doing. I could fix your breakfast while you shave. Jim, you'd love it. I'd make you so happy."

"Rose, no one can make someone else happy. Each person must be able to do that for himself. Besides, I don't love you, and when I marry, I'll love the girl. End of subject, okay?"

"Okay. I'm sorry. I just thought, well, I..."

"Rose, forget it. I like you, I really do. You're a nice person, great in bed and you have many other fine qualities. You'll make some lucky man an excellent wife. You're very pretty and before this war is over, you should be able to find an American husband, if that's what you really want. But, not me, okay."

Rose felt like a fool and was sure Jim figured all she wanted was a ticket to the States. The fact that he was partially right was the main reason there was very little conversation for the rest of the evening.

Later that evening, they had sex in different positions until Rose told him they had just 'pointed the compass'. He didn't tell her that he had never heard of pointing the compass. All he wanted to do at that point was go to sleep.

Jim awoke first and was relieved, though he didn't know why. By the time he was finished shaving and showering, Rose was also awake. They ate in the hotel dining room and Jim was surprised that their ham, eggs, coffee and orange juice cost almost as much as their lunch had the day before. After breakfast, they visited Old Fort Santigo, where Jim was impressed by the twelve foot thick walls. From there, they went to pick up Jim's suits. He tried each one on before paying and found both fit perfectly. As he looked at himself in the mirror he glanced at Rose standing behind him. The smile on her face told him he looked good, so he couldn't resist asking, "Well, how do I look?"

"Stunning, absolutely stunning. You'll have all the girls back home chasing you."

It was almost 2:00 when Jim asked the shop owner if he would keep the suits while they got some lunch. Not too far up the street they found a sidewalk cafe. Rose ordered a rice ball and shrimp for the two of them. When it came, the shrimp, rice and indistinguishable vegetable was all rolled into a softball sized wad. Jim's first thought was, "That looks awful." But he decided he should try it. Much to his surprise, it was very good and had a sweetness that he hadn't expected. After lunch, they went back and picked up his suits and from there Joe took them back to the hotel.

Jim had already decided he was going to have Rose one more time and then take her back to Manuel. Once in the room Jim hung up his suits. Rose started packing his bags, since she had packed hers while he had been in the shower that morning.

Rose was bent over at the end of the bed folding clothes when he took hold of the zipper on the back of her dress.

They were in Joe's taxi on the way back to Howard's when Jim decided that this was the best time and place to say good-bye. "Rose, I want to thank you for a wonderful time. I really enjoyed myself, largely because of you. I wish you the very best and honestly hope you'll someday find the husband you need."

"I'd be happy to take you. I love you and I could make you happy. I'm a great cook and I really enjoy it when we make love."

Jim felt like a rat. He liked Rose, he really did. And she was always ready and willing to make love, which greatly pleased him. "Rose, I'm not going to, so please just quit."

At Howard's they ordered dinner. As they were finishing, Manuel approached. "Good evening, I trust you have enjoyed Manila and Rose's company."

"Manila has been very nice, thank you. As for Rose, well, she has been an experience beyond words. She has been truly wonderful...a delight to be with and a very nice person."

"I'm pleased you liked her. I'm also curious. Why did you bring her back one night early?"

"Simply because I have to get up at four-thirty tomorrow morning and I would like to get a good night's sleep."

"You're sure that you don't desire her services tonight?"

"I'm sure."

"Very well. Rose, we have a new R & R group in tonight. Time to go back on line."

Rose and Jim's eyes met for the last time. "Good-bye Rose, and thank you."

"Good-bye Jim. I really enjoyed being with you. Remember me."

"Oh, I will. Of that you can be certain. Good-bye."

Manuel held out his hand to Rose. She took it, stood, and walked into a hidden corner of Jim's mind, where she would be remembered by him forever.

Four-thirty came before Jim was ready. In one hour, he was back in the R & R center going through customs. His suits were already packed in a shipping package. That way, once he got back to Vietnam where postage was free, he could send them home. At 0745 the DC-6 left Manila and arrived four hours later in Saigon.

At the airport, he sent his packages home and went to the R & R center. Jim picked up his M16 and, as he started out the gate, a jeep stopped.

"Hey, GI, need a lift?"

Jim looked at the M.P.* driving and figured, 'Why not'.

"Sure, if you're going the direction of Hotel Three**."

"Sure, that's my area. Hop in."

Once at Hotel Three, he headed for the dispatcher's office and asked about a possible ride to Tay Ninh. If not, were any of the Blackhawk ships in Saigon air space.

"Sorry, Specialist. No on both accounts."

"How about Cu Chi? Anything headed that way?"

"No."

Jim was beginning to wonder what to do next when a Major General walked up. "Specialist, you with the Blackhawks?"

"Yes, Sir. I'm a crew chief. I just got back from R & R this morning and thought maybe I could catch a ride back to Tay Ninh from here."

"Well, Specialist, you're in luck. I'm going to Nui Ba Den***, I'll give you a ride."

"Thank you very much, Sir." Jim picked up his gear and followed the General out the door and said a silent prayer of thanks for once again making things work out so well.

It was 1430 hours when he walked into the hooch. After getting clean bedding, the rest of the day was spent in the club drinking beer

---

*M.P. - Military police.

**Hotel 3 - Main heliport in Saigon.

***Nui Ba Den - Mountain just outside Tay Ninh. On top was a Special Forces Camp protecting a long range radio complex.

and writing letters. He wrote one long one to his parents telling them all about the things he saw. Then he allowed R&R to retreat into his subconscious mind. However, it would affect him in many ways for years to come.

5

"Do you not know that your body is a temple of the Holy Spirit?" I Corinthians 6:19 NIV

You Did It, Then You Talked About It—But Only Once

Once at Saigon, no one seemed to know they were coming; so again, the flight had to sit and wait. Finally, the bodies were loaded onto a quarter ton pickup.

The flight back to Tay Ninh took even longer than usual, with artillery fire coming from most every fire base. Finding a route home around it was tough. The cloud cover made it even darker than usual that night, but the flash of the big guns reflecting off the clouds was unmistakable as they flew along.

Jim shut off all his radios and turned his intercom switch to private. This allowed him to hear himself talk without anyone else listening, unless someone else on the ship had also turned his intercom switch to private. Then there would be a hot mike situation between their respective head pieces. Jim was mumbling to himself about nothing, interspersed with a short song every now and then when he heard, "Hey, Mac, is this a private party or can anyone join in?"

"Come on in, Broadnex. You getting lonely, too?"

"Yeah, I guess. It's funny how people get to the point where they simply need to talk to themselves and hear themselves respond."

"Especially after a day like today."

"Yeah, isn't that the truth. I'll tell ya, Mac, I still have that burnt flesh taste in my mouth."

"Me too, I keep wishing I could brush my teeth. I hope I never have to do that again."

"Yeah, look, could we, uh, change the subject?"

"Sure, Broadnex, that suits me just fine. What do you want to talk about?"

There was a long pause before Broadnex said very softly, "Look, Mac, I'm sorry about calling you a sissy for going to that chaplain's service earlier today. I know that's your way of coping mentally, and getting by, and I shouldn't make fun. Besides, there might be something to it."

"There is something to it, Broadnex, and thank you for the apology."

Once the flight was on the ground, Jim pulled the necessary inspections and headed for the showers. Much to his disgust, there wasn't any water, so he put on clean clothes and headed for the enlisted men's club. He got a beer and joined Green, who was already seated at one of the big tables.

"Hi, Mac, I heard about your day."

Jim gave him a surprised look, "How?"

"Broadnex was here, in fact, he just left."

"Well, Green, you can be glad you had to take a physical today. Which reminds me, did you pass?"

"Sure, the only time I had a problem was when this doctor put on a rubber glove and said, 'bend over.' I'll swear, Mac, that man had a twelve-inch finger. You wouldn't believe the hand this dude had on him. He wouldn't have any trouble palming a basketball. I'll bet he got picked for the job just because of the size of his hand. Of course, he just had to make a big production of putting this glove on and then sticking it over his finger. I'm telling you, that finger grew an inch right before my eyes. I almost asked if I could have something to bite down on when he told me to bend over. I don't know what he was feeling for, but I thought for a moment he was going to push it out my belly button."

As Green told his story, several other guys joined them at their table. Soon they all found themselves laughing so hard it hurt.

Two of the guys now joining the group were Hunter and Athia. Green decided to have some more fun. "Hey, Hunter, I see your favorite monkey is still around."

"That son of a bitch Kenny, I knew he wouldn't get rid of that damn monkey. Green, how did he get out of it?"

"I don't know, other than he was telling Gillett when I got back that he couldn't catch it."

"Well did he at least clean up my wall locker?"

"Oh, you mean you don't want to keep that little present that came this morning?"

Hunter's glare made everyone at the table laugh that much harder. Another round of beer was ordered and a general round robin started.

"Well, what are we going to do about that monkey?"

"I vote, kill him."

"Look, Hunter, I don't think anyone here would object to that. The question is how? We'd never get away with shooting him. Hey, Barkeep, bring us another round."

"We could put poison in its food."

"Okay, Genius, where you going to get poison?"

"I've got it! We could lace his food with enough pot to kill him."

"How about, if every time one of us walks in the door, we throw a couple of combat boots at him. Maybe he'll get the idea and leave."

"No, it would be our luck the bastard would think it was a game. I can just see it now, we throw a boot at him and he throws a fist full of shit at us."

"Look, Mac, you're Gillett's friend. Why don't you talk to him about it? Maybe you can get him to do something."

"Athia, don't you think I have? I've been trying to get him to make Kenny get rid of it for I don't know how long. However, if you're buying another round I'll have another talk with him."

"You got it. Barkeep, another round please."

While the barkeep was collecting Athia's money, Jeff Stihl came in and joined them. Jeff was probably the best looking crew chief in the company; 5'10, 185 pounds, blond hair and blue eyes with just enough of the man coming through the boy to make him a very striking person.

Dick Hunter turned the conversation in another direction by asking, "Jeff, weren't you in the chopper that was shot down today?"

"Yeah, talk about a day not worth remembering, this is it."

"Didn't you enjoy being a grunt for a day?"

"Not in the least."

"Well, come on, Jeff, tell us all about it! By the way, did you see that anti-aircraft gun?"

"Hey, look, if I'm telling the story, somebody else is buying the beer."

"Barkeep, set 'em up again!"

"To be honest, we were already on the ground when that gun opened up. The fifty was on the other side so I didn't see it, but, man, did I hear it! We were unloading when he first got us. He must have hit us a dozen times. Then, almost at the same moment, the flight lifted and must have diverted his attention from us. I'll tell you, I can still hear that ship's skin rupturing, thump, thump, thump. He had to have hit the engine. I could hear it die, and Mr. Marshall said, 'We lost the engine. Let's get the hell out of here.' I got the door open for Mr. Barr who was flying peter pilot. Just as he stepped out, Chalk Seven got it direct. Man, I was so scared I didn't know what to do first, crawl in a hole or check to see if I had shit my pants. Of all the days to get stuck flying with a couple of pot heads, you'd know this was it. I had Conrad for a gunner and he and Barr were so stoned, Marshall and I had to practically drag them to safety.

"I really had to laugh at Barr, he had left his camera in the ship and was going back after it. Marshall wouldn't let him, since the flight was gone and that fifty was taking target practice on my ship. I expected it to blow any minute, but it never did, and Barr was sitting there arguing with Marshall to let him go get his stupid camera. Anyway, I'm getting ahead of my story. Did any of you guys see Chalk Seven get it?"

Several of the men including Jim said they had. "Talk about an explosion, those guys never knew what hit them. One big boom followed by a fire ball and a bunch of burning pieces all over the place."

"Well, Jeff, what did you do all day?"

"Sat around mostly. When we first got in the woods we helped set up defensive positions with our M60's. The Captain in charge of the grunts was positive Charlie was going to come get us. When you guys put in the second lift and didn't draw any ground fire, the Captain didn't know if he should shit or play with himself. I don't know how long it was before he sent a scout team out, but it was quite a while. When they didn't make contact, he moved everybody out. There was absolutely nothing to show anyone had been there but us, no shells, nothing.

"I went back and checked out my ship. That poor baby looked like swiss cheese; you guys should have seen that thing. Every window in it was shot out. I counted thirteen holes in the tail boom and was ready to start on the cargo area when some lieutenant came up and told me Conrad and I had to lay the guys from Chalk Seven out. Man, talk about a sick job, that was it."

Jim said, "Hey, I know all about it. Broadnex and I had to put them in bags."

Jeff pointed his finger at Jim as he said, "I'll tell you, Mac, you couldn't have had it as bad as us, other than they had already started to swell when you got them. At least when you bagged them, 'rig' had already started to set in. When Conrad and I tried moving them, they weren't stiff yet, which made it twice as tough. Plus the smell, I don't think I'll ever forget that smell. I got so sick I ended up with the dry heaves. That damn Conrad was so high on pot he was making sick jokes. I'll tell you, I've had it with those potheads. I don't know what I'm going to do, but I'm going to do something."

Gillett had entered and approached the table unnoticed. Laying a hand on Stihl's shoulder he asked, "You're going to do something about what?"

"Gillett, I didn't see you. Grab a chair and sit down! Want a beer? I'll buy."

"Sure, I never turn down an offer like that."

"Barkeep, set 'em up again, please."

"Come on, Stihl, you didn't answer my question!"

"Oh, I was just talking about Conrad and the rest of the potheads in this company. I'm getting awfully tired of flying with these guys, Gillett. Sooner or later, one of them is going to get someone killed besides himself."

"Well, there isn't anything I can do about it unless I see one of them with a joint in his mouth."

"Come on, Gillett, if they're stoned they're stoned and you know it as well as anybody else."

"That's right, but I can't prove anything. Even if I could, the Brass isn't going to do anymore to them than they are to you guys. Look at you, every one of you is drunk on your butts. Not one of you is fit to fly. If we had to scramble in ten minutes you'd all be a health hazard. Yet, you'll get in those choppers and go and do your job. The Brass figures there isn't any difference between you guys who are drunk, and a stoned pothead, just as long as you or they get the job done."

Hunter spoke up, "Look, Gillett, why do we have to fly with them at all? Why can't you put the potheads on one ship and us on another?"

"The biggest reason is, I don't assign the officers. What are you going to do when a stoned pilot walks up to your ship and says, 'Hi, I'm your A.C.* for the day?"

"Okay, Gillett, I've got a question, and I'm not being funny. I want an honest, serious answer!"

"With a prep like that I can hardly wait. What's your question, Athia?"

"What could they do to us if we all stuck together and refused to fly with any pothead?"

"Other than throw your asses in jail, not much, I suppose."

"Come on, Gillett, if all of us at this table stuck to it, do you really think they would press it, especially since pot is illegal?"

"No, I suppose not. It would be very touchy though, and you guys would have to watch your mouths. Man, I'll tell you, the more I think about this, the less I want to do with it. I'm going to bed. You guys just forget I was in this conversation." Gillett drank the rest of his beer in one gulp and stood to leave. Jim finished his beer at the same time and also stood.

"Come on, Gillett, I'll stagger back to the hooch with you." Jim looked back towards the table, "If you guys decide to blackball the

---

*A.C. - Aircraft commander.

potheads, I'm with you all the way. I think if we stick together, we can beat 'em."

The two men walked out together and headed for the urinals, which were two fifty-five gallon drums cut in half with each half buried to an inch of the top, then filled with rock and covered with a fine mesh screen. The whole thing had a roof over it with wood walls on both ends and on the side facing the prevailing winds, leaving the back side open. After all, one would not want to pee into the wind. The two friends stood and relieved themselves as they talked.

"Gillett, I see everybody's favorite monkey is still with us!"

"Yeah, that damn Kenny, I don't know what I'm going to have to do to get rid of that thing."

"Put Kenny in the air one day and give it to the gook house maids."

"That's fine except for two things. One, since this Tet thing broke out, there are no more Vietnamese on post. Two, do you want to fly with him tomorrow?"

"Hell, no!"

"That's right, and nobody else does either. By the way, I wish you would have kept your big mouth shut back in the club. You gave them just enough encouragement, I'll bet they try it. If you hadn't piped up with, 'count me in', it would have died right there, but not now."

"How come they're not letting in the hooch maids?"

"Somebody up there figures they'll give aid to the enemy. So until this offensive dies down, no more hooch maids, K.P.* workers or detail people."

The two men finished their business and started to walk to their hooch. They both heard it at the same moment. The sharp, shrill whistle of the Soviet made 122MM** rockets. Their reaction was instantaneous and without hesitation. They dived for the ground and covered their ears as the grumbling and grating sound started, telling them it was going to be close, real close. The explosions shook the ground they lay on severely enough that Jim could feel his body bouncing. He looked up in time to see one hit about ten feet from the officer's

---

*K.P. - Kitchen police.

**MM - Millimeter.

shower. The concussion and shrapnel were enough to blow the shower walls down. Another rocket hit, almost at the same time, just outside one of the officers' hooches. The screams of pain and calls for a medic left no doubt that one of the pilots had been hit, probably while still in bed. One of the enlisted men's hooches took a direct hit and blew up like the proverbial match box.

Jim was scared, this was the heaviest bombardment in which he had ever been; plus, laying out where he could see everything didn't help any. It seemed like hundreds of those 122MM rockets were dropping on his company area. The sound was deafening. He closed his eyes and tried to get closer to the ground. Suddenly, it stopped. Jim's eyes felt like they were going to burst out of his head and his ears ached from the ringing.

"You okay, Mac?"

"Yeah, other than I've got a terrible headache. I'm just thankful I was leaving the pisser instead of heading for it. You okay?"

"Yeah. I was just thinking, you don't suppose we were lucky enough that Kenny's monkey was in that hooch that got it?"

"That's about as much wishful thinking as hoping it's not going to start again any second. You want to try to make it to the bunker?"

"No, Mac, didn't you notice? Almost all of 'em hit in the hooch area. They probably have a spotter in that church steeple at the end of the runway again. They had one up there earlier today, until a gunship put a rocket in its bell tower. We're probably safest right where we are."

Just as he finished speaking the shrill whistles started again. "Mac, in case we don't make it, I want you to know your name in on the list coming down tomorrow for promotion to E-5."

The company's buildings were once again the main targets. "Gillett, why the devil didn't you tell me that at the pisser? I could have been happy about it then!"

"I thought about it, but figured you might get so excited you'd pee down your leg!"

The two looked at each other and started laughing. Rockets exploded all around and they lay there laughing so hard at each other, their stomachs hurt.

After twenty minutes, the rockets stopped and almost immediately someone went running through the area shouting, "Gun crews, man your ships."

"Gillett, they'll just about get to those ships, and it'll start again."

"Yeah, but if they can get off the ground, they'll get it stopped."

"They'll have to go to Cambodia to do that and you know it."

"Ten bucks says they go, plus they'll probably make a run on that steeple again on the way out."

"I hope they blow the bastard down. Well, at least we stopped laughing. I'll bet we look like the drunken fools we are."

The gun crews were running across the area headed for their ships when it started again.

Jim and Gillett were still lying in the same spot watching when the whistles started sending shivers up their spines.

"Here they come, Gillett, this'll be the big one!"

"It can't be bigger than that first group."

It was. Rockets started dropping all around, not only in the living area, but also along the flight line. Jim watched one of the gun crew members running to the flight line, run right into the path of a rocket. One moment he was there, the next he wasn't. The noise was deafening as the rockets screamed and grated, followed by an explosion. Jim watched as three guys from maintenance tried to run from the club to a bunker. He couldn't believe they were up and moving. He kept thinking, why didn't they get down. Finally, they made it to the three foot deep drainage ditch in front of the hooches. Jim sighed with relief as he saw each man jump in. Then wincing with pain, he saw a rocket jump in behind them, throwing their body parts back out. Gillett poked Jim in the ribs and pointed with his head to what had just happened. His gesture was his way of asking if Jim had seen it happen. Jim looked him in the eyes and shook his head yes. Jim's ears began to hurt even worse and the ringing in his head was getting louder and more painful, so he pressed his hands even tighter against his ears in an effort to block out the spine shattering noise, and to help keep his head from exploding. He began to think that nothing could live through this pounding when, suddenly, off to the northwest corner of the post, it started to look like the Fourth of July: fire balls, flares and rockets were going off. He knew that it could only be one thing. What a magnificently beautiful display of grandeur, unlike anything he had ever seen. But the fact that he knew only the ammo dump going up could make such a display, caused a certain amount of anxiety to pass over him. After almost thirty minutes, the rockets stopped, just as though someone had shut off a water faucet. One moment rockets were exploding all around, the next, it was perfectly quiet.

"Mac, you okay?"

"Yes, you?"

"Yeah, other than I've got a splitting headache and my ears hurt."

"Gillett, some of those things didn't hit more than ten feet from us. At least that should be the last of it for tonight."

"I hope. Come on, let's go help clean those guys out of the drainage ditch."

"Okay, let me go take a leak first, though."

Gillett headed for the ditch and Jim for the urinal. Once at the urinal, Jim relieved himself again and then walked around behind the club. Staying in the shadows, he made his way to the back door of the hooch. He'd had all the bagging of bodies he could take for one day. Opening his wall locker, he found his box of post cards and thought, 'why not'. Using a flashlight to see, he addressed a card and wrote "free" where the stamp would go. "Dear family, Not much seems to be happening here, though I understand there's some trouble down at Saigon. I'm fine, enjoying flying, although it does get boring a lot of the time looking at nothing but rice paddies. Gillett and I just got back from having a beer at the club. Nothing new happened today. Spent day flying troops in and out of L.Z. Didn't draw any fire. Hope all is well with you, also. Love, Jimmy." He stripped, threw his clothes into the wall locker and was asleep within seconds of pulling the mosquito netting down over his bunk.

Deep within his subconscious, Jim heard an explosion, but it took the second one to bring him fully awake. Now, he was aware they were being hit again, and with that awareness, he simply rolled over and out of his bunk onto the concrete floor. As he hit the floor he heard Gillett call from the floor beside his bunk, "Mac..."

"I'm right behind you, Gillett, let's go!"

The two men low crawled out the door, around the corner and into the bunker. Like everyone else, they were dressed only in olive drab boxer shorts.

"Mac, you got your watch on?"

"Yeah, it's quarter 'til five. The bastards could have waited another fifteen minutes 'til it was time to get up."

By this time the shelling had stopped and the bunker slowly started to empty out. "Gillett, did all these guys spend the night in there?"

"Yeah, did you know we got hit again about three o'clock?"

"No! Really?"

"That's what I thought. You went to bed after going to the pisser last night, didn't you?"

"Sure, I was tired, I came in and went to sleep."

"Well the rest of the company worked 'til about two thirty cleaning up Charlie's mess. We lost the three guys in the ditch, plus Lolofft, and I don't know how many officers were killed in the bunker. Evidently a rocket hit right in their doorway; it killed a half dozen or more, and seriously wounded several others. There was also the pilot that got it right to begin with. He was still in bed. We saw that one hit, it got the officers' shower at the same time. We had to clean up the hooch to the south of us that took a direct hit. Anyway, we were just about done when it started again and everybody got in the bunker. They only hit us for two or three minutes, but everybody had decided to spend what was left of the night in the bunker. Everybody but you, that is. I couldn't find you. Finally, I looked in your bunk and sure enough there you were sleeping like a log. I figured I couldn't leave you there all alone in case we got hit again. You might sleep through it forever. I figured, 'what the hell', I couldn't have better company to go out with, so I stripped down and went to bed."

"Gillett, you're a real friend. Here, mail this for me please, while I go take a shower."

Gillett looked at the postcard and laughed. "Mac, you jerk! Your parents will hear on the six o'clock news that Tay Ninh got the hell kicked out of it last night. Especially since the NVA overran part of Manchu's bunker line."

"No shit, how far in did they get?"

"Clear into their company area. You mean you slept through that also? You couldn't have been in bed. That happened shortly after we split up last night. They even sent officers through all the hooches moving everyone out."

"Well, I didn't see anybody or, at least, nobody saw me. Back to the postcard, Gillett, who are my folks going to believe? Somebody they never met on TV or that postcard? Besides, they won't get it for four or five days."

Gillett just shook his head as Jim headed for the showers. 'Mac, wait a minute, there isn't any water."

"I know, I'm going over to the hospital."

"Don't get caught."

Much to his surprise, there was still water but it was very cold. He got in and out as quickly as possible and was glad none of the good doctors saw him.

There wasn't anyone at the mess hall, which allowed Jim to move right into the serving line. As he picked up a malaria tablet a voice behind him spoke, "Those things will give you the shits."

Jim laughed as he turned, "Green, if you've got the squirts you don't have to fly. Besides, after you've taken them as long as I have, they don't bother you."

"I better take two or three in that case. I didn't get any sleep at all in that bunker last night. We were packed in so tight you couldn't lie down or stretch your feet out. Where did you spend the night?"

"In more than one place. Hey, what did you guys decide about the potheads after Gillett and I left?"

"They decided to refuse to fly with 'em. As for me, I'll do whatever you do. By the way, did you hear two of 'em got killed last night?"

"No, who?"

"Holiday and Gomes, I'd just met them yesterday after I got back."

"How did they get it?"

"We had to clean up the hooch that took a direct hit and also the guys in the ditch. But Holiday and Gomes climbed up on the roof of the next hooch down the line. They were sitting up there watching the ammo dump go up. You know that place had fireworks all night. Mac, you should have heard those two. Gillett was trying to get them to come down and they were going on about this being the best Fourth of July fireworks display they'd ever seen. Anyway, they wouldn't come down. We started getting hit with rockets again so everybody else went to the bunkers. I don't know who found them this morning, but they were on the ground dead. The fireworks must have gotten too close."

"Come on, Green, eat! We have to get going."

6

"Your eyes saw my unformed body. All the days ordained for me were written in your book before one of them came to be." Psalms 139:16, N.I.V.

Just For The Fun Of It

Jim picked up the day's C-rations and his gear. On the way out to the chopper he couldn't help but feel good for being alive. He'd gotten a fair amount of sleep last night, so maybe things would go better today. He stowed his gear and had just finished pulling the preflight inspection when Green showed up with his guns, mounted them and helped Jim clean up the ship. They were finishing when Jim spotted Halsey approaching. "Oh happy day, Green, here comes Mr. Halsey, commonly called the Admiral. Let's hope he walks on by to another ship."

"Looks like he's drawn a bead on this one, Mac."

"Well shit, let's look like we're busy. Go fiddle with your M60, I'll climb on top and mess with the rotor head."

Both men went about their busy work in hopes Mr. Halsey would see their activity and not take time to harass them.

Jim's heart sank as it became obvious Halsey would be their co-pilot. Mr. Halsey put his helmet in the peter pilot's seat, and turning back around, his eyes lit upon an object laying on the ground next to the revetments wall. "MacLaughlin, what the hell is that laying there?"

Jim knew without turning around to what he was referring. "What's what, Sir?"

Mr. Halsey reached down and picked it up. Jim halfway expected him to put it to his mouth and blow it up like a balloon. As Halsey held it in front of his face giving it close examination, Jim had a terrible time not laughing as he answered, "I believe it's called a rubber, Sir."

"What do you find so funny, MacLaughlin?"

"Nothing, Sir."

"This is your revetment isn't it, Specialist?"

"Yes, Sir, but I didn't put that there."

"If you didn't, who did?"

"Sir, I can only guess that some officer has brought one of the nurses who sells it out here to my ship and screwed her. When he finished, he ripped that rubber off and gave it a chuck against the revetment."

Halsey's face took on an even greater expression of disgust. "Why didn't you throw it in the trash, MacLaughlin?"

"Because, Sir, I just didn't like the idea of picking up someone else's old used rubber."

"Look, MacLaughlin, this is your revetment, it's your job to keep it picked up. Here, put this thing in the trash!"

"Sir, it's right behind you. Would you please put it in the trash for me?"

Halsey looked Jim in the eye and threw it on the ground. As Jim saw his response he thought, "You bastard, you probably put it there to begin with." In fact, he wouldn't have been surprised if Halsey had picked his ship to use just so he could hassle him with it.

"I'm giving you an order, Specialist. Pick it up and throw it away!"

"Yes, Sir." Jim slowly climbed off the helicopter roof, picked up the rubber and threw it in the trash. "You happy now, Sir?"

"You're a real smart mouth aren't you, Specialist? Green, front and center. I want the both of you at attention." Halsey walked slowly around the two men standing side by side. "You two are a disgrace to the uniform you wear. Neither of you has a hat on. Where's your head gear?"

Jim responded, "In the helicopter, Sir. I was under the impression we were about to put on helmets and fly."

Halsey looked Jim in the eye. "Specialist, did you shave this morning?"

"Yes, Sir."

"You must not have used a blade in the razor. I've half a mind to send you back to shave again." Jim thought he had one thing right, *he only had half a mind*. "Your left breast pocket is unbuttoned, you need to button your blouse, and you have a pants pocket unbuttoned. Where do you think you are, MacLaughlin, back on the block? That's a uniform you're wearing. There is a correct way for it to be worn, but you don't seem to understand that, do you?" Jim made no response as anything he said at this point would be wrong. "How long has it been since you had a haircut?... Answer me, Specialist."

"I don't know, Sir."

"MacLaughlin, get a haircut tonight. I don't care if you have to shave it off, it's too long. Get it cut."

"Yes, Sir."

Halsey then turned to Green. "Private, you obviously haven't changed uniforms in the last week."

"Sir, I put it on clean this morning."

"You couldn't have put it on clean unless its been wadded up in a duffel bag for a month, which is about how long it's been since your boots have seen any polish. I'm afraid to stand close to you for fear your boots will rape mine for their Kiwi. Here come the pilots now or so help me, I would send both of you back to the hooches to straighten up your acts. Button your buttons and you're dismissed."

As Jim buttoned up he saw Mr. Walker put his gear in his seat. "Good morning, Mac, how are you this morning?"

Jim saluted and said, "Morning, Sir. I was fine a few minutes ago. Mr. Halsey, could I ask you a question?"

"Sure, what is it?"

"Are you flying peter pilot on my ship today?"

"Yes, I am." Halsey had a great big smile that told Jim he was looking forward to the day. Jim didn't say a thing. He just picked up his helmet, rifle and water jug and started to walk away. He could hear Halsey shouting at him as he continued to walk down the flight line. "Specialist, where do you think you're going?" Jim just acted like he didn't hear him. "Specialist, come back here. That's an order!"

Jim made no response, he didn't even turn his head. "Specialist, I'm giving you a direct order! You come back here or, damn you, I'll court martial you!" Jim just kept on walking down the flight line.

The thing to do now was find Gillett. He walked over to Athia's ship and asked if he had seen Gillett. "Yeah, Mac, I just saw him over at Captain Wolf's ship." Jim turned and headed for the captain's helicopter. As he approached he could see Gillett and Captain Wolf talking. Gillett turned to him with a look of surprise.

"Mac, what are you doing here?"

Jim saluted Captain Wolf as he spoke. "Captain Wolf, Gillett, I've got a problem. Mr. Halsey is flying peter pilot on my ship and the first thing he did was start on me. So I walked off because I'm not flying with him. You can put me back in maintenance. I don't care. I'm not getting in the same helicopter that Mr. Halsey is in."

Gillett turned to Captain Wolf. "Sir, could we switch crew chiefs with you for the day?"

"Sure, although I've got a better idea, let's switch co-pilots. It'll give me a chance to find out what Mr. Halsey's problem is." Captain Wolf walked around to the left side of the chopper where Mr. Gabrys was lacing his boot. "Hey, Dave, I want you to go with Mac and fly right seat on 925 today. Tell Mr. Halsey he's flying with me today. Okay?"

"Yes, Sir. Dave Gabrys picked up his helmet and without showing any signs of displeasure for being switched, looked at Jim. "Where you parked, Mac?"

"I'm on my way if you want to walk with me."

The two men turned and started back down the line. Once out of Captain Wolf's hearing Jim started the conversation, "I'm sorry about causing you any inconvenience, Sir."

"Oh, that's okay. For a West Point man Captain Wolf isn't bad. There's just something about flying with the boss that makes a person uneasy."

"It's been my experience, Sir, that the guys from West Point are usually pretty nice and easier to get along with than a lot of the 'ninety day wonders' walking around."

"I guess if a person puts up with four years of harassment at the Point they have a better understanding of what the troops go through.

What's your problem with Mr. Halsey, Mac?"

"We have what's called a personality conflict. It's not just me, Halsey has problems with all the enlisted men. The only difference is, since I refuse to fly with him, he feels it's his duty to break me."

"Why won't you fly with him?"

"Because my life and the lives of everybody in that ship depend on our ability to get along with and respect each other's opinion. Halsey and I don't respect each other and that's a prime ingredient for making four dead men." They walked the rest of the way in silence. Once at 925 Mr. Gabrys spoke to Mr. Halsey, who gave Jim a hate look and started collecting his gear. Jim wondered what Mr. Gabrys had told him. It was obvious he wasn't supposed to hear, or Mr. Gabrys wouldn't have taken Halsey aside and spoken softly into his ear. Mr. Walker and Green both welcomed Jim back and inquired as to how he had managed to get Mr. Halsey switched.

After Mr. Walker walked over to where Gabrys and Halsey were standing, Green looked at Jim and shook his head. "Mac, back in the infantry they didn't put up with guys like Halsey."

"Other than shooting him in the back, what would they do?"

"Oh, you could frag him, or almost as good, a fake fragging."

"What's a fake fragging?"

"That's where you fix a fragmentation grenade so it's a dud, then throw it at him."

"Throw what at whom?"

Both men turned in surprise to see Mr. Walker standing there, but it was Jim who responded without hesitation and thus convincingly, "Throw an open can of cold beans and weinies in Halsey's face."

Walker laughed and said, "That's a good way to get busted for sure." As Mr. Walker climbed in his seat he shouted back, "Untie it, Mac, Lead's starting to crank."

The familiar whine of turbine engines starting to turn reached Jim's ears at the same time he released the rotor blade from its tie down strap.

The day started off much the same as many others with the flight flying resupply to various outposts. As with the previous day, there wasn't any fuel anywhere except in Saigon, so it wasn't long before the flight headed south for Saigon and fuel. Artillery strikes were such that it was necessary to go around to the west and come up the

Saigon River. As they approached Saigon, flying at about twenty five hundred feet, Green came over the intercom, "Why do I suddenly smell something rotten?"

It was Mr. Walker's laughing voice that answered, "Why, Green, that's the Paris of the Orient you smell, usually called Saigon. We just flew into its upper air currents."

"Sir, why does it stink so bad?"

"Because, Green, they're burning their shit. That's how all the military posts get rid of their shit from the day before. You obviously haven't been on many details yet. When you take a crap in the latrine it falls into half a fifty-five gallon drum. The next morning some private drags it out, pours a couple gallons of fuel on it and lights it. With several hundred of them burning at once around Saigon it makes a pretty bad smell up here. In fact, on a clear day when there isn't any wind you can see the smoke rising up from Saigon at fifteen hundred feet over Cu Chi. It's strange though how it does just suddenly hit you."

The flight had started its descent as they crossed the Saigon River. Mr. Walker spotted an island floating down stream that gave him a thought. "Hey, Green, what do you suppose that island floating down the river is made of?"

"I suppose moss and sticks and various debris that float in any river."

"Wrong, it's shit. What happens is the good people of Saigon crap in the streets and alleys. Next time you're in Saigon notice the gutters in all the streets. Those people do their thing in the gutters, or else in a pan and then throw it in the gutter, then a rain comes along and washes it all away. Just like magic they have nice clean streets again. The only trouble is it all gets washed out to the Saigon River, where it collects along the banks until a bunch breaks off and floats out to that big septic tank called the South China Sea. The best part is, Mac and I have been flying along the river before Tet broke and could see people water skiing around that stuff. I checked it out after the first time I saw it. Come to find out, there used to be a French resort on the river here in Saigon which the Americans have turned into an officers club where all the male and female officers in Saigon can go to socialize and, as it turns out, to water ski and swim."

"Sir, do they know what they're swimming in?"

"I would certainly think so."

It only took a short time to refuel and the flight was back in the air, flying more resupply. As with most of these missions the boredom of landing, taking off with supplies, flying for a half hour, dropping off the supplies and then back again began to wear on most everyone. Jim looked at Mr. Walker who was driving, from there his eyes shifted to Mr. Gabrys. He was sitting there smoking a cigarette with his right arm stuck out his window.

"Hey, Green, what are you doing?"

"Oh, just thinking, Mac. Why?"

"What are you thinking about?"

"To be honest, last night. Tell me something will you? How long does it take till you quit thinking about getting killed? I mean, I lived through last night, but will I live through today and tonight, and if I do will I live through tomorrow, or is tomorrow the day I get it?"

Mr. Walker spoke first, "All I can say is get used to it, Green, because it's part of life over here." Mr. Walker looked back at Jim who shook his head slowly.

"I don't agree. It is true there are times when we're all sure we're going to die. There are times when we look back and think that by all rights we should have been killed. It's also true we have to deal with death most everyday, though not our own, others will have to deal with that. Green, I look at it this way, there is a book in heaven with my name in it and along side my name are many items including the time and date of my birth, also the exact time and date of my death. That is set by God. When my time is up, my time is up and there is nothing I can do short of suicide to change it. To spend time and energy worrying about it is a waste, since there isn't any difference where we're at when our time is up, it's up. Back in the States or here, we're still going to die and there isn't anything we can do to prolong it. It's up, it's up, you're dead, your family weeps, but life goes on."

The long period of silence that followed left each man to his own thoughts. Jim's were broken by something moving across the floor. He turned in time to see Mr. Gabrys' cigarette flutter across the floor and out the cargo door. Jim looked up to see Mr. Walker who looked at him and winked. Walker's hand reached down and switched his radio to private. Jim knew instantly that was his cue to do likewise. Reaching up, he switched his intercom over to private. "I'm on, Sir."

"Mac, let's give Mr. Gabrys a hard time about that cigarette."

"Okay."

Both men switched back their radios and Mr. Walker started. "Hey! I smell something burning!"

Jim picked it right up. "Yeah, me too! I just thought it was my imagination, we're on fire!"

"No, none of my instruments show it. It's getting stronger though."

"Mr. Gabrys, I think it's coming from you. Are you on fire?"

Mr. Gabrys spoke up, "I sure the hell hope not."

Mr. Walker decided to turn the screw a little tighter. "Dave, what happened to that cigarette you were smoking?"

"It was right here in the ashtray a moment ago."

Jim spoke, "Mr. Gabrys, your seat must be on fire, I can see smoke coming from it. I'll bet that cigarette is down there."

Mr. Gabrys hurriedly unbuckled his seat belt and frantically tried to climb out of his seat. He looked at Jim and Mr. Walker who were both about to burst with laughter. Mr. Walker was laughing so hard he could hardly drive. It was a good thing Jim was strapped in, or he would have laughed himself right out the door. Mr. Gabrys still wasn't sure if his seat was on fire or not, but seeing no smoke or flames, he decided to sit back down.

"Well, I hope you two had a real good laugh at my expense. Just out of curiosity, where did the cigarette go?"

Mr. Walker had gotten control of himself enough to say, "On the floor and out Mac's cargo door. You should have seen yourself, Dave. There you were at two thousand feet flying along with your ass stuck up in the window. It's a good thing you didn't fart just then, or you would've scared yourself right over the radio console and out the cargo door."

Gabrys spoke, "Well, at least we're not talking about getting killed anymore."

7

Another Single Ship Night Mission

Lunch was to be in a remote staging area just outside Saigon. All the pilots were to report to Lead ship, so each took a box of C-rations with him. Jim was glad he wasn't the crew chief on Lead's ship. He didn't like the idea of playing garbage man for all the pilots. Jim looked for Green but he wasn't to be found, so he picked up a C-ration box that read, 'ham and eggs' and headed for Hunter's ship.

Jerry Green had known for the last hour what he was going to do if time and chance permitted. On the next to the last lift he had talked a grunt into giving him a fragmentation grenade. Once on the ground for lunch, Green grabbed the frag and took off. He needed a place far enough from the flight that they wouldn't notice the bang from the percussion cap. It didn't take long to find a secluded spot where the engineers had piled up some dirt. Jerry climbed half way down a slope and sat down. He pulled out the grenade and, leaving the pin in place, very carefully unscrewed the top, thus separating the percussion cap from the explosive body of the grenade. He then sat the body down beside him and holding the percussion half so that the spring wouldn't pop, he pulled the pin. Jerry placed the pin beside the grenade and, watching for the spring, he gave the top a flip about twenty feet in front of him. The ensuing 'pop' attracted no attention and in a moment, Jerry had collected the top and the spring. He replaced the spring, folded the handle back over it and reinserted the pin. That done, he then screwed the body back into the exploded percussion cap and wiped off the powder burns. Jerry held it out in front of him and gave it a good inspection. He was pleased but a bit nervous. He hoped no one had seen what he had just done and that the grenade would pass visual inspection. Placing it in his pocket, he calmly walked back to the flight and his ship. Nobody was in his helicopter so he picked up the last carton of C-rations. Beans and weinies was the label on the box, and the idea of the cold, grease coated beans didn't really excite him, so he ate everything except the beans and weinies, cleaned up his mess and stretched out on the chopper floor for a nap.

Sleep came quickly and easily for him. The next thing he heard was Jim's voice. He came to as Jim shook his foot and said, "Wake up, Green, time to earn your pay."

Green slowly lifted his head and said, "I'm awake, Mac, we leaving?"

"Yeah, the pilots are on their way back to the ships. Hey, Green, where did you disappear to after we landed?"

"Oh, man, you wouldn't believe how bad I had to pee. I began to think my back teeth were going to float out."

Jim laughed so hard he had to hold his stomach. After all, he'd had the feeling in the past himself.

Mr. Walker approached and said, "Untie it."

Once in the helicopter and ready to take off, Mr. Walker spoke up, "Well, we've got a new mission. The Brass thinks Charlie is retreating from the Saigon area back towards Cambodia, so we're to put in a blocking force in the Hobo Woods and the Michelin rubber plantations just south of Saigon."

Jim had been listening to Saigon radio and had just heard the news broadcast before they had landed.

"Mr. Walker, from what I've heard on the radio, the Cholon District*

*Cholon District - Chinese area of Saigon.

of Saigon must still be getting hit pretty good."

"Yeah, I know, Mac, there's still house to house fighting in parts of Saigon. However, the people who should know, think it will be only rear guard personnel left by tomorrow with most of the NVA trying to slip back over the border."

The first two lifts were taken into the Hobo Woods. On the first insertion, they had received some small arms fire, but nothing that anyone considered out of the ordinary. Their last three lifts for the day were to go into the Michelin rubber plantation. They were completed without incident and the flight was released for the day. They flew north along Highway One up to Go Dau Ha where they would pick up Highway 22 to Tay Ninh. Jim started to think out loud. "Mr. Walker, considering where we put troops in this afternoon, would it be correct to assume that tomorrow we're going to be working in the Iron Triangle area?"

"They were talking about tomorrow during lunch today, and there are three possibilities; all are for putting in blocking forces outside Saigon. Someplace in the Iron Triangle is one, the sugarcane fields around Dong Hoa, or someplace in the Plain of Reeds between the Song Vam Co Dong River and the Parrot's Beak."

"Sir, the Parrot's Beak is in Cambodia. Were they talking about crossing the border?"

"No, unfortunately, there isn't much chance of that happening. The sad thing is we could end this war if we could cross."

It was well after dark when the flight landed for the night. Jim pulled his post flight and headed for the club. Green pulled his guns off the ship and took them in with the rest of the platoon gunners and started to clean them. He had just finished when Mr. Euclid walked up.

Mr. Euclid was a tall, lean, black man who looked like the former high school basketball, football and track star he had been. He was also one of the better liked peter pilots, because of his easy going attitude. Several of the crew chiefs who didn't have permanent pilots were hopeful that Mr. Euclid would be assigned to their ship once he made pilot.

"You Green?"

"Yes, Sir."

"I've been looking for you. Your ship's got a night mission to fly.

Come on, I'll help you carry your guns back out."

"Okay, Sir, they're both ready to go, you going with us?"

"Yeah, I've got the privilege of riding right seat. Gillett is looking for Mac and I don't know who's flying AC or left seat. It won't be Mr. Walker though, he left for the other side of the post to see somebody he knew."

Each man picked up an M60 and walked towards the waiting helicopter.

Meanwhile Gillett had found Jim in the club along with several of the other crew chiefs. Gillett had just come from Operations and figured this would be as good a time as any to pass the bad news. "Good evening, men."

Hunter turned and said, "I hope this is a social visit, Gillett."

"Yes and no, do you want the good or the bad first?"

"The good."

"Okay, I'll have a beer. Now for the bad."

"Wait a minute, where's the good news?"

"My drinking a beer with you guys is it."

"Oh, great, I just can't wait for the bad news."

"In that case, I'll get on with it. First, Mac, you have a night mission to fly. Before you go, though, I have to tell everybody: as you all remember last week, we had to take all the cargo doors off the helicopters. Well, this week the Colonel has decided that you should put them all back on."

The vulgarity that followed wasn't totally unexpected by Gillett. Athia spoke up, "Hey, Gillett, you can't be serious."

"Unfortunately, I am. The old man wants all the doors put back on."

"Well you can give him a message for us. Tell him to go screw himself, he's doing more to destroy morale than Charlie has done since I've been here. What the hell does he do, lay awake nights thinking up things for us to do?"

"Okay, okay knock it off. It's not going to do any good to get all upset about it, just do it. End of discussion, okay! Mac, I don't know anything about your mission except operations wanted a ship, so you had better get going."

Jim got up and headed out the door. As he walked across the company area Hunter joined him. "Hey, Mac, you going to put your cargo doors back on?"

"Hel-l-l-l, no!"

"How you going to get out of it?"

"I'm going to go to supply and order the neoprime rollers that hold the doors on. Since supply hasn't had any call for those in the past, they're not going to have them in stock. And, since they're not critical to the ship's safety or flying ability, they're not going to be put on rush order, so it should be three to four weeks before they come in. Once they're in I'll go back to supply and order the door tracks. If I'm asked, I can just say, 'gee whiz, I didn't realize I needed both 'til I got the rollers and saw how worn the track was.' It should take another three to four weeks to get the track into supply. Since it's going to take sheet metal work to put on the track, they'll wait 'til my ship comes in for a P.E.* to put it on. Since I've been having a P.E. about every six to seven days lately, it could end up being seven to ten weeks before my ship's got its doors back on. In that time span a lot could happen. I mean, I could have two or three helicopters by then. Or the old man could forget all about cargo doors and be hot on something else for us to do. For that matter, he could decide to take 'em all back off again in two months time. Just one thing, Hunter. If you do that, make sure you've got it written up in your log book that you have the parts on order. You could write something like, 'cargo doors removed due to excessive wear of gromlets, parts on order.' Make sure you put the order number in there also, Okay?"

"Sounds good to me, have a good time out there tonight, Mac."

"Right, see you later, Hunter."

The two men entered the hooch and went to their respective areas. Jim picked up his helmet and M16, then headed for the flight line. Hunter sat down on his foot locker and started to write a letter.

With pad and pen in hand, he paused to think before starting and happened to look up. There, watching him very intently was the monkey. "You son of a bitch, I'd like to cut your sorry ass throat." It was almost as though the monkey understood his every word. Instantly, he spread his lips, showed his teeth and gave off a loud screech.

---

*P.E. - Periodic inspection of ship which is done every one hundred hours. Takes five men about eight hours to do if they find no major problems.

He took his fist and started pounding against the rafters while shaking his head in every imaginable direction. Chattering wildly, the monkey's whole body went through contortions and gyrations. Hunter decided it would be easier and safer to write his letter in the club. Collecting his writing paper, he put the pen in his pocket and started down the aisle of the hooch. As he went by Kenny's bunk, he very smoothly and in the blink of an eye, reached down and picked up one of Kenny's combat boots and in the same motion, he raised and threw the boot in the monkey's direction. He missed, but the mere gesture was enough to cause the monkey to go wild. Hunter ran out the door, letting it slam shut behind him.

When Jim got to his ship, there sitting in the cargo area was Green and Mr. Euclid carrying on a conversation like old buddies. "Good evening, Sir."

"Hi, Mac."

"Where's Mr. Walker?"

"On the other side of the post, visiting some old friends."

"In that case, who's driving?"

"I don't know yet. Captain Wolf was trying to find someone who wasn't too close on their hour limit."

Jim turned on the inside lights and started to write in his log book when Mr. Hill walked up and said, "Ya all ready to go?"

Mr. Hill was one of your basic good ole southern boys from Georgia who had lost most of his accent, but not the drawl. He was well liked by both the enlisted men and the officers. His general attitude was 'you don't cause me trouble, and I'll not cause you any', and he'd built a good rapport and working relationship with the enlisted men. His five foot eleven height was built around a small-boned, petite frame that gave the first impression of belonging to a feminine-type person.

Jim looked up and closed the green, plastic covered log book as he spoke, "Mr. Hill, you driving tonight?"

"Yep."

"Aren't you supposed to rotate home tomorrow morning?"

"Yeah, well I just couldn't stand the idea of leaving without one more time in the sky."

"Mr. Hill, that's the dumbest thing I ever heard."

"Well, there isn't much I can do about it."

"You could refuse, you don't have to fly. My God, man, you're supposed to go home tomorrow; not get killed on some stupid ass single ship night mission."

"Look, Mac, I can't refuse and you know it. Captain Wolf came up and said he needed me to fly one last mission. One simply doesn't tell Captain Wolf, no; although I did kind of try by telling him I didn't have any flight gear—no helmet or gloves, nothing. He just told me to borrow some. So, I've got my roommate's."

"Mr. Hill, if you don't get killed tonight it'll be a miracle, you know that, don't you?"

"Look, I don't have any more choice than you do, so stop telling me I'm going to get it! Okay?"

The expression on Jim's face told all of them he truly thought Mr. Hill's flying was stupid. He had one more thought. "Sir, tell you what I'll do. Give me your left hand and I'll break your index finger for you. Just tell Wolf you fell down in the dark on the way out here and did it. That way, you'll still go home tomorrow without having to fly tonight."

"Mac, just shut up and untie this thing! Will you?"

"You're really going to fly it?"

"Yep. Look, Wolf said it's a simple resupply mission. All we have to do is go to Dau Tieng, pick up a load of beehives* and take them up to Loc Ninh, that's it. We should be back in a couple hours." A look of surprise came over Jim's face. Goose pimples rose on his arms and a shiver went up his spine.

Almost shouting he said, "Beehives! Mr. Hill, there's only one reason Loc Ninh needs a night resupply of beehives and that's because they're catching hell. Captain Wolf doesn't care about you. All you are to him is a warm body in the pilot's seat."

"Mac, that's enough! Captain Wolf is just like the rest of us. He has a job to do and he did it. Now go untie the rotor blades and let's go!"

Jim shook his head in a slow no motion as though to say one last time, 'this is dumb,' and stood up to go untie the rotors. The two pilots

---

*Beehives - Small needle like darts tightly packed in an artillery canister. Fired from an artillery piece as an antipersonnel weapon at close range. Approximately 20,000 needles per shell.

climbed into their seats and Green strapped on his chicken plate.

Dau Tieng was only a few minutes flight time away. The area between Tay Ninh and Dau Tieng was densely wooded forest with heavy underbrush. It looked during the day like a big, puffy, green canopy. At night, it was just one huge black expanse. Jim had often thought in the past it would be a most unpleasant place to go down, especially since the highway between Tay Ninh and Dau Tieng had become known as Ambush Alley. Like many of the military posts in Vietnam, Dau Tieng was named after the village next to it. The military complex was located directly on top of the mountain, with only a few two seat observation choppers stationed at Dau Tieng. Its main purpose was as a forward staging area for the 25th Infantry Division.

One of the interesting things about Dau Tieng for Jim, was a little house that looked like it was only big enough for one room. It had white, freshly painted walls and a bright red tile roof with a big white swastika painted on the red tile. Each time Jim saw that house, he wondered why a Nazi swastika would be painted on it. It was almost a month after he had started flying, that he found out that it was also a Buddist insignia.

Mr. Hill dialed 36.8 for Dau Tieng control, "Dau Tieng control, this is Blackhawk Niner Two-Five, we're inbound to your location. ETA, zero five minutes. Over."

"Roger, Blackhawk Niner Two-Five, you're clear to land. Winds are calm and there is no artillery fire at this time, over."

"Roger, Control, we're supposed to pick up a load of beehives, could you advise us as to their location, over."

"Roger Niner Two-Five, try the truck parked on the east side of the runway, over."

"Roger Control, Niner Two-Five, out."

Mr. Hill keyed his mike, "Well, Mac, if that truck really has our beehives on it, this part of the trip will have been easy enough."

"Yes, Sir, but then this isn't Loc Ninh and we both know Charlie is in love with Loc Ninh. To change the subject, I was just thinking things are looking up, I mean we could be going to Saigon for fuel if the Air Force hadn't brought up those fuel wheels today."

"Wonderful outfit, the Air Force. Did you hear, Mac, that the first day of Tet, Charlie had a gun set up at the end of Tan Son Nhut's main runway, so the Air Force had their F-4's taking off and dropping their payloads almost as soon as they were off the ground."

"No, I hadn't heard, but for that matter, I haven't heard much of anything in the way of news. Man, that would have been something to see."

The deuce and a half waiting at the end of the runway was loaded with beehives, and three GI's, who hurriedly loaded Jim's ship. Once loaded, the artillery sergeant supervising gave Jim a thumbs up sign, and Jim waved good bye as he spoke into his mike, "Mr. Hill, I just got a thumbs up, let's go see what's happening at Loc Ninh."

"Roger, Mac, have they got those boxes balanced and secure?"

"Yes, Sir."

"Okay, Dau Tieng control, this is Blackhawk Niner Two-Five at the northeast end of the runway, requesting clearance for takeoff and artillery, over."

"Roger Niner Two-Five, you're clear to take off and we now have artillery firing from the east end of post at a maximum altitude of two thousand feet going into Tango November. Out."

Mr. Hill spoke, "That's Tay Ninh. I wonder which bunker line is under attack tonight? Well, we can always look on the bright side. We could be back at Tay Ninh sitting in those damn bunkers, huh, Mac?"

"Mr. Hill, that's why I fly all these night missions. It's better than getting my ass blown off in a ditch. Besides, I get the message, Sir, and I'll tell you what, nothing would make me happier than to say at the end of this flight, 'I was wrong and you didn't get it.' I really, honestly, hope I get to say that."

"Believe me, I hope you can, too. Okay, we've got clearance to leave. We can fly east around those guns and then head north. Mr. Euclid, I'll drive, you keep us clear of artillery."

Niner Two-Five was airborne and headed north before anyone spoke again. Mr. Hill, like all the short timers, couldn't help rubbing it in. "Well, you guys, in about forty-eight hours I'll be on that big freedom bird heading home. You poor saps still have all that time left. Mac, how long you got yet?"

"Oh, about three months, too long to start a 'short timers' calendar. It's Green and Mr. Euclid that you should work on, neither one's been in country three months yet."

"Nine months, man, if I had nine months left over here I'd walk in to the club tonight and get so drunk I wouldn't wake up the whole time.

"I'll tell you what I'll do, just for you guys, in memory of this flight tonight. It takes about twenty minutes to get home from the airport, so just for you guys, I'll kiss my wife all the way home and, I promise, I'll not once think of any of you. Man, just think, in about seventy hours I'll be with my wife in my own bed. Oh, wow, I can see it now!"

Mr. Euclid broke in, "I hate to interrupt when you're just getting started, but I've checked Quan Loi artillery. They must have every gun in reach of Loc Ninh firing on it, they also have a Puff* operating in the area. I've got him on UHF and he'll give us a lead in. However, the only way I see we can get in and out is to come up along the Fish Hook** and swing in almost directly from the west. Loc Ninh sits at about two hundred feet altitude, so we'll have to maintain at least three thousand feet. The artillery is all going in on the south and east side of the air strip. With the Special Forces camp on the west side of the air strip, we shouldn't get within two hundred meters of any artillery. Now, did you get all that, Mr. Hill?"

"Yeah, three thousand feet, come in from the west and if I cross the airstrip we get blown to hell by our own artillery."

Mr. Hill moved the control stick so the aircraft would head toward the west and the Fish Hook. Unseen from the ground, it glided like a giant bumble bee, carrying its cargo of death northwestward into the night sky and the destiny that awaited its four masses of pollen, called humans.

Jim's voice broke the silence, "You know, this will be the first milk run I've ever been on where we had Puff give us an escort in. Besides, anybody got a coat I can use? Three thousand feet is going to be very cold."

"That's a fact, that's why I'm not taking her up there 'til I have to."

---

*Puff - Air Force C-47 aircraft with three mini guns on one side, each firing 6,000 rounds per minute. On each pass the C-47 fired 18,000 rounds per minute with every fifth round a tracer.

**Fish Hook - Nickname for an Eastern section of the Cambodian border.

Green spoke next, "I hate to be showing my ignorance, but what's Puff?"

Mr. Hill answered, "Green, it's an Air Force C-47 with three mini guns stuck out one side, each firing six thousand rounds per minute. There's no real way to describe what it looks like, other than it does look like a dragon spitting fire. It's quite a sight! Three thousand feet, here we are, Mr. Euclid, what's that thermometer read?"

"Five degrees centigrade, which would be about forty to forty-two in normal temperature."

Mr. Hill turned the ship sharply eastward and made a straight line for Loc Ninh. Jim sat there shivering, he was freezing. Between the temperature and the wind, it seemed like time was clicking by all too slowly. He was on his way and would just as soon get there, get it over with and get out. If Puff was there, plus all that artillery, he knew it wasn't going to be a pleasant visit. As they approached, they could see the flares light the night above and around Loc Ninh. Jim listened as Mr. Hill talked to the driver of Puff and to the radio operator on the ground in Loc Ninh.

"Loc Ninh control, this is Blackhawk Niner Two-Five, we're about ten minutes out. What is your status at this time. Over?"

"Niner Two-Five, this is Loc Ninh. We've had a few uninvited guests try to drop in, nothing we can't handle with the help of your cargo. We will get a C-130* drop first light. See you in zero nine minutes, winds are steady at five knots out of the south. Your approach should be from the west straight in and down, land with your nose on the flashlight and turn off all lights. Over."

"We're on our way, Niner Two-Five. Out. Mr. Euclid, where's Puff?"

"I don't know. I just talked to him and he'll give us an escort in. He said he has us on visual and promised not to shoot us down. Also, he had me dial up an air traffic controller in a Bird Dog**. I'm on hold now."

"Well, at least we've got a friendly Puff."

"Blackhawk Niner Two-Five, this is Bird Dog One over Loc Ninh.

---

*C-130 - Air Force cargo plane.

**Bird Dog - Fixed wing, single engine aircraft used for observation.

I monitored your call to Loc Ninh and there are some things you need to know that they didn't tell you. To start with, the place is under extremely heavy attack; Loc Ninh Village and the ARVN* Camp have already fallen, and the American Special Forces camp has had its perimeter breeched once already. I have two F-4's, one light huey fire team and Puff up here, plus artillery. To make a long story short, I think I can get you in! I'm not sure, and I won't promise, but I think I can put down enough fire power to get you down there. I will, however, almost guarantee you, if you get in, you'll not fly out! Charlie has several mortars firing on 'em, and there is a dual quad fifty set up and well sand-bagged in what used to be the Frenchman's swimming pool right beside the main house. I have two F-4's dropping napalm and five hundred pounders on it, do you understand what I'm trying to say to you? Over."

"Roger, I understand. Wait one." Mr. Hill then spoke to the crew of his ship. "Well, crew, I assume you all heard, so what do you think?"

Several seconds passed before anyone spoke. Finally Jim said, "Sir, we came here for a reason, if we don't take 'em their beehives will they be able to hold? I guess I vote to do what we came up here for. Let's take 'em their beehives and, what the hell, if we can't fly out, I always wanted to be a Green Beret—but I'm not the one going home tomorrow!"

Green and Mr. Euclid quickly agreed leaving the decision to Mr. Hill who said, "Well, what the hell, it might be fun."

Mr. Euclid said, "What about your wife?"

"Hey, she's done without this long, she can wait a couple more days if we don't make it out."

Keying his switch to broadcast outside the ship, Mr. Hill said, "Bird Dog One, if you can get us in we'll take out chances on getting out. Over."

"Roger, Blackhawk, follow same approach as given by Loc Ninh control. I have you on visual at about thirty five hundred feet and circling just west of Loc Ninh. Is that correct? Over."

"That's affirm. Over."

"Roger, most aircraft are in position, shut off your navigation lights

---

*A.R.V.N. - Army of the Republic of Viet Nam.

at this time. Thank you. Begin descent on my command." There was a short pause.

Both Green and Jim checked their monkey harnesses and pulled their M60's up into firing position. Mr. Hill spoke, "You two ready?"

"Yes, Sir. Yes, Sir."

"Blackhawk, this is Bird Dog One. Go! And good luck!"

"Okay, here we go. Mac, there's nothing friendly out there on your side. Green, you've got the village down the hill plus the ARVN camp. Don't be afraid to hit either one. We're at twenty five hundred feet and I don't hear either gun firing back there."

Both men knew that was their cue to open fire. Each pulled his trigger, bringing a small smile to Mr. Hill's face. Loc Ninh was now only a short distance away and Mr. Hill could see the star shaped perimeter by the light from the flares. Niner Two-Five was now on short final approach. All four men could see the flashes from the ground as the enemy troops opened fire on them. Jim had just decided that it would take a miracle to get them in and out when it happened—out of the black sky came a steady stream of red fire streaking towards the ground. Green came over the intercom with the almost typical response to the first time observer of Puff.

"What the HELL is that?"

Mr. Hill laughed and said, "That, Green, is Puff the Magic Dragon."

"I don't think Peter, Paul, and Mary would approve," said Green as he watched the tracers race to their destination below. He really couldn't believe anything could live through that onslaught, if unfortunate enough to be caught in its path. He watched as the last stream of burning hail balls streaked towards the earth just like a giant hand had shut off the flow of fire and was now pushing the last breath from the dragon's mouth downward with open palm. He realized his own gun was still firing into the darkness and that Mr. Euclid was calling out altitude and airspeed for Mr. Hill. Both Green and Jim stopped firing at about the same moment as the chopper settled gently down into a blanket of dust. Instantly two men dressed in combat gear and camouflage paint appeared on each side of the helicopter and started unloading the crates of beehives. Their movements were strained, and showed a forced hurriedness as they jerked the crates, weighing approximately one hundred sixty pounds each, out the door. Jim heard the pop but didn't make the connection until he heard the second pop at the same time he saw the explosion, followed by another and another as the mortars were slowly walked their direction. All four Special Forces soldiers were now lying prone on the ground, starting to low crawl to protective cover.

"Mr. Hill, this place is getting mortared and we're empty, let's get out of here."

Mr. Hill turned up the RPM and started to talk to Bird Dog One. Mortar shells were falling all around them as Bird Dog One came over the radio. "Roger, Blackhawk, please wait as the gunships aren't yet in position."

Jim could feel the chopper leap up and forward as Mr. Hill shouted, "Fuck you, Bird Dog!"

"Puff, this is Blackhawk Niner Two-Five, we're on our way out, give 'em hell!"

"This is Puff, Niner Two-Five, hell's on its way," and indeed it was as the dragon's breath spewed forth lead and fire. Mr. Hill had Niner Two-Five red lined as he tried to make good their escape. Tracers flashed over their ship as it sped away giving them the necessary protective lead curtain. Jim, looking back, could see the explosion at the swimming pool and two gunships starting their run with rockets and mini guns blazing.

"Puff, Bird Dog One, everyone, this is Niner Two-Five, we're homeward bound, thanks for the help out."

"Niner Two-Five, this is Bird Dog One, we were all glad to be of help. Too bad you can't stick around for the show."

Mr. Hill was ready to get back and had nosed it over to the one hundred twenty knot red line; with any luck he could get back before midnight.

"Loc Ninh, this is Blackhawk Niner Two-Five, we're out safe and homeward bound, sorry we couldn't stay for the party, but your uninvited guests weren't being very nice. Niner Two-Five, out."

"Niner Two-Five, this is Loc Ninh. You're always welcome here at sunny, scenic Loc Ninh. Come back again and thanks for the supplies, without them, we wouldn't make it. Loc Ninh out."

"Thanks for the invitation but I go home tomorrow morning, I'm SHORRT." Mr Hill laughed as he yelled short, short, short into the mike. "Well, Mac, we made it much to your chagrin."

"My chagrin? Bullshit! I'm just as happy we made it as you are, besides, where did you get that ten dollar word in this land of the fifty cent vocabulary?"

"Hey, I'm almost a civilian again, I've got to start acting like one.

"You know, gentlemen, there are a lot of reasons I'm glad to be leaving this place, not the least of which is our new XO. Any of you guys met that man yet?"

All three said, "No." "No." "No."

"Mr. Hill, I didn't even know we had a new XO; what happened to the old one?"

"He got promoted and given a command someplace down in the Delta. I'll tell ya, Mac, you E.M. are just going to love this guy." The sarcasm in Mr. Hill's voice was obvious as he continued, "I met the man this afternoon in the officers' club, he's a Major. I can't remember the name but the guy thinks he's John Wayne. I'll give him this much, he is a big dude, about six foot six and I'd guess two hundred fifty pounds, blond hair with a flat top and he eats nails for breakfast."

"Mr. Hill, could I ask a question before I forget it?"

"Sure, Green, shoot."

"At Loc Ninh they said something about a Frenchman. What Frenchman?"

"Didn't you take history in school, Green? This place belonged to the French. A handful stayed on after the French Army got kicked out, primarily to run the various plantations. There's one that lives in a mansion at the far end of the runway. He's got a swimming pool located between the house and the Special Forces camp, or at least, he used to. Next time you're up there during the day look for it. There's a pretty good sized little village on down the hillside with his mansion about halfway up the hill. Anyway, the Frenchman who lives there runs the rubber plantation that's all around Loc Ninh. He, of course, pays the Viet Cong protection money. Whenever they're going to have an offensive against the Special Forces camp, he gets the word. Then he moves all his valuables into the basement, drains his pool, packs his bags and climbs in his little yellow airplane for a few days vacation."

"Sir, how does he know when to come back and where does he go?"

"Oh, they probably tell him how long the offensive will last and he probably goes down to Saigon or Vung Tau. You see his plane around every now and then. He could even go over to Bangkok. I've heard that the Special Forces guys know if he's leaving on business, or if he's getting out before an attack, by whether he drains the pool first or not, but that's not important.

"There is one thing, Green, you should remember about tonight. In fifteen or twenty years when you tell this story, no one will understand or comprehend what it was like seeing all those tracers going by you. In fact, most people won't even believe we went in there with a helicopter. There are a lot of pilots who wouldn't have gone close to Loc Ninh tonight, let alone landed there. For that matter, in this company you'll go a lot of places people won't believe you've gone. Isn't that right, Mac?"

"Yes, Sir, we'll fly into a hornets nest if someone needs help. Just out of curiosity, Mr. Hill, tell me more about our new XO."

"Oh, he's got more good ideas than a cat has lives." The sarcasm in Mr. Hill's voice was obvious as he continued, "I think the one all you guys will like the most is, he wants all the cargo doors put back on the ships."

"That's where that idea came from!"

"Oh, you've already heard about that one?"

"Yeah, Gillett told us about it tonight before sending me to the flight line."

"You going to do it, Mac?"

"Why, Mr. Hill, you know I'd never disobey an officer's order."

"Yeah, just like I'm not going home tomorrow. You'll do whatever you damn well please. The thing I want to know is how you are going to get away with it. Cause I know you're not going to put those doors back on."

"Well, you're right. I'm not happy about it, they are a big pain in the neck. I have to shut the right door every time I put fuel in, then open it again and snap pin it open, plus I'll have to unhook the ammo belt and then hook it back up again every time the doors are opened or shut. Of course, every time I want into the engine or storage compartments, I'll have to shut the door. It wouldn't be so bad if it wasn't for the fact the machineguns are on the outside and the ammo is inside."

"So, how'll you get out of it?"

"Hard to say, Sir, something may come up. What else does he have up his sleeve for us?"

"Oh, cute little things like painting the rocks, raking the sand, police call* before the flight takes off, washing and waxing the helicopters and their blades. He's got this idea that waxed rotor blades give a chopper ten percent more lift. He was saying in the club today that Colonel Appleton and he decided to split the duties. Appleton would have the flights, and he would have the company area. It will be his mission to clean the place up and make it look like the first class unit it should be, which means a lot of painting, raking and shoveling."

It wasn't quite midnight when Mr. Hill sat Niner Two-Five down in its parking revetment. Everyone was in a hurry to get back. Mr. Euclid immediately climbed out and walked off, while Jim was tying the main rotor blades down. Green came around to the tail of the ship and asked, "Mac, do I have to take those guns in tonight?"

"You're supposed to, but why don't you hide them in the corner of the revetment?."

Jim walked forward to the pilot's door. He wanted to talk to Mr. Hill before he left and was glad to see he was still there writing in the log book.

"Well, Sir, I was wrong. We made it, you made it,and I'm glad you did. You've been a good officer and a good pilot. I always enjoyed flying with you."

"Thank you, Mac, that's very nice of you to say. For the most part, I've enjoyed the year I've spent here, but then I've been really lucky. You know I wasn't shot down that first time, although I have to admit, I really figured we'd never get out of Loc Ninh tonight. Speaking of Loc Ninh, did we take any hits tonight?"

"Not that I know of, but then I haven't really checked it out yet. You know, Mr. Hill, it's kind of strange how we can fly through Hell like we did tonight, not take any hits and yet be in a flight of ten and come out looking like a peg board."

"Yeah, that's one of the benefits of being a member of an all combat

*Police Call - Picking up everything that isn't supposed to be in the area, such as cigarette butts.

assault team. We go places and do things other general purpose units wouldn't touch."

The two men shook hands and said good bye. Mr. Hill headed back to the company area and officers' club while Jim started his post flight inspection. Green had already hid his guns and headed back.

Aircraft parked on flight line.

Local kids were always a welcome sight as it meant there were no V.C. around.

Hueys in for maintenance.

Author and Blackhawk 925.

Flight in trail position.

Blackhawks company area and hooches.

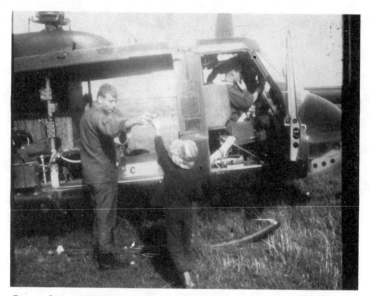

One of Author's doorgunners playing with local kid.

Huey on dirt road.

They weren't all bad times.

Cu Chi after Tet.

Cu Chi before Tet with cemetery on the left.

Author with Dave Smith, one of his pilots.

8

"Whatever a man soweth, that shall he also reap." Galatians 6:7, KJV

So You Want To Play Games

On the way to the company area, Green fingered the grenade in his fatigue pocket. He knew what he was going to do, he just didn't know quite how to go about it. He knew if he got caught, he'd go to jail. So he just didn't dare make any mistakes. Suddenly he had to pee something terrible. Squeezing all the way to the urinal, he still almost wet his pants while trying to get it out. Control, that was the key, he had to get control of himself and his nerves. If he couldn't, he might just as well forget the whole thing.

Taking a deep breath, Green moved into the shadows and started working his way into the officers area. As he walked, he tried to look as casual as possible, like he belonged there. Staying in the shadows, he passed the officers club and latrine. The area in front of the officers quarters was well lighted. Green stood and looked at the L-shaped building that made up their two-man quarters. There wasn't any way to get closer without exposing himself to the light and possible discovery. He stood and watched for several minutes before deciding the only thing to do was walk down the row of doors and read the names on the outside. Hopefully, he wouldn't be seen by anyone. There hadn't been but a couple officers in sight the whole time he'd been standing there. He looked around very carefully for other people and, seeing none, started toward the row of doors. As he walked he was struck by the similarity between this building and some of the fleabag motels he'd seen in the states. He was now close enough to spit on the first door and he still couldn't see any names. There was enough light for him to see a few doors down the row and they were all the same, no name, just numbers. Turning quickly, he moved rapidly away and back into the shadows. He was visibly shaken and now very uncertain just what to do next. It had never occurred to him that the doors wouldn't have the officer's names on them. Now he had a real problem, how could he go about finding Halsey's quarters without anybody knowing he wanted to know. One thing was sure, after he made his move, everyone would hear about what had happened. If he asked questions, someone would surely remember.

Somewhat dejected, Green sat down. Not really knowing why, he just sat there looking at the empty space in front of him. Finally, he decided he might just as well go to bed. As he started to get up, the officers club door flew open and a group of officers staggered out. Searching each face, hoping to locate the one belonging to Halsey, he again felt the disappointment of failure.

As he watched each man enter his hooch he also saw two female nurses leave the club together. They went straight to the latrine, almost as though they had been there before. Green was really surprised when they walked right in. After all, it was an officers' latrine, for men. As he thought about it, it did make sense. There wasn't a female latrine outside the hospital area, and that was a quarter mile away. It did strike him somewhat strange though as he pictured those nurses sitting down on the pot beside some pilot. The more he thought about it, the more he became convinced it was probably so dark in there that they would have a hard time finding the pots, let alone seeing who was next to them.

Again the club door opened and two men walked out. Green's heart jumped—one of them was unmistakably Halsey. Suddenly Green felt chilled and he again struggled to control his nerves. After all, it was a dud. He wasn't going to kill him—just scare the hell out of him.

As Halsey walked by he thought about just throwing it and then running. No, that simply would not do. There were far too many people around; the guy with Halsey and the two nurses still in the latrine, who surely would be coming out any second now. Green watched and waited as the two men headed to their respective doors. Halsey's was the second from the inside corner. That meant he would have to walk by a lot of officers' doors in the light before getting to Halsey. Then he would have to get out. He'd run to the shadows and then make his way back to the hooch as quickly as possible without being seen.

He looked back toward the latrine, not understanding why the nurses hadn't yet emerged. To his surprise there they stood just outside the door, partly hidden in the shadows of the latrine wall. He would have missed them, if not for one of them moving. Now why were they standing there? It was almost as though they too were watching for something or someone and not wishing to be seen. Maybe they had spotted him. That was it, they had seen him! It just didn't make sense. He had been very careful not to move anything except his head and that only slowly. He watched two of the pilots emerge from the club and move quickly to the latrine. Not spending but a few minutes in-side, they left by the door where the two nurses stood. Now he knew what the nurses were doing. The four people exchanged words, looked around for others and holding hands as couples often do, moved quick-ly, almost at a run, towards the officers' quarters. Green almost broke out laughing as both couples entered the door beside Halsey. He knew that was one door that wouldn't open, no matter what. Almost at the same moment Halsey's light went off.

Green knew this was it. Carefully, he looked for any signs of some-one else in the area or about to enter the area. He was moving quick-ly now like a man with a purpose. Stopping in front of Halsey's door he looked around to see if anyone was about. Seeing no one, he gave two quick firm raps on the door, ripped the pin from the grenade, opened the door and threw the frag inside. In the same movement he turned and ran back to the shadows as though the devil himself was behind him. He'd only taken three or four steps when he heard Halsey's voice yell, "Grenade".

He was in the shadows now and his whole body was shaking so badly he could hardly run. Once back in the protective darkness, he

slowed to a brisk walk. Still his nerves kept his body shaking so badly his knees would hardly function. He fell twice before finally
reaching his hooch's back door. The back door was his choice of entrance so he wouldn't have to pass by Gillett's bunk. Finding his bunk
in the darkness wasn't easy, but he didn't want to fall over anything
and wake someone up. The army cot he slept on felt good, like a
child's security blanket. Yet his heart continued to pound violently.
So fierce was its beating, he thought it might burst. Even breathing
deeply to try to regain control of himself was almost an impossible
effort. Yet, he knew he must get into bed as quickly as possible before
bed check. The combat boots had to come off. He struggled with
the strings, with fingers shaking uncontrollably. Finally, the boots came
off and the shirt pulled over his head without unbuttoning. The pants
weren't too much trouble and he found himself in bed. Still shaking,
he wondered if he would ever get control, would he really get away
with it? Man, he wished he hadn't done this. It was the dumbest thing
he had ever done. His heart was still pounding as though trying to
escape his chest cavity. So fierce was the pounding and shaking that
his whole bed was moving. Finally, after some time he began to set-
tle down and fatigue was once again setting in. Ever so slowly, like
a slowly melting snow, he began to relax. The shaking and pounding
had stopped and his eyelids settled gently over his eyes.

The squeak of the main entrance door being opened shot through
Green like a spear. He lay there trying to pretend he was asleep, certain they had come for him. Yet nothing happened. He lay there strain-
ing to hear what was going on. For some reason someone had awakened Gillett, who was now getting out of bed.

Mr. Halsey hadn't been in bed but a short time and sleep was rapidly
shutting down his bodily functions. The knock on his door irritated
him more than anything else. After all, he was comfortably in bed.
As he threw off his sheet and flipped up the mosquito netting he
mumbled under his breath, "This better be good." He was never sent
on any of the night missions so that wasn't it. Who would be knocking on the door. His roommate would just walk on in. Besides, he
was probably still in Bangkok on R&R and wouldn't be back for a
while. The grapevine claimed that Bien Hoa had been closed since
Tet started. As a result, all R&R activity had stopped, with the guys

still out of country being held over.

Mr. Halsey had just stood up when his door opened. With the light in the background, he could just make out something small and round being thrown in. He could tell it was something relatively heavy the way it traveled through the air. It was the spring throwing open the handle that told him what. In that same flickering of a heartbeat he yelled, "Grenade" and dived into his bunk. As he hit the bed, the mosquito netting over it became tangled in his arms and body, breaking off three of the four poles holding it up and ripping a big long tear in the netting where it was attached to the fourth pole. Realizing his bed wasn't the safest place he could be, he allowed his momentum to roll him over onto the floor. Trying his best to hug the floor, he covered his ears with his hands and awaited the pain he knew would come. His only hope now was to live through it because he was going to be hurt, yet there was no ear shattering explosion. Why not? Was it possible he had misjudged what had come in his door and bounced like a steel ball onto the concrete floor? He searched the floor with his eyes trying in vain to find the mysterious object. If it was a frag, it should have blown long before now. He began to wonder if he should stand up or try to low crawl to the door and the light switch. Finally, he started to move, slowly at first, almost as though his very movement might set off the awaited explosion. As he moved closer to the door, he moved faster and faster until he resembled a bug on a hot surface. Once at the door, he stood up and turned on the lights. There it was in the far corner, just as big and black and ugly as a fragmentation grenade could be. He stood there staring at it for several minutes trying to figure it all out.

Why had it not blown? The spring was off and the handle lay several feet away. It was obviously a dud, but had someone made it so; or was someone disappointed he wasn't dead? But who? MacLaughlin, of course. He really couldn't picture MacLaughlin doing this—it just didn't fit his personality—but he was the only logical one. It had to be MacLaughlin. That son of a bitch, he'd send his smart ass to jail for the next twenty years.

The thing he had to do now was make sure he did everything the right way. The first thing he did was bang on the door next to his. Mr. Halsey's heart was still pounding pretty hard as he shouted, "Hey,

you guys, wake up! There's a live frag next to your wall in my room."
The response from behind the closed door was strained.

"Get lost, Halsey, we're busy."

"I'm not kidding you, guys. Somebody threw a frag in my door
and it's laying against your wall."

With that he could hear a woman's squeal and a great flurry of activity. The door flew open with a bang and a disgusted Mr. Lucas
stood there, a bulge protruding from the pants he was hurriedly trying to buckle. Halsey knew the activities had already started. That
knowledge, plus the sight of Lucas standing there with nothing on
but his pants almost made him laugh. Lucas was a tall man, over
six foot, but thin as a rail. His most distinguishing characteristic was
his prematurely bald head. He kept the rest of his head and face shaved,
which gave a very strange appearance.

"Halsey, you know something? You're an asshole."

"Hey, man, I'm just trying to help you out. I'm going to go report
that grenade to Captain Wolf, and you know how he feels about
hookers."

Mr. Lucas looked down at Halsey standing there in nothing but
his green boxer shorts. There wasn't any question in his mind that
Halsey would pull this kind of trick, just out of meanness. Yet there
was something about the pathetic little bastard that told him his story
might just be for real.

"Halsey, don't jive me. Nobody in this outfit would do something
like that."

"Hey, I'm not going to stand here and argue with you. I was just
trying to be a nice guy."

"Halsey, I'll tell you what. There damn well better be a grenade
in there, or I'll kill you myself."

Lucas turned and slammed the door behind him. Once inside he
looked at both girls who had finished dressing. "Come on, girls, he
was just kidding. If there was a frag in there it would have blown
long ago."

"I don't care! Either way we're getting out of here. We didn't ask
for this, and we're not staying."

Lucas found himself wishing the grenade had blown Halsey's ass off.

Once the door had been closed in his face, Halsey turned and started towards Captain Wolf's quarters. He had only taken a few steps when Captain Wolf and Major Hobbs came out of the latrine. Major Hobbs was indeed a big man, as Mr. Hill had said. He had a dark complexion with blond hair, cut in a half-inch flat top. Worst of all, he tried his best to give everyone the impression he ate nails for breakfast.

It was Captain Wolf with a big smile on his face who spoke first, "Halsey, what are you doing out here in your shorts?"

"Looking for you, Captain! Someone just tried to frag me!"

At that moment, Mr. Lucas' door came open and out ran the two nurses. Almost running into Wolf and Hobbs, the two nurses came to an abrupt stop. Wolf spoke, "At attention, Ladies."

"You happen to be speaking to a Captain, Mister, and I expect to be treated like one."

"Then you should try acting like one. Furthermore, I'm also a captain, the difference is, you're on my turf!" Captain Wolf's voice continued to build in force and volume.

"Lucas, Euclid, get your butts out here!"

Both officers came through the door fully dressed acting like two little boys who had just been caught with their fingers in the pie. Captain Wolf's voice was now back to normal, but still very forceful. "I've told you guys before, no women in the rooms. As long as you're in my platoon, you'll follow my orders, or wish you had."

Mr. Lucas spoke up, "Captain, it's not what you think. I just invited the girls in for a minute to look at some pictures I'd gotten back."

"Lucas, unless you want to be put on every asshole flight or shit detail for the rest of your stay, don't treat me like I'm stupid." Turning to face Euclid he asked, "How much did they charge you?"

Euclid shrugged his shoulders and looked at the ground, then said, "one hundred dollars each." Wolf's eyes bulged and his mouth dropped as his head slowly turned to the two nurses. In a soft, but forceful voice he asked, "One hundred dollars each! What were you going to do, gold plate it for 'em?"

Neither nurse said a thing as one looked at the ground and the other looked hatefully at Halsey, who was standing a few feet behind and to the side of Hobbs.

"Okay you two, because of this fragging, I don't have time to mess with you now. Just get out of here and don't ever come back. Not here, not to the club, not anywhere in this company area, or I'll personally see to it you stand court martial for prostitution. You're a disgrace to your country and your uniform. As officers, your conduct is inexcusable, and insulting. There are countless fine women who serve as military nurses, but you two are scum. Now get out of my sight and stay out."

Major Hobbs had moved close enough to Wolf so that he could speak in his ear without any of the others hearing and without it being obvious he was speaking, "I hope you never have to spend time in one of their hospital beds."

Captain Wolf slowly nodded his head in agreement and said, "Right."

Wolf now turned to Lucas and Euclid still standing there watching as their dreams walked rapidly away. "As for you two, it is going to be a very expensive night. You can sign the papers in the morning in the orderly room. Shall we say another two hundred dollars each? That'll make it a three hundred dollar night for you two love birds."

Neither man said a word but both looked straight at Halsey, who had now moved behind the massive body of Major Hobbs. Halsey's attempt to hide was unsuccessful, and seeing their stares, simply shrugged his shoulders and curled his mouth in such a way as though to say, 'I'm sorry, fellows.'

Captain Wolf now turned to Mr. Halsey and said, "Now, tell me about this fragging."

Mr. Halsey related the story as best he remembered it. At the end Major Hobbs said, "Let's go see it."

The light was still on as Halsey opened his door, allowing Wolf and Hobbs to walk in. Major Hobbs spotted the ominous looking grenade and said, "Well, Captain, I used to be in the infantry. This sort of thing is one of the reasons I transferred to aviation. You fly boys aren't supposed to have this type of problem."

"To my knowledge, Major, it's a first, at least in this company. What do you think, Major?"

"I think it's an intentional dud. In fact, I'm willing to bet on it." He walked over and carefully picked up the frag. Gripping the top with one massive hand, he gingerly turned the bottom off. Once the two parts were separated and the Major could see the exploded percussion cap, his face lit up with a big smile. Turning to face the two men still standing in the doorway, he flipped the spent percussion cap over to Captain Wolf, who caught it and quickly examined it. Standing fully erect now, Major Hobbs turned to Halsey, "Didn't I hear your name is Halsey?"

"Yes, Sir, that's right."

"I've got a question for you, Mr. Halsey. When this thing bounced across your floor, what did you do?" Adding very sarcastically, "Jump in your bed?"

"Sir, it was dark in there. The lights were off and when I realized what had just come through my door, I just dived for the floor and hit the bed in the process."

"I can see that. Did you pull your covers over your head also?"

"Major, this isn't a joking matter, someone tried to kill me, and..."

"Wrong! Mr. Halsey, somebody tried to scare the hell out of you, not kill you. At least not this time. That cap has been previously exploded, intentionally. Someone's gone to a lot of trouble to separate the body, blow the cap, pick up all the parts, and then put it back together. You didn't see who did this?"

"No, Sir, but I've got a real good idea!"

"Who?"

"A Spec Four named, MacLaughlin."

"Any particular reason why him?"

"Yes, Sir, we've had problems in the past, and this morning was just a typical example of his arrogance and insubordination."

Mr. Halsey started to relate a very shaded account of Jim's refusal to fly with him that morning.

Captain Wolf just couldn't feature MacLaughlin doing something like this. Yet somebody had, so until he knew more, he wasn't about to say anything one way or the other. He did notice that Halsey's account of this morning's activities wasn't quite correct. Yet again, he felt it best to listen and remember.

Once Halsey had finished, Major Hobbs suggested they go talk to Colonel Appleton after Halsey put on some clothes. As they headed out the door, Mr. Euclid reached over and tapped Captain Wolf on the arm. The Major and Halsey were already on their way as Euclid spoke to Captain Wolf, "Captain, Mac was on a night mission with

Mr. Hill and I tonight 'til after midnight or later. I don't believe for a second he did this. For one thing, whoever did it has been sitting out there someplace for a long time, watching for Halsey. Mac just hasn't been in the company area that long."

"Okay, go on back to bed. By the way, I'll draw up the papers for you and Lucas to sign before I go to bed. See you in the morning."

Colonel Appleton walked through the orderly room into his office, followed closely by Major Hobbs, Captain Wolf, Mr. Halsey and shortly thereafter, by Mr. Walker. Colonel Appleton positioned himself as comfortably as possible in his office chair. He'd had a long day and was sound asleep when Captain Wolf pounded on his door. Why in Heaven's name did it have to be his company? In the infantry, one could maybe expect it, but not an aviation company. Not an outstanding company like his. There had never been any trouble before this. Oh, sure, the usual amount of Article 15's. All for small time things like insubordination, mostly talking back to one of the officers; but nothing of this magnitude where a man's life was threatened.

The biggest question he had to answer besides who, was how should he handle it. He sure didn't want the publicity and problems that went with this kind of thing. If at all possible, Appleton wanted to keep it right here within the company.

Halsey was positive MacLaughlin did it. Maybe he'd get unbelievably lucky and MacLaughlin would confess and he could be on his way to the L.B.J* before morning. Well, he'd better get this thing started so he could get back to bed. Leaning back in his swivel chair, Colonel Appleton shouted at the CQ**. "Hey, Sergeant, come in here!"

The CQ quickly jumped up from his chair and headed into the old man's office. He didn't know what was going on, but at this time of the morning it had to be something big for all that Brass to be up walking around.

"Sergeant, I want you to get Sergeant Gillett up and have him find Specialist MacLaughlin. Don't tell them anything except I want to

---

*L.B.J. - Long Binh jail.

**C.Q. - Charge of quarters, always an E-5 or above, usually there was a lesser ranking E.M. used as a runner.

see MacLaughlin in my office at once."

"Yes, Sir!"

"One more thing, Sergeant. Don't send your runner. I want you to go personally. I also want you to pay close attention to MacLaughlin's reactions."

"Yes, Sir!" He saluted the Colonel, turned and headed out the door. Once in the outer office, he checked the duty roster. Finding Gillett's name on it, he glanced across the board to find his hooch number and was on his way.

"Now then, Mr. Walker, do you know why we're all gathered here in the middle of the night?"

"Yes, Sir. Mr. Halsey told me when he got me up."

"Okay, you probably know MacLaughlin better than any other officer. You are his AC, aren't you?"

"Yes, Sir, I am."

"What kind of soldier is he? What kind of person is he?"

"Well, Sir, as a person, he's very religious. He's a nice guy and well liked. He's intelligent and disciplined. In fact, I'd say he does nothing on impulse. As a soldier, he's one of the best crew chiefs in the company. He does his job and doesn't bitch, no matter how bad things get. He knows that Huey inside and out, and how to fix anything on it as a result of his having been in maintenance before becoming a chief. I believe Captain Wolf will verify that he flies most every single ship night mission we have. They used to ask for volunteers and he always went, so they just quit asking. Now they just go get MacLaughlin. As to whether I think he would do something like this, no, Sir! There's no way he'd frag someone, not even Mr. Halsey! His personal conduct and appearance is always what you would expect. One other thing, Sir, as a pilot, he makes my job a whole lot easier. I know I can depend on him no matter what. I personally don't believe for a second that he did this. It's against everything he stands for. I've never once heard him advocate anything even close to this.

"As you know, Sir, Mr. Halsey and MacLaughlin haven't gotten along since Mac turned him in for falsifying those records. I wonder if that hasn't clouded Mr. Halsey's judgment in this matter?"

"Mr. Walker, you obviously like the man a great deal."

"Yes, Sir, we're very close. We've gone through a lot together. He has never shown any disrespect, for myself or any other officer. He has, however, given me a lot of reasons to greatly respect him."

"All right, Mr. Walker, you can go back to bed now. Thank you very much for coming in and giving me some background information."

Mr. Walker was stunned at being so quickly dismissed—but having no choice, he came to attention, saluted, turned and left. Once outside, he thought about waiting for MacLaughlin, but decided against it. If the CO found out he'd talked to Mac before going in, he would find himself in almost as much trouble as Mac.

The CQ had no trouble locating Gillett's bunk. It was right where all platoon sergeants bunks were supposed to be; the first bunk on the right after entering through the main entrance. His flashlight shone in Gillett's face and with a gentle shaking, Gillett came to enough to say only, "What?"

"Sergeant Gillett?"

"Yeah, what do you want?"

The CQ had moved his light from Gillett's face to help ease his reintroduction into the waking world, "Sergeant, I'm the CQ. Colonel Appleton wants to see Specialist MacLaughlin ASAP."

"What's he want with Mac?"

"You'll have to ask the Colonel that, Sergeant."

"What time is it?"

"Almost two."

Gillett stretched and slowly sat up on the edge of his bunk. He couldn't imagine why the CO wanted to see Mac at this time of night. Oh, well, at least Mac wasn't hard to wake up. He'd had a real education about waking people up since he'd become platoon sergeant; some guys you didn't dare touch or they'd get upset and start swinging, always under the pretense of being startled out of sleep. With others, he had to exchange verbal blows each morning. Not Mac, though, he always woke easily and without a hassle, all he had to do was shake his foot or shoulder gently and say, 'Mac, wake up,' and he would, without a fight of any kind.

Gillett turned on a flashlight and walked over to Mac's bunk. Reaching down to Jim's foot he gave it a gentle shake and said, "Mac, it's me, Gillett. Wake up!"

The CQ had positioned his light so it shone directly in Jim's face causing him to squint and turn his head to one side.

"Gillett, get that light out of my eyes!"

"It's not me, it's the CQ."

"I don't care who it is, just get it out of my face, will you?"

The CQ lowered his light slightly, enough to allow Jim to remove the hand which had been shielding his eyes. "Gillett, where're you sending me now, Loc Ninh again?"

"No, Mac, the CO wants to see you."

"The CO! What time is it?"

"Two, or there about."

The CQ had put the direct beam of his light full force in Jim's eyes once again. As Jim sat up he said, "I don't know who you are, but I'm not going to tell you again to get that light out of my face. I'm about ready to stick it down your throat."

"Look, Specialist, I was told to get you up and watch your reaction and that's what I'm doing."

Jim was now seated on the side of his bunk, so it was a simple, and seemingly natural move to gradually reach for a boot. Gillett spotted the movement and realized the potential problems it could cause if Jim put his boot up alongside the CQ's head. At the same time Gillett spoke, he reached out and moved the light, "Forget it, Mac, it's not worth it. Look, Sergeant, go on back and tell the CO we'll be there just as soon as we finish dressing."

"Okay, Gillett, but if you two aren't there in five minutes, I'll be back for you."

The CQ turned and left. Once out the door, Mac asked Gillett, "What's the CO want with me at this time of night?"

"I don't know anymore than you do, Mac."

"One thing is for sure, he didn't get me out of bed to give me a promotion!"

"Right! Did you get in trouble going up to Loc Ninh tonight?"

"No. I gave Mr. Hill kind of a hard time about flying a night mission when he's going home tomorrow. That's it though, hardly something major."

"Well, one thing is for sure, the CO isn't going to get himself out of bed for something that isn't serious. Did you and Halsey have more trouble?"

"Just this morning and you know about that. Gillett, maybe it's not something bad."

"I'm not so sure. That CQ said he was told to watch for your reaction when you were told the CO wanted you. Now, I ask you, why would he be told to do that if it was something good?"

"Gillett, I can't figure it. You about ready?"

"Yeah, just as soon as I finish tying this boot."

Jim stood and walked to the door where he waited for his friend. Gillett finished, picked up his light and walked out the door with Jim. The two men walked in silence with the aid of Gillett's flashlight to the orderly room. As they approached, yet still out of hearing range, Gillett took Jim's arm and shut off his light. "Look, Mac, I don't know what this is all about so let me give you some advice before we get there. First, it might be something good, it might be something bad, and it might be neither, so until you know exactly what's going down, don't do or say anything you don't have to. Give, 'Yes, Sir,' and 'No, Sir,' answers, don't volunteer anything. Remember your military procedures for saluting and your physical stance. Stay at attention until he tells you otherwise. If by some remote chance, and I can't think why there would be, but if there is anybody else there, you talk only to and respond only to the CO. Unless, of course, the question obviously has the CO's blessings. You got any questions?"

"No, I guess I'm ready. Let's go find out what the old man wants."

Gillett turned his flashlight on and the two men resumed their walk. Jim kept searching his brain for any kind of clue—his continuing struggle with Halsey was what he kept coming back to. This morning's refusal to fly with him must have been the last straw. Still, that didn't make sense. The CO would just have waited until morning...

After leaving Gillett and MacLaughlin, the CQ walked directly back to the orderly room. As he walked in the door, Colonel Appleton, Major Hobbs, Captain Wolf and Mr. Halsey were all coming out of the old man's office. Colonel Appleton spoke before the CQ had a chance to do anything but shut the door.

"Well, Sergeant, did you find him?"

"Yes, Sir. He was in bed asleep."

"Tell me everything you did just as it happened."

The CQ told his every action in great detail including the fact that Gillett was going to accompany MacLaughlin. This pleased the CO. After all, it is a platoon sergeant's responsibility to assist his men in this type of situation. He smiled to himself as he thought about what a fine example Gillett was making. He'd have to remember Gillett.

After the CQ had finished, the CO thanked him and turned to Captain Wolf. "Captain, let's go over these duty rosters and see where we stand on personnel."

The two men looked at the roster of names in each platoon trying to get some idea of how to shuffle people around. "Colonel, as I see it, we have one extra gunner in second platoon and one extra crew chief in the first platoon. If we lose Mac, we'll have to leave a ship on the ground anytime one of the crew chiefs gets sick or can't fly for some reason."

"That only leaves us with two options. One, take a man out of maintenance to fill a crew chief's spot or start making the two flight platoon sergeants fly."

"Colonel, the flight platoon sergeants have too much to do as it is. Those guys have to work on the next day's flight schedule after everyone else is in bed. They have to coordinate ships in and out of maintenance with the personnel available. They often don't get to bed until 0200 or later, then get up at 0445 to get their people up and going. Those men have to be able to rack out during the day. We put them on a chopper and they'd sleep most of the time."

"Captain, maintenance is almost as bad. They used to have five work crews of five men each; three day crews and two night crews. They're down to one five-man night crew and two day crews of five men each. I've already eliminated all supervisory personnel in maintenance, every crew leader works just like one of the crew. I even told the the sergeants they had to start helping out. They're to find a crew they like working with and stick with it until they have to go inspect someone's work. It's to stay that way until we get some replacements. Oh, well, we can make a decision after we talk to MacLaughlin."

Everyone but the CQ followed the Colonel back into his office. As they walked by the last hooch, Jim could see the bright lights of maintenance; several sets of those lights were set up and burning brightly. Jim knew it was going to be another long night for the guys in maintenance. He could remember spending many a time working under those lights all night long. Maybe it was the loner in him, but he actually preferred working at night. There was never any Brass around to hassle you, just a sergeant, and they always left you alone, as long as you did your job. He could still remember as though it were yesterday, being told he was going on the night crew. He hadn't liked the idea but the sergeant hadn't given him any choice. Besides, he told Mac, they only put their best people on night because they were expected to work without much supervision. Man, that had been an understatement. The only time he'd seen any supervision was when he'd picked up his job assignment along with the rest of the crew, or when the crew he was on needed a tech sergeant to okay something they were doing and then sign it off. Tech would leave and the crew would be on their own again. Jim very quickly saw the advantage of working on the night crew. Almost as quickly, he'd really learned to like working nights. It really did have a lot of advantages; no hassling, the work pace was flexible and you had the next day off. Not to mention the night crew missed most formations due to the working hours. Oh, well, that was in the past.

Gillett and Jim walked up the steps and entered the orderly room. There sat the CQ, who stood up as soon as he saw the two men walk in. "Wait here and I'll tell the CO you're here."

The CQ turned and knocked on the CO's door. The CO's voice was heard, "Come in."

The CQ opened the door, stepped in and said, "Sir, Sergeant Gillett and Specialist MacLaughlin are here."

"Send them in, Sergeant."

Jim wasn't nervous or apprehensive. He couldn't think of any reason why the CO wanted him so he was as relaxed as any enlisted man could be, going to see the CO. The fact that he was still partially asleep helped. Gillett poked him and said, "Remember what I said."

Jim nodded his head and thought about the CO's office. He'd been in it once before when he'd been a CQ runner one night. The old man's desk sat off to the right so that one had to enter the door, take two steps forward, make a right turn and face the CO behind his desk.

Jim figured the CO probably put his desk there just to intimidate those entering the room.

Gillett entered first and made a straight path to the CO's desk. Jim noticed that he had made a very unmilitary diagonal path to get there. If he wants military, I'll give him military, Jim thought.

Gillett reported, "Sir, Sergeant Gillett reports."

"At ease, Sergeant."

Jim figured Gillett being told to stand at ease was a good sign. He entered and took a quick glance to his left and there, to his surprise, stood Halsey. The sight of Halsey struck Jim like a hundred needles pricking his spine. Halsey meant trouble and he knew it. Gillett was right, he would have to be very, very careful. Jim took two steps forward, executed a perfect right turn, took two more steps and found himself squarely in front of the CO's desk. Standing perfectly at attention with his eyes straight ahead he brought his right arm up to a snappy salute, "Sir, Specialist MacLaughlin reporting as ordered!"

Jim could see standing off to the left and behind the old man was Captain Wolf, seated to the right and slightly behind the CO was a Major whom Jim had never seen. It was impossible to read the name tag without turning his head or eyes, so he didn't. Something was very wrong, this almost looked like a court martial hearing. Jim was now scared. If Wolf and Halsey were both here, he was definitely in trouble. The unknown Major bothered him almost as much or more than the others, yet the location of each man indicated their importance, and the Major held no more important position than did Captain Wolf. The CO brought his arm up to return the salute and the moment he started back down, Jim whipped his hand down in a lost effort to beat the CO's.

Both men were impressed with the other's salute. Most officers gave a lackadaisical type of salute and Jim had expected to beat the Colonel's arm down. Colonel Appleton, on the other hand, often measured an enlisted man's military sharpness by his salute and MacLaughlin had certainly passed with high marks.

The Colonel sat there looking up at Jim's face as though trying to read his mind. Jim was aware of the significance of his being left standing at attention. No one spoke and Jim knew no one would until the CO did. All the CO was doing was staring at him, if his intent was to make him nervous, he was being very effective. Finally, after what seemed like a lot longer than it really was, Colonel Appleton spoke, "Specialist, how long have you been in country?"

Jim wondered why in the world he wanted to know that. It had to be a lead in, after all Halsey and Wolf weren't here to find out what they could read on his personnel records. "Going on nine months, Sir."

"Of that time how much has been spent with the Blackhawks?"

"About four months, Sir."

"Specialist, I've looked over your record. It's very impressive. You're obviously a good crew chief. Tell me, do you have any problems?"

"Problems, Sir? Well, Sir, between the long hours, the night missions and the CQ waking me up, I don't get enough sleep."

"That's not what I mean, Specialist, and you know it. Do you want to talk about it?"

"Sir, I don't know what you mean."

Colonel Appleton just sat there giving Jim a very stern look. Very slowly he leaned back in his chair allowing the swivel rocker to tip backwards. Placing both hands behind his head he allowed himself to show a small smile. In a soft friendly voice he spoke, "At ease, Specialist."

Jim moved very smartly into the more comfortable 'at ease' position.

"Did you fly a night mission tonight, Specialist?"

"Yes, Sir."

"What time did you get back?"

"About 1230, Sir, I'm not real sure."

Colonel Appleton leaned forward, opened a desk drawer, pulled out an object, sat it abruptly on his desk and said, "Ever see this before, Specialist?"

The surprised expression on both Gillett's and Jim's faces registered with all the officers in the room. Even Halsey, who had slowly worked his way around the room to where he could see everyone's face, hadn't expected that reaction. Jim shrugged his shoulders, "It's a fragmentation grenade, Sir. Everybody in the army has seen one of those."

"Specialist, the question was, 'have you ever seen this particular one before?'"

"I have no way of knowing that, Sir. I would say right off the top, no, Sir, I haven't, because I simply don't handle that many frags."

"Disassemble it for me, Specialist!"

Jim looked down at the Colonel as though he were crazy, then looked over at Captain Wolf, who was taking in his every reaction. Looking back at the Colonel, he spoke, "Colonel, that thing is not a toy. It has one purpose and that's to hurt people. So if it's all the same to you, Sir, I'd rather not play with a live grenade."

"I didn't give you a choice, Specialist, I said take it apart, now!"

"Yes, Sir." Jim picked up the grenade, looked it over and looked back down at the CO. "Sir, having never done this before, I'm not sure one can take a frag apart without blowing one's self into very small pieces."

The expression on the CO's face told him he should start disassembling the frag. Firmly gripping the base with his left hand, he turned the cap off with his right hand. Clearly showing the apprehension he felt, Jim removed the cap and saw the spent percussion clip. The look of surprise on his face was obvious to everyone in the room. Holding the cap in his hand so that it was visible to the others, Jim searched each man's face for some kind of answer. "Colonel, I know you didn't get me out of bed to play a practical joke. Sir, I would appreciate it if you told me what is going on."

"I had hoped you could tell me, Specialist."

The questioning look on Jim's face had convinced the CO by now that Jim wasn't their man, or else he should get an Oscar for his performance. "Sir, I am obviously missing something. I don't know what you want from me."

"Specialist, someone took this grenade earlier tonight and threw it into Mr. Halsey's quarters."

Jim's eyes enlarged, his jaw dropped open and his general look of surprise and shock was clear. "Colonel, you obviously think I did it. I'll be the first to admit Mr. Halsey isn't one of my favorite people, but I didn't do it. In the first place, I wasn't in the company area until sometime around 0100, when I got back from a night mission. You can ask Mr. Hill or Mr. Euclid. They were the pilots."

Halsey spoke up, "You had plenty of time after you landed!"

"Sir, I did a post-flight inspection, took a shower and went to bed."

"I'll bet."

Jim turned to Halsey, "Sir, you can check my log book and ship on the post flight, and smell my arm pit to verify the shower!''

A quick glance at Gillett who was shaking his head "no" and saying, "not now" with his lips, moved Jim's glance to Captain Wolf,
who gave him the same glance and facial expression. He then turned
back to Colonel Appleton and the unknown Major. It was only the
Major whose body was moving as though laughing, and who had
covered his bowed face with one hand. The Major quickly regained
his composure and looked up, showing only a small smile.

Gillett spoke up, "Sir, may I speak?"

"Go ahead, Sergeant,"

"Sir, Specialist MacLaughlin was on a night mission tonight. I don't
know what time he got back, but I came in the hooch to go to bed
at 0115. I know the time because I had to set my alarm. Mac's bunk
is right across the aisle from mine and I checked on him just to see
if he was back. He was in bed, sound asleep. When the CQ came
in, he was still asleep, and the CQ stood there and watched me wake
him up. Could I ask the Colonel what time this fragging occurred?"

"About 0100, which makes it pretty unlikely that you were the guilty
party, Specialist."

Jim's mind was saying, "Thank you, Gillett!"

"Do either of you two have any idea who might have done this?"

Gillett slowly shook his head and said, "No, Sir. I can't think of
anybody who would do something like this."

The Colonel looked at Jim, "How about you, Mac. Any ideas?"

Jim was struck by the sudden difference in attitude...suddenly he
was good old Mac. "No, Sir, none of the enlisted men I know would
do anything like this." Jim saw a small chance to get Halsey off his
back and decided to take it, no matter how far out it sounded. "Colonel, I would like to suggest one possibility for your consideration."

"All right, who is it?"

"Well, Sir, it's common knowledge that Mr. Halsey hassles me every
chance he gets ever since I turned him in for falsifying those reports.
Sir, the man hates my guts, and has been trying everything he can
think of to put me in a situation where he could get me into trouble.
Sir, I can't help but wonder if Mr. Halsey didn't fake this whole thing.
That would explain why it was a dud instead of a live grenade. Mr.
Halsey didn't want his room all messed up."

The rage on Halsey's face was apparent to Colonel Appleton, who spoke before Halsey could, "Specialist, nobody in this room including yourself believes that's a real possibility." The Colonel paused and looked around the room. "Okay, we don't seem to be getting anyplace tonight. Captain Wolf, you and Major Hobbs sit tight, everyone else is dismissed."

Gillett and Jim came to attention, saluted and left, followed out the door by Halsey. No one spoke as the two enlisted men picked up their caps and walked out into the night. Once out into the darkness, Jim grabbed Gillett's arm, as the two men turned and watched Halsey walk down the orderly room steps. Halsey paused at the foot of the steps, looked around, pulled out a cigarette and lit it. After taking a long drag, he turned and walked toward the officers' quarters.

Jim felt a great sense of relief. The darkness gave him a sense of confidence and security; he felt a freedom to do things that he would never do in daylight. As Halsey walked away, Jim flipped him the bird, Gillett laughed softly and said, "If I had a grenade right now I might just use it myself. Mac, you didn't really do it, did you?"

"Hell, no, I didn't. By the way, Gillett, thanks for speaking up for me in there. I appreciate it."

"Well, I just hope the CO doesn't check out our stories too closely because, if he does, he'll poke some holes in mine."

"Why do you say that?"

"Mac, I lied through my teeth in there. I didn't lay eyes on you or your bunk from the time I sent you on that mission until I woke you up with the CQ. I just didn't think you did it and I wasn't going to let Halsey hang your ass for it. For that matter, I wouldn't have let him have you even if I thought you had done it. It's just a shame Charlie doesn't shoot that son of a bitch for us."

"Yeah, the only trouble is, that's the kind who makes it all the way through without a scratch. Thanks, Gillett."

"Forget it, Mac, but I would like to know if not you, then who?"

"I don't really know, but if I were to guess, I could think of six or eight guys who wouldn't mind seeing him dead."

"Gillett, how about Green? He's from the infantry, and that's primarily an infantry problem. Plus, he was saying something about fragging this morning."

"I doubt it, but let's go ask him. He just hasn't been in the company long enough."

They walked into the hooch and Gillett turned on his flash light as Jim made his way down the aisle to Green's bunk. Gillett approached from the other side of the bunk with his flashlight on. Both men raised the mosquito netting on their respective sides and Gillett handed Jim the light. "Here, hold this."

Jim took the light and directed it in such a way as to see Green's face without shining it directly into his eyes. Gillett shook Green's shoulder and as Green started to open his eyes, Gillett spoke, "You certainly have had a busy night haven't you, Green?"

"Hey, man, I don't know what you're talking about. I didn't do anything." Green's heart was pounding so hard that both Gillett and Jim could feel it. Green was obviously very nervous about something and both men knew it.

Gillett put his face down close to Green's and said, "You threw that frag, Green, and we both know it. Listen to me, you son of a bitch, make damn sure you stick to that story about not knowing anything and for sure don't do anything for the next month to draw attention to yourself! Above all, don't be throwing anymore, you got that? Or, I'll turn you in myself, even if it is Halsey. Understand me, asshole?"

"Yes, Sergeant." Green looked at both Jim and Gillett and asked, "Does anyone else know?"

"Not yet."

"Sarge, how did you know it was me?"

"We didn't."

Jim walked back to his bunk and went quickly asleep. It was Halsey who had the most trouble getting to sleep. He'd locked his door behind him yet was startled by every creak and sound. MacLaughlin obviously hadn't done it, yet the little creep had really turned the screws on him there in front of the old man. It was just a good thing the CO didn't believe him; he very easily could have. The thing that bothered him most was, if it wasn't MacLaughlin, then who? Certainly, he'd have to start being a little more careful, and he'd watch all the EM for even the slightest indication of guilt.

In the CO's office, Wolf and Hobbs moved two chairs in front of the CO's desk. As always it was the CO who started, "Well, Gentlemen, what do you think?"

Both men's facial expressions said, "You go first." Finally Hobbs spoke, "Since I just got here today, maybe I could give a more balanced opinion. I was more positively impressed with MacLaughlin than I was with Halsey. I don't think MacLaughlin did it, he was just too surprised. I have to admit, I didn't think I'd keep from laughing when he asked Halsey if he wanted to smell his armpit!"

Appleton and Wolf both started to laugh as they remembered the scene and Halsey's face. "If Halsey really does hate MacLaughlin as much as he claimed, perhaps we should take more seriously the possibility that Halsey faked it."

Wolf jumped in, "I don't think Halsey has the guts to try something like this. I do agree, though, I don't think Mac's our man, so how do we find the guilty party?"

"Without a major interrogation of all the enlisted men, the only thing we can do is to wait for the guilty party to start telling people he did it. Once the secret is out, it'll get back to the officers, then we can make our move. So, unless one of you two have something more to add, I suggest we all go back to bed."

Everyone was in agreement; flying tomorrow would be a real effort for everyone after tonight's activities.

Colonel Appleton was the only one besides Halsey who had any trouble getting back to sleep. As he lay there in his bed, he kept thinking, Of all the units in country, why his? Halsey was an ass, he knew that, nobody much cared for the man, but he hadn't realized the men hated him so much. Of course it was a dud, so whoever did it meant it only as a warning. Still, it couldn't be tolerated regardless of who, or how bad the officer was. He wondered how often this kind of incident occurred. It was common knowledge that the infantry had a problem with fraggings—but not aviation companies. He wondered if there were any accurate statistics available. Furthermore, if he didn't have anyone to court martial, he certainly wasn't going to report it. He only had a short time left in country and unless something went wrong, he had a real good chance of being promoted to full bird before his tour was up. The last thing Appleton needed was a bunch of TV people running around doing a story. The army sure had changed in the years he'd been in it. Who would have thought ten years ago that there would be daily TV coverage of a war? Worst yet, that a company commander would be somewhat inhibited by it in the handling of his troops. The fear that some TV reporter would want to take pictures and do a story changed a lot of things. He would just bet there would be more than one perfectly good officer's career ruined by the TV coverage of this stupid war.

It was 0500 when Gillett woke Jim and the rest of his platoon much too early as far as Jim was concerned—yet there was nothing to do about it but yawn and get up. One of the benefits of flying was not having to stand morning formation, which meant an extra fifteen or twenty minutes of sleep, making the morning a lot slower and easier. Gillett came back through just as Jim finished tying his boots.

"Mac, you ready to go eat?"

"Yeah, let's go,"

Once outside the door and headed for the mess hall, Gillett spoke, "I switched your gunners today. I got to thinking about it and decided it would be best if Green flew with someone else for a while."

"That's fine with me, if you don't think it will draw attention to Green."

"Quite frankly, Mac, I really don't care if it does. In fact, I'm halfway tempted to turn him in myself. The only reason I don't is I figure he did it to get Halsey off your back." Both men displayed their meal cards which allowed them to eat without paying, and picked up their trays. Jim put the malaria tablet on his tray alongside the usual utensils.

"Hey, Cookie, the war must be swinging back our way. That actually looks like food!, I halfway expected to get nothing but dry cereal for breakfast again."

"Gillett, we have a vast wealth of food this morning. The Air Force got a C130 full of food in here last night. Up until then, you were getting cold dry cereal for breakfast this morning."

Jim looked over the selection. There were the ever-present individual packages of cereal, eggs cooked to ones' specifications, toast and creamed chipped beef on a bun at the far end. Gillett took a couple of overeasy eggs and some toast. Jim put four toasted buns on his plate and poured a plate full of creamed beef over them, then followed Gillett to a table where no one else was seated.

"I'll swear, Mac, you'd eat shit on a shingle every day if it was available."

"Hey, man, I like it!"

"Mac, it's gross! It looks like it should be coming out the other end of somebody sick, not something being eaten."

"I don't care how it looks, it tastes good, it's filling and I like it. Besides, I don't cut on your hard boiled eggs that the cook called overeasy."

Both men laughed as they started to eat. Before anything else was said, Kenny walked to their table, put his tray down and asked, "Mind if I join you guys?"

Jim looked at Gillett who had a, "if you have to" look on his face.

"Hey, Mac, I hear you tried to frag Halsey last night."

Jim's shock was apparent. "Kenny, how did you hear that?"

"The guy who was CQ runner was telling me as we stood and pissed on Vietnam together this morning."

"I didn't do it, Kenny. I think Halsey faked it and I hope that isn't an accurate account of what he told you."

"Well, that wasn't exactly what he said; it was more like the Old Man pulled you in last night because he thought you did it."

"Well, it looks to me like Halsey set the whole thing up, so if you tell anybody else about it keep it accurate, will you! Say, Kenny, while I'm talking to you, I'd like to know where you got the water you put in the shower yesterday."

"We had to get it straight out of the river, Mac, why?"

"Because it had half the river bottom in it. I didn't know whether I was washing the dirt off or just recycling it. It was terrible, dirt, sand, and the way it smelled, a good percentage of it had to be shit."

Kenny said, "I'm surprised there was still water in the tanks."

"Yeah, I was, too. Man, I still remember the first time I took a late night shower and the water ran out; all that grit and grime came pouring out just as I was rinsing my hair. I had to go get a steel pot full of water out of the drinking water trailer and pour it over my head to get the sand out." The three men laughed together as each remembered a similar experience. It was Gillett who finished eating first, he turned to Kenny and spoke, "Kenny, didn't I tell you to get rid of that monkey?"

"Gillett, I can't catch him!"

"Bullshit!"

"No bullshit, Gillett, you know how wild it is!"

"I'll tell you what, Kenny, if you cage it up, you can keep it, but otherwise it goes."

Kenny's face lit up like a child's on Christmas morning, "Hey man, that's great! Thanks, Gillett, I really appreciate it. I'll get him caged up today. Man, I promise."

"Well, you better, because I'll give it to the gooks as soon as they get back on post. If that monkey isn't caged, it'll be their dinner. You understand me, Kenny?"

"Sure, Sarge, I'll get a cage today, or maybe I'll just make one—but somehow I'll get it caged up, I promise."

Gillett looked over at Jim and saw the disapproving look on his face, but before Jim could say anything, Gillett asked if he had finished eating. If so, he would walk out with him. Kenny stayed at the table and continued eating his breakfast as Jim and Gillett picked up their trays and left. Once outside, Jim turned and said, "Gillett, why did you let Kenny keep the monkey?"

"Oh, a couple of reasons. First, he is the only one who can catch it. Second, once it's caged it won't be throwing shit on anyone and, finally, if it's caged and Kenny goes on a convoy to Saigon it's hard to say what could happen to his poor monkey while he's gone."

"How soon are the highways supposed to be open for traffic again?"

"The last I heard, in a day or so. All they have to do is put up a couple more pontoon bridges where the VC knocked out the old ones and I guess we're back in business."

"Let me guess. You've already volunteered Kenny to go on the first convoy out, right?"

"Right!"

"Gillett, he'll just love to hear that."

"Now, you don't have to be so sarcastic, Mac. Besides Kenny has gone on several convoys in the past. I think he kind of enjoys it. He gets to spend the night in Saigon, where he can get good and drunk, plus have some broad to lay him."

"Gillett, you're all heart." Both men broke into laughter.

Once back in their hooch, Jim opened his wall locker (which was similar to everyone else's with clean uniforms hanging in no particular order), to get his toothbrush, paste and shaving gear. One of the few nice things about a true combat area was that enlisted men seldom had to stand inspection of their personal area. As a result, most all wall and foot lockers were very unmilitarily organized, if organized at all. Jim had all his underwear in his foot locker where it was out of the way. Like most men in his company, he long ago had quit wearing underwear. It only retained more heat and held the sweat against his body causing crotch itch. Also, it wasn't at all uncommon to get back underwear from the cleaners which looked like it had been cleaned in the Saigon River. Whenever one can tell that olive drab underwear isn't clean, it really isn't clean. Jim kept his socks and spare footwear on the floor of his wall locker, he hung up his dress uniforms and clean fatigues and, on the top shelf, he kept his toiletries and hats. On the inside of the door he had taped only two pictures. One was his family, the other his home. He didn't like to hang up nude pictures, as it only made him want what wasn't available.

Jim headed straight for his ship as the crews were all beginning to gather, including a few of the officers flying peter pilot, so he stowed his gear and pulled out the log book. Once satisfied that all the paperwork was in order, he got out his flashlight and started pulling his preflight. The last thing he checked was the rotor head and he couldn't believe there were no holes. It was almost as though a blanket had been thrown over them which nothing could penetrate. As was often the case, he simply stood there on top of the helicopter looking out over the area. From the direction of the company area, Jim could see the trucks bringing the officers out towards the flight line, their preflight briefing was obviously over. With the pilots on their way, Jim climbed down off the chopper's roof as Kenny drove up in the platoon's quarter ton jeep and dropped off the door gunners and their guns. Green and Sp-4 Wright climbed out, but it was Wright who carried his guns over to Jim's ship, where he could set them down, along with his gear, on the chopper's cargo floor. Green picked up his guns from the revetments corner and left.

Sp-4 Wright wasn't that much different from the rest of the guys in Jim's company, standing 5'10" and thin as a skeleton, with brown hair and eyes, and a nose as big as Jimmy Durante's. His nickname, as a result, was 'The Beak.' With a happy-go-lucky personality and almost always in good spirits, it was hard not to like him.

Once the pilots arrived, the rotor blades were untied and the aircraft started. They didn't go far, however; only to the runway where troops were loaded, then into the air, where they formed a trail-right formation and began circling Tay Ninh while one other company landed and put on troops. Once everyone was loaded, Blackhawk Lead turned and headed north to Loc Ninh. It was Mr. Walker who broke the silence, "Mac, you awake back there?"

"Yes, Sir, bright eyed and bushy tailed."

"Yeah, I'll bet! How much sleep did you get last night?"

"Oh, I don't know, about an hour or two."

"You know where we're headed?"

"No, Sir! Where?"

"Loc Ninh! Does that send shivers up your back?"

"Yes, Sir, it does! I take it you heard about last night?"

"Yeah, Mr. Hill was telling everyone about it at breakfast. Sounded like you guys had quite a ride."

The sarcasm was obvious as Jim replied, "Hey, man, that's what we're paid extra for! Why do we have to go back this morning?"

"We're going to be the lead company on a three company insertion into Loc Ninh. We're supposed to land just seconds after daybreak and the two companies behind us will follow us in and, hopefully, out on ten second intervals. Which means we're not going to have time to do anything. If we can't find a place to land, we'll have to hover and let the troops jump."

"Mr. Walker, I've never heard of landing on a ten second interval before."

"Well, don't feel bad, the only other time I've heard of it was in flight school, and they told us then not to sneeze or someone would land on top of us. The whole idea is to put in as many troops as possible, with as much cover fire as possible, in as short a time as possible.

"Looks like the lights of our third company forming up on our right. If you guys aren't strapped in, you'd better get ready, because I put us only three minutes out of Loc Ninh."

Jim checked his seatbelt and pulled the visor down on his helmet. He was beginning to see daylight, and could just make out trees below.

"Flight, this is Lead. We're on final approach to the runway with touch down in ninety seconds, please advise door gunners not to hit the Special Forces camp, everything else is a free fire zone. Also, be advised the Air Force hasn't received any fire from the swimming pool for about an hour now, but we'll still brake right on take off as planned to stay away from it. Here we go."

It was now just past daybreak and everyone could see the bodies and parts of bodies all over the ground below. All door guns were now firing and Jim concentrated his fire on the distant tree line which had been shredded by bombs, artillery and small-arms fire. He could make out the bodies of dead NVA nailed to the rubber trees by the darts from the beehives. There were so many bodies on the runway that landing was impossible, so the troops quickly jumped out and started to throw bodies aside to allow the flight on its way in to land. As the Blackhawks turned right and away from Loc Ninh, Jim could see the Special Forces camp with bodies of dead NVA stacked two and three deep on the wire surrounding Loc Ninh.

"Blackhawk Lead, this is Loc Ninh Control. Do you copy, over?"

"Roger, Loc Ninh, we copy. Over."

"Roger, Blackhawk. Sir, my commanding officer wishes me to convey the following message to the men from your company who brought in the beehives last night. We would like to extend our thanks and appreciation to the men of that aircraft, for without their courage we wouldn't have received the beehives, and without the beehives we could never have held. Thank you, from all of us, Loc Ninh, out."

Mr. Walker came over the radio, "Mac, did you hear that?"

"Yes, Sir!"

"Hey, you're a real hero!"

"Yeah, and they'll probably give Mr. Hill a DFC for it."

"Yeah, I know it's unfair. You and Green will probably get V-devices on an air medal for it."

"Yeah, that and ten cents and I can buy a cup of coffee. We going to work up here all day, Sir?"

"No, we're supposed to go back to Tay Ninh, refuel, and go someplace else."

The trip back was quiet except for when Lead came over the radio to say that the troops hadn't made any contact other than rear ground action, and that they'd gotten to the swimming pool and found it empty. Not so much as a spent shell had been left by the NVA.

Once at Tay Ninh, Jim quickly removed his helmet and started to pump on fuel and was surprised when he heard the engine start to wind down and die.

"Hey, Mac, come on, we're supposed to have a formation at the CO's ship."

Jim walked around the nose of the ship. "Wright, did you say formation?"

"Yeah, our new XO wants a formation. Mac, have you met this guy yet?"

"Yeah, I think I had the pleasure last night. Wright, as long as I've been here, I haven't stood formation on the flight line. I don't even know where to fall in."

"Well, I've got a feeling you'll find out."

"Why does he want a formation?"

"All I know is Lead came over the radio and said to have all crews meet at the CO's ship for a formation."

"Okay, let's go."

There was quite a crowd gathering at the CO's ship when Jim and Wright arrived. Officers and enlisted men were mingling with each other grumbling about having to stand formation. Even Mr. Hill in his Class A uniform* was there, holding his records and departure orders. Jim walked over to where Mr. Hill stood reading through his records. As Jim snapped to attention and saluted, Colonel Appleton and Major Hobbs walked around the revetment unnoticed by Jim or Mr. Hill. It was the big smile on Jim's face that caused Mr. Hill to return the salute and extend his hand. Jim shook the officer's hand and spoke, "Sir, I just want you to know I'm glad we made it last night and I was wrong, plus, I can't think of anyone other than Mr. Walker I'd rather have had driving than you."

"Mac, you're a hell of a soldier and one of several enlisted men I can honestly say I really like and respect. Just between you and me, I can't think of any crew chief I'd rather have had in the back than you."

---

*Class A Uniform - the light, short sleeved khaki dress uniform.

"Thank you very much, Sir. That's very kind of you to say."

"I mean it, Mac, I truly hope you make it back alive and all in one piece."

"I will, Sir."

"Not if you keep flying all those night missions you won't. Besides, that's what every GI who ever stepped foot in country said."

The two men shook hands again as Jim said, "It looks like they're starting to fall into formation, so I'd better go. Good luck, Sir!"

"Good luck, Mac. Stay alive!" As Jim turned to walk away, he saw Major Hobbs and Colonel Appleton standing within hearing distance. He looked both of them in the eye, saluted, and continued on his way to where Gillett was trying to assemble a formation.

Major Hobbs looked at Colonel Appleton as Jim walked toward his platoon, "Colonel, when I get my own ship, I want that man as my crew chief."

"MacLaughlin?"

"Yep."

"Why, for heavens' sake do you want him? He's constantly on the edge of trouble."

"Wolf says he's one of the best crew chiefs in the company. I've got a suspicion that Halsey is the problem, not MacLaughlin, and if you'd transfer Halsey, you'd probably find that out. To answer your question, I guess there are several reasons. First, the man impressed me last night. He's obviously smart, he's got a quick mind and he is not afraid of danger or he wouldn't be flying single ship night missions. Also, he's got a sense of humor, I woke up this morning laughing at him asking Halsey if he wanted to smell his armpit to verify his taking a shower. The man has brass and isn't intimidated by officers, yet he knows his place and how to conduct himself in a military manner. The conversation we just overheard with that warrant officer tells me that. So far, I like everything I've seen from him. He's one sharp GI and the kind I want to surround myself with. He's the kind that I'll have to earn his respect, but once I've earned it, he'll follow me to Hell and back without a moment's hesitation or complaint."

"I can tell you right now it's not going to be easy for you to get him. Walker won't want to give him up and he won't want to quit Walker."

"Oh, that's no problem, just send Mr. Walker on R&R. Put MacLaughlin on my ship as crew chief, temporarily, of course."

"Of course!"

"By the time Walker gets back, MacLaughlin will have seen all the advantages of being the XO's chief. He'll ask to stay with me."

"If he's all you think he is, when Mr. Walker gets back, he'll go back to him just out of friendship."

"In that case, Colonel, I'll transfer Walker to guns and if MacLaughlin decides to go to the guns, I'll transfer Walker to another company."

"Of course you know if MacLaughlin finds out you're behind Walker being shipped out, you'll never get his respect."

"True, very true."

"One final thought, Major, you don't think there is any chance of being fragged, do you?"

"None, he didn't do that job last night anymore than I did."

Major Hobbs and Colonel Appleton moved out in front of the formation as the company first sergeant called the formation to 'ten hut.' The flight company slowly came to attention after which the first sergeant continued, "Men, your Company Commander wishes to address you."

The first sergeant stepped aside as the CO stepped forward, "Men, I've called you together this morning to introduce you to your new XO. He is a former infantry platoon leader. While serving his first tour of duty in Vietnam, Third Corps Area, he received several citations for valor including the Silver Star. Men, I'm very pleased to introduce the man who will probably be taking my place in a few months, Major Hobbs."

As the Colonel stepped back, Major Hobbs stepped forward. He spoke with a strong, deep and husky voice, "Men, I want to tell you how happy I am to be here as a part of such an outstanding company."

Jim could hear faintly an unknown voice behind him say, "If he's so happy to be here, he can take my place."

"The record you men have compiled as an all-combat assault company is truly outstanding. You pilots have never refused to go anyplace you're sent. There isn't an outfit in the area that doesn't know that if the Blackhawks are on their way they'll get there, no matter how much or what kind of enemy fire tries to stop you, you get through.

"However, you men are a lot like a tooth that is beginning to show some decay. You need some minor work so you can continue to function in the high tradition you have come to accept as a standard. Colonel Appleton and I have discussed it, and it is the Colonel's desire that I make every effort to make this company look as good as it really is.

"Men, together we're going to clean out the bacteria that is causing our tooth to begin to decay; let's start with this sloppy formation." The Major paused, then shouted, "Dress, right, dress!"*

Jim again heard the unknown voice behind him say, "Dress, right, dress? I haven't done this since basic training. What is with this guy?"

After completion of the dress, right, dress, the Major spoke, "Men, that's much better. Now, we're going to paint the choppers, the hooches and anything else that needs it. We're going to clean up the company area and these revetments where our hueys are parked; we're going to replace the rotten and busted sandbags with new; we're going to restack every sand bag pile in the company area and do it in such a way that it will look like you have used a plum line. We're going to fill in all these rocket and mortar holes, so that this place doesn't look like a teenager with an extreme case of acne. We're going to put those choppers back in mint condition. Those without doors will have their doors put back on, all bullet holes will be patched and painted OD.

"I started to count yesterday how many choppers we have with more than one greenish yellow bullet patch on it, and finally decided that most all of them do. Those choppers without the soundproofing or part of it will have it reinstalled. I have already talked to the supply sergeant and he has assured me there isn't any problem getting us paste wax and rags to wash and wax the helicopters and their blades. Some of you may not know that waxing the blades and ships will give ten percent more lift.

"I've noticed that several of you men need haircuts. It's always been my opinion that one can tell a great deal about a soldier by his

---

*Dress Right Dress - Means of obtaining proper spacing in a group formation.

personal appearance. Therefore, I want you men to look as sharp as you are. I've found a man in maintenance who has assured me that he gives excellent haircuts. So I've instructed him to set up a barber shop each day for an hour after the flight has landed. That way, there will be no problem keeping both officers' and enlisted men's hair properly clipped. There isn't too much we can do about the condition our uniforms are in when returned from the laundry. However, each man will be expected to have enough uniforms, so he can put on a clean one each morning.

"Well, men, that gives you a basic understanding of how I will be changing a few things, plus some of the things I'll be expecting from you." The Major stood there for a moment looking as though he was as proud as he could possibly be, then turned to the first sergeant and said, "Dismiss the men, First Sergeant."

The first sergeant stepped forward, came to attention and since the troops were still at attention he simply shouted, "Officers, platoon, dismissed! Enlisted men, fall in for police call of the flight line."

Almost in unison a number of voices moaned with, "Police call! You can't be serious." Someone else said, "I've never done a police call of the flight line as long as I've been here." Still another voice was heard, "This guy has to go, fellows!"

Jim and Athia were beside each other as the troops spread out at the end of the flight line, so it was only natural that Hunter found his way over to their location. Just as Gillett started the slow movement of walking vacuum cleaners through the flight line, Hunter started the conversation. "Well, how do you two like our new XO?"

"I can't speak for Mac, but I think he sucks the green weenie."

Jim laughed and said, "He sucks it? My man, the green weenie has just taken up permanent residence at the Blackhawks!" Very sarcastically Jim continued, "I really loved how he kept saying 'we' knowing full well how 'we' are going to do things. He's going to give the orders and all of us underworked, EM are going to do it!"

Hunter jumped in, "The part I liked was how he started out telling us how great we are and ended up telling us we stink."

"Yeah," said Athia. "The only trouble is the man isn't any flash in the pan. This guy just got here and obviously plans on taking Appleton's place when he rotates home."

"You know," added Hunter, "He and Halsey should get along just ducky."

Jim added, "Oh, isn't that just a wonderful thought. Halsey was bad enough but at least he didn't have any real power or authority. All he could do was chicken shit stuff compared to this joker. You know, fellows, I think I'll put in for emergency R&R. By the time I get back, he'll have most of this worked out of his system."

"You can't, Mac. They're not letting any flight crewmen or maintenance personnel go on R&R until we get some new people in. I'll tell you what, I don't know about you and Hunter, but I can't see myself out there washing and waxing those stupid helicopters. I mean, give us a break, we fly every day, usually until late at night and this guy wants us to wash and wax those ships. I mean, I can just see all of us out there between midnight and 0200 washing and waxing our little hearts out. Oh, well, now we know why Gillett told us to put our cargo doors back on last night. What a pain in the ass! Every time we put fuel in, we'll first have to unhook the ammo belt and shut the door."

"Hey, Athia, not just when you put on fuel but whenever you want in the engine compartment, or the storage area, anytime you get tools, rags, C-rations, or anything out of the storage compartment, you'll have to go through that same procedure."

"Yeah, Mac, you're right. I'll tell you what I think I'll do. The first LZ we land in after I put those stupid doors back on, my chopper's going to loose its right cargo door. I'll just put it back on so that all I have to do is unhook the safety pin, slide the door forward a little and give it a good, big, kick! Bingo, Chuck just got a new roof for his shack, courtesy of Major Hobbs."

Jim and Hunter looked at each other and wondered if that wasn't a better plan than the one both of them had already put into play.

The now jagged row of men reached the end of the flight line and started to mill around. Gillett, seeing that the police call had reached its destination, ordered the troops to fall out to their respective helicopters.

"Well, Mac, how many tons did you pick up?"

"Wright, I picked up the same thing the little boy shot at, nothing."

"Mac, you suppose that guy's so damn dumb he doesn't know the choppers blow everything away that isn't tied down or weighs at least fifty pounds?"

"It sure looks like it. It also looks like whatever little esprit de corps there is left in this outfit will be lost if he keeps this kind of chicken shit stuff up."

Every man on police call had developed an instant dislike for Major Hobbs. Somehow the idea of policing the flight line didn't make much sense, especially when they all knew sometime today they would be caught up in what was now being called, 'The Tet Offensive.' Jim and Wright walked around the rear corner of the L-shaped revetment and up along the open side. There, in the cargo door, sat Mr. Walker just looking out at nothing in particular, "Mac, you okay? You look terrible."

"Mr. Walker, I feel like I'm on the verge of total exhaustion! I've had very little sleep the last few nights, I've gone through hell the last couple of days, and last night I thought sure I'd get killed at Loc Ninh. Then, I have to get up in the middle of the night because some asshole was out playing games with Halsey."

Wright interrupted, "Mac, didn't you really throw that frag?"

With total exasperation Jim looked at Wright, "Hell, no, I didn't." Turning back towards Mr. Walker he continued, "Then I have to go for this silly ass walk this morning. I'll tell you what, to me, that was the height of insults, to make us go police the flight line. He has to know that anything on the flight line gets blown away by our props during take off. It's almost like he feels he has to show us that he has the power and authority to make us do anything he wants. It was just his way of saying, 'Fellows, get used to the changes I'm going to make, whether you like them or not, they're here to stay and there isn't a damn thing you can do about it!' He might just as well have said in that speech of his during formation, 'Bend over, fellows, cause here it comes and there isn't anything you can do about it!'"

"Come on, Mac, it's not all that bad. In a couple of weeks he'll have it worked out of his system."

Walker and Jim looked each other in the eye, neither man smiled. After a few seconds, Jim turned to see Mr. Mace walk up with his helmet in hand. Mr. Mace, a small man, stood only 5'2", with small bones, small fingers and feet. His frail one hundred ten pounds made something of a comic appearance. "Hi, Mac. Hey, I hear you scared the hell out of Halsey last night."

"Mr. Mace, I didn't do that, and if I had a Bible on me, I'd swear to it. Furthermore, if you ask me, I think Halsey did it himself."

With disbelief, Mr. Walker said, "Come on, Mac, Halsey may be an asshole but he isn't stupid; besides, he made Euclid and Lucas mad as hell at him last night."

Jim looked questioningly at Mr. Walker, "How did he do that?"

"You really haven't heard, have you?"

"No!"

"Well, I'm not sure I've got this story straight. But as close as I can figure it, Halsey caused each to get an Article 15 for two hundred dollars."

"How?"

"Well, Lucas and Euclid had a couple of the nurses in their room fucking their eyes out when Halsey started yelling, 'Grenade.'" All four men started laughing as Mr. Walker continued his story, "The nurses decided they wouldn't spend the night after all. Of course, you always have to pay before you play, so they just packed up and left with their one hundred dollars each. Only trouble was, Captain Wolf walked up as they walked out the door. Now, Captain Wolf has this thing about whores. He must have read those four the riot act. Anyway, he kicked the nurses out of the company area and hit Lucas and Euclid each with a two hundred dollar Article 15."

The laughter from the four flight crewmen made them all feel better. Jim and Mace were seated on the chopper floor laughing so hard they were holding on to each other. Wright had climbed up in his seat and was laughing also as Walker continued, "Needless to say both Lucas and Euclid are a tad bit upset with Halsey right now. Not only did they not get laid, but what started out costing them one hundred dollars each ended up being three hundred dollars each and no ass to brag about!"

Jim stopped laughing, "Mr. Walker, isn't one hundred dollars a little steep?"

"I'd say so personally, but they seem to have a steady business."

Mr. Mace spoke up, "Yeah, you talk about setting on a gold mine, there's more than one broad who'll come out of Nam a millionaire.

You know, Walker, that blond one's a good looking whore."

"You're telling me. She's almost worth a hundred dollars, but the other one she buddies around with isn't much."

"For a couple of guys who've never used their services, you two sure know a lot about 'em."

Mr. Walker and Mr. Mace looked at each other and started to snicker, Mr. Mace responded, "Well. . ., Mac, you have to understand, our officers club is THE PLACE to hang out. The fact that we're so close to the hospital, and we have more officers than any other company on post, makes ours the ideal place to drum up business. As a result, that's where a lot of the nurses hang out, which makes it impossible for Mr. Walker and me not to know what's going on."

"Sir, how many nurses are whores?"

"Oh, really not many, most of them are nice girls. But like any large group of people, they run the whole gamut. Some won't put out for anybody or anything, others will if you work at it hard and long enough. Then there's the three or four pros who sell it and the price starts at one hundred dollars and goes down the longer it's been since payday."

Jim spoke, "Well, Sir, I guess that's one of the nice things about being an officer instead of an enlisted man, you get the opportunity to waste your money on some sorry broad's ass."

Mr. Mace just looked at Jim, not sure if he was being sarcastic. It was Walker who spoke next, "Mac, go untie it. I see Lead starting to crank."

"Yes, Sir." Jim untied the main rotor blade from its secured position as the other three climbed into their respective seats. Jim put the tie down rope in the ship's storage compartment, put on his chicken plate and helmet, plugged in his headset and climbed into his seat behind the ever present M60. Mr. Walker started to crank the engine over as soon as Jim untied the blades and gave him the thumbs up sign. By the time Jim was in his seat, the aircraft was running and both Mace and Wright had checked in with Mr. Walker, just as Jim was ready to do, "I'm in, Sir, and ready to go."

"Okay, Mac." Pushing his mike switch down to broadcast outside the ship. Mr. Walker spoke again, "Lead, this is Chalk Five. We're up."

"Roger, Chalk Five."

9

"Because he loves me," says the Lord, *"I will rescue him; I will protect him, for he acknowledges my name."* Psalm 91:14 NIV

To Hunt And To Be Hunted

Jim listened as each ship's A.C. checked in with Lead and received the same response. In less than a minute all ten A.C.'s had checked in and Lead came back over the radio, "Flight, this is Lead. Everyone's up, so I'm now pulling pitch and on my way." One after another, the Hueys moved down the flight line until all ten were airborne. Once in the air each A.C. maneuvered his ship into its flight spot, and it wasn't long until the Blackhawks were headed south in a V formation.

"Lead, this is Trail, we're all up and in formation."

"Roger, Trail." It was an unwritten rule that until this message was given there was to be no unnecessary conversation.

"Mr. Walker, where are we working today?"

"We're going down to Saigon to pick up troops, then put them in the Michelin rubber plantation just outside of Ben Sue."

"Oh, great, another day of fun and games inside the heart of The Iron Triangle."

"Does that bother you, Mac?"

"Naw, if we got to be here, I figure we might as well be where the action is. I don't understand though why we have to go to Saigon to get troops and then all the way back to Ben Sue?"

"Intelligence says the offensive is over in Saigon and the NVA and their VC buddies are pulling out, so we're taking the troops who have been defending Saigon out and putting them in as a blocking force."

Jim figured the flight down to Saigon would take about forty-five minutes to an hour, depending on artillery. He pulled his seatbelt up good and tight, pulled the dark visor down on his helmet so Walker couldn't see his eyes, and then leaned back to get some sleep. It took only a matter of minutes for him to drop off; this kind of flight was always boring and Jim had learned shortly after starting to fly, the value of a quick nap. One of the gifts he knowingly possessed was his ability to fall asleep quickly anywhere and through most anything.

Mr. Walker, aware of all the night missions Jim flew, let him sleep. Unlike the gunner and peter pilot, who could not easily look at Jim, Walker had only to glance over his right shoulder. It wasn't uncommon for Walker to glance back at Jim during long flights and see him cinched up tight with his dark visor down. It was a dead giveaway because the only time Jim pulled his visor down was on their way into an LZ, or when he didn't want anyone to see him sleeping. However, it was a simple matter for Walker to wake Jim without anyone else on the ship knowing he had been asleep or that Walker had known it. It seemed Jim's ears were tuned to Walker's voice so he could simply start talking, but slightly louder than usual.

The flight to Saigon was uneventful with no radio chatter, until Lead told the flight to change into a trail formation as they would be landing shortly at the fuel dump.

It was the sound of Mr. Walker's voice that woke Jim up.

"Mr. Mace! Would you like to drive for the rest of the way into Saigon?"

"Sure, but you don't have to yell. I've got it."

"Sorry, Mace, I was thinking about something else." Walker glanced back over his right shoulder and saw MacLaughlin had raised his visor. The next time Walker looked back, Jim had removed his seatbelt and put on his monkey harness.

Mr. Walker had flown in and out of this area of Saigon several times. He was struck by all the destruction that had taken place since Tet. Engineers were busy with the earth moving equipment making new perimeter fortifications. They were on short final approach now, and Walker could see troops waiting off to the side. It looked to him like there were enough troops there for four or five lifts. At that rate, this would be an all day affair.

Once on the ground, Jim unhooked his monkey harness tail and stepped out. First, he threw the tail over his shoulder then opened the fuel cap, letting it dangle on its chain. Next he dragged the fuel hose to his ship and started pumping fuel. Meanwhile, the pilots kept their ships running at idle speed while fuel was being added and the grunts started to load. Jim looked up and saw a staff sergeant seated there watching him. Each man looked the other in the eye and knew the other had been there and come back.

"Hi, Sarge."

"Hi, how are you?"

"A little tired but other than that, okay."

"You guys been flying a lot lately?"

"All day and half the night."

"Yeah, we've been busy, too. Until yesterday, then suddenly. . . nothing, just like Charlie packed up and left. You know where we're going?"

"Not exactly! You?"

"Yeah, we're on our way up to Ben Sue. We're to set up a blocking force in the Michelin plantation to keep what's left of a NVA battalion licking its wounds up there from escaping."

"You don't look too happy about going."

"Hey, man, I'm not. I just hope we don't find a thing when we get there."

"You will. We haven't flown in there yet and not caught hell."

When the fuel tank was full, Jim replaced the hose and cap. He gave Walker, who was looking back at him, a thumbs up sign as he climbed in. Walker reported to Lead that they were up, and after all the flight had checked in, Lead called Six in the C and C ship. In only seconds the engines began to pick up RPM, and they were on their way.

No one said much during the flight to Ben Sue. It sometimes amazed Jim that he could sit for long periods of time with a totally blank mind.

"Flight, this is Lead. Our destination has been switched to Highway

14 just south of Rach Bap. The LZ has been prepped with artillery
and we'll have gunship escort all the way in. Let's form a staggered
right formation at this time. We'll be landing on the road and in the
brush off to the right. Make sure your door gunners understand there
are NO friendlies on the ground or in the area at this time. Six advised that when we lift off from the LZ, we'll have to fly straight
ahead for a ways due to the height of the rubber trees. Once up, we'll
be banking hard left and over the Mekong River. If anyone goes down,
try to get it across the river first. There are mostly rice paddies over
there where we can make a pick up. Over here you're in trouble. Lead,
out."

They were now on short final approach. Jim saw the gunships fly
by firing their rockets and mini guns. This was the signal for all the
doorguns to open fire, and they did. All twenty machine guns were
spitting lead into the rapidly approaching LZ. Trees lined both sides
of the dirt, one-lane road, yet there was plenty of room for the flight
to land. Jim's chopper hadn't quite touched down, when the grunts
started jumping out. Small arms fire was coming from the trees to
their right as their flight lifted and started to fly out.

Jim heard their engine make a funny sound but continued to fire
his M60 as they departed. In only seconds, he could tell by the engine
noise they had taken a round through the engine intake. It probably
had been sucked on through the engine, taking some of the turbine
blades out the other end with it.

"Lead, this is Chalk Five, we're rapidly losing engine power. May
Day, May Day, we're going down in the trees, no power!"

"Chalk Five, this is Lead, I read you. Trail, do you see Chalk Five?
Over?"

"Roger, Lead, they're down in some trees. There's no way we can
put a ship in to pick them up where they are."

"Lead, this is Chalk Five. We're down, nobody's hurt and I didn't
hit anything larger than some large twigs with my rotor blades."

Once on the ground, Jim and Wright went quickly to work, taking
off their M60's and opening the pilots doors. Mace climbed out at
once and started collecting ammo for the M60's.

"Chalk Five, this is Blackhawk Six. I have you spotted. Do you
read me? Over?"

"Roger, Six. Over."

"Chalk Five, you're in trouble. The ground troops have encountered heavy resistance from the area between you and them. Your best chance for a pick up is to continue north along the river bank for about a half mile. There are some rice paddies up there where we can put in a chopper."

"Six, be advised we have a scrambler* on board."

"Why the hell!? Never mind! Look, under no condition is that unit to be left. Understood? Over."

"Understood, Six. It's on board because of all the night missions my crew chief flies. Walker out."

Walker looked around and saw Jim grab his M16 and pistol belt.

"Mac, get the scrambler unit out, we have to take it with us."

"What the hell for?"

"Don't give me any mouth, MacLaughlin, just get the damn thing out. Six doesn't want it left under any circumstances."

"Yes, Sir! Mr. Mace, get me my tool box out of the storage compartment, please, while I start unhooking the quick disconnects."

Jim turned and headed for the ship's nose. Mace, who was already standing beside the storage compartment door, turned and pushed the two snap buttons that unhooked the latches. He reached in, grabbed Jim's tool box and turned to leave as Wright walked around the tail section carrying his M60, with his M16 slung over his shoulder.

Jim never saw it, but knew instantly to hit the ground when he heard the AK47 open fire. Walker, who had climbed out his door, dropped beside Jim. Both men looked back at Wright when they heard his M60 open up. Jim's eyes went from the still standing and firing Wright to Mr. Mace who was lying face down on the ground.

"Mac! I got the three VC but Mr. Mace is hit!"

Jim started to move in a crouched position towards Wright. He could see the three dead VC not more than fifty feet away. Looking down at Mace, he recognized the grotesque signs of a sucking chest wound.

"Wright, cover us! Mr. Walker, pick Mace up and get him out of here! I'll get some ammo and be right with you."

---

*Scrambler - Radio unit that garbles all radio transmissions on that wave length. Makes it impossible to understand unless the receiver also has a scrambler.

Walker picked Mace up in a fireman's carry and headed in the opposite direction from the dead VC. Wright grabbed as much M60 ammo as he could quickly loop over his shoulder and followed Walker into the brush and trees. Jim strapped on his pistol belt, reached up and grabbed one of the two first aid kits above the cargo door, and, picking up the pilot's map laying in Mace's seat, he jumped out the door and started to run. Then he remembered the fragmentation grenades he had hidden in his storage compartment. He turned and ran back to the ship. The storage compartment door was still open. He reached in, removing the rags covering the frags and pulled out all four, taking only seconds. He put the frags in his jungle fatigue pockets and picked up two smoke grenades, one violet and one yellow, from under his seat. Once again, he started to leave as he heard Wright's M60 open up. This time he dropped to one knee, laid down his M16, pulled out a fragmentation grenade, jerked the pin and threw it at his chopper. Grabbing the M16, he ran like hell. Then, tripping over a branch, he fell just a few feet from Mr. Walker.

The first explosion went off as he was falling, followed almost immediately by the secondary explosion of his Huey. Jim picked himself up and looked back at the fireball that was once his ship. Stepping over a fallen tree, he joined Walker and Mace. Wright had set up his M60 on that same tree log and was watching for VC moving on the far side of his field of fire. The burning Huey started erupting with smaller secondary explosions, as the ammo left on board became hot enough to blow.

Jim knelt beside Mace and unzipped the small, green first aid kit. Walker had his left hand over the entrance hole in Mace's chest and his right hand over the exit hole. Blood was flowing out both holes and had covered Walker's hands and back from carrying Mace. The bubbling and gurgling that came from Mace's mouth told Jim that he was having extreme trouble breathing, as he knew he would. Jim's switch blade cut Mace's shirt open and, as best he could, Jim wiped the entrance hole dry of blood. Walker dried his hands on Mace's clothes and held the plastic envelope from the bandage in place as Jim tried to tape it down. The continual flow of blood made it difficult at best. The wheezing from the exit wound in Mace's back was expelling blood and body fluids with each choking breath he tried to take. Walker rolled Mace over onto his chest, exposing the full extent of Mace's wound. Unlike the small thumb sized entrance hole, the jagged exit hole was not quite the size of a hard ball. Jim cut what was left of Mace's shirt off and tried to wipe a dry area where tape could be applied. There was flesh, meat and even a piece of bone sticking out of Mace's body. Jim picked the bone chips out so they wouldn't rupture the plastic that Mr. Walker then placed over the hole. Once the plastic was in place, the almost impossible breathing of Mace became much more normal, as air now could enter the lungs only through the mouth. Jim dried the back area with Mace's clothes and taped the plastic down as Walker applied the cloth bandage. It was at this point the first word was spoken by either man.

"Mac, Six said we should go to the river and walk north to some rice paddies for a pick up."

"Sir, that's the direction the VC came from."

"Yeah, I know. They're also between us and the ground troops we put in."

"Oh, great! Does that radio you're wearing around your neck work?"

"I don't know yet."

Walker started to open the radio up as Jim reached in his pocket. He pulled out a violet smoke grenade and handed it to Walker along with one of his three remaining frags, and the map. Walker put each in a different pocket as Wright's M60 started to bark once again.

"Mac, I thought you weren't supposed to carry any frags in the ship."

"We're not, but I'm glad I didn't get around to taking them out yet!"

"Me too!"

Wright had quit firing and joined them.

"Mac, where's the other M60?"

"I left it on the ship! I figured we couldn't carry two M60's, Mr. Mace and ammo."

"You're right, come on. We have to get out of here, they're trying to flank us."

Jim picked up his M16 and put Mace in a fireman's carry. Walker took Wright's M16 and several belts of ammo, and followed Jim. Wright, with the M60, brought up the rear walking in a circle as he followed Walker. Jim could hear Walker speak into his radio as they moved deeper into the heart of the Iron Triangle.

"Six, this is Walker, come in, Six! Six, this is Walker, over! Six, please come in! SIX! Anybody! Please, does anybody hear me, over."

Silence. Their hearts sank as they realized their sole means of communication didn't work. It was Walker who verbalized what they all thought. "This damn thing doesn't work."

"Mr. Walker, just keep trying. It only has a fifteen kilometer range. The flight's probably getting more troops and C&C ship could have gone back for fuel."

"You're right, Mac. At least let's hope that's what happened."

"Mr. Walker, is Mr. Mace going to make it?"

"Wright, if we can get him to a doctor in time he should be okay."

"He has blood coming out of his mouth and looks like a ghost."

"He's probably in shock. We just can't stop now and treat him for it."

Walker raised the radio to his lips to try once again. "Walker to Blackhawk Six. Over!"

The radio cracked and to everyone's relief, Colonel Appleton's voice was heard. "Mr. Walker, this is Blackhawk Six. Your situation down there has changed."

Wright spoke, "He's telling us!" Walker motioned Wright to be quiet.

"I've been in touch with the gunships, they spotted VC along the river bank and have sunk one sampan. There's a road that you should intersect about six kilometers ahead if you follow a heading of seventy-five degrees. We can make pick up there. Over."

"Six, be advised Mr. Mace took a chest wound. Over."

"Where's Mr. Mace now? Over."

"We're carrying him. Over."

"There's no way we can get him out until you reach that road. Did you bring the scrambler with you? Over."

"Negative, Six. We didn't have time. It was on the ship when my crew chief blew the chopper. Over."

There was a short silence before Six's voice broke through the radio again. "What did you bring out? Over."

"I got my map and pistol, Mace's pistol, one M60, two M16's and ammo. Over."

"Walker, we'll try to maintain one gunship in the area with orders to monitor this frequency and give whatever support possible. If you need ammo, we can try to drop it through the trees, otherwise, you're on your own 'til you get to that road. The flight's on short final with its second lift into the LZ. We'll put the next lift in on the road you're headed for. They'll sweep your direction, so you should be able to link up. One more thing, are you being pursued? Over."

"Affirmative. Over."

"By how large a force and how close? Over."

"Unknown to both questions, Sir. Over."

"Good luck, Walker, Six out."

The group had already stopped moving and Jim, as gently as possible, laid the unconscious Mr. Mace down. Jim's face was scratched from the tree branches. Sweat was dripping into his eyes, and the salty wetness burned as it came in contact with his scratches. Mace didn't weigh much, for which Jim was thankful, yet he had quickly tired under the burden Mace presented. Walker and Wright sat down facing Jim, who spoke first.

"Mr. Walker, do you really think they're following us?"

"Wouldn't you be, if in their position?"

"Yeah."

"Look, we can't stay here very long, how much ammo have we got?"

Wright responded first. "I've got six magazines full for my M16 and, I suppose, between you and me we have about three hundred rounds for the M60."

"Sir, I've got eight magazines in my pistol belt plus these three I always carry taped together. And I've got two more frags."

"Okay, that's pretty good, three frags, two smokes and seventeen magazines for the M16's. At twenty rounds each we should be okay."

"Sir, you only put nineteen rounds in each or it'll jam."

"Okay, Mac, that's not important right now. Look, let's get going. I'll carry Mace for a while. One of you take Mace's pistol."

"You can have it, Wright, I don't want it!"

"Okay, I'll take it." Wright took the shoulder harness containing the snubnose 38 off Mace and looked up at Mr. Walker.

"Sir, I think he's dead."

Walker kneeled down and felt for the carotid artery. Finding no pulse, he turned Mace's face so he could look at his still open eyes. "You're right."

Jim looked at his watch for the first time since being shot down, ten after ten. Walker took one of Mace's dogtags, positioned the chipped part between two opposing teeth and pushed his mouth shut, wedging the dogtags in place. Wright spoke as Mr. Walker started to pick up the lifeless body.

"Mr. Walker, wait a minute will you? I've got to take this chicken plate off."

Walker waited while Wright flipped it over his head, then he pulled up his shirt, exposing his black and blue and obviously sore ribs. Most of Wright's left side was bruised and starting to swell. Walker and Jim were amazed.

"Man, am I sore, but I sure am thankful for that chicken plate." Jim pulled the fiberglass plate from its cloth wrapping. There in the left center of the plate was an AK round.

"Wright, when did you get hit?"

"I got it the same time Mr. Mace did, fortunately, I hadn't gotten around to taking my chicken plate off yet." Jim found himself wishing he still had his on. "It knocked me back against the tail boom and I started firing the M60 I had."

Suddenly, Walker grabbed Wright's arm and put his index finger to his lips. Now they all heard it—Vietnamese! Walker quickly picked up Mace and motioned Wright to lead. Jim grabbed the M60 and pointed for the other two to head up a gentle slope. The two took off in a run as fast as they could move. Jim took a frag from his pocket, pulled the pin and carefully placed it under the chicken plate. Then he picked up the M60 and moved quickly up the slope. Once on the top, he moved behind a big tree off to his right and lay there prone. For the first time, he realized they weren't in the rubber plantation any more; in fact, as he looked at the trees and bushes, it didn't seem much different from the woods he had hunted rabbit and squirrel in ever since he could remember.

Jim's mind drifted back to his childhood and a cold winter day with a new fallen snow, and his dad saying, "Hey, Jim, how about you and me going rabbit hunting today?" Off they'd march into the crisp, sparkly clean Ohio winter. Everything was good then, and natural and safe, with his dad carrying a 12 gauge pump action shotgun and him carrying a stick.

He remembered clearly the Christmas his parents gave him the BB gun. That afternoon his dad and he made a search of the fence rows for some poor unsuspecting rabbit who would be skinned, gutted and carried home with the greatest pride. Many a rabbit had been fired at with that BB gun, and occasionally, one would even be hit and sent jumping in a different direction before his dad, who rarely missed, would drop the floppy eared creature with the first shot. His dad had been taught to shoot by his father, who had been taught in turn by his father, who had lived in the days of Wyatt Earp and Doc Holiday.

In a few years, Jim progressed to a 22 rifle and squirrel hunting. Then, there was the magic year that he'd saved every penny to buy a shotgun of his own. Finally, with rabbit season approaching, his dad took him one fall day to the local gun shop. The salesman showed him several different guns he could afford before finally bringing out a used, double-barreled 20 gauge Winchester. Its blue steel shone with the luster of a cold, deadly breeze, and the intricate carvings were impressive. The stock was made of a polished dark wood with a rubber butt. The salesman said, "Go ahead, pick it up and bring it up to your shoulder to see how it fits. Good, good, looks just like it was made for you, son. How's she feel?"

"Just fine, Sir."

"Well, young man, that is a mighty fine weapon. She's been used a little but she's been well taken care of. You can tell by the fact there aren't any chips in the stock, and if you'll open her up, you can see the inside of the barrel is as clean as the day she was made. Plus, for a young man like yourself, a 20 gauge is the perfect size; it's big enough to kill anything you'd want to hunt, yet it isn't as heavy or overpowering as the 12 or 10 gauge shotgun. You'd need several more pounds before you could fire one of those without being knocked down by the kick. I'll tell you what let's do, let's go out back and fire both barrels and see how you like it."

Jim was so proud and pleased, he could hardly wait for hunting season to begin. His dad bought three boxes of shells for practice, and a tin can of any size or shape would soon find itself being thrown in the air and shot full of holes. By the time hunting season arrived, he was the scourge of the woods. If a rabbit jumped, he dropped it, but the climax came the last season before he entered the Army. His dad and he had been sitting under a hickory nut tree watching two squirrels go about their business of collecting nuts for the long winter ahead. His dad wanted to take the one on the right and Jim the one on the left but Jim said, "No, wait. I want to try for both at once." And so it was. Jim thought he'd always remember with pride the day he'd killed two squirrels with one shot of his own gun; a piece of wood and steel that made him feel big and strong and powerful and invincible.

Now he lay behind a tree with an M60 machinegun, which fired a 7.62MM round at 600 rounds per minute for more than 300 meters, and he felt like the terrified rabbit he was. He was so scared he wanted to cry but forced himself not to. He felt more and more like the rabbit—it had certainly gone full circle for him. It was then that he decided, if he lived through this, he'd never go hunting again.

As the enemy troops became visible he couldn't believe it; they had on uniforms just like him, complete with boots and helmets and carrying AK47's. These weren't VC—these were North Vietnamese Regulars. He had an overwhelming desire to pee as he counted one, two, three, four, five, six, seven. Seven NVA, man did he have to pee bad! They'd stopped right next to his frag and now two more showed themselves. One had a back pack with an antenna sticking up so the other one had to be the group's leader, with a radio man. Jim had to pee so bad he started squeezing his legs together. He couldn't understand why they hadn't picked up the chicken plate yet. He was going to pee his pants if he didn't get it out in time. So he rolled over onto his left side and opened his fly. The nervous pressure shot a good stream out and for the first time since he'd been shot down, Jim realized he was scared to death.

The shouts from the gooks, followed by an explosion, told him they had found his booby trap. Damn, he wished he'd seen it. He was only about one hundred fifty to one hundred seventy-five meters away with a real good line of vision. Oh, well, he hadn't, now he had to get himself put away and zipped up. That done, he rolled back over where he could see the NVA. There must have been at least one hit since he could hear shouts of pain. Carefully, he placed his M60 where he could watch and then fire without moving again. He was so nervous he didn't dare put his fingers on the trigger. Now he wished for the standard handle and butt instead of the two handled aviation system.

Man, he had to pee again, but he knew it had to be nerves, he'd just gotten done peeing! Watching closely, he could see one gook start to give orders and others start to fan out. Now there was a group of three in one spot, one of which was their officer. Jim figured they were working on the wounded gook and this was going to be his best shot. Just as he was taking aim, one of the NVA who had fanned out stepped behind a tree between Jim and his target. The gook behind the tree had to go. He was just too close and Jim knew he'd never be able to escape with him there, so he waited and watched as the gook peeked around the tree. Jim drew a bead just beyond the tree and waited. At least they hadn't seen him yet. Over and over in his mind he said, "Oh, God, help me! Please help me!", when the gook started to move quickly to the next tree.

The blast from Jim's M60 caught the NVA full in the midsection, throwing him backwards and rolling him over. In only a flicker of a second, he shifted his aim to the group with the officer. Everyone in that group had started to dive for cover already as Jim opened up on them. He was sure from watching his tracers he'd hit at least one more. He continued to fire into the same area hoping to hit another one. Suddenly the dirt all around him started to explode and tree bark began falling on him. His first thought was, 'What?', then he realized his every fifth round being a tracer, had drawn a direct line to where he was—he was being fired at. Instantly, he rolled over behind a tree and then started to low crawl away. Once far enough away, he got up and ran in a crouched position to a big tree. From there, the elephant grass and bushes would give him enough cover to run standing up. He looked around behind the tree to where he had just been and off to the left he saw a movement. He aimed the M60 and waited for only a second until the gook started moving to the next tree—then he opened fire once more. Again he watched his tracers fly to their target and then suddenly stop as the body they had hit lifted into the air and flew backwards. Jim turned and ran through the woods in the direction Walker had gone.

It wasn't hard to find their trail. Jim's adrenalin was really flowing, so it didn't take long for him to catch up to where he could see them moving ahead of him. He figured he was about three hundred meters behind and just hoped they didn't shoot him.

It was certainly strange going through these woods. There were all different types and sizes of trees, there were places with no undergrowth at all, and other places where there were briars, vines and thick, coarse grass that cut his skin. He had to jump over an ancient rotting tree and tripped in the process. Jim lay there for a moment, his legs ached and his breathing strained. Slowly, he picked himself up and then the ammo belt that had fallen off his shoulder. He tried to wipe the dirt from his face and found blood on his hand. His shirt was totally soaked with sweat, and his panting and gasping for breath made him feel all the more like a scared rabbit fleeing for its life. Breathing was still difficult, especially since he was now crying silently, causing his chest to heave. Cradling the M60, he started moving through the underbrush once again.

He caught up with the others a short time later seated along the bank of a small creek. Walker was looking at his map and Wright was keeping watch. Walker looked up when Wright spoke. "Mac! Man, am I glad to see you! What happened back there?"

Jim told him briefly and then asked whose turn it was to carry Mace. Wright spoke in a soft, dejected tone, "Mine."

"Mr. Walker, which way?"

"I don't know, Mac. This creek isn't on the map."

"In that case, let's go up stream, we know the NVA are downstream behind us. If we walk in this creek, we'll quit leaving a trail a blind man could follow. How are the ribs, Wright?"

"Sore, Mac, really sore, but I'm alive!"

They all cupped their hands and drank from the creek, then Wright picked up Mace and moved into the middle of the creek followed by Walker and Jim.

"Mr. Walker, I'll trade you this M60 for those two M16's." Walker laughed and handed Jim his M16 with the three magazines he'd taped together and took the M60.

"You look like you could use a break. I'll carry the M60 and Wright's 16 slung over my back—it's no problem."

"Thank you, Sir. Do you have any idea which way we're headed?"

"No, not really. It has to be in the general direction of the road though."

After a while they came to a place on the bank where they could climb out on some rocks without leaving a trail. Each man was glad to finally leave the creek and the mosquitoes, which were eating them up. Walker led them up the bank, followed by Wright carrying Mace and Jim bringing up the rear. They walked around a small clearing not large enough to land a chopper in, and sat down under some trees on the other side. Speaking almost in a whisper Jim said, "Well, if they're following us, that little trip should lose them. At least it does in the cowboy movies. I'm glad that creek wasn't any more than a foot or so deep."

"Mac, did you get any C-rations out of the ship? I'm hungry."

"No, but now that you mention it, so am I."

Jim looked at his watch, ten after one. They'd been on the ground for over three hours. Each man sat there totally exhausted and saturated with sweat. They all knew they should start moving again but nobody wanted to.

"Mr. Walker, rig's got Mr. Mace already."

"You're kidding me? He's stiff already? He hasn't been dead more than an hour."

"He's beginning to smell and the flies are already all over him."

"Well, for God's sake, Wright, don't unhook his belt!"

Jim grabbed Walker's leg and motioned for him to be quiet. He'd seen something move off in the woods and motioning only with his hand, pointed in the direction of the movement. Now, they all saw a NVA moving slowly through the trees. Walker motioned to Wright to pick up the M60, his M16 and move out slowly. Jim grabbed Walker and whispered, "Take Mace. I'll try to hold them one more time."

Walker nodded, picked up Mace and moved into the woods after Wright. Both men tried to keep the trees between them and the NVA. Once out of sight, Walker told Wright to drop back and give Mac some cover.

Jim moved slowly into a prone position beside a large tree with several smaller ones behind him and waited. Fortunately, the NVA hadn't seen them move, and by now Walker and Wright were out of sight. Jim watched as the single NVA moved closer along the bank to where they had come out of the creek. When the NVA got to the clearing, he suddenly crouched down and yelled for what Jim knew had to be his comrades in the creek. This guy had to be a flank man.

The NVA officer had learned his lesson. Jim was sure he was now using a point man and flankers on each side, and this guy had found their path. "Well, you smart son of a bitch, you just had to see it, didn't you. Now I'm going to give you a sucking chest wound, you bastard!" The NVA flanker had just finished yelling for his comrades when Jim flipped his selector switch to semi automatic. Taking careful aim, Jim squeezed the trigger firing a single round into the body of the crouched man knocking him over on his side. Jim flipped the switch to full automatic and waited for the NVA troops to come through the tree line from the creek. Nothing. Why didn't they come to help their buddy? Had he hit the panic button and fired too soon? Maybe he should spray the tree line with lead and then run like hell? No, that would just be a waste of ammo and give away his position. He had to get out of there—something was definitely wrong. Those NVA should have moved out of the creek by now. Jim started to low crawl backwards when he heard an M60 open up behind him. "Hallelujah! They've found the road and American troops." No more had this thought cleared his head than he heard Wright yelling, "Mac, they're flanking you. You hear me?"

Jim's heart sank as he yelled, "Yes!"

"Mac, I'll fire five second bursts. You move when I open up!"

Wright's M60 opened fire and Jim started running toward him, trying to move so he'd come out behind Wright. As he ran from tree to tree he counted one thousand one, one thousand two, one thousand three, one thousand four and he stopped behind a big old tree. It was a full two seconds before Wright stopped firing, but Jim just stayed behind his tree and panted. Boy, what a sucker he'd been. That gook officer was a smart son of a bitch. He'd just have to be a whole lot more careful from now on. Thank God Wright hadn't left him. He heard the M60 open up again and instantly started running and, once again counted as he ran.

When Walker heard the M60 open up and Wright start yelling, he dropped Mace and started to move back. Then he had another thought. Appleton had said he'd keep a gunship overhead. Turning on his radio and extending its antenna he spoke, "May Day. May Day. This is Blackhawk on the ground, does anybody up there copy? Over!"

"Hey, Walker, I've been trying to reach you. This is your friendly gunship Triple Nickel on station. What can I do for you? Over."

"You can give me some fire support, ASAP. We just moved out of a creek and are approximately one hundred fifty meters west, I think. Over."

"Walker, give me a count. I don't know where in the hell you are. I don't see any creek. Over."

"Roger, one...two...three..." As Mr. Walker counted, he continued to move towards Wright's M60 sound. Once in position, he stopped counting and asked, "Do you have me yet?"

"Affirmative. Where do you want what—and be exact. Over."

Walker took the violet smoke grenade out of his pocket, pulled the pin and tossed it as far as he could. "Smoke's out and I want one rocket ninety-five meters northeast. Over."

"I see violet smoke. Over."

"You got it."

The Blackhawk gunship rolled in and placed one of its 2.75 inch rockets between the trees as requested.

"Triple Nickel, you're twenty meters too far west and fifteen too far north. Fire for effect this time, smoke is between us and your rocket. Over."

"Roger." The gunship had already turned to start its second run when Walker gave the corrections. On this run, they started firing early and continued a little past where they usually would quit, since they knew where the Americans were.

"One more time, Triple Nickel. Same place, please."

"Roger, roger."

Walker watched with satisfaction as once again the rockets started exploding on target. Giving him even more satisfaction was the sight of Mac and Wright running towards him as the rockets hit. Walker put down cover fire with his M16 just on general purpose.

Once Jim made his second run, he knew that was all the further he'd ever get. Even with Wright's M60 fire, Jim knew he was being fired at for the last couple of steps. When he got to the trees, he tried to make himself as thin as possible and hoped they couldn't cut his tree down with AK fire. This was it, he knew beyond a doubt, this was where he would die. The next time he tried to move he'd be the one cut in half. He was surprised at how much he was in control of himself. Yet he wondered how his parents would take the news, and why he'd been brought to this place to die all alone. He'd just made up his mind to make them come and get him so he could take as many with him as possible when he heard the chopper overhead. He didn't know what was going on but, hearing the explosion, he assumed they'd put a rocket in. He didn't know how or why, but was so thankful it had shown up. Once more, he checked his selector switch to make sure it was on full automatic and hoped that gunship would make another run. If it did, he was going to make another break for it and hope Charlie kept his head down. He could hear the chopper coming and got ready to move. Jim was quite pleased with himself; he was totally in control and perfectly relaxed. As soon as the rockets started to hit, Jim began to run. By the time the rockets quit, he was about ten meters behind Wright on Walker's side.

"Wright, you okay?"

"So far!"

"If that gun makes another run, let's try to get to Walker."

"I'll be right behind you, Mac."

Once more the gunship could be heard coming in on its last run. Wright opened fire from behind his log just as the rockets started to hit. Jim and Wright instantly started running in the direction of Walker's firing M16. What a beautiful sound that thing made as it burped, and in the process, led Jim and Wright by its sound to where Walker was hidden. There wasn't any activity from the area where the NVA had been. Once the three were together again, Walker pointed in the direction of Mace, and without saying a word they moved out.

Jim handed Wright his M16 and bent over to pick up Mace. Instead, Jim turned to Walker, who was about to speak into his radio. "Mr. Walker, thanks!" Walker only nodded.

"Sir, Mr. Mace smells terrible."

"I know. Pick him up and let's get out of here. Walker to Triple."

"Nickel, over."

"Go, Walker."

"Thanks for the help. Now, could you tell me where the hell we are?"

"Not anywhere near where you're supposed to be, that's for sure. But that's good. The flight put in troops on the road you were supposed to be headed for, and after being on the ground about fifteen minutes, found some heavy resistance. There's a major war going on down there. We've put in most of the 25th infantry that's available, part of the Big Red One, and parts of the 199 Light Infantry. To put it bluntly, you're in the middle of a big box that's being squeezed from three directions. How you got turned around, I don't know but you were supposed to be headed northeast and you've been going southeast. You're only about eight kilometers southeast from where you went down."

Wright looked at Jim and asked in a whisper, "How far is eight kilometers?"

"I don't know, about five miles, I'd guess." "How far have we walked today?"

Jim shrugged his shoulders and said, "Feels like twenty miles."

Both men turned their attention back to what was being said on the radio as they walked.

"There's a thinly wooded area about half a kilometer ahead of you. Once you pass through there, I'll be able to see if you're still being pursued and give you directions to the pick-up sight, which is about five kilometers further. Over."

"Triple Nickel, we're exhausted down here. Could you drop some water and C-rations to us? Over."

"I'll see what I can do. There's one more thing you should know. The pickup sight is so small it'll be straight down and straight up, so get there before dark! Over."

Jim looked at his watch, quarter after five. That meant they had about two hours to travel five kilometers. Under normal conditions they would be able to do it easily.

He'd had it, and Wright's ribs were so sore, he was holding his arm strangely and Walker's feet kept tripping over every little stick. Mace felt like he weighed twenty pounds more than when this day began and man did he stink, the flies were all over him.

"Mr. Walker, I can't carry him anymore, I've had it."

"Okay, I'll carry him for a while."

Jim put Mace down and Walker bent over and picked him up. "My Lord, he stinks. That's enough to make a person sick. What would you two think of leaving him?"

"I think it's a great idea."

"Me too."

"So why haven't we done it yet?"

Walker's radio came on just then, causing all three to turn their attention to it as they walked. "Walker, this is Triple Nickel, do you copy? Over."

"Roger. Over."

"You're starting into the thin part now. Veer a little to your left. There, that's good, try to maintain as straight a line as possible. I'll be turning you over to 714 at this time. See you back at Tay Ninh, Triple Nickel, over."

"Thanks for the help, Triple Nickel. Walker out."

"Walker, this is 714, we have a canteen of water for each of you and three chocolate candy bars from the C-rations. Six said to tell you he'd have the mess sergeant fix supper for you once you're out. I'll make the canteen and candy drop on the edge of the thickest jungle. That way you can move into a more protected area more quickly. I'll maintain a watch over this area to make life unpleasantly short for anyone still on your tail. Do you copy? Over."

"Affirmative."

Once they started into the thinner jungle, the grass and brush seemed to increase in size and thickness. Jim wondered if the giant ant hills, some as high as six feet with eight to ten foot bases, had anything to do with the thinness of the jungle in this area. Certainly they were doing their best to stay clear of all the ant hills, big or small.

Each man found a great deal of comfort in the whopp-whopp-whopp of the Huey blades as it flew across the tree tops. It was like having a big brother who would beat up on anybody picking on them. The NVA had to know they had communication with the chopper, how else could that rocket attack have been put down with such accuracy. The single rocket on the first pass was a dead giveaway of communication with the ground people, who would have given corrective information if necessary.

The area they were now passing through was only about two hundred meters wide. Once they were within fifty meters of the thicker jungle, Walker got back on his radio. "714, this is Walker, we're ready for your drop. Over."

"Roger, we're on our way."

Because of the trees, the chopper had to stay about sixty to seventy meters up. It moved slowly, almost in a hover until directly above them. Then, as the chopper slid slowly on by, a package dropped from each side. Walker had already put Mace down and all three ran for the canteens and candy. The canteens had been put in a pillow case and stuffed with wadded up paper. The candy was in an old C-rations box that burst open upon hitting the ground. The stuffed pillow case landed on an ant hill and rolled part way down the side.

Without stopping to think, Wright climbed up and returned with the bag. Walker picked up the candy bars, and all three men returned to the thicker jungle. Jim's switch blade quickly opened the pillow case and the three men drank like the water-starved animals they were. After drinking their fill, Walker handed each a candy bar and that, too, was quickly eaten. More water helped wash down the extremely rich candy that they each had finished off. Jim hooked the canteen on his pistol belt and offered to put one more on it. Walker and Wright put the remainder of their water into one canteen and Jim added it to his now full pistol belt.

As they sat on a log to eat and drink, they could see and smell Mace's body. Each had his own thoughts about Mace, and were torn between leaving him and carrying him on further. It was Wright who finally spoke, "Mr. Walker, I've been thinking about Mr. Mace. We don't have that much further to go. I can't help but think if it was me, I'd want you to carry me out. After all, I'd like to go home, even if it is in a rubber bag."

Walker simply nodded his head in agreement and looked at Jim, "Me, too, I'm just tired of carrying him and it's so damn hot and humid, plus the mosquitoes and flies." They all looked at each other and at Mace's body. It was Jim who spoke next, "Wright, how much ammo is there for that M60?"

Wright looked at the ammo belt in the machinegun and the one on the ground. "Oh, I'd say about forty to fifty rounds."

"Okay, let's leave the M60, we could strip it and put the barrel in one of those ant hills and the firing pin in your pocket, then give the rest a toss. It would mean that much less to carry. I used all three magazines in my Y clip, but I've still got eight full magazines left."

Walker shook his head in disagreement and said, "You can't leave a weapon."

Jim spoke, "I don't care what you say unless you want to carry it. Look, each of us have only been able to carry Mace for ten to fifteen minutes."

"Mac, we can't leave a weapon."

"It's the M60 or Mace!"

Wright immediately went to work. First he handed Jim the barrel and then gave Walker the ammo. As Wright continued to strip the M60 down, Walker broke the ammo belt apart into single rounds. Jim took the barrel and headed back to the ant hills. The gunship 714 was still circling overhead when Jim started out for the ant hills. The first one he came to over four feet tall would do. With the nose of the barrel he made a shallow slit in the side of the hill, placed the barrel in it and covered it up as the small red ants emerged. By the time he got back, Walker and Wright were throwing bullets in every direction and the M60 was gone.

"Whose turn to carry Mace?"

Walker looked at Wright, who looked at the bloated body a few feet away and said, "Mine."

Walker, with one M16 took the point and Jim with the other M16, brought up the rear. Once on the move again, Jim looked at his watch and knew they'd never make it by dark. He didn't know what time sunset was, but it had to be within the next hour. With the sun down, it would get dark fast in this jungle, and the idea of walking in the dark didn't appeal to him.

As they walked, Mace was passed from one to the other with each turn lasting a shorter time, as they became more fatigued; stumbling and falling more frequently.

Once the sun set, darkness came quickly, and they each kept thinking about Triple Nickel's telling them they had to make it to the pickup before dark. Walker had been on the radio most of the time he wasn't carrying Mace, each time hoping to be told they were almost there. Finally, it was just too dark to continue trying to move any further and Walker sat down against a fallen tree stump. He was joined shortly by Jim and Wright.

"Take a break you two, and I'll get hold of 714."

Walker pulled out his radio and extended its antenna, "714, this is Walker. Over." There wasn't any doubt that 714 was up there, they'd heard the whopp-whopp-whopp of its blades all afternoon. "Walker, this is Triple Nickel, we're back on station over your location. What can we do for you? Over."

"It's too dark to walk down here, we're falling over every little stick. How much further to go? Over."

"Well, Walker, that's a problem. I think you're only about one hundred to one hundred fifty meters out yet. We knew you would be close, so Six got a flareship rigged and on its way, along with a heavy fire team. Major Hobbs called a company formation and told everyone your station. He said he was going in to get you out, that it would be a night extraction with only about two feet clearance for the rotors and they would probably get fired at. Then he asked for volunteers to go with him, and I'll be damned if the whole company didn't volunteer. I never realized how popular you guys are. Anyway, the Major then asked who the best pilot in the company was and since I was already assigned to gun duty, he picked Lucas to fly AC with him! He's got Gillett and Athia in the back with him. Hold on a minute." They waited in silence for only seconds, then, "I'm done entertaining you guys. My co-pilot says the Major is on final approach and the flareship is in position. You guys ready to make one last run for it? Over."

"Anything to get us out of here. Over."

"Okay, flares will be out shortly, start moving ASAP and let me know the moment you hit the clearing. Walker, you'll have to talk Lucas down. Understood? Over."

"Affirmative."

They waited and watched skyward for the first flare to light. The noise from the choppers had increased considerably, telling them there were more than two helicopters up there. Suddenly, as though God himself had struck a match, the first flare lit, then a second and a third, a fourth and finally a fifth. Jim picked up the terribly rancid remains of Mace for what he hopped would be the last time. Then, just as they had done all day, Jim fell between Walker and Wright.

The light wasn't great but for coming through the trees, it wasn't bad either, and the final few meters were traveled without much trouble. They could hear the gunships making their runs ahead of them and knew the LZ would be hit with rockets along the area on three sides. Only the side they were approaching from would be untouched. The jungle would be hit in case the VC were there waiting on them, and the LZ would be hit to explode any booby traps. It was common knowledge that many of these small jungle openings were booby trapped just to discourage helicopters from landing, dropping off, or picking up reconnaissance teams.

Walker stopped before Jim realized they had reached the clearing. He almost bumped into Walker and had to step around him. He looked out into the pickup spot. It was long and narrow, with elephant grass higher than their heads. Yes, it was definitely going to be tight. Walker was already on the radio telling the people upstairs they had finally made it. Then the gunships made a run behind them and more flares popped above.

"Walker, this is Lucas, I'm on my way in. I'll be coming straight down so talk to me 'cause I can't pick up my rotor blades. Over."

"I got you, Lucas, you're looking good, bring it on down." Wright stood there beside Jim, who was still holding Mace. Their faces were pointed upward as they watched the red and green lights slowly descending. Suddenly, a blinding light struck all of them in the face as Lucas turned on both his landing lights and search lights. Still, they watched as the Chariot that would take them home settled on down. "Lucas, take it left a foot, that's good, back a couple inches, set it down."

The rotor blast flattened the grass and almost flattened Jim before Wright caught him, and helped him toward the now waiting chopper. Jim very rudely dumped Mace on the floor and climbed in, followed by Walker and Wright. They weren't yet seated when Lucas, who hadn't slowed the engine down, put pitch in the rotor blades and started to lift her straight up. Jim was seated on the left end of the bench with Walker in the middle and Wright beside him.

Once the ship was on its way back home, Jim felt a pat on the shoulder. It was Gillett who was flying gunner welcoming him back. With that pat, Jim relaxed for the first time since being shot down. The relaxation of the tension and stress slowly gave way to the well of emotion he'd suppressed all day. He could feel it building low in his chest and steadily swell to consume his whole chest cavity. Tears began to leak from each side of his eyes and, unwilling to suppress it any longer, he lowered his head to his knees and wept. Like a chain reaction, Walker, then Wright broke down and cried.

Once the ship was safely at altitude and on its way home, Major Hobbs looked around at the three men he had just plucked from the jungle. He wasn't surprised to see all three in a state of uncontrollable weeping. He'd known the feeling himself once. Major Hobbs, unseen, turned back around and didn't look back again.

10

"And then he will reward each person according to what he has done." Matthew 16:27 NIV

Games, Games And More Games

Mr. Lucas slowly guided his helicopter into its revetment and gently sat it down. Remaining seated, the three passengers waited for the ship to completely shut down. Fatigue had taken its toll and it wasn't until the hospital people had removed Mr. Mace, that they slowly climbed out.

Athia tied down the rotor blades, Gillett pulled the guns and the two pilots finished the log book and then climbed out. Major Hobbs stood on one side of the chopper and watched as Mr. Mace was removed. He, along with everyone else, just stood there quietly while Mace's body was placed in a black rubber bag and removed to the waiting truck. Major Hobbs, the ranking officer, was the one who broke the silence.

"Well, gentlemen, you can't stand there all night. The CO has the mess sergeant fixing you supper, which should be ready by now. There's a company formation at 2200 hours in the E.M. Club and I'm sure at least one of you is on the promotion list that'll be announced then."

For the first time that night, Jim looked at his watch and was really surprised to see it was only a quarter after nine.

Kenny arrived with the platoon truck and everyone climbed in for the ride back. Wright and Jim locked up their M16's, washed their hands and faces and put on a clean shirt before heading for the mess hall. On the way, they were greeted by several of the guys who wanted to congratulate them and just say, "Welcome back!"

Once at the mess hall, they were instructed to go over to the officers' side to eat. The mess sergeant had fixed them a good meal: roast beef, brown gravy, mashed potatoes, peas, fresh rolls and coffee. The servings were ample and both men were eager to dig in. Jim, unsure where to sit, waited for Wright to finish filling his plate so they could walk to a table together. It was Major Hobbs who pointed at the empty chairs at his table and said, "Hey, you two, sit down over here!"

The officers' side of the mess hall was the same as the enlisted men's with two long tables placed end to end, and sixteen chairs total at each table. All the chairs were placed on the table tops upside down for the KP's to sweep and mop the floor, except the ones at the Major's table. Jim looked at Wright as though to say, "Are we really supposed to eat with those officers?" Wright shrugged his shoulders and proceeded to their table, taking the open chair on Mr. Walker's left, which forced Jim to sit on his right. They were now seated facing Colonel Appleton and Major Hobbs, who made the expected small talk trying to put the enlisted men at ease. After telling about their day, and having nearly finished their meals, both Jim and Wright felt more comfortable. It was at that point Colonel Appleton asked, "Mac, why did you blow your ship?"

Jim looked directly into the Colonel's eyes. He couldn't believe he was being asked that question. Surely the answer was obvious. "Well, Sir, I didn't think I had any other choice. Mr. Walker told me you had given him an order not to leave the scrambler behind. I was in the process of removing it when Mr. Mace got hit. Once he went down, we had one less man to share the load, plus Mr. Mace to carry.

"I just didn't think the three of us could carry two M60's, two M16's, a scrambler, Mr. Mace and the ammo. It was a split second decision I made because I thought it was better than leaving it for the VC."

"Specialist, did Mr. Walker order you to blow your ship?"

"No, Sir."

"You just took it upon yourself to do it?"

Jim was still staring into the Colonel's eyes. "Yes, Sir."

"My problem, Specialist, is that I have to account for each and every one of those choppers. Believe me, you have no idea how much paperwork I've got to do because you fragged that helicopter. And, speaking of frags, where did you get them?"

Jim turned to Major Hobbs and started to chuckle. Almost at once, his eyes moved back to the Colonel. "Specialist, I don't know what you find so funny, or do you just find everything funny?"

The smile on Jim's face disappeared, and his voice became serious. "Sir, there was nothing about the last twelve hours that I found funny."

The Colonel paused for several seconds before he spoke again. "So, where did you get the frags?"

Jim was in trouble and he knew it. If he admitted to having the grenades in his ship, he was guilty of disobeying the CO's order to remove all the frags from the helicopters. If he lied, the CO would know it. The Colonel wasn't stupid, he knew where those frags came from. If he refused to answer, the CO would just order him to tell and then he would be right back where he was; lie, tell the truth, or refuse to obey the Colonel's order. The two men held each other's eyes, yet without malice. It was more a sizing up for both of them.

"Colonel, what do you want me to do, lie to you? I could tell you the grunts left them in the helicopter before we dropped them off. But you're not stupid and you're not going to believe that. And furthermore, I'm not in the habit of lying and I'm not about to start now."

"Mac, I want to hear you say it."

Jim knew he was back in the Colonel's good graces or he would never have addressed him as, 'Mac.'

"Sir, I kept four in my storage compartment for just such an emergency."

"Four! Where are the other two?"

Jim reached in his pocket and pulled out two remaining grenades and the one smoke grenade. He placed all three on the table directly in front of the CO. "Right here, Sir."

As the CO slowly shook his head, Jim glanced at Major Hobbs from the corner of his eye. The Major was sitting there with a half smile on his face. Jim put the last bite of roast beef in his mouth, as the Colonel cleared his throat.

"MacLaughlin, you really enjoy living on the edge, don't you? That's why you fly all those night missions, you just enjoy living on the edge! I mean, you've been on the verge of trouble ever since you joined this company. First, you had problems with the maintenance officer. What was it you told him to his face, 'He didn't know what he was talking about?' You came close to getting it on that one, the only thing that saved your ass was that it turned out you were right. Then there was Mr. Halsey. You couldn't just let it go, no, you had to turn him in for what was it again, 'falsifying records and flying too low?' He's been on your back ever since, and it's hurt the company as a result. You two have got to stop carrying on your own private little war. I'll tell you right now, Specialist, it stops and it stops now!"

"Sir, I had nothing to do with last night."

In a slightly tense voice the Colonel continued, "I know that, but the two of you agitating each other constantly precipitated it. Now, you have disobeyed a direct order from your commanding officer to remove all the fragmentation grenades from the helicopters. You blew up a helicopter worth about a half a million dollars without being ordered to do so, plus an M60 against your officer's orders, I might add, plus ammo, plus radios, plus a scrambler! Do you have any idea how hard it is to get a scrambler unit? You know, of course, I could make you pay for that helicopter and everything in it! But you also know you're right on that edge again. Just a little bit one way or the other, I could push you right off! I'll give you this much, you've always got your ass covered! Okay, you get away with it one more time but so help me, don't show up in my office in any kind of trouble ever again! One more thing, if there are any medals passed out for this day's activities, you won't be getting any. That's the trade off. Understood?"

"Yes, Sir."

The Colonel looked at his watch and then back at the three men seated across from him. "I see you men are finished with your meals and it is nine fifty-five. We'd better head on over to the E.M. Club."

Colonel Appleton stood, followed by everyone else. He took his hat from the table behind him and looked back at Jim. "Specialist, you're a good crew chief and if I'm ever shot down, I hope you're with me, but I just can't allow enlisted men to make the decision to blow up a helicopter. Worst of all, you disobeyed my orders about the frags. Now, you're going to get away with it because of the way things turned out. But you damn well better pass the word, I'm going to personally check each of those helicopters and any crew chief who has frags on his ship loses a stripe, understood?"

"Yes, Sir! About the cost of that helicopter, Sir?"

For the first time Colonel Appleton smiled, "Oh, you don't have to pay for it, you made the right decision—this time!" Pointing his finger at Jim, Appleton continued, "Mac, climb off that edge before you get knocked off."

As everyone followed the CO out, Major Hobbs took Jim's arm, "Mac, I'd like to speak to you alone." The Major waited until everyone else was out the door before he spoke, "Mac, I'm going to make you an offer you're going to love, I'll send Halsey to another company if you give me the name of the person who fragged him last night."

"Sir, do you think I know who did it?"

"Probably not yet, but you will before too long and when you do, I want him. Do we have a deal?"

"How soon after I rat will Mr. Halsey be gone?"

"I'll have him out of here in a week's time, and don't call it ratting— call it maintaining military discipline."

"Will Mr. Halsey know why he's being shipped out?"

"Do you want him to?"

"Sure!"

"Okay, I'll even let you be there when I tell him if you want, do we have a deal?"

"If you'll get him off my back until I find out who did it, sure, you got a deal."

Hobbs laughed, "You drive a hard bargain. How much more do you want?"

"That's all."

"Well, I can't guarantee that but I'll tell you what I will do. I'll talk to Mr. Halsey and tell him I think it's time for this silliness to stop, and I'll try to impress upon him that I mean it."

"Major, can I ask you a question?"

"Sure."

"Sir, why does the Colonel hate my guts?"

With a look of surprised disbelief the Major replied, "He doesn't hate you at all, quite the contrary. If he hated you, he'd be busting you to PFC instead of promoting you to an E-5."

Jim looked up with surprise, "I'm really on the promotion list?"

"Yep!"

"In that case, I'd better get over there or I'll be in trouble for missing my promotion."

Major Hobbs laughed and opened the door motioning Jim out. Once outside, Major Hobbs put his left hand on Jim's right shoulder. "Mac, Colonel Appleton told Mr. Walker he could go on R & R as soon as that channel opened back up, which will probably be ten days to two weeks. By that time I should have made AC. Would it be all right with you if I flew AC in your ship while Mr. Walker's gone?"

"It would be fine with me, Sir. In fact, I'm honored that you even asked me instead of just doing it."

"Oh, I realize I'm not the most popular person around here right now, and it's not going to get a lot better."

"Why do you want to fly with me, Sir?"

"Because you're good and I like your personality. You know the difference between an officer and an NCO*, which you'll be shortly, and you'll talk to me without pulling any punches. I like that and respect an enlisted man who can carry it off, in a respectable manner, of course. I like the way you handled yourself with that Halsey thing and the way you handled yourself when shot down. You've got a set of balls all right. Just out of curiosity, how come you don't mind flying with me? I have to be on all the E.M.'s lists by now."

"As a matter of fact, Sir, you are about one step below Mr. Halsey. Nobody likes the idea of painting rocks or putting the cargo doors back on the choppers. I mean, it's a real pain to unhook the ammo belts so I can shut the door and put fuel in the chopper, or get into the engine compartment, or the storage area." Jim could tell from the look on the Major's face it was time to stop on that subject.

*N.C.O. - Non commissioned officer (E-5 and above).

"You didn't answer me, Mac. How come you don't mind flying with me?"

"Because with your rank you're only going to fly lead or trail. Those are the two spots in the flight that are never sent on single ship missions after the flight is released. As a result, I'll be able to finish my post flight inspection earlier and maybe get a little more sleep." Jim opened the club house door and followed the Major in. The place was crammed with all the officers and enlisted men in the company; there was hardly enough room to stand, let alone walk, so Jim simply followed the Major towards the stage at the west end.

Colonel Appleton had already started handing out the promotions and was in the process of shaking Gillett's hand, along with two other men. All three had obviously just been promoted to Staff Sergeant. With promotion orders in hand they stepped off the stage leaving only the CO. As they climbed off, the First Sergeant climbed up. From a sheet of paper in his hand, he read the names of all the men being promoted to E-5. Jim, whose name was about halfway down the list, quickly joined the others on stage.

Happy didn't describe how Jim felt. He was elated! He'd finally been promoted to Specialist E-5. Sp/5 meant a lot of things besides the obvious increase in pay. It meant no more K.P., no more guard duty, other than the possibility of sergeant of the guard and that was an easy job and only pulled about once a year. It meant no more crummy details like filling sand bags or burning shit. Officers, and for that matter most everyone, treated a Sp/5 with considerable more respect than a Sp/4 and that would be nice. It also meant he'd be able to get away with a lot more as a Sp/5, things he wouldn't even try as a Sp/4. Plus, he'd be an NCO. That did sound good to him—Jim MacLaughlin, a non commissioned officer. He'd almost forgotten that meant he'd be able to get into the NCO side of the E.M. Club, where he could buy hard liquor. He was only twenty years old and he'd be drinking whisky when guys who were twenty one or older couldn't if they weren't E-5's.

Colonel Appleton stepped in front of Jim, who was already standing at attention. The CO held out his hand to shake Jim's, than handed him a copy of his promotion orders and said, "Congratulations, Mac!"

"Thank you, Sir."

The CO and Jim saluted, then Colonel Appleton turned to the next man in line. Once the Colonel had completed handing out the E/5 promotions, those men were released and everyone else being promoted had their names read off by the First Sergeant. Everyone from E/2 to Sp/4 was lumped together and quickly handed their promotion orders.

Once the CO was finished, he asked that all the new E-5's meet him in the NCO side of the club—he was buying. There was monumental confusion as people tried to leave and others tried to make their way to the just-opened bar. Others, like Jim, were trying to make their way through the NCO doorway. Once in the NCO side of the club, Jim didn't know quite what to do, so he stood along one wall looking around. It was a fair sized room with several small tables where people were already seated. There was a great deal of activity as men moved from table to table, and some were just looking for a place to sit. Others just enjoyed talking to several people and moved from table to table. The wall to his left housed the bar itself, behind which was the usual display of bottles and glasses. There was one American GI tending bar who Jim recognized as having come to Tay Ninh with him from Bear Cat. He'd heard that during the day two fairly attractive Vietnamese girls tended bar. The thing that held his attention most was the silk parachute used as a ceiling adornment. Major Hobbs was standing at the bar trying to get everyone's attention and for the first time Jim realized how smokey and noisy it was.

"May I have your attention please...thank you...thank you. Just in case somebody doesn't know me yet, I'm Major Hobbs, your new XO. I'd like to congratulate all of you who were promoted tonight and be the first to buy all of you a drink. Barkeep, the first round's on me for everyone who just got promoted."

Jim felt a hand on his arm and turned to see Gillett standing there. "Mac, you stink!"

"No kidding! What did you expect? I've had a hell of a day and haven't had a chance to shower and change yet."

"So I understand. I can't wait to hear all about it! Come on, let's go get our free-bee. What are you drinking?"

"I don't know, beer I guess."

"Beer! You have to be kidding. Mac, you're not going to drink beer anymore! I want you to get a Jack Daniels Black and Coke. In fact, since the Major's buying, you should buy a bottle and keep it here behind the bar."

"I'll tell you what, I'll try the Jack Daniels and Coke, but I get the feeling I've got a friend in Major Hobbs, so I'm not about to pull a stupid trick like sticking the man for the price of a whole bottle."

The two men made their way to the bar and Gillett ordered a bottle of Jack Daniels and a can of Coke. Jim stuck to a single drink of Jack and Coke and followed Gillett to a table where Mr. Walker, Mr. Euclid, Hunter and Athia were seated. Congratulations were passed all around along with inquiries about their day. Several comments were made about the way Walker and Jim smelled and looked, followed by a general discussion about what it was like to spend the day running from Charlie while carrying a dead man. Their table seemed to be one of the main centers of attention, with several officers stopping by to shake hands with Jim, Walker, and Gillett.

It was Major Hobbs who moved most of the flight crews out by getting everyone's attention and then giving final congratulations to all those newly promoted. He then announced that he had to fly tomorrow along with several others in the room, and it would be a good idea to get some sleep.

Once the flyers had left, there were only about a dozen guys remaining. Walker, Gillett and Jim remained at their table only because they knew the line at the urinal would be immense.

"Well, Gillett, I'll tell you this, you were right about the Jack Daniels, this stuff is nice."

"Mac, would I steer you wrong? I'll even make you a deal. Since the Major was nice enough to buy the bottle, I'll share it with you two if you'll buy the Coke."

"That sounds like a good deal to me."

Since the bar was empty it didn't take him long to get back. "Sorry, Gillett, they're out of Coke so I had to choose between Pepsi and root beer."

Gillett looked at the can in Jim's hand, half afraid he'd be holding root beer. "Well, I'm glad to see you made the right choice. While I'm thinking about it, Mac, I want to give you these since I won't be needing them any longer." Gillett reached up to his collar, un-snapped the Sp/5 insignias and handed them to Jim. Genuinely pleased, Jim pinned the insignia onto his collar in place of his Sp/4.

"Thanks, Gillett, I really appreciate this."

"You're welcome."

Walker poured the last of the Pepsi into his glass and with a puzzl-ed look said, "I'd like to know something, Mac, what's with you and Hobbs?"

"I don't know, I guess the guy just plain likes me. Why?"

"I don't know for sure, but before you got to the mess hall tonight, the Major pumped me for everything I knew about you. From the questions and comments he made, he'd obviously looked your 201 file* over very carefully."

"What did he want to know?"

"It's hard to say, but my guess is he wants to know why you do the things you do. If you know the risks and do them anyway, or if you're just too stupid to know better."

"I'm too stupid to know better."

"I'm sure that's what you'd like everyone to think and there are times when you do a real good job of playing that part! That little act has probably kept you out of a lot of trouble, but there's nothing stupid about you. You always know exactly what you're doing and all the possible consequences. Nobody knows that better than the three of us sitting here, right, Gillett?"

Gillett nodded, "I think there are others who know it or he wouldn't have gotten promoted. But you're right about Major Hobbs, he's after something. He was asking me a bunch of questions about Mac earlier today."

"Well, he must not dislike me too much or he wouldn't have asked me to fly with him when you go on R & R, Mr. Walker."

"I'm not going on R & R for a couple weeks. Appleton said tonight in the mess hall that I would be the first person to go but that won't be for awhile."

Gillett took a swig from the bottle of Jack, handed it to Jim and said, "Maybe he's decided he wants you as his crew chief."

---

*201 File - A person's personnel records giving all known information on an individual.

Jim shook his head but Gillett continued, "Just think about it, in about a month Appleton rotates home and Hobbs is the new CO. He'll be flying C and C ship and will need a crew chief." Looking at Mr. Walker, Gillett continued, "Why else would he be so interested in sending you on R & R?" In two weeks he should've made AC and you'll be gone so Mac has the choice of flying with every loose pilot in the company or with him. You're gone a week and by the time you get back Mac's learned all the benefits of flying with the CO, and bingo, he's only too happy to stay with Hobbs!"

"You know you're just about right; I know he was really impressed with the way he handled himself last night. Hobbs told me this morning he had to bite his tongue to keep from laughing when Mac asked Halsey to smell his armpit, or something like that!"

Jim and Gillett exchanged glances and broke out laughing remembering the moment. Jim, who, like Gillett, was now drinking straight from the bottle of Jack, took another gulp. "I think you're both crazy! He has to know I'd never quit flying with Mr. Walker."

Walker looked Jim in the eye, "Listen to me! If you get the chance to fly as the CO's chief, you'd better grab it."

"Why? I don't want to spend the rest of my time flying in circles at thirty-five hundred feet!"

"It would be a lot better than getting shot at all the time or flying all those night missions."

"But I like flying night missions."

"Do you have any idea what the casualty rate on those single ship night missions is?"

"Zero for me, I've gone down lots of times but never on a night mission."

"You're lucky, that's all."

"Divine protection."

"Look, it's irrelevant. What's important is you keep flying all of them and you're dead. With Hobbs, you're out of it; you get more time off, you'll fly less hours, you'll get back to base before anyone else and you'll get first class service from maintenance. Further, if you won't do it for yourself, do it for me. If Hobbs asks you to crew for him and you say no, he could send me to the guns or to another company."

"Hey, there are a lot of pilots who would give their left nut to be in the guns, besides we're just guessing anyway. Hobbs could have something entirely different in mind."

"Mac, if you could go to the guns, would you?"

"No, I like flying slicks. Besides, I'm too lazy to fly guns, they're just too much work."

"Ditto! But you're right. He might not ever ask. I've got to pee. See you two in the morning."

Jim took another swig from the bottle and handed it to Gillett who did the same. Once Walker had left, Jim felt it was safe to tell Gillett about Major Hobbs' proposition. "Gillett, just between you and me, I think you're probably right about Hobbs. He offered me quite a deal on the way over here tonight. Basically, if I turn in the guy who's responsible for fragging Halsey, he'll ship Halsey out to another company."

Gillett looked shocked, "You kidding me?"

"No."

"What are you going to do?"

"I don't know for sure."

"Have you told Green?"

"No and I'm not going to. In fact, I haven't told anyone but you and I don't think I will either. If Halsey finds out, he'll go crazy. Gillett, tell me something, will you? Why does he want me? I know I'm good at my job but no better than most of the guys in this company. And, I'm always closing in on trouble. So why me?"

"I don't know, Mac. The only person who does is Hobbs. If he ever does ask, and we might be jumping the gun, before you say yes, ask him—why you?"

They both heard it at the same time—the unmistakable scream of a 122MM rocket. Both men jumped under the table as someone in the background yelled, "Incoming". It only lasted a couple of minutes, but everyone stayed under their tables for several minutes more. Finally, after the first person stood up, everyone else followed. Jim looked over at Gillett who was still holding his bottle.

"Mac, you want this last swallow?"

Jim shook his head and said, "No, thanks. My stomach really doesn't feel too good. I think I'm going to go take a leak and go to bed."

Gillett smiled a knowing smile. "Wait a minute and I'll go with you!" Jim stood and watched as Gillett downed the last of his Jack Daniels.

Jim's stomach was feeling progressively worse. The fall he took going down the club's steps didn't help any. Fortunately, it was a short walk from the enlisted men's club to the urinals. He was so drunk he couldn't stand without holding himself up. Yet walking didn't seem to be any real problem, though his head kept going around in circles and things looked a bit fuzzy.

"Mac, can you get to the hooch okay without me?"

"Sure, Gillett. You know, I've never been this drunk in my life and I'm never going to be again. I feel terrible."

"Well, look on the bright side, you don't have to fly tomorrow."

"Does that mean I have to stand formation in the morning?"

Gillett laughed, "No, I'll cover for you, go to bed. I've got to run out the few guys who do have to fly and are still in the club."

Gillett turned and headed up the steps of the E.M. club and Jim headed on to the hooch. He was only a few steps from the pallet used as a bridge across the drainage ditch when Kenny bumped into him. He almost fell over but somehow managed to maintain his balance. "I didn't see you. Where'd you come from, Kenny?"

"The club." Kenny had positioned himself in such a way that Jim couldn't cross the pallet.

"Hey, Kenny, get out of my way!"

"To hell with you, MacLaughlin, just because you made E-5 tonight doesn't mean you can push people around."

"Kenny, you're drunk."

"So are you. So what are you going to do about it!"

Jim was making every effort to be as alert as possible. Something told him Kenny was working up enough courage to take a swing at him.

"And I'll tell you one more thing, get off Gillett's back about my monkey."

"Kenny, you and your monkey can both go to hell for all I care. Besides, what are you going to do about it if I don't?"

"How about busting you in the face for starters?"

"You're drunk, go to bed!"

Jim knew exactly what Kenny was going to do as he watched him make the exaggerated motion with his right arm. Jim's mind flashed with all the moves he'd been taught as a high school wrestler and later refined without the rules, by the army. Kenny's right arm had swung behind his back and started forward with fist clinched. Jim raised his left arm with open hand and caught Kenny's blow. His right hand came up and caught Kenny's armpit at the same time his left hand slid up Kenny's arm and grabbed his wrist. Then, pivoting on his left foot, he turned, bent over, bumped Kenny with his hip, pulled his arm down and flipped Kenny over his shoulder.

Kenny landed with a jar which hurt him physically as much as it did his pride. It had all taken place in a matter of seconds and Kenny hadn't even landed yet when Jim vomited. Jim straightened up only to jerk forward once more, spewing chunks of his supper and slimy Jack Daniels all over Kenny's chest and stomach. Jumping up as quickly as possible, Kenny lowered his head and charged like a bull. Jim stepped to his left and stuck out his right foot, tripping Kenny; who then fell in the drainage ditch. Jim vomited one last time and turned to where Kenny lay. "Kenny, I'm sick, could we finish this tomorrow? I promise. You let me go to bed and we can finish this tomorrow if you want. I just really don't feel like fighting you right now."

Kenny picked himself up out of the ditch and looked down at the vomit all over his front. Somewhat dejectedly he said, "I think you'd better go on to bed before I end up with vomit down my back as well. I'll tell you one thing I've learned, I'm never getting in a fight with a drunk again!"

Jim took off his shirt as he entered the hooch and wiped his face with it. Fortunately, he hadn't gotten any on himself. He sat down on the edge of his bunk, took off his boots and lay down. His head and stomach were still spinning, but feeling much better after having vomited, he was soon asleep.

11

"Do you not know that we will judge angels? How much more the things of this life!" I Corinthians 6:3 N.I.V.

Situation Ethics

The first thing Jim was aware of was someone shouting in the background. Then he realized how much his head hurt and his lips were swollen and dried out. Next his brain became aware of a mouth full of cotton and, finally, opening his eyes, he had trouble focusing.

"Mac, come on, wake up, get up!"

Jim slowly sat up on the edge of his bed, holding his head with both hands. He looked up and to his right at Gillett standing beside his bunk. "Welcome to the world of the living, Mac!"

"You don't have to shout, Gillett! Besides, you said I didn't have to fly this morning."

"I'm not shouting and you didn't go with the flight. It's ten o'clock."

Jim looked down at his watch, Gillett was right. He felt terrible and something stunk. All he wanted to do was lie back down. As he started to fall backwards, Gillett spoke and reached out, grabbing Jim's shoulder. "Oh, no you don't, get back up and go take a shower. You stink! Now that you're an E-5, you can go in the mess hall anytime you like and I suggest after the shower you go get a cup of coffee. At 11:15 the courier ship is supposed to land here and you're going to be on it along with Walker and Wright." Jim looked up questioningly. "You're supposed to pick up a Huey from Depot at Vung Tau. You got it?" Jim slowly nodded his head. "Mac, you really tied one on last night. How do you feel?"

"Like shit!"

"Well, you smell like it, too. Go get in the shower. Kenny just filled it up."

Jim watched Gillett walk out the door before starting to strip. For the first time, he saw Mr. Mace's dried blood, now an ugly blackish color, caked on his legs, shoulder and arm. Looking at the blood, he felt only a moment's sadness for Mr. Mace. Realizing how close he'd come to death himself, he decided to be thankful he was alive and not to think about Mr. Mace anymore. Jim put on his flip flops, and had just finished wrapping a towel around himself when Gillett walked in holding a cup of coffee.

"Here, drink this. It'll make you feel better!"

"Gillett, thanks, but I really don't think I could drink anything right now."

Gillett pushed the cup forward and said, "Drink it!"

Jim took the cup and drank it in two gulps. "Gillett, I swear to God and anybody who'll listen, I'm never going to get that drunk again as long as I live."

Gillett laughing said, "Sure, Mac, at least until tonight."

"No, I'm serious. I may get a little tipsy, but never totally wiped out, stoned-ass drunk again." Jim picked up his shower bag and headed for the shower. The water was still cold, so he didn't spend any more time than necessary. Once showered and dressed in clean fatigues, he felt a lot better. He still had almost an hour before meeting the courier ship, so he decided to go declare his losses from yesterday to supply.

Supply was nothing more than a big hooch. The first thing he saw once inside was a long counter top with various types of clothing piled on top. There was conversation coming from the shelving just behind the counter.

"Anybody home?"

"Be with you in a minute."

The conversation stopped and Jim waited for more than his minute. Finally, a large, overweight staff sergeant with his gut hanging over his belt buckle approached, "What can I do for you?"

"My name's, MacLaughlin. I was shot down yesterday and I lost some stuff when my Huey caught on fire."

"From what I heard, you blew it up; it didn't catch on fire!"

"Does it make any difference, Sarge?"

"Not as far as I'm concerned. I've got your records right here. What did you lose?"

"How did you know I'd be in? For that matter, how did you know about my ship?"

"Mr. Walker and I just finished pulling inventory on Mr. Mace's gear and boxing his personal belongings for shipment home. In fact, that's what I was doing when you came in, putting his gear back in stock."

Jim looked at his watch and decided he'd better get on with it. "Okay. Well, let's see. I lost my ballistics helmet, field jacket, flight gloves, five magazines for my M16, one baseball cap, canteen and my big water jug—I don't know what you would call it, it held five or eight gallons of water and had a bottom spigot."

"Okay, I know what you mean, but I don't have any more in stock and probably won't get any for a while. What else?"

"All my tools."

"You're out of luck there, also."

"You're kidding, how am I supposed to fix anything?"

"Well, you won't have to worry about that until you get a ship. Then I guess you'll just have to borrow, what else?"

"I guess that's it."

"Be right back." The staff sergeant walked off with paper in hand. Shortly, he returned with an arm load of items to replace what Jim had lost. "Here you are, Mac, everything but the water jug and tools, including tool box. Try the helmet on and see if it fits." It did. Shoving the receipt form in front of Jim, the sergeant said, "Sign on the line!"

Jim signed, picked up the gear laying on the countertop and walked out. From the supply room, he went to his hooch and put the gear in his wall locker and headed for the mess hall.

It was now five minutes before eleven and Jim figured he didn't have a chance of getting anything to eat. But then, nothing ventured, nothing gained. Once inside he looked around until he saw a mess sergeant. "Hey, Sarge, I've got an eleven-fifteen flight to Vung Tau.

Could I get an early lunch?"

"Oh, I think we can fix something up for you. I just wish you'd given me more time. I'll tell you what, Sarge, about the best I can do for you is heat up some C-rations real quick."

"That would be fine." Jim got a cup of coffee and sat down.

It wasn't long before the mess sergeant hollered, "Hey, Sarge, here's your lunch; potato cakes, peas, with beans and weenies."

Jim picked up a plate, "Thanks a lot, Sarge, I really appreciate it."

"You're welcome, Sarge, have a good flight and you had better hurry."

Jim ate quickly, thanked the mess sergeant again on his way out and returned to his hooch, where he picked up his M16 pistol belt, flight gloves and helmet. On his way to operations, he took a detour through maintenance. There he found a roll of gray tape used to temporarily patch bullet holes in rotor blades. In less than a minute he had taped three M16 magazines together, two down and one up, and slammed the single magazine home in his M16. He thanked the maintenance crew for the tape and moved at a brisk pace to operations.

The courier ship was already on the operations pad when Jim got there. Not seeing Mr. Walker, he went on into the operations bunker just as Mr. Walker and a second lieutenant were starting out. Jim could tell the lieutenant was the courier by the combination lock attache case he had handcuffed to his left wrist. The lieutenant was about 5'10" with dark hair, eyes and complexion. He was big boned and Jim figured he weighed over one hundred eighty pounds. Like most all couriers, he had an Army 45 on his right hip. Since Jim was outside headed in, he decided he'd better salute. Both Walker and the lieutenant returned his salute, but it was Walker who had the big smile.

"Cut it a little close didn't you, Mac?"

"Sir, I was told to be here by the time the courier was ready to leave and here I am." Jim knew that wasn't quite the truth, but he didn't feel like being hassled about not being there on time. After all, the important thing was not when he got there, only that he was there and ready to leave before the courier.

"I'm surprised you can even function this morning. I understand you really tied one on last night."

"Guilty as charged, Sir."

"How do you feel?"

"Oh, I feel okay after getting cleaned up and having something to eat. I'm a little sore from carrying Mr. Mace. But I'll tell you what, I'm never getting that blown away again. You know, I've been drunk on beer before, but never anything close to last night."

"Mac, that's the difference between beer and whiskey. I kind of figured you wouldn't feel too good after watching you drink straight from the bottle."

The three climbed on board, joining Wright who had been there waiting. The Huey engine picked up speed and soon they were airborne. Jim knew there wouldn't be any conversation because of the flight noise, so he leaned back in his seat and watched the scenic view below.

Heading south, they would follow Highway 22 to Go Dau Ha, where they would pick up Highway One to Saigon, from Saigon they'd probably pick up Highway 15 just outside Bien Hoa, and follow it to Vung Tau.

Jim had flown courier flights several times before their company had been changed to an all combat assault unit. He'd always enjoyed flying courier because they went to every outpost that had a landing pad and some that didn't. After all, how else was the military to get their important papers from one post to another? Jim's hope now was that Tay Ninh would be their last stop before lunch. If it wasn't, it could take a long time to get to Vung Tau; if it was, they'd probably head straight for Saigon to eat lunch. Afterward, the courier ship would head back out and spend most of the afternoon flying more papers.

Jim was right about Tay Ninh being the courier's last stop before lunch. Heading south, the jungle, green and lush around Tay Ninh, quickly turned to rice paddies outside Go Dau Ha. There was an occasional farmer working his rice paddy as they flew overhead. Twice he saw farmers working their water buffalo. Jim laughed to himself as he remembered eating water buffalo once in a fancy restaurant in Saigon. He and three other guys had paid perfectly good money for the most terrible steaks they'd ever eaten. To say it was strong and tough would be a major understatement. Catsup helped the flavor, but he couldn't cut it thin enough to help the toughness.

It wasn't long until they landed at Hotel Three and the three

Blackhawks headed for the Operations room. Mr. Walker got them a ride on a chinook leaving in ten minutes for Vung Tau. Once outside, they found a shady spot and sat down to wait.

"Wright, have you ever been to Tay Ninh?"

"Nope."

"How about you, Mr. Walker?"

"I've flown in and out of it, but never done any walking around. How about you, Mac?"

"Yeah, I've been there several times. When I was in the 191st, my maintenance crew won an in-country R & R at Vung Tau."

"You're kidding me?"

"No."

"Man, you're just full of surprises! Well come on, tell us all about it."

"Okay. They were having trouble getting aircraft out of maintenance, so the maintenance officer decided to give the crew who completed the most jobs in thirty days a trip to Vung Tau. Oh, yeah, to get credit, the aircraft had to pass inspection the first time. The guy I had for a crew leader was really good; he was on his second tour of duty in country, so he knew what he was doing. He said right to begin with that we were going to win it and we did. Don Sunday was his name.

"Our crew was also the recovery crew. If a ship went down, they sent us to fix it or rig it to be sling-loaded home by a Chinook. You know, I haven't thought about that crew for some time. I was on K.P. one day when the crew went out. For some reason, they couldn't find me so they got someone else to take my place. Everybody in that helicopter was killed." The others just sat there with blank looks on their faces. "I guess that's one reason I believe in divine protection. Anyway, one of the guys I came to Tay Ninh with said one of the pilots in this company found Don's ship shortly after we came to Tay Ninh."

"Was it a Boomerang ship?"

"Yeah, why?"

"I was the pilot."

Jim, obviously surprised, looked up, "Now who's full of surprises? Are you serious?"

"Yeah! I was just flying alone one day, I don't remember what I was doing or where I was going. You know—one of your basic milk runs back when we were a general purpose company. Anyway, we were just outside of Blackhorse when I thought I saw a helicopter crash down in the trees. So I circled around—you had to fly over it just right to see it—but there it was. I could make out a Boomerang on the nose so I radioed Saigon to see if the Boomerangs had lost a ship. Sure enough, about three months before, their maintenance ship had gone down and they never found it. They happened to be working in the area so they came and got the skeletons, which I understand, was all that was left."

"Had they been shot down or what?"

"I really don't know, Mac. I heard that they'd hit with enough impact that the pilots' seats had been ripped out of the floor. The pilots were still strapped in and they found the passengers some distance away. From the way that chopper was busted up, it had to hit those trees well over red line. My guess, and it's just a guess, is they got caught in a monsoon and were blown into those trees. But who knows, their transmission could have frozen for any one of several reasons including a bullet hole letting out the oil." Mr. Walker shrugged his shoulders and continued, "That's all I know, Mac. I'm sorry I don't have more information."

"Did Charlie find them?"

"Mac, I just finished telling you, I don't know! I don't even remember if they found their weapons."

"I wonder why it didn't blow?"

"Who knows, maybe they were about out of fuel. Besides, not every Huey that crashes, burns."

"That's true."

"I'm sorry, Mac."

"Hey, don't be. I know more now than I did before. You know, Mr. Walker, one of the things I don't understand now is, I was on the serving line that night in the mess hall. When our First Sergeant came through he was really surprised to see me, since he thought I was dead. He had me leave the serving line right then, much to the annoyance of the mess sergeant and report to the company commander, who was in the process of writing the letter home to my parents. Now, what I don't understand is, how did he know they were dead?"

"I don't know, what time of day did they go down?"

"Early morning."

"Maybe they'd been lost without contact long enough, I just don't know!"

Wright spoke for the first time. "So tell us about Vung Tau!"

"There's not much to tell. We went down on the maintenance ship early one morning. Don had been there before, so he took us to a motel he knew about, named, The Thunderbird. We each got a room and spent the rest of the day on the beach."

In unison Wright and Walker said, "On the beach!"

"Yeah, there's a pretty nice beach area where you can swim and just lie around. Then that evening, we went to a fancy hotel for dinner and had buffalo steaks. After that, we hit the bars and got picked up on base the next day about noon."

Walker smiled and said, "Did you ever spend any time on the base?"

"Sure, I used to go with the maintenance ship two or three times a month to pick up parts."

"Good, then you know right where we're going."

"Sure, I've been there several times, it's not hard to find."

"How about passenger pick up area, do you know where that is?"

"Sure, we used to give guys rides out of Vung Tau all the time as long as it was on our way. Why?"

"We're supposed to have a Lieutenant Carson waiting for a ride back to Tay Ninh."

"We getting a new pilot?"

"I don't think so. We're supposed to deliver him straight to Headquarters at Tay Ninh. So I don't think he's a pilot."

"Mr. Walker, do you know what he looks like?"

'I have no idea. I don't even know if he's black or white."

"Well, it shouldn't be any problem to find him, he's probably waiting at Operations. I can show you where to go sign for the Huey, and then I'll go look for our lieutenant."

The three turned to their left and watched a Chinook land and lower its back door, which doubles as a cargo ramp. Out walked several GI's, including one that still had a flight helmet on. Mr. Walker approached the man, figuring him to be the crew chief and asked if he was headed to Vung Tau. Receiving a thumbs up sign, Walker motioned for the other two to join him. In only minutes they were once again airborne and headed south.

The inside of a Chinook is like a very noisy, rectangular box. Much of the super structure is visible, as are hydraulic lines and electrical lines. There are fold down seats on either side for passengers to sit on, and several steel tie down rings in the aluminum floor. Unlike a Huey, passengers can't sit and look out the sides because they are solid, with only a few small windows to look out.

It wasn't long until they landed at Vung Tau. Jim showed Mr. Walker and Wright how to find the maintenance offices, with the understanding that he would join them with Lieutenant Carson at the helicopter. Wright was to stand out in the open so Jim could see him.

It was only a short walk for Jim to the Operations office, and he was glad. The sun was directly overhead and it was getting very hot. He knew Operations was air conditioned so once in the door, he removed his hat and just stood there cooling off.

Seated on the bench on the far side of the room was a Wac Lieutenant. It only took one glance to see she was a real knockout of about twenty-four or five years of age. She had on a dress uniform, complete with hose which accentuated a pair of gorgeous legs. She'd crossed those legs with her skirt hem resting a good three inches above the knee. Jim couldn't help but think, Man, the things I'd like to do with her. He decided he'd better quit staring before she looked up from her paperback book.

Moving over to the counter, he looked for the first time at the staff sergeant standing there. In a whisper, the staff sergeant spoke, "Didn't strain your eyes did you?"

Jim chuckled quietly. The sergeant continued, "Makes a man wish he was an officer, doesn't it?"

Jim puckered his lips slowly, blew out some air, closed his eyes and nodded. "What can I do for you, Specialist?"

"I'm looking for a Lieutenant Carson."

The sergeant stood up straight and broke into a big grin. With his eyes he pointed to the Wac Lieutenant. It took Jim a moment to recover and only then did he turn around. The first thing he looked for was her collar insignia, which would tell him her job. It was a gold diamond. She's in finance? There aren't any finance people at Tay Ninh! The broad is a whore! Jim was really disappointed, but her beauty still held him captive.

Jim walked over to the bench and positioned himself only about two feet from the Lieutenant. He felt sure she had been aware of him and probably had checked him out just as he had her. For one thing, he didn't remember her turning a page of that book she seemed to be reading. He had to admit, she was truly a beautiful woman, even in military clothing. One thing he'd learned, if a woman was attractive in military clothing, she was gorgeous in civilian clothes. Her short brown hair had every strand in place and her makeup was perfect. Unlike so many Wac's he'd met who either didn't wear any makeup or put so much on it looked like Indian war paint, hers was truly perfect.

Jim stood there not saying anything, waiting for her to respond to his presence. Very slowly and deliberately she raised her head showing a slight smile.

Lieutenant Carson had been waiting most of the morning for her ride to Tay Ninh. Her rear end and back had long ago begun to ache from sitting on the wooden bench placed against a wall.She was bored to death with the wait, and the novel she'd brought along didn't hold her interest.

There'd been a parade of men through that door and with each one she'd hoped her chariot was parked outside waiting. Instead, each man ogled. Some even went so far as to stand and leer. One, a captain, had even had the nerve to try to pick her up. She didn't mind though, she knew she was very attractive, and in the military she rated higher. In fact, she usually got a kick out of the men's reactions. She had, after all, worked very hard to perfect her ability to get the reaction from men she wanted.

When Jim had walked in the door, she'd shifted her eyes to the top of the page, that way she could watch him without being obvious. He was young, but then weren't they all. He carried an M16, which meant he was stationed out in the boondocks someplace, and there was the pistol belt with ammo packs on it. Of all the guys who had walked through, not more than a couple had weapons, and none had a pistol belt. This guy was either a basic Saigon warrior or the real thing. Somewhat to her surprise, he'd removed his hat and placed it under his arm. Only a few of the officers had removed their hats while inside. As he was walking across the room to the counter, she took the opportunity to look him over good. Not bad looking, not great, but not bad, A shame he's only a Spec-Five, and not the pilot sent to get her.

She moved her eyes back to the book and started to read. Much to her surprise, this Spec-Five started to walk towards her, stopping only a couple feet from her. This was obviously her ride but she was a lieutenant and not about to appear anxious. He just stood there with his feet slightly apart. He didn't seem intimidated by her looks or rank or he would have spoken her name from the counter, not walked over and stood directly in front of her. Slowly and very purposefully, she raised her head to look directly into his eyes. Dark brown eyes. It's too bad it's only in the movies that you can read things in people's eyes. His soft boyish smile caused the woman in her to respond instead of the lieutenant. I think I'll give him a thrill.

Softly and very pleasantly, she spoke, "Is there anything I can do for you, Sergeant?"

Jim thought, but didn't say, *There's a lot you could do for me, lady!* But something told him she knew exactly what she was saying. So, in a slightly deepened voice, Jim replied, "Yes, Ma'am! And I believe there is something I can do for you. My name is, MacLaughlin, but most everyone calls me, Mac. I'm with the 187th Assault Helicopter Company stationed at Tay Ninh. I understand you need a ride!"

She thought, It is just a shame this one isn't an officer. It was such a rarity to meet a man who wasn't intimidated by her looks. Well, he wasn't an officer, so she'd just have to take this cocky young Spec-five down where he belonged. Without smiling, and in a curt tone, she said, "You're right, Specialist, I'm waiting for a ride. Get my bag and let's go!"

"Yes, Ma'am. Lieutenant, Ma'am. Anything the Lieutenant Ma'am wants, Ma'am."

Lieutenant Carson was instantly sorry she'd pulled such a cheap trick. She could have asked nicely. For that matter, she probably hadn't even needed to ask. He probably would have done it on his own. As it was, his response made her feel small. Then there were his eyes.

His soft boyish eyes had in an instant turned hard and mean. She wasn't sure whether it was his tone of voice, his eyes, or the M16 he held that made her feel so slightly threatened. There wasn't any doubt he'd been there and back, you could see it in his face, in his eyes. Only an instant had transpired since her command. Since he hadn't yet picked up her bag, she started to stoop to do so when his M16 moved in front of her, blocking her hand's path.

With his left hand, he picked up the bag and said softly, "I'll get it, Lieutenant."

Jim was very pleased with himself. He'd put just the right inflection in his voice when offering her a ride to Tay Ninh. Then she'd barked that command to pick up her bag; it was almost as though she didn't like the idea that he wasn't scared to death of her. What did she expect him to do, stand there with his knees knocking? She was beautiful, that was for sure, but he thought she was also a whore, even if she was a lieutenant. And if she wanted to play hardnose with him, he could play, too; even if it was her game. When she started to reach for her bag he figured two things: first it was her way of saying she realized she'd made a mistake; secondly, she had given him an order and he'd better obey it.

Jim reached down and picked up the small overnight bag, which was surprisingly light. He had to smile to himself. His mother would have packed the kitchen sink in this thing and it would have weighed a hundred pounds. That was the worst thing about going on a vacation, carrying the bags his mother packed. Not this bitch though, she couldn't have more than a toothbrush and negligee in her bag.

He wasn't sure if he had overstepped his bounds with all the "Lieutenant, Ma'ams" he'd used, so to make amends he had smiled and said, "I'll get it, Lieutenant."

Lieutenant Carson smiled faintly and replied, "Thank you."

Jim only nodded and motioned with his M16 for her to lead. Once out the door, the heat and humidity hit them full force. Lieutenant Carson, not sure where to go, had to wait for Jim. In fact, she would be following him, a small but significant role reversal. Jim watched her fidget as he put her bag down and placed his hat back on his head.

"May I call you, Mac?"

"I wish you would."

"Mac, where's your helicopter?"

"Lieutenant, I'm not really sure. Someplace in the maintenance area, I hope."

"What do you mean, you hope?"

"My helicopter blew up yesterday when I was shot down, so my pilot, gunner and I were sent here to pick up a new one."

"No co pilot?"

"He died of a sucking chest wound and shock and there aren't any other pilots in the company."

Lieutenant Carson looked at Jim and held his eyes for a full heart beat. There wasn't any question but what he'd said was fact.

She walked directly to his left and allowed him to set their leisurely pace. The maintenance area was a good walking distance away and she, for some reason, was enjoying his company. Since he wasn't an officer, he wouldn't try to get into her pants, and with his self confidence, it was a good thing he wasn't.

"Lieutenant, what do you know about Tay Ninh?"

"Not a whole lot. It's supposed to be a good-sized base. Why?"

"Do you know we get hit with rocket and mortar fire almost every night? We sleep in bunkers, and the base was partially overrun only a few days ago. Tay Ninh is a dirty, dusty hole where people get killed …in their beds! It's not a nice place to visit."

They walked on in silence for a while. "Lieutenant, could I ask why a finance officer is going to Tay Ninh? There isn't any finance operation there."

Somewhat embarrassed, she replied, "That's really none of your business!"

"No, Ma'am, it's not. I just can't help wondering since there isn't any finance and you're all dressed up like you're going to your college R.O.T.C. graduation dance. Don't misunderstand me, you're my idea of a truly beautiful woman. In fact, I hope I end up married to someone who looks like you. But somehow I just don't think you belong at Tay Ninh, let alone dressed like that."

"Specialist, that's enough!"

"Yes, Ma'am!" They walked a ways further. "Lieutenant, I don't understand something. You could have most any man you want, so why?"

"Specialist, that's enough. I'm giving you a direct order, just shut up until we get to your helicopter! You understand me, Specialist?"

"Yes, Ma'am." Jim started to laugh as he shook his head.

In a slightly irritated voice, Lieutenant Carson said, "And just what do you find so damn funny?"

Jim's thought was, *Ah, so, permission to speak,* but said, "You. First, who, besides the two of us have heard this conversation? Secondly, you're not going to court martial me. If you do, it would greatly embarrass you, but more than that it would greatly embarrass the guy you're meeting."

"You're an insubordinate son of a bitch with a smart mouth. Just how do you know I'm not meeting my husband?"

"Because there isn't any wedding ring and any man who really loved you would never take you to Tay Ninh, not for any reason!" She just looked at him. He was on a roll and decided to make one last push in something that really wasn't any of his business. "So what do you get out of it, Lieutenant, Captain's rank?"

"For a Spec-Five, you've got a smart mouth and a lot of brass that'll get you in a lot of trouble. Okay, Mr. Smart Mouth, let me ask you a question! Have you been on R & R yet?"

Jim understood her point. "Yes, Ma'am."

Lieutenant Carson was obviously upset. "And you're pointing the finger at me?"

"There's a difference."

"Oh, you bet there is, you're a man and I'm a woman, that's the difference!"

Jim tried to respond calmly. "No, the difference is the seller is considered a cheap, slut-whore. The buyer, he's considered just a good old boy and whether it's right or not, that's the way it is, at least in the military and most of society. That's the difference, Lieutenant."

Nothing more was said the rest of the way. Jim spotted Wright and waved his recognition with the M16 and made a direct path in his direction. Three helicopters were parked in a row just behind Wright. Mr. Walker was seated in the cargo doorway of the middle one.

The first thing Jim noticed about the chopper was the First Cav insignia on the tail boom, the next was the lack of passenger seats or sound proofing.

"Mr. Walker, Specialist Wright, I'd like you to meet Lieutenant Carson. Lieutenant Carson, Mr. Walker, my pilot, and my door gunner, Spec Four Wright."

Jim laughed as both men struggled to regain their composure. Still stunned by her beauty, Mr. Walker said, "Lieutenant, you're going to Tay Ninh?"

"That's right and please save the lecture, I've already had the full course from your crew chief."

Walker smiled. "Mac never was one to mince words. I just want to be sure you know what you're going to. Tay Ninh isn't a nice place to visit. If you're accustomed to Saigon or Vung Tau, you're in for a real shock when you reach Tay Ninh."

"Believe me, Mr. Walker, Mac's told me all about it!"

Jim had picked up the log book and was looking through the various pages. "Mr. Walker, is this ours?"

"Yep."

"Did you see how many hours this thing has on it?"

"Yes, but I wasn't given a choice. Besides, I didn't know what I was getting until I got out here and looked at it. Is it really flyable?"

"According to the log book it is, it just looks like the devil. It's been test flown and signed off, but I'll still give it a thorough preflight inspection. Major Hobbs will have a hemorrhage when he sees this thing."

"Well, Mac, what do you want to do?"

"I'll tell you this, I don't want to fly in it. The log book says it came in because of structural cracks in the transmission mounts. This thing has so many hours on it, metal fatigue is going to be a real problem. Wright, go over to the maintenance area and find a Specialist Six named, Dill. He's the Tech Inspector who signed this crate off. Tell him your pilot would like to speak with him. Lieutenant Carson, you might as well sit down, this is going to take a while. Mr. Walker, here's the log book, as I list them, you write 'em up. Remember, each item gets its own line and don't sign 'em or give anything a status symbol."

Mr. Walker picked up the log book as Lieutenant Carson gave him a dirty look and spoke, "Wait just a minute, Specialist. This man is a Warrant Officer in the United States Army and is not to..."

Mr. Walker interrupted her by placing his hand on her arm, "Lieutenant, could I have a word with you, please?"

"Sure."

"Lieutenant, has Mac done something to irritate you personally?"

"As a matter of fact, yes. He's an insubordinate smartmouth who disobeyed a direct order I gave him on the way over here."

"Just what did he say to you, and what was the order he disobeyed?"

Lieutenant Carson thought better of going through the whole thing so she simply replied, "Just forget it, it's not important anyway! Okay?"

"Whatever you say, Lieutenant. I just don't think you understand. He would never be disrespectful to me. Where he and I have been, you'll never go, and the things we've done to stay alive while there, you'll only read about in books or see in the movies. And furthermore, you should give thanks to God above you'll never be put to the kind of test that man has already passed. Try to understand our relationship. We're in combat every day. We get up in the morning knowing we'll be shot at that day. There are times when we just don't have time for military courtesy. As a result, a crew chief and his pilot develop an understanding about a lot of things. How we talk to each other is just one of many examples. Look, if we're going to fly in that helicopter it better be safe, because I can't pull over to the side of the road and park until it gets fixed. Lieutenant, every time I get in a helicopter, my life depends on that man. If you fly to Tay Ninh with us, yours will, too. From the looks of that chopper, we both better hope Mac knows what he'd doing. Sometimes it's necessary for me to help him with his job and I'm happy to do it. Do you get my drift, Lieutenant?"

"Yes." Lieutenant Carson picked up her book and sat down on the crew chief's seat.

Mr. Walker picked up the log book and walked around the tail boom to where Jim was checking the tail rotor. "Find anything serious, Mac?"

"No, Sir, well, at least no one thing. I've found a whole lot of little things though that'll keep a crew chief busy for months. You ready to start listing?"

"Yep."

"Okay, first item: four bullet hole patches, tail boom left side needs spot painted O.D. Same for right side: screws missing from tail boom inspection panel, two snap openers missing on tail rotor drive shaft cover, several rivets loose in tail boom on both right and left sides, all sound proofing missing, passenger seats missing, both cargo doors missing, both cargo door tracks have excessive wear, both first aid kits missing, fire extinguishers missing, left pilot seat not safety wired, magnetic compass missing." Jim climbed into the pilot's seat. "There's play in the foot pedals and I get drag which shouldn't be there."

"What causes that?"

"Oh, there are several things that can cause that and none of them are good." Jim climbed out of the pilot's seat. "Window missing in pilot's door, left side, window broken in right door, snap release broken on door to radio nose compartment." Jim continued to list every little thing he could find wrong with the helicopter. It was up on top that he found the most serious problems. Maintenance had put back on the old dampers that had so much moisture in the hydraulic oil, he couldn't see through the sight gauge. There were push-pull rods with a lot of play in their bearings, and several other things which caused him concern.

Lieutenant Carson had never started to read her book. She'd been more interested in listening to Jim list all the things wrong. The longer the list grew, the more she thought about what Mr. Walker had said. As a result, her respect for him grew. She watched Jim climb off the roof and jump into the cargo area, landing in front of her. Pointing with her head she said, "Mac, I think we're about to get company."

Jim noticed the friendliness was back in her voice and that she called him, Mac, instead of, Specialist. All these things, plus the fact she was giving him advance notice had to mean she was softening towards him, at least partially. Jim glanced back to see Wright and another man approaching.

"Thank you, Lieutenant. I appreciate it."

Lieutenant Carson smiled and said, "You're welcome, Mac. Is this thing safe to fly?"

"Technically, I suppose so, but personally, I wouldn't fly in it from here to the other side of the post. May I sit down?"

Lieutenant Carson smiled and moved over to give him room. Walker came around the aircraft's nose at the same time Wright and a

Spec-Six approached.

Wright spoke, "Specialist Dill, this is my pilot, Mr. Walker and my crew chief, Specialist MacLaughlin, and Lieutenant Carson."

Spec-Six Dill was a tall man about six foot six and thin, not weighing more than one hundred fifty pounds. Dill saluted, then placed both hands on his hips and developed an all business expression. "What seems to be the problem, Sir?"

"Are you the Tech Inspector who signed this aircraft off?"

"Sir, if you looked in the log book you know I did."

Jim looked at Lieutenant Carson seated beside him and in a soft voice said, "And you called me a smart mouth."

She only smiled. Walker's voice was now all business. "Specialist Dill, I'm really not in the mood for any smart ass answers, you got that!"

"Yes, Sir."

"Do you let all the aircraft you work on out of maintenance looking like this?"

"No, Sir."

"Then why this one?"

"Because, Sir, that's the way we got it. All we do is depot level maintenance. In this case that meant replacing the transmission mounts. We don't paint or put missing sound proofing in or replace loose rivets. All that type stuff is done on a company level."

Jim said, "You mean to tell me that those push-pull rods on top shouldn't be replaced?"

"I didn't tell you anything of the kind, all I said is we don't do it."

"Not even if its got excessive play?"

"They don't have excessive play!"

"I think they do! How about the dampers? You can't even see their sight gauges they're so cloudy."

"I don't remember looking at 'em."

"Specialist, would you fly this thing?"

"Sure."

"Just like it is for ten hours a day for ten days?"

"I don't know what that's got to do with anything."

"The point is that there isn't any one thing the aircraft can be grounded for maybe, but all together it's an accident waiting to happen. As a Tech Inspector you should be ashamed of yourself for letting the thing be test flown, let alone released!"

The two NCO's simply stared at each other until Mr. Walker said, "Specialist, I don't understand how this crate can look so terrible and that chopper right beside us look brand new."

"Sir, the biggest reason is that it is almost brand new. As I remember, it doesn't have two hundred hours on it yet."

Jim asked, "What is it in depot for?"

"It came from the 195th Skychiefs up at Long Binh. It had a sudden stoppage."

Lieutenant Carson asked, "A sudden stoppage, what's that?"

Dill looked at Jim and replied, "You're such a hot shot and think you know my job better than I do, you tell her!"

In a very pleasant voice Jim said, "Specialist, I am a Specialist E-5, which, in case you have forgotten, makes me an NCO just like yourself. Therefore, I would appreciate not being insulted in front of two officers and an enlisted man. Furthermore, not because you want to know how much I know, but because I happen to like Lieutenant Carson, I'll answer her question for you. Lieutenant, a sudden stoppage is when the rotor blades hit a solid object, like a tree, causing them to stop suddenly. The problem, Lieutenant, with a sudden stoppage is there isn't any place in the power train to allow for any slippage. Power is delivered from the engine into a shaft called a short shaft, from there, directly into the transmission, directly into the mast, directly into the rotor head; where it is finally delivered to the rotor blades. Since there isn't any place in the system for slippage when the rotors hit something solid enough to suddenly stop them, it causes a massive internal hemorrhage. Gears break, bearings rupture and bolts pop. As a result, everything that turns has to be removed and replaced: engine, transmission, drive shafts, bearings, everything. And that, Lieutenant, is what a sudden stoppage is all about."

Dill nodded his head and said, "Very good, Specialist, very good indeed."

Jim had an idea. "Specialist Dill, who's supposed to get that ship?"

"The 195th gets it back. When we're done with them, they're test flown and if everything checks out okay, they're parked here 'til picked up by the receiving company."

Mr. Walker said, "In other words, Specialist, you're not going to fix anything on this helicopter to make it safer to fly?"

"Sir, it's been test flown and signed off as safe to fly."

"I guess that's a matter of opinion, isn't it?"

Dill just stood there and looked at the ground before finally saying, "Sir, if there isn't anything else, I'll be going."

Dill was standing between Mr. Walker and Jim, who was still seated beside Lieutenant Carson. Mr. Walker glanced at Jim, who shrugged his shoulders and shook his head slowly in disgust. Walker looked back at Dill and said, "That will be all, Specialist."

Everyone sat there in silence and watched as Dill walked off. It was Wright who broke the silence. "Well, what are we going to do now?"

Jim and Walker looked at each other and both knew what the other was thinking. Jim spoke, "Lieutenant, would you rat on us if we committed a little grand larceny?"

Lieutenant Carson laughed and answered, "After listening to you two talk, I'm not interested in riding in this one."

Walker said, "Mac, we'll have to get the log book somehow."

"I can think about that while I preflight the chopper. Keep an eye open for somebody who might see me." In a few minutes Jim returned. "Well, I don't see anything wrong with it and Dill is right, that ship's almost brand new. I've got an idea about the log book. Mr. Walker, tell me what you had to do and how many people were there when you signed for this crate."

"There was only a staff sergeant seated at the front desk. There was another desk behind him but no one was there. I told him who I was and what company I was from and that I was to pick up a Huey. He got the papers I signed from a file cabinet, and the log book was with a stack on his desk."

"How many times did you sign?"

"Just twice."

"What did he do with those papers?"

"I'm not sure. One was in duplicate. In fact, I think I left before he did anything with them."

"What drawer did he get the papers from?"

"Top."

"Okay, Mr. Walker, you can't go back in there because they'll recognize you. So if you and I trade shirts and hats, I'll go in and try to find the papers you signed. I'll leave this log book here and pick up 647's book. I'll have to sign your name to new forms."

"Mac, one wasn't a form, it was like a sign in sheet that was on a clip board on the front desk. Besides, you'll never get away with this. That sergeant isn't going to sit there and let you go through his files."

"That's where a beautiful lieutenant dressed to knock your eyeballs out comes in handy."

Lieutenant Carson interrupted, "Just wait one minute! I'm not going to have anything to do with this!"

"Lieutenant, please, all you have to do is go in, ask the desk sergeant to show you where the ladies room is and have him escort you there."

"No! You're talking about stealing a helicopter, impersonating an officer, forgery and enough other things to send you and anyone involved to jail for thirty years. I don't want any part of it!"

"There isn't any forgery unless Mr. Walker presses charges, which you're not going to do, are you, Mr. Walker?"

"I'll swear it's my signature."

"As for the impersonating an officer, who's going to say, hey, you, you're not an officer! Nobody knows Mr. Walker or me, so no one's going to question me. As for stealing a helicopter, if I sign all the forms, it's not stealing. It'll be a simple case of the sergeant giving the wrong forms to Mr. Walker to sign. As for you, nobody will ever connect you with it. After all, you're just a damsel in distress who asked the nice sergeant to show you to the ladies room."

"You two are crazy, you know that! What if someone walks in on you?"

"I'll have Wright standing outside to warn me." Jim could see Lieutenant Carson warming to the idea. "Come on, Lieutenant, you see this type of thing done in the movies all the time. Now's your once in a lifetime chance to be part of a military operation, usually called something like, 'a midnight requisition'."

"Yeah, except this is in broad daylight."

"And that's the biggest reason it'll work. Come on, be a sport!"

Lieutenant Carson looked at the three men standing there staring at her. "You're crazy, you really and truly are crazy, all three of you!" Looking at Jim she said, "Especially you." She paused for a moment then continued, "You won't go off and leave me?"

Walker answered, "I give you my word as an officer—you'll leave with us!"

"Your word as an officer! You're talking about stealing a helicopter amongst other things and you're giving me your word as an officer?"

"Please, Lieutenant."

Lieutenant Carson smiled and shook her head, "Well, I do need to use a latrine, but I'm not going to help you guys."

Jim smiled at her and said, "Thanks, Lieutenant."

Lieutenant Carson stood up and brushed her clothing. "I'm giving you guys a direct order, forget about this whole idea." With that she turned and walked towards the office. Jim and Walker traded hats and shirts.

"Mac, I sure hope we get away with this."

"If we don't, you can always fly us out of here in this crate and hope it holds together 'til we get home."

Jim and Wright were almost to the office door when Lieutenant Carson walked out talking to a staff sergeant. "Wright, you wait outside. If someone comes, rap on that door twice and once more when the coast is clear."

"Mac, don't take too long!"

Jim walked in the door and everything was just as Walker had said. He headed straight for the first desk and started frantically hunting for Walker's forms. Surprisingly, it didn't take him long to locate both. This done, he pulled open the file cabinet's top drawer, pulled out the first blank form he found and ripped out the carbon paper. He threw the blanks in the trash and placed the carbon between the two forms. Moving to the typewriter, he picked up the correction fluid and wiped out the helicopter number. As he blew it dry, he was glad he'd thought of this because once he'd seen the forms, he knew there were far too many things to fill in. Once dry, he placed the forms with carbon in the typewriter and typed in the new numbers. Quickly, he threw the carbon away and placed the forms back where he found them. Last, he switched the log book from the sergeant's desk with the one in his shirt, and changed the number on the clip board

form beside Walker's name. As he walked around the desk, he heard
Wright rap on the door twice.

Jim walked outside just as a staff sergeant approached. The sergeant
saluted and Jim returned his salute. "Sir, can I help you?" the sergeant
asked.

Jim responded just as any other officer, "Is your CO around,
Sergeant?"

"No, Sir, but I can get him for you in just a second, if you'll stop
back inside."

"Thank you anyway, Sergeant, I've got a couple of other things to
do, I'll just stop back in an hour or two."

"Yes, Sir."

Jim looked over at Wright, "Let's go, Specialist."

Jim and Wright walked away as the staff sergeant entered the
maintenance office. "Mac, you didn't forget the log book did you?"

"Nope, it's inside my shirt. Man, you talk about being close, I'm
sure glad he didn't get back thirty seconds sooner!" Jim, hardly able
to control his excitement, slapped Wright's hand, "We did it, Wright,
we really did it."

"Mac, let's don't celebrate yet, we still have to get out of here. I
just hope that staff sergeant doesn't notice he's got a log book missing."

"I'll drink to that."

They moved quickly back to Walker, who saw them coming and
moved to the new ship. Jim handed Walker the log book and said,
"It worked like a charm, let's get out of here!"

"Lieutenant Carson isn't back yet, give me my shirt back and go
untie the rotor blades."

"Yes, Sir."

Lieutenant Carson approached as they were changing shirts and
quickly climbed into the chopper.

"Well, Mac, I see all went well."

"Yes, Ma'am, thank you, we couldn't have done it without you."

"Somehow I get the impression you'd have found a way."

Walker, who was already strapped into his seat, yelled, "Clear!"
Jim responded, "Clear."

Walker hit the start switch and yelled at Jim, "Mac, you want to
drive?"

Without responding, Jim climbed into the co-pilot's seat. He strapped himself in and plugged in his helmet. Walker knew keeping a crew chief happy was easy; give him some stick time and treat him like a person should be treated and you got along just fine. Walker asked ground control for permission to taxi. Permission was given along with instructions for the path to be followed to the runway. As they taxied out of the maintenance area they went by several choppers parked off to the side. Jim had been looking each ship over carefully and on the next to the last ship he saw what he was looking for.

"Mr. Walker, set it down quick! I'll be right back."

Walker, who didn't know what had happened, instantly dropped the chopper to the pavement. By the time Walker had it on the ground, Jim was unstrapped and climbing out of his seat. "Mac, what's wrong?"

Jim didn't answer as he unplugged his helmet and jumped out the door. He ran to the Huey parked only slightly behind and off to the side. In one leap, he jumped through the ship's open cargo doors, grabbed the large water jug and started to leave when he had another thought. Setting down the water jug, he ran around to the right side of the chopper and opened the storage compartment door. There it was, a tool box. Jim grabbed it and ran without even closing the door. The tool box was so heavy, he knew it had to be well stocked. With the tool box in one hand and the water jug in the other, it was all he could do to walk fast. Wright saw him coming and jumped out to help. As Jim threw the tool box on board 647, he looked back to see two enlisted men running towards them as fast as they could. He jumped on board and motioned to Walker to take off quickly. Jim sat in the cargo door briefly and watched the two men grow smaller and smaller as Walker moved it down the runway. As he turned to climb back into the co-pilot's seat, Jim saw Lieutenant Carson smiling at him and slowly nod. Jim returned her smile and winked quickly at her. He then climbed back into his seat, plugged in his helmet and said, "Hi, I'm back."

"I can see! You're crazy, you know that?"

"Yes, Sir, but I got us a water jug and a tool box, neither of which I could get out of supply back at Tay Ninh."

"Any idea who the two trying to run us down were?"

"My guess is they were Skychiefs and that was their aircraft whose load we just lightened. Come to think of it, this was probably their aircraft also. I'll bet that's why they were parked there, they'd brought a crew down to pick up their ship."

All three men laughed a good, deep, hard laugh. Lieutenant Carson, not having a helmet, just sat there wondering what was so funny. Once they'd stopped laughing, Walker said, "Mac, you've got it."

Jim took hold of the controls. "I've got it. We have enough fuel to make it to Tay Ninh?"

"No, but it doesn't make any difference; we have to stop at Long Binh Replacement and pick up some new pilots. We can get fuel there."

"You didn't tell me about that."

"Mac, I don't tell you everything I know, and in case you've forgotten, I am the officer in this crew!"

After refueling, they made the short hop to Long Binh Replacement Depot. Once on the ground, Mr. Walker told Wright to go over to a group of men seated not too far away and ask if any were headed for the 187th. Shortly, Wright returned followed by six warrant officers carrying their duffel bags.

"Mac, are we going to get off the ground with all that weight?"

"I don't know, Sir. If I had known there'd be six of them, I wouldn't have topped it off with fuel. They probably average one hundred sixty pounds each with another eighty in each duffel bag. That's two hundred forty times six, or fourteen hundred forty pounds, plus the three of us and Lieutenant Carson. Of course, we don't have the guns and ammo, and this thing is supposed to have a brand new engine, but the thermometer says forty-two degrees. That's awfully hot, well over one hundred degrees Fahrenheit. I don't know how much humidity there is, but you can bet a bunch. I guess there's only one way to find out, give it a little try and if you can't get it off the ground all we can do is kick one of them out, which should make it light enough to get airborne."

As Jim talked, he and Walker watched the new pilots load their duffel bags and eyeball Lieutenant Carson as they climbed in. It was obvious she was becoming very uncomfortable with the looks. Lieutenant Carson looked up in time to see Jim and Walker looking back over the radio console. Unsnapping her seatbelt, she climbed over the duffel bags and leaned over to talk to Mr. Walker. Walker pushed his lip mike out towards her and keyed his switch to make it easier to hear what she had to say.

"Mr. Walker, take me back to Vung Tau."

"What?"

"You heard me, take me back to Vung Tau."

"Lieutenant, I can't do that. I'm supposed to take you to Tay Ninh. Besides, I'm not really anxious to take this ship back to Vung Tau right away."

"Come on, Mr. Walker, I've changed my mind. I'm not going to Tay Ninh. I want to go back to Vung Tau."

Walker turned just enough to look Jim in the eyes. He shrugged his shoulders and gave an 'Oh, brother' look, then spoke into the mike so she couldn't hear. "Sir, she does outrank you."

"Yeah, I'm painfully aware of that." Walker turned back to Lieutenant Carson. "Lieutenant, I've got orders to take you and these men to Tay Ninh. I can't go back to Vung Tau."

"Mister, I don't care what your orders are. I'm giving you new ones. Take me to Vung Tau!"

"Yes, Ma'am." Walker turned around, looked out the windshield, and spoke to himself. Jim didn't need the intercom to tell what Walker had said. He was getting better at lip reading and the 'well, shit' came across Walker's lips as clearly as if he'd keyed his mike.

Jim wasn't very happy about going back to Vung Tau, either. He'd been looking forward to getting home before the rest of the flight and having a couple hours of daylight. He could take a nice hot shower then hit the club before anyone else got there. That was out now. They'd be lucky to make it home before dark. Walker was already on the radio getting the necessary flight clearances. Once airborne, Walker said, "You wanna drive?"

"Sure."

"Okay, Mac, you got it. Keep it on this heading and just shy of red line. I'm not going to fiddle around taking this bitch home. I just hope some bastard at Tay Ninh doesn't raise hell with me because his piece of ass for the night changed her mind."

Jim held it just shy of the one hundred twenty knot red line all the way down to Vung Tau. As a result, it didn't take long to get there.

There's a lot of difference between one hundred twenty knots and the casual eighty knot cruising speed.

Once on the ground, Lieutenant Carson jumped out with her bag and took only a couple of steps before setting it down and returning to the ship. She had gotten out on Jim's side, so it was his door she opened. He pushed his lip mike out for her to speak and keyed it so Wright and Walker could also hear what she had to say. "I just came back to thank you guys for a very interesting and unusual day." Looking at Jim, "I'm glad I met you." Glancing over to Walker, "Both of you." Jim smiled as she stepped down and shut his door. She waved good-bye as she stooped to pick up her bag. Walker watched Jim wave good-bye slowly, and with a strange look on his face, turn the wave into a salute. Lieutenant Carson, whose eyes hadn't moved from Jim's, broke into a big smile and returned the salute.

Walker, who couldn't believe what he was seeing said, "What the hell was that all about?" There was only silence for a response. "Mac, what'd you do, fall in love with that whore?"

Jim laughed and said, "Don't be silly."

The two men sat and watched her back side as she moved briskly across the pavement. "I'll tell ya, Mac, that's one hell of a lot of woman!"

"Yes, Sir."

Only slightly sarcastically Walker asked, "Be okay if we go home now?"

Jim, still not wanting to take his eyes off her, nodded his head and replied, "Yes, Sir."

As Walker pulled pitch to the rotors and headed down the runway Jim asked, "Mr. Walker, can we red line it going home, too?"

"Yep. You got it, and I'll get us as straight a path home as artillery will allow."

Sign that greeted all persons coming from flight line to company area.

Huey wrecked by drunk pilot on way to test fly after being released from maintenance.

Hot LZ pickup. Note troops behind protective cover.

Author on doorgunner's side of ship. Note brass catcher on M60 to prevent tail rotor damage.

Author and one of his ships with Blackhawk symbol.

View of pilots' heads as seen by Author during flight.

Officers' shower after 122mm rocket hit a few feet away.

Hueys parked in revetments.

Left to right: urinal, latrine (white building), and enlisted men's showers, with flight platoons' hooches behind the photographer.

Chaplain holding worship services at Cu Chi.

Members of 187th AHC on flight going over.

12

"For he will command his angels concerning you to guard you in all your ways." Psalm 91:11 NIV

What's In
A Hand?

In the west, orange and red rays streaked skyward from the rapidly setting sun. It was beautiful, even though the black bellowing smoke from the burning fuel dump in Saigon made a sobering contrast. VC sapper* squads had blown and burned a large part of the Saigon fuel storage area the night before. As a result, from fifteen hundred feet above Tay Ninh, one could still see the flames that leaped skyward changing into clouds of deep, rolling black smoke, which rose several thousand feet.

Jim was glad they were on short final approach. It meant they'd be on the ground ahead of the flight and with enough daylight left to pull his daily inspection. With just a little luck, he could even get a warm shower and still have plenty of time for a drink at the club.

Once on the ground, Mr. Walker parked beside the fuel pumps for Wright to top it off. From there he took it to their revetment and started shut down procedures. Once Wright had opened the pilots' doors, Jim climbed out and saluted each new officer and shook hands. He

---

*Sapper - V.C. and NVA demolition people. Usually willing to blow themselves up along with their target.

introduced himself and was giving them directions to the company area when Mr. Walker turned around and shouted, "Hey, Mac! Put your helmet on!"

Jim excused himself and motioned to Wright to tie down the rotors. He noticed the new pilots just stood around as though they didn't know what to do. As he put on his helmet, then plugged it in he said, "Yes, Sir."

"Mac, the flight's on long final and Chalk Two has lost tail rotor control!"

Jim jumped into the cargo area and flipped the switch allowing him to hear the flight.

"Chalk Two, this is Lead. I've got clearance from the tower for you to put it down on the runway. Flight, the rest of us will move directly into the revetments. Chalk Two, good luck and remember to keep your airspeed up."

"Roger, Lead, see you in the club."

Jim, looking out the cargo door, could see the single ship headed for the runway as the flight approached short final on the revetments. The brave words of Chalk Two's pilot didn't hide the nervousness in his voice as he called out his airspeed and altitude.

The tail rotor's sole function was to prevent the helicopter from spinning like a top at slow speeds. Once the helicopter reached a speed of about sixty knots, the air flowing by it would hold a Huey straight, so to land a Huey without a tail rotor required landing on a pair of skids at about sixty knots. Jim knew the procedure. Twice he'd come in without tail rotor control. Fortunately, on both occasions, his pilots had the skill to do it right; one little mistake meant a crash and roll. There wasn't any question in his mind it was the most dangerous of all the emergency landing procedures. Perhaps it was even more dangerous because the pilots never practiced it. Whatever the reason, Jim was glad he wasn't on board Chalk Two.

Everyone's eyes were glued to the single ship as it rapidly approached the runway. Mr. Walker broke the silence, "He's too high. He'll never make it. I know what he's done, he's forgotten the runway's at twelve feet above sea level and his altimeter is set at zero. He hasn't made the mental twelve foot subtraction. He's twelve feet too high! He thinks he's at twenty-four feet and he's really at thirty-six!"

Jim ripped off his helmet as Walker switched the radio over so he could talk to Chalk Two. Jim yelled in terror, "Wright, he's going to crash! Come on, let's go!" Pointing his finger at the closest pilot still standing there holding his duffel bag, Jim ordered, "You, get the fire extinguisher out of our ship and follow us!"

As they ran, Jim kept praying the pilot would touch down with both skids at the same time. If he didn't, he'd bounce and flip over.

Jim, and the rest of the group behind him, stopped running about a hundred feet from where the broken machine first bounced. They stood and watched as it slid only a short way before spinning and skipping sideways. Then like a giant wounded monster, it flipped over onto its right side and died, throwing rotor blade pieces and various other parts of its anatomy in all directions. Jim and Wright ran to the wounded chopper and started climbing up its skids. Screams of intense pain could be heard inside as Wright opened the pilot's door to help him out. Jim climbed inside to find the gunner struggling to climb out. Shouting at the gunner over the continuing screams of the injured crew chief, Page, Jim asked, "You okay?"

"I see two of everything."

One of the new pilots had climbed up to help, "Sir, help him down he's got a concussion."

That done, Jim climbed on down inside. The screams of pain coming from both the crew chief and peter pilot caused Jim to lose precious seconds wondering if he could get both out. As he looked at the peter pilot he could see through the window the others were working from the outside to free him. Jim turned to the crew chief. The smell of JP-4 fuel penetrated his nostrils and he knew all caution had to be discarded.

The crew chief's left hand was pinned between the ground and the edge of the ceiling. Two bones protruding from the compound fracture made it a grotesque sight with blood seeming to be everywhere. Jim heard the psst!psst! of the fire extinguisher as he ripped his belt from its loops.

"Page, this is going to hurt!" Page only nodded his head and continued to moan. Quickly, Jim slipped the belt under Page's arm, hooked the webbing into the buckle and pulled it as tight as he could. Page let out a scream that caused Jim to look back at him lying there gritting

his teeth. But the bleeding had pretty well stopped. Looking up at
Wright standing on the skid looking in, Jim shouted, "Wright, try
to rock it so we can get his hand free!"

"You got it!"

Looking back at some officers standing there watching Wright, he
shouted, "Hey you guys, give me a hand!"

Jim looked at Page and said, "Pull." It was useless, the hand wouldn't
budge. Then it happened—Jim heard someone yell, "Fire!"

Wright, still on the skid shouted down, "Mac, it's on fire! Get the
hell out of there!"

Jim felt his heart jump and the adrenalin rush through his system.
Page almost in tears cried, "Mac, don't leave me!"

Jim's hand moved swiftly in and out of his pocket. In the same flick
of a second that the blade flashed from its handle, Wright shouted,
"Mac! Get out! It's going to blow!"

As though in that same fraction of a second Page shouted in panic,
"Do it, Mac! Do it!" The blade was sharp and Jim struck where the
bone protruded. With the first slice, Page let out a scream that came
from the very depths of his soul, and collapsed into a state of unconscious shock.

As a farm boy Jim had helped butcher hogs and cattle since
childhood. He knew how much force it took to cut raw meat and with
the second slice the hand was completely severed. Next, he cut the
two shoulder straps on Page's chicken plate, with each requiring only one quick stroke. At the same time but with his left hand, Jim ripped open the velcro strap at the waist allowing the chicken plate to
fall free.

Only a few short seconds had passed since Wright's first shout of
fire. Now there were several people yelling, 'Fire!', but Wright was
still standing on the skid waiting to help get Page out. Jim quickly
refolded the knife and slipped it back into his pocket. With the
adrenalin still flowing in his body, he threw Page over his shoulder
in a fireman's carry. Using the pilot's seats as steps, he climbed high
enough for Wright to reach the still unconscious Page. With the help
of a pilot who had joined Wright, they got Page over the side and
into the arms of others. Now there was only Wright left on the skid
to help Jim out as the others had all started to run away from the

burning aircraft. As Jim threw his leg over the side, Wright jumped and Jim saw the flames leaping up from the engine compartment. He could feel the heat and hear the crackling of the fire. Jumping as far away as he could, he hit the ground and fell, rolling over once and coming to his feet on a run. Only two steps had been taken before the explosion behind him knocked him once again to the ground. This time Walker was there to help him up and the two moved quickly to a safe distance where the rest of the group greeted them with applause and cheers. Everyone wanted to shake Jim's hand and pat his back. Yet the fire behind him drew their attention like a magnet. Jim also turned and looked back and for the first time, heard the screams and realized they hadn't been able to get the peter pilot out. The burning blob of human flesh caused his heart to sink rapidly, and the screams of pain caused shivers to race up and down his spine. The burning body twisted and jerked and its face contorted with pain making it look as though its eyes would jump from their sockets. Someone off to the side asked, "Major, should I shoot him?"

Major Hobbs said, "Give me your M16. I'll do it." Before the major's hand could reach the offered rifle, a second explosion sent a giant fireball skyward. With that explosion the pilot's pain ended.

Jim turned and walked through the crowd hypnotized by the burning mass in front of it. As he passed through the back of the group, he saw Halsey approaching and thought, *I hope I don't have to put up with any of his shit.* Mr. Halsey was unaware of all that had just transpired, other than the obviously burning aircraft.

"Mac, what happened?"

Jim, with tears in his eyes, only looked at the ground, then slowly shook his head and shrugged his shoulders, "MacLaughlin, you're a mess, no hat, no belt. Where the hell's your belt, anyway?"

Jim never knew why he did it. In fact, it happened almost before he realized what he'd done. Maybe it was just a gut response which caused his right hand to fly up with all the force left in his body and strike Halsey in the left cheek, sending him sprawling to the ground. Halsey looked up in an expression of shock that changed to a smile. Finally, he sat up and laughed as he said, "Thanks, MacLaughlin, you don't know how happy this makes me."

Jim didn't respond. He simply turned and walked away, sure that by morning he'd be, at the very least, a Spec-Four again. Jim hadn't gone very far when Kenny pulled up in the platoon quarter-ton pickup.

"Mac, you've got blood all over you. You hurt?"

Jim looked at himself for the first time and realized how bad he did look. Blood was on both hands, arms and down his right pant leg. "I'm okay, Kenny. Do me a favor, will you?"

"Name it."

"Give me a ride back to the revetment so I can pick up my stuff, and the new ship's log book."

"Hop in," Kenny turned around and drove off quickly.

Once at the ship, Jim collected his gear and was back in the pickup in less than a minute. As Kenny drove towards the maintenance area he said, "Mac, I saw you hit Halsey. I just want you to know I'll swear he fell down on his own if you want."

Jim smiled and patted Kenny on the shoulder replying, "Thanks Kenny, but you don't want to end up in the brig with me, do you?"

"Hey, if it gets rid of Halsey..."

Once back in the company area, Jim showered and put on clean clothes. He was in the mess hall eating when Gillett came in. Their eyes met and Jim knew it wasn't good. "Mac, the CO wants to see you."

"Would it be okay if I finish eating first?"

"Sure, I've got to go find Kenny anyway. He wants to see both of you. Why don't you meet me in the hooch?"

Jim entered the hooch and heard muffled sobs. Walking back through the hooch, he found Green sitting on his bunk crying, "Green, what's wrong?"

Green only shook his head and said, "Nothing."

Jim noticed the letter in Green's hand and sat down beside him, "Come on, Green, you might as well tell me."

"I got a letter from my mom. Mary Ann, she's my girl; we were going to get married when I got home. My mom says she announced her plans to marry some guy she met at college. In two months she'll be Mrs. Somebody Else. Oh, Mac, I loved her so much. My chest, the pain . . .the pain! Why couldn't she wait? I waited for her. I never messed around, not so much as a flirt. I love her so much!" Green lowered his head into his hands and cried.

Jim patted his shoulder and said, "I'm sorry, Green, I know how you feel."

Green, between sobs asked, "You got a girl, Mac?"

"No, she dumped me when I joined the Army. I wrote her letters but she wasn't even kind enough to write back."

"She get married?"

"Not yet. She marries the day before I get home. I get the privilege of thinking about her on her honeymoon my first night home."

"How long did it take you to get over it?"

"I haven't. The pain's still there but I go on. They say time heals all wounds; maybe it will, maybe it won't. Right now, Green, I think when I'm fifty I'll still love her, but maybe by the time I'm fifty I won't even remember she ever was."

"Thanks, Mac, but somehow it doesn't help."

"I know, Green. I know. Try getting drunk and passing out, when you're unconscious or asleep, it doesn't hurt anymore."

Green sat there and cried with Jim holding him. Shortly, the hooch door opened and Gillett hollered, "Mac, you in there?"

"Yeah, I'll be right there."

Green fell flat on his bunk and covered his head with a pillow as Jim stood to leave, but turning back he said, "Green, you might as well have it straight. The hurting doesn't go away, it just gets to the point where you think it's normal. Once you reach that point, you'll forget what it feels like not to hurt. Then you'll think you're back to normal and who knows, maybe you are. At least you don't realize you're still hurting."

Jim joined Gillett and Kenny waiting just outside the door, "Hi, Mac."

"Hi, Kenny. What's the Old Man want you for?"

"Oh, Halsey probably told him I saw something."

Gillett interrupted to say. "You two go ahead and go on over to the orderly room. I've got to take a leak. I'll be right with you."

Kenny and Jim headed in the direction of the orderly room. "Mac, this has to be a rather familiar walk for you."

"Yeah, one I'm getting tired of."

"Mac, tell me what you're going to say so I'll have the same story."

"Look, Kenny, tell him the truth. There isn't any point in lying, there were too many other guys standing around. All you'll do by lying is get yourself in trouble, and it won't help me in the end."

They entered the orderly room and were told to sit down. Kenny leaned toward Jim and whispered, "I'm going to tell him I didn't see a thing. I was watching the fire."

Jim nodded his head. The two sat silently for what seemed like hours. Jim tried to think of all the possibilities and decided his only chance was to plead memory lapse, due to what he'd just been through. Gillett came in shortly after they'd been seated and was called into the CO's office. Finally, he came back out and said, "Kenny, Major Hobbs will see you now."

Kenny entered, had the usual problem walking to the CO's desk, came to attention and saluted. "Sir, Specialist Kenny reports."

Major Hobbs returned the salute but kept Kenny at attention. "Specialist, tell me what you saw happening on the flight line this evening."

Kenny told the Major everything just as he remembered it, except he left out seeing Jim hit Halsey.

"Specialist, did you leave anything out?"

"No, Sir."

"You didn't happen to see Specialist MacLaughlin hit Mr. Halsey, did you?"

"No, Sir. Did he do that, Sir?"

"Yes, he did!"

"Well, Sir, I was watching the fire and driving at the same time and didn't see anything like that."

"Specialist, have any of the other enlisted men said anything about seeing him hit Mr. Halsey?"

"No, Sir."

"Very well, you're dismissed."

Kenny saluted and left. As he walked by MacLaughlin he whispered, "I told Hobbs I didn't see a thing." With that, Kenny walked outside and found a place in the dark, where he could wait unseen and watch the door.

In the meantime, Major Hobbs turned to the three men standing along the wall, "Captain Wolf, what do you think?"

"Well, Sir, he could be telling the truth, or he could be lying. Either way, as long as he sticks to that story, he's worthless as a witness."

"Mr. Halsey, how about you?"

"Sir, I think the man's lying through his teeth. He was in that quarter ton headed straight for us. He had to see it!"

"Yes, so you said. Sergeant Gillett, your turn."

"Yes, Sir. Well, Sir, I agree with Captain Wolf."

Hobbs smiled and said, "Very diplomatic of you, Sergeant."

Captain Wolf turned to Mr. Halsey and said, "Too bad none of the officers saw it."

"Yes, Sir, it is. But just like you, they were watching the fire."

"There wasn't anyone besides you who could possibly have seen anything?"

"No, I don't think so. I got there after everyone else, and MacLaughlin had started to leave by himself."

Captain Wolf, with the irritation he felt showing, barked, "Mr. Halsey, stand at attention! Damn it, you play this game with the enlisted men all the time and that's part of the reason we're here now. I am a Captain, and your superior, and you will address me as such! We're not in the club having a beer and you damn well better remember it!"

"Yes, Sir! I will, Sir. The point is, Captain, I was struck by an NCO and I want him jailed for it!"

Major Hobbs broke in, "Captain, Mr. Halsey, this isn't getting us anywhere! Sergeant, did you tell Specialist MacLaughlin why he's here?"

"No, Sir."

"Okay, Sergeant, bring him in."

"Yes, Sir." Gillett walked out to the orderly room where Jim was waiting. Jim's mind had been at work and he had decided several things. One, he wasn't going to admit to hitting Halsey. Two, they must not have any officers as witnesses or they wouldn't have messed with Kenny. Third, and the thing that bothered him only slightly, was Kenny had said Hobbs, not Appleton. Why would the Major be running things?

Gillett looked at Jim and said, "Your turn, Mac."

"Gillett, can I talk to you first?"

Gillett glanced over to the CQ seated only a few feet away at the company clerk's desk. "I don't think that would be a good idea. Let's go, Mac."

Jim nodded his head only slightly and knocked on the door.
"Come in."

This time he wasn't surprised to see Halsey standing alone against
the far wall with Captain Wolf seated in the chair Major Hobbs had
occupied only the night before. Once again, he made a sharp entrance
and came to attention directly in front of Major Hobbs. "Sir, Specialist
MacLaughlin reports."

Jim raised his right arm in salute and it was a real race to see which
man got his arm down first—Hobbs returning the salute, or Jim.

"Specialist, I assume you know why you're here."

"I haven't been told, Sir."

"At ease, Specialist. Mac, we're all very proud of what you did
to get Page out. You put your life on the line. Captain Wolf wants
to put you in for a Silver Star. Personally, I think you deserve it. The
only problem is, Mr. Halsey thinks we should send you to jail. What
do you think?"

"Sir, I think the medal would be very nice."

Major Hobbs slowly shook his head.

"Perhaps, Sir, it would be best if we just forgot about the medal
and also Mr. Halsey's idea. I'm even willing to transfer to another
helicopter company, if that would be acceptable, Sir."

"Did you hit him, Specialist?"

There was a long pause, during which Jim tried to figure what Hobbs
had in his hand that he was willing to play verbal poker. "Sir, I'm
not in the habit of lying and I'm not going to start now."

"That doesn't answer my question, yes, or no."

Jim looked over at Captain Wolf, "Sir, do I have any trouble with
any officer except Mr. Halsey?"

"Mac, you're not answering the Major's question."

Major Hobbs spoke, "Yes, or no, Specialist!"

"Sir, if I say 'yes', what happens to me?"

"We'll talk about that after you say 'yes.' We're not playing poker,
MacLaughlin, because your hand's exposed. Now I want a straight
answer out of you."

"Sir, can I tell you what happened?"

"Specialist, I'm trying to be nice. Now, I'm giving you a direct
order, yes or no?"

"In that case, no, Sir."

"Okay, now that we've finally got that out, tell me what happened."

"Sir, I've changed my mind. I don't care to explain."

"Just who the hell do you think you're talking to, MacLaughlin? I gave you an order. Now I want an explanation, and I don't want anymore of your smart ass answers. You got that, Specialist?"

"Yes, Sir."

"Well, you'd better, or you'll find yourself a PFC just because of your mouth. Now everyone in this room knows you hit Mr. Halsey, so we might just as well find out why!"

"Sir, I'll not admit to hitting Mr. Halsey and I don't think you'd expect me to. I knew their chopper was going to crash, and in my hurry to give aid to the guys in it, I didn't take the time to get my hat out of the chopper I was in. Mr. Halsey stopped me afterwards and dressed me down for not having a hat on or a belt. I'd used my belt as a tourniquet on Page's arm. He also didn't like my uniform being so dirty. It was Page's blood and the dirt from being knocked down when their ship blew."

Jim could see both Major Hobbs and Captain Wolf look over at Halsey. It was obvious he hadn't told them some or all of it. Major Hobbs spoke, "Mr. Halsey, is there anything about Specialist MacLaughlin's story you disagree with?"

"Only that he could have explained, instead of hitting me, Sir. He didn't even try to explain..."

Jim interrupted, "Sir, you could have fallen down and busted your nose and blamed it on me."

Halsey shouted, "MacLaughlin, you've got more brass than a fuckin' monkey. You know that?"

Hobbs interrupted, "Okay, stop it! Both of you, at attention! Mr. Halsey, you're dismissed. Wait in the other room."

"Yes, Sir." Halsey saluted and left.

Jim, still at attention, waited for Major Hobbs to speak, "At ease, Mac. How old are you?"

"I just turned twenty, Sir." There was a long pause before Hobbs spoke.

"He's right, you know. You're brass, for one so young. It's really gotten you in trouble this time. I understand you also stole that helicopter today. Oh, don't look so worried. I know all about it. You switched shirts with Mr. Walker and forged his signature. You've had quite a day, haven't you: stole a Huey, cut a man's arm off, and busted Mr. Halsey in the mouth."

"Sir, I never said I did that and unless there is a witness..."

"MacLaughlin, shut up before I chew you up and throw you to the dogs."

Jim stood there silently. "Specialist, I'll tell you what I'll do. You accept an Article 15 and I'll only take one stripe and a couple hundred dollars."

"And if I don't accept it?"

"Mr. Halsey will probably insist on a court martial. Which would mean jail if convicted."

"Can I think about it, Sir?"

"Hell, no, you can't think about it! You know that. Make up your mind. Now!"

"Sir, are there any witnesses?"

"That's not necessary and you know it. All you have to do is look at his swollen black eye."

"Sir, I'll take the court martial."

"That's the stupidest thing you could do and you know it!"

"Yes, Sir, but a lot could change between now and then. I could be killed or wounded by then and, if not, I'll go into it denying everything."

"That's enough, Specialist, I get the message! Now let me give you one: right now, you're only looking at thirty days down at LBJ. You kill Halsey, or even try, I'll see to it you spend the rest of your life there! You got that?"

Jim allowed himself to let only the slightest smile cross his lips. "Yes, Sir, I've got it."

"Very well, you're dismissed." Jim saluted, turned and left.

On his way through the orderly room Halsey's eyes met his. Jim smiled broadly at Mr. Halsey and walked on by. Neither man spoke. Jim stepped outside and took a deep breath. Kenny walked up, "Mac, how did you come out?"

"I took a court martial."

"Damn that Halsey! It's too bad that frag the other night wasn't live."

"You know, Kenny, I'm beginning to think the same thing."

"Come on, Mac, I'll buy you a beer."

Jim put his arm around Kenny's shoulder, "Kenny, that's the best offer I've had tonight."

Back in the CO's office, Major Hobbs looked at Gillett and said, "Sergeant, you're dismissed. On your way out tell Mr. Halsey to step in."

Gillett came to attention and saluted, "Sir, could I speak openly to you?"

"I wish you would, Sergeant."

"Without repercussions, Sir?"

"What do you want to say, Sergeant?"

"Sir, do you know how this feud between Mac and Mr. Halsey got started?"

"I believe it was the broken window incident, where Mr. Halsey ended up paying for the window and getting an Article 15."

"Yes, Sir. Ever since then Mr. Halsey has made life unpleasant for MacLaughlin. I'm surprised he hasn't punched him out a long time ago."

"Or thrown a frag under his bed?"

"Major, you know as well as I do, Mac didn't do that."

Major Hobbs looked startled, "Gillett, you know who did it, don't you?"

"No, Sir."

"Don't lie to me, Sergeant!" He paused, "Wait a minute, you did it!"

"No, Sir, I didn't and I've got enough witnesses as to where I was to prove it."

"Well, then, you know who did!"

"Yes, Sir, I do! And so does MacLaughlin. In fact, he knew when you offered him your deal. But as much as he hates Mr. Halsey, he refuses to burn someone else for trying to help him."

"How did he find out?" "He guessed and, after leaving here the other night he simply tricked the guy into admitting it."

"You really like MacLaughlin, don't you?"

"Yes, Sir, I do. And I don't think he deserves what he's going to get out of this. The whole company would be better off without Mr. Halsey. It wouldn't be better off without Mac."

"Who did the fragging, Sergeant?"

"No, Sir. You said I could speak freely. Sir, you and I both know in the States Mac wouldn't stand a chance. But here, Sir, you're the law. You don't have to send him up regardless of what Mr. Halsey wants. Sir, you won't have any more trouble from Mac, he's only got about two and a half months left in country. He's put up with more than he should have had to already. You can hold this over his head if he gets out of line, which he won't, and I think Captain Wolf will agree. That's all, Sir."

"Very well, Sergeant. You're dismissed, and thank you for your honesty."

Gillett saluted and left.

In the club, Jim, Kenny and Athia were all on their way to a good drunk. Gillett walked in, sat down, and was the first to speak, "Well, Mac, how you are going to get out of this one?"

Jim laughed and said, "Something will come along, you have to have faith."

"Mac, I don't think you truly grasp the severity of this situation."

"You're wrong, Gillett, I grasp it. I just don't know what the hell I'm supposed to do about it."

"Well, for starters, you could have taken the Article 15."

"No, I'll get to the court martial and drag out every little shitty thing Halsey has ever done. I may go to jail, but I'll fix it so he never gets promoted again."

"Mac, don't kid yourself; besides it's not worth it."

Kenny interrupted, "Gillett, I've got a question. Do you think we could scare Halsey out of pressing charges?"

"Not without the officers' help."

"They'd help, there are several of them who don't like Halsey any more than we do."

"I don't know. I'm not sure they'd risk it for an NCO. What kind of scare do you have in mind?"

"Well, you know Mr. Lucas is always running some kind of lottery. Maybe we could get him to run one on when Halsey gets killed."

"That's enough! I don't want to have any more of that kind of talk!"

"Gillett, I wasn't going to suggest we really kill him, just talk like we will."

"It could backfire, too, and make the bastard determined to send Mac up, regardless of what happens to him."

"But, Gillett, if the officers will help, they could convince him to drop the charges."

"I don't know. What do you think, Mac?"

"Sounds like the best idea I've heard so far."

Gillett saw Wright walk in and said, "By the way, Wright will get a Bronze Star for helping get Page out of that chopper."

Jim looked at Gillett and said, "Big deal. He can take that Bronze Star and it'll still cost him a dime for a cup of coffee."

Wright walked up and sat down, "Hi, fellows." Everyone returned Wright's greeting before he said, "Hey, Mac, did you hear the good news?"

"What's that, Wright?"

"I get a Bronze Star for this afternoon!"

"Hey, that's great, Wright! I'm really glad, you deserve it! Congratulations."

"Mac, could I fly as your permanent gunner?"

"Wright, I don't really think you'd want to. For one thing, I probably won't be flying more than a day or two."

"What are you talking about?"

Jim and Gillett exchanged glances. "Wright, you get a Bronze Star; I get a court martial."

Wright couldn't believe it. "What in the world for?"

"Halsey says I hit him."

"When did you do that, and why?"

"Why, Wright? I'm surprised at you, not even asking if I hit him." Jim smiled and added, "You know I'd never hit a superior officer."

Wright sat there looking stunned as Gillett said, "Mac, let's go see what's happening on the other side."

The two got up and walked through the door to the NCO side. Both drank Jack Daniels Black and RC as they talked, figuring it would be their last chance. The hours slipped by quickly. Finally, Gillett reminded Jim he had to fly tomorrow and it was past midnight.

Jim used the latrine and was almost back to the hooch when, on impulse, he made a right turn and headed for the hospital.

Walking through the big double doors, he entered a brightly lit hallway. Not sure where to go he started to walk forward slowly, when a nurse, carrying a tray, stepped out of a door just in front of him, "May I help you, Specialist?"

"Yes, Ma'am, I'm looking for a Spec-Four Page. He was brought in earlier, with his left hand cut off."

"Oh, yes! I remember him. He's two doors down but you can't go in there now, it's almost twelve-thirty. He's had major surgery and wouldn't be coherent."

"Lieutenant, please. I'm the guy who cut his hand off."

"Oh!" There was a short pause before she said, "In that case, we can check and see if he's awake." The Lieutenant led the way to Page's bedside and turned on a bedside light. Very softly she said, "Specialist, if you're awake, you have a visitor."

There was no response, so the Lieutenant turned to Jim and said, "I'm sorry, but he's asleep and you'll have to leave."

"Lieutenant, could I just sit here in a chair for a while?"

"No, I'm afraid not."

As they turned to leave, a Captain walked in. The Lieutenant addressed him, "Doctor, this is the man who cut Specialist Page's hand off."

The Captain looked at Jim and said, "Tell me about it."

"There's not much to tell, Sir. He was pinned inside a Huey that was on fire. The only way to get him out was to cut off the hand where the arm bones were sticking out."

"What did you use?"

Jim reached in his pocket and slowly pulled out his knife. He held it out slightly, pushed the button and the blade sprang into a lock position with a clang, "This."

The Lieutenant's eyes bulged only slightly larger than the Captain's, whose mouth was also hanging open. The Captain closed his mouth and swallowed, then said, "Where did you get that thing?"

Jim answered as though it wasn't any big deal, "Supply. It's Army issue. Sir, did you happen to save the belt I used as a tourniquet?" The doctor looked down at Jim's waist and then back up questioningly, "Sir, I had another belt, but I would like to have the buckle back."

The captain turned to the nurse and said, "Lieutenant, see if you can find his belt and buckle, please."

"Yes, Doctor."

Looking back at Jim he said, "You can put that thing away. I'd also like to say, you did a good job. Are you going to get a medal?"

"No, Sir, I'm getting court martialed."

"For cutting his hand off?"

"No, Sir. Could I speak to you in confidence, Captain?"

"You bet! I want to hear this. Just a minute, I'll take off my gown. Come on over here and sit down."

Jim told the doctor the whole story, leaving out nothing. He added the necessary background information on Mr. Halsey and had just finished, when the nurse walked in. "Specialist, here's the buckle. I don't think you'd want the belt."

"Thank you, Lieutenant."

The Captain stood and said, "Lieutenant, set a chair up beside Specialist Page's bunk for this man. How soon is his medication due?"

The Lieutenant took the chart from Page's bunk, looked it over and answered, "In about ten minutes, Doctor."

She handed the chart to the doctor, who looked it over and hung it back, "He gets a couple of shots so he'll be waking up. You can talk to him then. Just don't stress him. If he falls asleep, let him sleep."

"Yes, Sir. Thank you, Sir."

"You're welcome, Specialist. What did you say your XO's name was?"

"Major Hobbs, Sir. Captain, are you going to talk to him?"

"Oh, I might remind him he could find himself in my care one day."

"Thank you, Sir." The captain only smiled as he left.

Soon the Lieutenant returned pushing a medical cart. She woke Page and gave him his shots, then told him he had a visitor. Jim walked over and sat down in the chair she'd provided. Page saw him coming and smiled, "Mac!"

"Hi, Page, How ya' feel?"

Page spoke slowly and with great effort, "Not very good." And yet Jim could see a faint smile as Page continued, "but better than the alternative."

"Page, I'm glad you're not mad at me. I was afraid you'd hate me for cutting off your hand."

Page started to cry softly as tears crept down his cheeks. "You didn't have any other choice. Mac, that chopper was on fire when you climbed in."

Jim slowly shook his head, "No, Wright and I got there at the same time and there wasn't any fire. I probably wouldn't have climbed inside if it had been on fire."

"Mac, I can remember hearing fire extinguishers."

"Yeah, so do I, but not until I was already inside."

"Mac, did everyone else get out?"

There was a second's hesitation before Jim spoke, "No, Page. Your peter pilot didn't make it."

"Mac, tell me everything, just as you remember it, including what I said."

Jim started at the point where Mr. Walker told him to put his helmet back on and finished with his getting into the quarter-ton with Kenny. Page smiled and slightly laughed, "Mac, I would have loved to have seen that. It's just too bad you didn't use a live grenade on him the other night."

"Page, I swear, I didn't do that."

"True?"

"True!"

"Did Halsey get mad about being punched out?"

"Yeah, you should have seen him lying there on his ass. The only problem is, it looks like I take a court martial for it."

"Mac, I'm sorry."

"What for, you didn't hit him."

"I kind of feel responsible."

"You're not!"

"Mac, I may not get another chance—so I want to say, thanks." With broken voice and tears visible, Page continued, "Thanks for my life."

"You're welcome, I'm just glad I could get you out."

"Mac, I feel kind of stupid asking this, but do you believe in God?"

"Absolutely! Why?"

"I once saw a Huey burn! Did you ever see one go up in flames?"

"Three times now."

"It's quite a sight, isn't it?"

"It sure is."

"Mac, the one I saw was up at An Loc. I don't think it was on fire more than thirty seconds before it was completely consumed and exploded. You had to be inside my chopper for a good three minutes. You'd been in there over two before I passed out. So why didn't it go up a lot faster and blow before it did?"

"Well, Page, in the first place, I don't think I was in there that long. Maybe I was, I don't know. I guess the reason it didn't go up was Jesus wasn't ready for us to die yet."

"Us or you? I mean, the second you're out, it goes up."

For the first time that night it dawned on him. Jim knew in his heart that the hand of God had once again reached out and restrained the Angel of Death until they were safe. What was there in his future he was being spared for? Maybe it wasn't him. Maybe there was someone in his life whose prayers for him had been answered. He didn't know which it was but he knew Jesus is no respecter of persons—He cared as much for Page as He did for him.

"Mac, you didn't answer me."

"Page, we're alive tonight because of the divine protection of Jesus Christ. I know nothing more."

"Were you raised in the church?"

"Yes, I was raised a Lutheran, but it was here in Nam that I really came to know Jesus. Now, I'm really thankful for all the Bible background and training that Lutherans stress, because I know what I believe—I'm not perfect by far, but I know Him."

"Mac, tell me about Jesus and what you believe."

Jim took a deep breath, "I believe in Jesus Christ as my personal Lord and Savior. He died on the cross and rose from the dead to take away my sins. In other words, even though I sin, and I know I do, Jesus is able to wipe my sins away as though I'd never sinned, each time I ask Him to forgive me. Because of that, I'm allowed into heaven when I do die."

Page asked questions and Jim answered as best he could late into the night. Finally, Page fell asleep as Jim continued to tell him about Jesus. Even though he knew Page was asleep Jim said, "Good-bye, Page, and may the peace of Jesus Christ be with you always." Jim looked at his watch, quarter after two. He'd have a hard time staying awake tomorrow. He shut off the light beside Page's bed and returned the chair to where the nurse had gotten it. He saw no one on the way out, and even though he thought about looking for that doctor, he simply left, unseen by anyone.

(There are many ironies about the Vietnam war. Howard Page would return to the States and enter school at Capital University in Columbus, Ohio. After being accepted by the Lutheran Seminary at Capital, Howard started writing letters to everyone and every organization he could think of in an effort to find Jim MacLaughlin. He was the one person Howard really wanted at his graduation and also his ordination service, when he would receive the full rights of a Lutheran pastor. Letter after letter came back getting him no further than when he started. Howard even visited the Pentagon one summer in hopes of finding some of Jim's records with a home address. His search was fruitless, as he never found Jim MacLaughlin. Yet, Jim lived only a short distance north of Columbus; his name, address and telephone number were listed in the Columbus phone book.)

News of MacLaughlin's court martial traveled fast. It was the only topic of discussion at the officers club by the time Halsey came in. He saw Captain Wolf already seated and headed for a table close by. Changing his mind, he approached Captain Wolf, "Mind if I join you?"

"Yes, as a matter of fact I do, but sit down, anyway, I want to talk to you." As Halsey sat down, Mr. Lucas walked up. "Hey, Captain, you want in the pool?"

"What pool?"

"Well, Sir, I'm calling it the Halsey pool. You see I think Halsey is a walking dead man. "They're going to kill him just as sure as the sun rises in the east." Halsey sat there almost in shock. "The pool works like this, Sir. You can place a bet on the day they kill him and how they kill him. Each bet costs you fifty dollars. For example, I've got bets they hit him tomorrow and with a door gun in the first hot LZ we hit. The winner of the pot is the person who gets both right. In case of a tie, I'll split it even. You in, Captain?"

"No thanks, I'll pass this one up. Although if I were going to bet, I'd bet on tonight with a frag—a live one this time."

"You know, Captain, that's where most of the money's at. Second high is he gets it in the showers with a grenade tomorrow."

Halsey interrupted, "Lucas, you'd bet on anything!"

"You bet; my old man was a pit boss in Vegas."

"Just what makes you so sure they'll try to kill me?"

"Haven't you heard? Walker was looking for MacLaughlin in his hooch and overheard some of the men talking about how to do it. Plus the barkeep in the NCO Club was here about ten minutes ago and said your demise was the only topic of conversation over there. See ya, Captain, try to make it through tonight would you, Halsey?"

Lucas turned and left as Walker sat down, "Captain, Admiral, how's it feel to be a walking dead man?"

"Walker, don't call me that, and I don't believe any of this shit!"

"Oh, you can believe it all right. Personally, if I was in your shoes, I'd drop all those charges and see to it the word gets passed before people start going to bed. Did Lucas tell you he's moving into my room for the night? Just in case a grenade does go off in your room, he doesn't want to be sleeping beside it. You know, Halsey, you don't have one friend in the enlisted men's ranks. Mac could have hit any other officer in the company and the rest of those guys wouldn't raise a finger to help him. But with you, they see it as their chance to get rid of you. Try to remember, everyone of those guys hates your guts. You know, I've spent a lot of time with Mac. He believes he has a guardian angel, and I've been flying with him long enough to think he may be right. I've seen too many things that did or didn't happen, which should have gone the other way. I'm telling you, Halsey, the man isn't alone, Somebody's looking after him Who's more powerful than either of us. Somehow, I just can't see him ending up in jail. Just look at what happened earlier today. Halsey, that ship was on fire, but it didn't spread until he stepped out of it—then suddenly BOOM, the whole thing erupted into flames and blows—almost like it was waiting for him to get out."

"You're crazy!"

"Halsey! You ever see a Huey go up?"

"Once."

"And how long did it take?"

"Not very long."

"I rest my case. In fact, do me a real favor and stay away from me from now on, I don't want to be too close when it happens."

Walker stood up and said, "Good-bye, Halsey. See ya, Captain."

Halsey looked at Captain Wolf and said, "Captain, you think they're serious? I mean in the infantry, sure, but not in aviation!"

"Halsey, you're a hell of a slow learner. What do you think that fake fragging was all about the other night? That was somebody's way of telling you to back off. These guys aren't any different than the grunts; they all came from the same United States. If I were you, I'd drop those charges before the men go to bed."

"Can't you have MacLaughlin locked up tonight, Sir?"

"I could, but I'm not going to. Besides, it wouldn't do any good. If he doesn't get you, somebody else will. Anyway, you have to sign the papers and the Major said he wouldn't have them ready 'til tomorrow."

"Captain, I refuse to be intimidated. Just to be safe, though, could I bunk with you tonight?"

"HELL, NO! I'm like Walker, I don't want you anywhere near me. You change your mind, you go tell Major Hobbs. I don't want you close to me after I leave this club."

Halsey had heard all he wanted to and decided to leave. When he got to the door, Walker was standing behind him. "Well, Admiral, it's a long walk and those lights are perfect for a sniper."

"Walker, you don't scare me!"

"I'm not trying to scare you, man, I'm trying to keep you alive."

"Look, they won't try anything here because of the company area guards."

"Halsey, those guards are enlisted men from our own company. Look, you and I've had our problems, but I don't want you killed, especially by our own men. Come on, let's sit down and talk it over."

Once at a table, Walker ordered two beers. "Okay, let's look at the pros and cons of this situation. First of all, if you drop the charges, you lose a little pride and have a black eye for a while. Hey, get somebody to take your picture and send it home, then you can tell everybody at home you got it in a crash. At least you're alive. I mean, man, is the risk really worth it? Halsey, if I'd been fragged, even with a dud, I'd thank God I was still alive and become the nicest guy in the company."

Halsey sat there and looked Walker in the eye, then took a big drink of beer and said, "Okay, I'm convinced, but the SOB shouldn't get away with it."

"He will, Halsey, because you got greedy. If you had asked for company punishment, you'd have gotten away with it. Plus, you could have laughed at him every day. But, no, you had to play hardball and go for the court martial. One final piece of advice, Halsey, your life depends on those men every single day. They fix the helicopters you fly in. You get shot down, who do you think's going to be out there walking through the jungle with you, with a loaded weapon? There've been more than one officer shot by his own men in this war. You get in a fire fight on the ground and, believe me, you want enlisted men around who like you. Man, you don't want to hide from Chuck and your own men. Come on, I see Hobbs over there, let's go talk to him."

Kenny was seated on his bunk when Mr. Walker came in and sat down beside him, "Well, Kenny, we got Mac off the hook!"

"Great, that's really great! How'd it go?"

"Just like we talked about. Now look, nobody knows about this but Mr. Lucas, you and me, and it damn well better stay that way or we could all find ourselves in a sling. You got that?"

"Yes, Sir."

"One more thing, it worked once, it'll never work again. By the way, where is our golden glove friend?"

"Probably still in the club. He and Gillett were beginning to really tie one on."

Walker hadn't been gone but a minute when Gillett walked in. "Hey, Kenny, they're going to try to get a convoy through tomorrow. It'll be a five day trip, so pack a bag. You'll take the company truck and you're to leave at 0500. You got any questions?"

"No. Where's Mac?"

"He should be along any second. We left the club together. You know, I wonder where he did go? He should have been here before now. Oh, well, he can't get lost. See ya in the morning, Kenny."

Jim carefully felt his way into the hooch. It was pitch black in there and he didn't want to wake anyone by falling over something. He made his way to the wall locker, felt for the lock and without much trouble, unlocked it. The flashlight he kept on the top shelf almost fell as he groped for it. Instead, he was able to lay it quietly on his bunk after turning it on. Jim sat down and started to untie his boots when the door opened and an unseen face called, "Sergeant Gillett?"

"He's in the bunk straight across."

The intruder turned his flashlight in Gillett's direction and approaching his bunk said, "Sergeant Gillett, wake up."

"Uh, what? I'm awake, I'm awake, get that light out of my eyes!"

"Sergeant, we need another crew and the names of the men you sent on the earlier mission."

"I don't know who went. I couldn't find MacLaughlin any place! I went next door to see if he was over there and their platoon sergeant said not to worry about it; he had a guy who's been wanting to fly some of those night missions. So I said fine, I'll just let you fill the crew and he did. Why?"

"We've got a dead crew chief, a wounded co-pilot, and a broken ship we have to go get."

Jim said, "Gillett, I'll go."

"Mac, you just getting back? Where the hell you been?"

"At the hospital with Page. Hey, runner, how'd they get it and where are they?"

"I don't know. All I know is they left here about a quarter 'til one to pick up a long range recon group. The next thing I know I'm being woke up and told to go find Sergeant Gillett, to get the name of the dead crew chief, and have him fill another crew."

"Okay, Gillett, I'm dressed, get me a gunner. I'll go preflight the ship. By the way, what am I flying?"

"Take the new one you brought in yesterday! Hey, runner, you getting officers?"

"Yeah, I woke Captain Wolf before coming here; he had me wake up Major Hobbs. He said the Major had been upset that he hadn't been able to go on the earlier one. The Major said he'd get a co-pilot. I've got to go."

The runner walked out the door and Gillett turned to Mac, "Mac, how's Page?"

"Under the circumstances, pretty good. He'll make it."

"Mac, you realize the only reason you're not that dead crew chief is that I couldn't find you?"

"I realize. Maybe that's why you couldn't find me."

"You've got no idea what you're going into out there! You don't know where you're going! All you know is the guy who took your place is dead and so you jump right in there and say, 'I'll go!' You got a death wish?"

"No, it's just that I'm already dressed. I just walked in the door. There's no point in waking someone else. See you later, Gillett." Jim locked his locker and left as Gillett tried to wake somebody on down the hooch.

Jim had just started with a preflight of the ship when two officers walked up. He knew from what the runner had said that one of them would be Major Hobbs. Acting like he hadn't seen them approach in the dark, Jim continued with his inspection until Major Hobbs spoke, "Hey, up on top, this is Major Hobbs. Who am I flying with tonight?"

"MacLaughlin, Sir. Sir, I'm almost done and then I'll be right down. I don't know who the gunner will be."

The two officers climbed into their seats. Jim didn't think anything of it when Hobbs climbed into the peter pilot's seat, since he hadn't been made an AC yet. Wright came around the revetment carrying his M60's, so Jim helped him mount them and, since it was already untied, the pilot started to crank the engine. Jim climbed into the cargo area and for the first time looked at the AC who was busy starting the aircraft. Jim felt a streak of panic leap through his body as he recognized the form of Halsey. Now he knew why Hobbs had been watching him so closely as he'd put on his gear. Jim plugged in his helmet and said, "Mr. Halsey?"

"Welcome aboard, Mac!"

"Go to hell! I'm not flying with you!" Jim unplugged his helmet and started to get out of the chopper.

Hobbs, who had been watching him, moved faster than Jim could believe possible; especially for a big man. By the time Jim had removed his helmet and chicken plate, Hobbs had gotten out and grabbing Jim by the shirt, flung him against the revetment wall. With his massive size pinning Jim against the wall, and the Major's two fists holding him by the shirt a couple inches off the ground, Hobbs spoke in his most forceful and commanding tone, "Listen to me, you smart mouth little son of a bitch! I've just about had it with you. I'm not real sure how, but you managed to get Halsey to drop the court martial. So you're off the hook, but I'll not allow you to talk to my officers like that! You got that?"

"Yes, Sir!"

"Now, I'm going to tell you something else. You'll fly with whomever I tell you to fly with, when I tell you to fly with him, and as often as I tell you. Now, you get your insubordinate little ass on that chopper before I stick my size twelve boot in it!" Still holding Jim's shirt, the Major stepped aside and half threw Jim into the chopper. Both climbed into the cargo bay and Hobbs gave Halsey the thumbs up sign. In seconds they were airborne. Major Hobbs, with some difficulty, worked his way over the radio console and into his seat. Jim had replaced his chicken plate and helmet and, like Major Hobbs, returned to his seat.

"MacLaughlin, you on line?"

"Yes, Major."

"Good, flip it over to private."

"You there?"

"Yes, Sir."

"Good! How do you feel right now, Mac?"

"Oh, slightly humiliated, upset and confused. We both know I shouldn't have spoken to Mr. Halsey the way I did, and you could get in as much trouble for shoving me around."

"But I won't, will I?"

"No, Sir, I won't rat."

"Speaking of ratting; who fragged Mr. Halsey?"

"I don't know, Sir."

"Yes you do, and I know you knew it when I first made you a deal. So why didn't you take it, Mac? Then all this unpleasantness wouldn't have happened."

There wasn't any response, so the Major pushed him a little harder. "Don't think too long, Specialist, because I only want two answers. One, the name, and two, why you didn't rat earlier."

"Sir, I don't know what you're talking about."

"The hell you don't."

"Major, what makes you think I do?"

"That's unimportant, just give me the name!"

"I don't know it."

"You're lying!"

"Major, this isn't going to get us anywhere, because you're just going to say, yes, you are, and I'm going to say, no, I'm not. So, if you don't mind, would you tell me what you meant by 'no court martial?'"

This time it was the Major's turn to pause, "You mean you haven't heard?"

"No, Sir. I spent the evening at the hospital with Page. I just got back to my hooch when they came looking for a crew for this mission."

"Okay, well, it seems that Mr. Halsey has decided that in the interest of 'esprit de corps,' he'll make the first move towards burying the hatchet by not pressing charges against you."

"That's very generous of Mr. Halsey, Sir."

"Yes, it is and you had better decide to reciprocate."

"Sir, it wasn't me who had the problem to begin with. The mere fact that he's the officer and I'm the NCO should tell you who had been harrassing whom."

"Yes, I know, but you're not entirely blameless. Okay, Specialist, I'll tell you what I've already done and you damn well better not tell Halsey. He's not going to find out until tomorrow morning. As of then, Mr. Halsey will be in the other flight platoon. I decided not to enter anything into your records. That means you won't get any medal, but when you get to the States nobody will ever know how much trouble you've been in over here or how close you came to jail."

"Thank you, Sir."

"Mac, have you ever considered extending your tour over here?"

"No, Sir!"

"Well, consider it. You're made for it. The Colonel's right, you simply enjoy living on the edge and this is the only place you'll be able to. Besides, you've got fifteen months left in the service when you get back. With that much time you'll get sent back over anyway—so you might as well stay to begin with; at least for another six months. That way you'll go home with less than a year left and not get sent back. You can fly with me as my crew chief, once I'm made CO. I'll see to it that you get the medals you deserve, and you won't have to worry about people like Mr. Halsey."

"I don't know, Sir. How can I live on the edge as you put it, flying in circles at three thousand feet? As for the medals, they don't mean that much to me anyway. I don't doubt for a second you could get them, after all, Colonel Appleton got a Silver Star a couple of months ago for flying courageously at thirty-five hundred feet while the rest of the flight got the hell kicked out of them in the Hobo Woods."

Major Hobbs sat there and slowly shook his head, "Mac, you don't respect anybody or anything, do you?"

"Sir, only if it's earned. So let me ask you a question, Major. Why me? Of all the guys in the outfit, why do you want me?"

"Who knows! Look, we're almost to Dau Tieng. Think about extending, Mac. Better switch back to intership commo."

Jim saw the Major reach down and heard the click of his going off private. Reaching up, he turned his switch back to intercom also and sat there quietly listening to Mr. Halsey update the Major on their status. Soon they were on the ground not far from the UH-23 chopper's hanger. Two warrant officers and a Spec-Four approached, then one warrant stuck his head in the Major's window. Major Hobbs directed them to get in as he said, "Their ship's at the far end of the runway. Let's go see what's wrong. Fortunately, we're not going to lose a pilot; he's just got some small shrapnel in his right arm."

Everybody but Mr. Halsey jumped out almost as soon as they were on the ground, leaving him to shut down. The lone Huey was only about twenty feet away but, for some reason, nobody approached it until Major Hobbs spoke, "Okay, let's go find out what's wrong with it."

Jim turned to one of the warrant officers and asked, "Sir, why did you land here? I mean, did you lose power or hydraulics or what?"

Major Hobbs shouted, "Don't answer that! Mac, you're supposed to be good at your job, let's find out how good—you tell us what happened!"

Jim shrugged his shoulders and shook his head, "Okay, Major, whatever makes you happy." Jim returned to his chopper, climbed in and turned on the searchlight, lowered it and shined it in the direction of the other chopper. Now he had plenty of light but, just in case, he held on to his flashlight.

The whole right side of the Huey was pot-marked with shrapnel holes. Jim looked underneath and saw a puddle. He put his finger

in it and then smelled it—fuel. He then opened the engine compartment and, after checking it, climbed on top. After about ten minutes,
Jim walked up to Major Hobbs, snapped to rigid attention, saluted
and said, "Sir, Specialist MacLaughlin reports."

Major Hobbs smiled, returned the salute and replied, "I guess I
deserved that. Okay, Mac, as you were. Now what did you find?"

Turning to the wounded officer, Jim said, "Sir, you either took a
mortar round or a grenade on your right rear side. Which?"

"I don't know."

"Was your crew chief killed instantly?"

"Yeah, along with two of the long range recon people."

"You must have had your arm out the window?"

"No, just my elbow."

"Okay." Turning back to the Major, Jim continued, "Sir, I believe
a mortar round hit just off their right side and slightly behind the
crew chief's seat. As a result, there's a massive rupturing of the chopper's skin, including the right upper and lower fuel cells. They're supposed to be self sealing and some of the smaller holes have sealed
but there are just too many that are too large. Therefore, I suspect
they ran out of fuel. Also, the engine shows it's taken a small piece
of shrapnel through the intake, breaking and chipping off some of
the blades. I also suspect they had a drastic loss of power. There's
hydraulic oil all over the place but I can't see a ruptured hose, so
I suspect it's a small break somewhere. Without the lines being under
pressure I can't tell where the break is." Turning back to the warrant,
Jim continued, "If you hadn't lost hydraulic assist yet, you would have
very shortly." To Major Hobbs, he said, "The tail boom has several
holes in it. Without taking the time to open the inspection panels,
I'd say there's probably structural damage; possibly damage to the
tail rotor control cables. It's unimportant, anyway, because the ship's
unflyable. We'll have to get a Chinook to take it home. The only other
thing I found was a hole in one of the main rotor blades which probably gave you a vibration. That's all, Sir."

Turning to the Warrant Officer Jim asked, "How correct am I?"

"I'm impressed. We landed here because we were losing fuel so
fast we couldn't get any further. Hydraulic pressure was taking a steady
drop and we didn't have more than two thirds power, plus a pretty

good vibration in the stick."

Jim, with a big smile, looked Major Hobbs in the eye, "Will that be all, Sir?"

"Yes, There's no way it'll fly home, right?"

"No, Sir! You might just as well call for a hook."

"You did a good job, Specialist. Let's go home. We'll have it hooked in the morning."

Mr. Halsey was standing beside Major Hobbs. As everyone started to walk away, Jim touched Mr. Halsey's arm, causing him to turn around. Extending his right hand Jim said, "Mr. Halsey, peace?"

Halsey looked at Major Hobbs and then back at Jim, "Yeah, why not, Mac? Peace." Mr. Halsey extended his hand and, somewhat begrudgingly, shook Jim's.

Everyone but Jim and Major Hobbs had climbed aboard. Jim untied the rotor blades and walked around to hold the Major's door for him, "Mac, I bet you play a mean game of poker!"

"Major, I don't particularly like the game."

"Well, you've played one hell of a hand tonight."

Jim, not sure of what he meant, showed a puzzled look as he replied, "Sir?"

"Never mind. You been to bed yet, Mac?"

"No, Sir."

"Flying tomorrow?"

"Yes, Sir."

The Major looked at his watch and said, "Well, you're only going to get about an hour's sleep, I put the word out last night, everyone has to stand reveille from now on."

"Sir, I thought this was a combat zone, not basic training. Do you have any idea how important those extra few minutes of sleep are to me?"

"I've got a real good idea, but that's no reason to relax military discipline. Get in. Let's go home!"

Jim motioned for the Major to climb in, which he did. Jim pulled the armor plating on the seat forward to the lock position and shut the door. Halsey had already started the engine, so as soon as Jim was in his seat, he gave Halsey the thumbs up sign.

13

"The spirit is willing, but the body is weak." Matthew 26:41, N.I.V.

Sure I'm Mean—
But Don't Make
Me Prove It

Both men were only a few steps from the hooch door when they heard the now familiar whistle of the Russian built 122MM rockets. Jim, who was closest to the bunker, turned and headed through the doorway. Tripping, he fell over a body as he entered. Wright, who'd been directly behind, fell on top of him. Both were startled at landing in an entanglement of hot, clammy bodies that had already started cursing and making unkind references about their mothers. Finally, a flashlight was turned on, showing a bunker packed so full of men they were sitting on top of each other, with no place to stretch out their legs. It had been hot outside, but the added body heat made it unbearable inside.

By now the rockets were falling so fast, one couldn't be distinguished from another. The continuous whistle and grumbling of the incoming rockets had all blended into an ear shattering sound, made even worse by the explosions as the rockets hit. The very ground on which they laid began to shake and vibrate as the pounding continued. Each man pressed his hands to his ears in a futile attempt to ease the pain. This was undoubtedly the worst bombardment Jim had ever been in. Though it seemed to each man that hours had passed, it had lasted only twenty minutes. Suddenly, as though someone flipped off a switch, it stopped.

The first sensation Jim felt was the ringing in his ears. Slowly, almost as though someone was tuning in a radio, his ears began to pick up other sounds and tune out the buzzing and ringing. A couple of guys were crying and another was shouting obscenities at the VC, at the Army, at Lyndon Johnson and anybody else who came to mind. Someone turned on a flashlight and the shivering in Jim's spine began to subside. He could see several guys still holding their ears and shaking. Most everyone was wearing only their underwear as they had obviously gotten out of bed. It wasn't much longer before someone said he couldn't stand the smell of mildew and rot any longer; besides, his legs were aching from someone sitting on them, and he was getting out. It was the signal they'd all been waiting for and the bunker slowly emptied. Jim was close to the doorway, and therefore, one of the first outside. Once out he waited for Gillett, who came crawling out wearing only his green boxer shorts.

"Gillett, how long you guys been in that bunker?"

"Since shortly after you left. This last one was the worst by far. How'd you get along?"

"No problem. In fact, I'm glad I went. I wouldn't have gotten any sleep in that bunker. I'm going to bed. See you later, Gillett."

"What time is it, Mac?"

Jim shone the light on his watch and answered, "About five 'til five."

Gillett shouted to anyone within hearing distance, "Listen up, you guys! You might just as well get dressed, because everybody who's still walking and has it swinging has to stand formation in five minutes!"

There was much cursing and moaning from everyone in the area, but it was Hunter who hollered from the far side of the hooch, "Hey Gillett, if I bind mine up, do I still have to stand reveille?"

"Yes!"

Gillett left to start the generator and shortly the hooch lights came on. Almost at the same moment Kenny started screaming. His wall locker had a six inch hole in it. Jim looked at his own bed. The mosquito netting had been destroyed by a piece of shrapnel, but the bed itself had been untouched. Looking up at the metal roof that now had more holes in it than a block of swiss cheese, Jim saw Kenny's monkey still alive and cowering in the far corner.

By the time the company was called to attention, the confusion over where to stand had yet to be worked out. Major Hobbs could hardly believe it; he had a whole company of people and two thirds of them had never stood formation since joining the company. They didn't know where their platoon was, or where to fall in once they'd found it. Others didn't even try to find their platoon, they just fell in the end of the first line they came to. Very few people were happy about the formation. For one thing, it would only take one rocket to wipe out the entire company. Finally, at 0517, the reports were given and the Major stepped forward to address the troops.

Jim heard Hunter behind him say, "I hope he makes this short. I'm getting hungry."

Jim smiled to himself at the typical lack of respect for officers. Major Hobbs spoke, "Men, I know we've all had a rough night, but I'll not accept this kind of slop for a formation. Tomorrow morning every man in this outfit BETTER know where he belongs and be there! We've lost so much time getting into formation that we can't have a police call of the company area—so what I'm going to do is this: you can just get up fifteen minutes earlier tomorrow morning, and you'll get up fifteen minutes earlier every morning until you get it right. By the time the flight lands tonight, I want all the holes in the company area made by those rockets filled. First Sergeant, I also want a work crew to start filling more sandbags and stacking them around the living quarters. Both clubs will be closed until the hooches are patched and the sandbags are raised to at least six feet from ground level around all the living quarters. You might just as well find out now that I've ordered enough paint to paint all the buildings in the company. There are going to be a lot of improvements in this company in the next few days and I know you men can handle it. Finally, I think it's important that you know we're going to be part of one of the largest operations of the war to date, Yellowstone*. First Sergeant, dismiss the company!"

"Yes, Sir. Company, ten hut! Fall out!"

Gillett and Jim were among the first in the mess hall. Each looked at the other with an 'oh no' type look, as they listened to the conversation in front of them.

"Hey, Cookie, what's the idea of hamburgers for breakfast?"

"Look, it's just this simple, Charlie blew up our powdered eggs, powered milk and boxes of cereal, along with most of our other supplies. About all we've got left is bread and hamburger. I can't even make creamed beef!"

Gillett had just sat down when Major Hobbs approached from the kitchen area that divided the officers' side from the enlisted mens'. "Sergeant Gillett, there are some things I need to go over with you. Why don't you bring your tray and join me on the officers' side?"

"Yes, Sir."

Hobbs turned to leave as Gillett stood up. Gillett looked down at Jim and said in a quiet, yet commanding tone, "What did you do now?"

Jim looked up and speaking through his teeth, answered in a slightly forced manner, "Nothing!"

Jim was standing outside the hooch, his steel pot half full of water, resting on top of the wall of sandbags protecting the hooch front. Being careful not to lose any of the toothpaste he was applying to his toothbrush, he didn't see Gillett walk up and slap him on the back. "Well, Mac, I've got good news and bad news, which do you want first?"

"Give me the good and somebody else the bad."

"Sorry, you only had two choices. But to show you what a nice guy I am I'll give you the good news first, anyway. Halsey has been transferred to the other platoon."

"Is that it?"

"Yes."

"Hobbs told me that last night. What else you got, Gillett?"

"Well, aren't you just full of little surprises. That's all the good.

---

*Yellowstone - 79 day operation (8 December 1967 - 24 February 1968) small in size and duration - conducted in Tay Ninh Province (War Zone C) with units of the 25th Infantry Division, 1254 known enemy casualties.

The rest is bad."

"And I'll just bet there's a lot more of it, isn't there?"

"Yes. Well, to start with, Hobbs will be flying your right seat* today."

"That's okay, he's not bad to fly with. Besides, as long as he's on board, there are only two places we'll be flying, lead or trail. I won't get stuck on some side mission."

"You're flying trail."

Jim finished spitting out the rinse water and gave the remaining water in his steel pot a fling. "I hope that's the worst of the bad news."

"It's not. Hobbs has ordered in enough soap and buckets so that we can start washing the helicopters."

"The man is crazy!"

"Mac, that's not the half of it. He also ordered in enough paint to completely paint all the choppers and enough paste wax, in fifteen pound cans, no less, to paste wax all those suckers."

"The man is totally insane! What time does he want us to do all this? Let me guess, midnight to two o'clock?"

"I don't know, Mac. I also don't know what we're going to do about it. Any ideas?"

"Not right off the top." The two friends stood there looking disgusted. Jim had a thought, "Hey, Gillett, did he also order in rags or sponges?"

"No, he didn't."

Gillett's face broke into a smile. He knew there weren't any sponges in the company, and supply was so tight with rags they had to be signed in and out. An old rag to wipe your hands with was something jealously guarded.

As Jim walked to the flight line, he took time to look over the company area. The place was a mess. Although, for the pounding they'd taken during the night, they'd gotten off pretty cheap. One other hooch had taken a direct hit and been turned into kindling. Another hooch had lost its front and several had roof damage. There were countless pot holes and one place where the drainage ditch had been widened. Most every hooch had some holes in its sides and several had roofs that looked like someone had tried to open a can with a screwdriver

---

*Right Seat - Co-pilot's seat.

instead of a can opener. The flight line, for some reason, didn't look like it had received more than a few strays.

It was only a little after six and already the heat and humidity had caused sweat beads to roll down Jim's back, soaking his shirt. The sun was up and serving notice. It would be unpleasant today.

There were places the dust was ankle deep, making it hard to walk. In a few weeks it would start raining and that dust would become ankle deep mud, which would be even harder to walk through.

Jim was glad his helicopter was still there. Once up in the air it would be a whole lot cooler; just one of the little benefits of being a flyboy.

Jim opened the left cargo door and put his water jug inside, directly behind the console. Next, he pulled out the green, plastic-covered log book. His entry from just a few hours before was the last one. There wasn't any reason that something should have been added, but one always checked the log book anyway. He could remember more than once going to the ship he'd been assigned, checking the log book and finding anything from a radio to an engine had been pulled out during the night. He'd finished his preflight and was having some water when Gillett drove up in the quarter ton. Wright jumped off the back and pulled out two M60's. Gillett waved a greeting as Jim shouted, "Hey, Gillett, where's Kenny?"

"I sent him on a convoy to Saigon. By the way, I've some more good news. They decided to let the gook K.P.'s back on post today."

"You don't suppose one of them would like to have monkey stew tonight, do you?"

Gillett smiled broadly and said, "I'd had that thought myself." Gillett drove off.

Jim helped Wright mount his guns as the pilots approached. Wright spoke, "Man, oh man, Mac. Kenny is sure going to be mad when he gets back and his monkey is gone."

"Yeah, he'll flap around like an old rooster that's just been wet on. Won't it be wonderful?"

Major Hobbs, who had just walked around the ship asked, "Won't what be wonderful?"

Jim and Wright came to attention and saluted both Hobbs and Walker, "Good morning, Sir. Wright and I were just talking about how nice it will be to finally get rid of Kenny's monkey."

Major Hobbs smiled, "You mean one of the men has a pet monkey?"

"Yes, Sir, and it's disgusting. It's like living in a zoo. The damn thing shits on people or shits and then throws it at somebody. It jacked off the other day and dumped its load all over Hunter's wall locker."

The Major was laughing so hard he had to sit down.

"Sir, I'm glad you find it so funny. Believe me, you wouldn't if you walked in the door and WHAM! A load of monkey shit hits you between the eyes!"

The Major regained his composure long enough to ask, "Mac, did you preflight this thing yet?"

"Yes, Sir."

"Do it again. This time, though, I want you to show me everything you're looking for. I want to learn as much about a Huey as I can while I've got the chance."

"Well, Sir, let me be the first to welcome you to Mac's school of preflights." Jim showed the Major everything he did on a preflight, and during that time there was a running conversation between the Major and the SP-5. Jim asked about Colonel Appleton, since he hadn't seen him for a while. Major Hobbs was pleased to inform him that the CO had been called to Saigon for a few days but would join them today as C and C, thus explaining Hobbs being in the command position. The Major was very friendly during the preflight even though Jim took a jab at him when asked about extending. He explained to the Major he didn't have any time off as it was, and the idea of washing and waxing Hueys when he could be sleeping didn't excite him. Jim told him that was stateside-type duty, not combat zone. That if he was going to pull stateside duty; he might as well be there. They hadn't finished the preflight when Lead ship started to crank. Hobbs quickly climbed inside, called Lead and informed them his ship had been on a single ship night mission and would need fuel. Jim laughed to himself as he could picture the lieutenant flying Lead ship kissing Hobbs' ass by politely telling him to go refuel. Anybody else would have received a not-so-polite chewing out. It wasn't long until they were parked at the fuel dump.

Jim had just climbed back into his seat when Hobbs came over the intercom. "Men, take a good look, because the first day I'm made

CO of this company, that's something you'll never see again."

Jim looked up to see a hog* making its usual struggle to take off. A hog was a classic example of the American adage that a little is nice, but a bunch is a whole lot better. It always amazed Jim that a hog could get off the ground at all. Hog pilots had their own routine; they always refueled first, then hovered to the opposite end of the flight line where the ammo bunker was located. There the gunner, crew chief and, if in a hurry; the co-pilot rearmed the ship with rockets and grenades. Once fully fueled, armed and crewed, a hog was about one thousand pounds over maximum gross for take off. Thus, the pilot always landed at the ammo bunker with the ship's nose pointed down the runway, because he couldn't hover to change directions. Whatever direction he was pointed, he had to go. Take off wasn't so much a thing of graceful beauty, as it was an accident full of explosives on its way to a happening. The pilot had to bring the engine and rotors up to full RPM, then tip the ship over onto the curved, forward part of the skids, which made it look like it was standing on its nose. Then, by jerking pitch into the rotors giving it lift, the pilot could literally hop down the runway until he had enough airspeed to make the transition into flight. Even then, he had to stay close enough to the ground to use the prop blast from the rotors to help him in the air. Only after most of the runway had been used did a hog ship have enough airspeed to raise its nose and gain altitude.

After topping off with fuel, Major Hobbs informed Lead he was ready to go. Instantly, Lead pulled pitch and hovered out of his revetment. Everyone in Jim's ship waited patiently as each ship slowly flew by, then the ninth one went by and it was their turn.

Walker pulled pitch into the rotors and hovered away from the fuel dump. He turned the ship to the right and started out over Tay Ninh Village. The Major had just finished calling Lead and telling him the flight was up when it happened—there was a crashing sound and Jim instantly knew they'd been hit. In that same fraction of a second, he saw pieces of plexiglas fly out the doorway and the aircraft rocked

---

*Hog - Huey gunship, equipped with an XM3 tube type rocket pod system (24 tubes 2.75 inch rocket) on each side. Plus an M5 nose mounted 40MM grenade launcher. Both the door gunner and crew chief had an M60 machinegun hung by bungi cords.

as Walker tried to regain control.

It was a startled Major Hobbs who shouted into the mike, "What the hell?"

Jim could see Hobbs trying to climb out of his seat backwards and then sink back down. Walker spoke, "You okay, Major?"

"Yes, I guess. Turn it around, Mr. Walker, we'll have to change ships while maintenance replaces this windshield." It was then the Major picked up the dead duck in his lap and threw it onto the cargo seat.

Jim came over the intercom, "Major, what happened?"

"That damn duck just flew through my windshield and hit me in the chicken plate. I don't mind telling you, it scared the shit out of me."

"Well, Sir, I've heard of a man shitting a brick before, but this is the first time I've ever seen anyone shit a duck."

Jim could see Walker laughing so hard he could hardly drive. Hobbs, now laughing also said, "I'm just damn glad I had on a chicken plate or that stupid duck would have broken every rib I've got."

"What kind of duck was it, Major?"

"Hell, I don't know, but it's a dead one now!"

Walker called Lead and told him what had happened, assuring him they'd be back in the air just as soon as they changed ships. Lead wasn't very happy; so after talking to Lead, Walker called Operations and asked where to land and where another ship could be found. They were told to park it on the maintenance pad to get the window fixed because there weren't any other flyable aircraft. Lead had been listening in and made it clear he couldn't understand anyone flying into a duck. Once on the maintenance pad, three men hurried their direction. One carried a tool box, one had a new window still wrapped in its protective paper and the third was a Spec-Six tech inspector. Jim couldn't help but be impressed. Service like this he'd never had before. Maybe flying with a Major wasn't so bad after all. He'd put windows in by himself before and it wasn't that easy, plus it took a long time. Something told him this job would be done in less than twenty minutes.

Jim tied down the rotor blades and walked around to where the maintenance men were attacking the broken windshield like ants after a cube of sugar. Since there wasn't any room left for him to work on the windshield, he decided to get out of the sun. The large maintenance tent was only twenty feet away, so he casually walked over and found an empty spot inside on one of the work benches and sat down. Directly overhead was a large NO SMOKING sign that someone was using as a shirt rack. It might just as well have been used as a dart board, since he was the only man in the tent who didn't have a cigarette hanging out of his mouth. It was slightly cooler inside the tent, but only slightly, with a faint, hot breeze moving through the open ends.

There were two slicks parked beside each other having their P.E.'s pulled, each with cowling off, inspection panels open, and in various stages of being broken down and put back together. Jim leaned back against the stiff canvas wall of the tent and closed his eyes. At the sound of heavy footsteps approaching, he opened one eye and saw Major Hobbs standing there looking at him.

"They said I'd find you in here. If you were sleepy, why didn't you rack out on the chopper's seats?"

"Because, Sir, there was a dead duck on it that belonged to you and it's a lot cooler in here."

Hobbs smiled, "It is at that. Mind if I sit down?"

Jim moved over to make room. "You know, Sir, I came over with a company as a maintenance man; I pulled many a P.E. Man, am I glad I'm out of that routine. I may not get any sleep, but it's a lot more fun flying. I mean, Major, how many of these guys can go home and tell about having a duck fly through their window? By the way, Sir, you going to have it stuffed or what?'

"I just took it to Cookie and let him know I wanted it dressed and ready to eat the night I make AC. I'll have a special party for you, Wright and Mr. Walker. You do eat duck don't you, Mac?"

"It couldn't be any worse than the zoo I've eaten with the Special Forces before we were made an all combat assault company. Those guys eat whatever their Montagnard friends cook, which could be anything from dog, monkey, rat or snake, to the water buffalo that died of old age, or hoof and mouth. You know, Major, I'll just bet the cook was tickled pink about having to cook that duck."

Hobbs laughed as he replied, "He didn't say much."

"I can imagine that! Major, do you mind if I ask you a question?"

"Go right ahead."

"Sir, you've got infantry written all over you. What are you doing in aviation?"

"Well, to make a long story short, I took ROTC in college, liked it, and decided to make a life of it. I graduated in '63 and was getting nowhere fast in the States, so I went to jump school and then volunteered for 'Nam. I was sent to Okinawa in January of '65 and joined the 173rd Airborne Brigade. We came to Nam on May 7th that same year and operated out of Bien Hoa. It was a hell of a good unit. You know we were one of the first units into Vietnam. In fact, I remember General Williamson, he was Brigade commander, telling us we were only here temporarily until an airborne brigade from the States relieved us. They're still here, up at An Khe, but we were supposed to be temporary because we were the only Pacific command quick reaction unit around. Anyway, I ended up spending eighteen months over here before rotating home. But I hadn't done too badly; I'd been a platoon leader and hoped to make company XO. In fact, that's what I'd stayed for. The only problem was every other officer who had been commissioned since the Korean War saw Nam as a chance for promotion. So I ended up at Fort Bragg with the 82nd Airborne Division behind a desk, doing nothing but reading the newspapers and being bored to death. After about a year of that, I decided this war wasn't going to end in a year or two, and I might just as well get back in it while the getting was good. Besides, I loved it here. This is where it's at. You and I are alike in that respect. You just haven't admitted it yet. You get back to the States, you'll realize this is reality and there's nothing else like it. It's just one hell of an ego trip. Anyway, after my first tour over here, it was obvious that helicopters were where the action was, so I put in for flight school. I'll tell you what, it didn't take that request long to come through. So I was off to Fort Rucker in Alabama and Huey flight training. From there I joined the 101st Airborne at Fort Campbell and we arrived at Bien Hoa on November 19, 1967. I made Major in January. About a month ago, I happened upon an old friend of mine in Saigon who worked in Corp Headquarters. During the course of the conversation, he mentioned this unit needed an Executive Officer, and here I am."

The tech inspector walked in and told them their ship was ready. Jim couldn't believe it. Only seventeen minutes had passed since he had tied the rotors down. Jim picked up a strange looking device that he'd asked one of the guys in sheet metal to make for him a few days ago, and headed for the ship. He explained to Major Hobbs how it was used to cook c-rations. He was also impressed with the speed of maintenance. Hobbs was really pleased when Jim told him it would have taken an hour or more for him to do it by himself. Then, pointing out all the rivets that went all the way around the windshield to Hobbs, he explained how they were removed and then replaced with new ones. The man seemed genuinely interested in learning everything he could and Jim enjoyed teaching him.

They were airborne again and he had a chance to think about the Major's story. Jim had been in the Army long enough to be able to read between the lines and there were sure some big holes in that story. Oh, he was probably telling the truth about not getting anywhere after college. It was a peace time Army with several Korean veterans still around, and if you're an infantry officer, you just about have to be airborne in order to make it up the ladder. Plus, old Hobbs had been smart enough to see a chance to get that all important combat experience. And it's not too hard to believe that bit about every officer since Korea volunteering for Nam, also. I'll bet he stepped on somebody's toes or he wouldn't have ended up behind a desk doing nothing in the States. If he went over in January '65 that means he went home in June '66. The buildup was underway by that time, new companies were being formed from scratch, and there's just no way a Captain with experience as a platoon leader in combat would get filed away. I wonder what he did. He should have been in a position to climb right up the ladder, quick. Whatever it was, he must have been passed over for promotion at least once back in the States because of it; possibly even once before that in Nam, with the 173rd. That would have been twice, once more and he'd have been riffed out of the service. That's why he put in for flight training. If he'd really loved combat as much as he let on, he'd have put in for Ranger school instead of flight school; although helicopters would get him out of the infantry and give him a chance to start fresh. The Army needed helicopter pilots badly, so he got in quick, but I'll bet he shit his pants when he ended up with the 101st Airborne. That's why he went to Saigon and happened upon a friend. Happened upon, my butt, I'll bet he's gone and hunted him up. Old Hobbs had to get out of that infantry unit. Even if he was driving helicopters for them, he was still in the airborne. That friend of his at Corps had enough rank, or else had the right job, with access to records and information to know we needed an XO. I'll even bet he arranged the man's promotion to Major. Hobbs did say he'd been promoted in January. I'll bet his buddy's got the promotion and orders sending Hobbs up here all on the same set of orders. After all, if Corps knew we needed an XO, it knew we would need a CO in about a month. If the buddy in Corps had that ability, then there wasn't any reason to believe he couldn't purge Hobbs' records for him, also. Not a bad deal, really. Hobbs had taken out of his records whatever it was that kept him from being promoted, never to be seen again; he gets orders sending him up here, and the promotion to Major. When he goes home at the end of this tour, he'll have one of the most important flags on his 201 file an officer could have, command of a company during combat. One thing was certain, any officer who gets a star in the next twenty years will have to have that flag on his records. No combat leadership command, no star. For that matter, it's going to be just about as important for an enlisted man to have Nam on his records. After all, the officers who are promoted will be Vets and they'll surround themselves with enlisted men who are Vietnam Vets also. I wonder what Hobbs had to give his buddy at Corps? That might explain Hobbs' attitude towards Halsey and me. Maybe he's walked in my boots. He just might have had a Halsey back in the 173rd without anybody to protect him.

By the time they had rejoined the flight, one lift had already been made. Mr. Walker pulled into the trail position as Hobbs advised Lead of their presence. Troops were picked up at Dau Tieng and added to those already in position. There had been no contact made to this point, so it was beginning to look like another long, quiet, boring day. From the LZ they flew to Tay Ninh and picked up more troops. These were put in a different location and the flight headed back to Tay Ninh.

By this time, Major Hobbs was getting wise to Mr. Walker's way of waking Jim up before each landing, but Hobbs was so tired he didn't really care. In fact, he wished he could rack out also.

They were almost back to Tay Ninh when Six called Lead and told him their mission had been changed. Nothing was happening with the troops they'd put in, and all hell had broken loose up north a ways; so they'd been released from the 25th Infantry and Operation Yellowstone. They were to pick up troops from the 1st Infantry Division at Lai Khe and put them in at an LZ just northeast of Song Be.

The flight up to Lai Khe took half an hour, during which Jim woke up long enough to say, "clear right" just prior to touch down. Jim noticed Major Hobbs was asleep while he put on fuel and troops. Having been to Lai Khe before, Jim recognized the place, but since he'd been asleep he had no idea why they were there, where they were going or why they were picking up troops from the Big Red One. He turned on all his radios after refueling, except AM Saigon, so it wasn't long before Lead's conversation with Six in C and C told him just about everything he wanted to know. Jim figured the flight all the way up to Song Be would take a little over an hour, so once again he pulled his visor down, turned off the radios, and put on his seat belt. Sleep came quickly as he sat there watching the rice paddies turn to woodlands.

Just outside Song Be, Mr. Walker had to wake not only Jim, but Wright and Major Hobbs. The Major was very apologetic about dozing off, even though Mr. Walker told him not to feel bad about it and had made light of his sleep-talking.

Song Be was a small village only a few miles from Cambodia and almost to the Second Corp area. It was heavily wooded and slightly rolling; some would say picturesque best described the area. It was also a U.S. Special Forces Camp. Yet for everyone in the flight of ten Hueys on long final approach, it was just another place to land, be shot at, and for some, to be wounded and die. They all knew it wasn't going to be good. An ARVN unit had gotten things started by sending out a patrol that was ambushed and ran. This upset the ARVN commander, so he sent his entire unit out to engage Charlie. The only problem was his men had back bones made of a substance slightly softer than mush. As a result, once the shooting started, they fell in behind the largest trees they could find and had been screaming for help ever since.

Mr. Walker called the roll to make sure everyone was awake. Major Hobbs was upset that Mr. Walker would be checking on him again, and made it clear Walker wasn't to do it again.

"Major, would you like to drive? This LZ is going to be good and hot!"

"Mr. Walker, I'd be glad to drive. What makes you think it's going to be so hot? The gunships didn't get any ground fire during their prep."

"Yes! Sir, that's one reason I think it'll be hot. We know they're down there. I mean somebody kicked the shit out of that ARVN unit. If they've got enough training and discipline not to fire on our gunship, then they're NVA. Believe me, it'll be hot. Okay, you two in the back, we're on short final, once we cross that road just ahead, open up. ARVN is supposed to be all on this side of the road so, Wright, if it moves down there cut it in half!"

"You got it, Sir."

"Mac, you copy?"

"Yes, Sir."

"Okay, there goes the road."

Both door guns opened up, causing the usual vibration. The grunts on board knew that was their sign. They all shifted in their seats and looked a lot more alert: some tightened their chin straps, some checked their weapons, one even retied his left boot. It was eight seconds from the time the doorguns opened up until Hobbs sat it down and the grunts jumped off. Walker had been right. It was hot. It was very hot. There was a steady flow of muzzle flashes coming from both tree lines. As the grunts jumped out, Jim's M60 was working perfectly. He gave the usual one word signal that the troops were all out, "Go!" and instantly the Huey started to lift. Out of the corner of his eye, Jim saw the grunts start to move forward, when one stood up straight, threw both his arms up and out, with his M16 being released and flying through the air. His face showed the pain his scream expressed. In that same movement his arms came back in, clutching his midsection as his knees buckled and his head jerked forward; collapsing his body in a roll on the ground.

Jim shouted into his mike, "Major, put it back down! Now!"

Like any good pilot, Major Hobbs instantly, and without question, followed his crew chief's command and sat it down only ten yards from where they'd dropped off the grunts. Jim waved to the two grunts who had come to their wounded buddy's aid to put him on board. At the same moment, he started firing his M60 into the trees and talking to his pilots. Less than two seconds had elapsed since he'd told Hobbs to set it down.

"Major, I've got a WIA back there!"

"Well, tell 'em to hurry up! We're sitting ducks here!"

As the two grunts helped put the wounded but still conscious GI on board, Mr. Walker called Lead. "Lead, this is Trail, you've got nine ships up. We're still on the ground putting on a wounded grunt."

"Roger, Trail. Take him to Phuoc Binh, Lead, out."

The wounded GI was a large black man with an unusual pot belly for a grunt. He was losing a lot of blood fast as it flowed freely onto his shirt and pants. There was a small white man under his right arm, and another black under his left arm. They quickly lifted him into the chopper's cargo area, with Wright's aid. As they pushed his legs inside, the short white man slammed face first onto the floor as though pushed by some unseen force. He struggled to stand, only to slide off the edge of the chopper's floor. The black man beside him reached down and pulled him to his feet. Blood was now making the back of the little man's shirt soggy. In one big push, the black man shoved the smaller white man onto the Huey and then threw in his M16. Mr. Walker had taken the controls and run the RPM up enough so when Jim said, "Go! Go!", the ship literally jumped into the air and disappeared.

As Jim climbed over the seats to help Wright give first aid, Mr. Walker said, "How many hits did we take, Mac? And how bad are those two?"

"Sir, I heard at least two hits, but I was kind of busy, so I wasn't really listening for them. How many did you hear?"

"I counted at least three. Check it out close when we get to Phuoc Binh!"

"You got it! Sir, you asked about these two." Jim had been working as he talked, and it didn't look good. "The white guy's not too bad, he took a slug in the right shoulder. If you can turn around and look at this black guy you should. I've never seen anything like it before."

With that, both officers turned in their seats to look back. Major Hobbs spoke instantly, "Holy shit! He's going to need major surgery, we better get him to Tay Ninh."

Jim said, "Major, he'll never make it to Tay Ninh. I don't know what's at Phuoc Binh, but even if there's only an aid station with a doctor, he can do more than we can to stabilize him until a med-a-vac can transport him."

"You're right, Mac, it would take us a half hour to get to Tay Ninh, and we're on long final to Phuoc Binh now."

Jim had bandaged the shoulder of the wounded grunt who, still conscious, had positioned himself so the black man's head rested on his lap. Tears slowly rolled down his cheek as he softly stroked his black friend's head. Wright had removed the flak jacket and opened the Black's shirt only to have his intestines fall out. The bullet had made a perfect incision just below the belly button. What Jim had thought was a pot belly were, in fact, the man's guts hanging out. It was at times like these Jim marveled at the punishment the human body could endure and still survive. Neither Wright nor Jim knew what to do. Every time they tried to push his guts back in, more came out. There was blood all over the place but no place to put a tourniquet. Likewise, there wasn't any place to apply direct pressure as could be done with a muscle wound. Every time they tried to apply direct pressure to the jagged edges of the tear, more guts and blood came out somewhere else. For some reason, there didn't seem to be any sensation in the area because he never once showed any signs of pain. He was obviously in shock. One look at his badly dilated eyes and dazed expression confirmed it. Yet, he never made a sound.

Finally, they landed. A man with a stethoscope around his neck and only an olive drab t-shirt met them. Jim figured he was the doctor. There were three other bare chested men who were taking orders from t-shirt. Jim could hardly believe his eyes as he watched the black hold his own guts on top of himself as the others placed him on a stretcher.

Both crewmen had removed their flight gloves to work on the wounded grunts, but had wiped their hands on the shirts of the infantrymen as t-shirt and his men arrived. Walker was in the process of shutting it down as Jim and Wright threw dirt and sand on the floor to help dry up the blood. Jim opened Major Hobbs' door and slid his seat's armor plating back. He was somewhat surprised when the Major climbed out and said, "Well, Mac, it's turning into quite a day. First we have a duck fly through our windshield, then we have some poor grunt spill his guts all over the floor."

"Sir, I feel sorry for him."

"Mac, me too. You've got to give him credit though, he's got balls of steel. There aren't too many men who wouldn't have passed out. Then when they put him on that stretcher he just gathered in his guts and held on." Hobbs laughed as he added, "Just like he was saying, 'By God, they belong to me and nobody else can have 'em!'"

"Major, you are hard! I mean really, making fun of some poor guy who's had his guts shot out." Jim shook his head and walked around the aircraft's nose as Hobbs followed laughing. There was one bullet hole in the fiberglass lid that housed some of the radios and a battery. Jim pointed the hole out to Hobbs. "There, Major, another two feet in your direction and you'd have had that one in the leg. You might have even gotten a free ride to the States out of it."

"I'll be damned! I'd have put a band-aid on it, and maybe taken a couple days off just to help the guys in the company area get things straightened out, and been right back at it."

"Sir, if you want, I'll find you some old rusty nails for breakfast!"

Hobbs at first was taken back, then a small smile crossed his lips, followed by his larger than necessary laugh. "Mac, you're alright, you know that? I like a man who's not afraid to give it to me straight. Something tells me you'd walk right up to General Westmoreland, himself, lay it on the line and not give a shit how many stars he's got. You and I'll get along just fine."

They found the second hole in the tail boom. There wasn't any damage to anything except its skin. They looked and looked for the third one that Walker was sure he'd heard hit, but couldn't find. Jim had even started to climb on top for a second look when Wright hollered, "I found it."

One round had passed through the soundproofing in the ceiling, almost in the middle and above the cargo door opening. It had then exited through the track on which the cargo door hung. Once Jim saw it, he tried to shut the cargo door, but it wouldn't go past the bullet's exit hole. Looking over at Major Hobbs, who was standing there watching, Jim said, "Major, we'll have to take this door off once we get back to Tay Ninh, or we won't be able to get into the engine compartment on the left side. Plus, it'll have to stay off until maintenance can get a new track put on."

The Major took another drag from his cigar, frowned, slowly nodded and more slowly said, "Why do I get the impression I'm going to have to crack some nuts to keep the doors on all the helicopters?"

"Because, Sir, the cargo doors are a pain in the ass. Besides, I didn't put that bullet hole there."

It wasn't long before they'd joined up with the flight on their way out of the same LZ. Another Huey company had joined the Blackhawks on this lift and what should have been a major battle, was underway. The NVA found themselves in a box. On one side, American troops, on another, ARVN, and both were to be pushing the NVA towards Cambodia. But between Cambodia and them stood the American Special Forces camp of Song Be, and all their mountain friends who hated the North Vietnamese more than anything or anyone else.

There was one more lift put in a different LZ by each Huey company. These were to dig in and hold in an effort to force the NVA towards Song Be. There was only one small problem, the ARVN troops weren't moving. This had irritated the American Commander to the point he'd ordered his troops to hold until they'd received confirmation that ARVN was on the move. Thus, the Blackhawks had been ordered back to An Loc.

The flight was on short final approach when Mr. Walker spoke, "Hey, Mac! Sounds like we might have a little time, how about cooking our C's?"

"You got it, just don't shut if off too quick."

Once on the ground, Walker kept the Huey running at idle speed. Jim quickly jumped out and closed his cargo door. Then, opening the storage compartment door, he pulled out the four C-ration boxes, and the metal holder he'd just picked up earlier that day after having one of the guys in sheet metal make it for him. He took the main meals from each box, placed them in his pockets, opened the engine compartment and climbed onto the platform. Then, using Wright's asbestos glove (used for changing gun barrels), he placed the rack with the C's in it inside the engine's exhaust pipe just after Mr. Walker shut it off. The heat still radiating from the turbine engine quickly heated their lunch. Still using the asbestos glove, he carefully removed each can and placed it on the platform beside his feet. Then he removed the holder and threw it on the ground to cool, but it didn't hit the ground until after bouncing off a highly polished combat boot. Jim looked down at a short, slightly plump little man wearing a uniform that looked like it had come from a dry cleaners in the States with extra starch. It was then that Jim saw the star in the center of the baseball cap.

Jim saluted as best he could and at the same time glanced at the tall, straight-backed first lieutenant standing with a clipboard behind the general.

"Good afternoon, General."

Both officers returned his salute as the General spoke, "Good after-noon, Specialist. What were you doing?"

"Sir, I was cooking our C-rations."

"Very ingenious. Did you make this, Specialist?"

"Yes, Sir, with the help of some of the guys in sheet metal."

"Everyone in your company have one of these?"

"No, Sir, just me. That's the second one I've had. I lost the first one after only using it a couple of times when my ship was shot down and burned. My friend in sheet metal knew it, so he made this one and I just got it this morning."

The General bent to pick it up and burnt his fingers.

"Sir, that's why I use my gunner's glove."

The General looked up disdainfully and said, "Get down from there!" Looking inside the aircraft, the General saw Major Hobbs and Mr. Walker still in their seats talking, with the Major smoking a cigar. In no time the General had all four crew members standing at attention in front of him. "At ease, men. Do any of you four know who I am?"

The General searched each man's face. Getting no response he started to speak when Jim said, "Sir, I do."

The General turned to Jim, who was standing there looking like he wished he didn't know. "Very well, Specialist MacLaughlin, is that pronunciation correct?"

"Yes, Sir."

"Very well, Specialist, why don't you enlighten your fellow crew members!"

"Sir, you're Brigadier General Anber, Commanding Officer 1st Aviation Brigade."

"Very good, Specialist, and how is it you know that when your Major doesn't?"

"Well, Sir, he hasn't been in country that long."

"Specialist, I didn't ask you to make excuses for your officers."

"No, Sir. I was a member of the 191st Assault Helicopter Company at Bear Cat before being sent up here. We had a formation one day, complete with TV cameras and you were there passing out medals. After you'd finished decorating people, you climbed up on the platform to speak, when you were handed a note. I remember your asking our Operations Officer if this was for real and he assured you it was. Then, you somewhat disgustedly spoke into the mike and told us a tactical emergency had been declared and all members of the flight crews were to man their ships. I think almost everybody in that formation let out a scream of joy and half of us threw our hats in the air. It was nothing personal, Sir, we just didn't want to stand out there in the sun and listen to speeches. I guess, Sir, I remember your face from that day."

"You mean you remember my nose." Jim didn't respond, but couldn't help but smile. "It's okay, Specialist, I know they call me Hook-Nose-Six. But with a horn like this, I can't blame anybody but my old man. You know, I remember that day also. It sure was hot. Believe it or not, I felt so sorry for you guys I'd decided to cut my speech from fifteen minutes down to just a couple. After all, I've stood in a few of those formations myself. If I remember right, you guys flew all the way down to Cau Mong that night. Got yourself into quite a fight, too, didn't you?"

"I don't really know, Sir. I was in maintenance."

The General simply smiled and said, "Hmmm. This your ship, Specialist?"

"Yes, Sir."

"Why isn't your name on it as crew chief?"

Jim glanced over at Walker, and the Major then replied, "Sir, it was just transferred to us yesterday."

"Do you smoke in your aircraft when it's on the ground, Specialist?"

Jim knew what the General had in mind. "Sir, I don't smoke at all, but if I could add, Sir, Major Hobbs has been very kind to me, Sir. I'm convinced he'll make an excellent pilot and commanding officer. He hasn't been in the company long enough to know one isn't supposed to smoke in the ship on the ground."

Again there was only the 'Hmmm' from the General before he said in a very commanding voice, "Lieutenant!"

"Sir!"

"Lieutenant, it appears we have three Article 15's to pass out here. Major, you get the first one for smoking in an aircraft on the ground with its engines shut off. That'll cost you one hundred fifty dollars. One hundred dollars for smoking, fifty because you're the company XO and should set a better example for your troops. Give the Lieutenant your full name, rank and serial number!"

If looks could kill, General Anber would have dropped dead on the spot. As the Lieutenant took the information from Major Hobbs, General Anber asked, "Mr. Walker, you're the Aircraft Commander?"

"Yes, Sir."

"Then you alone are responsible for everyone on board your ship regardless of whether they're crew members or passengers. They're your responsibility. As a result, they take orders from you even if they are majors. I understand your problem with rank, but you have no choice but to make it clear that you disapprove of their actions. Did you say anything to the Major?"

"No, Sir."

"Because you didn't say anything at all to the Major about his cigar, it'll cost you one hundred dollars. Give the Lieutenant your full name, rank and serial number."

Turning to Wright who was next in line, Anber continued, "You seem to be the lucky one today. You get off scot free. Just have a seat in the aircraft and see to it you don't move up the line. By this time everyone in this flight who smokes has lit up and I'm going to get every one of them for one hundred dollars. So just have a seat and enjoy your lunch. I'm sure it's still warm."

Then turning to Jim, the General said, "And as for you, I don't know. At least you had good motives."

Jim took this opening as his only chance. "Sir, have you ever eaten cold beans and weenies or, even worse, cold pork slices with so much grease it looked like lard? Then when you ate it, even after scraping off the greasy lard, it stuck to your teeth and mouth until you were willing to use a GI brush to get it off?"

"Yes, Specialist, I have and so have thousands of others and there'll be thousands more after you're gone. Give the Lieutenant your serial number."

"But, General, I wasn't doing it just for myself. If everyone could cook their C's, we'd all be a lot happier. Happy troops make better troops, and Sir, I wouldn't keep it for myself. I can very easily see the Army putting one of these in each chopper."

"You're a real humanitarian, Specialist. Now, before you become a Spec-Four, give the Lieutenant your serial number!"

Jim decided it wasn't going to do any good to continue on, especially after being threatened with the loss of a stripe. In a voice that clearly conveyed his displeasure, Jim said, "RA* and I USED to be proud of it!"

The General shouted, "Specialist, one more smart ass remark out of you and you'll be an E-1**. Aren't you afraid of me at all?"

"No, Sir. I always thought a General was supposed to have the good of his troops at heart. So why should I be afraid of someone who's supposed to be looking after me?"

"Just give the Lieutenant your serial number."

"Yes, Sir. RA11701118, Sir!"

The two men's eyes held each other's for a full second before the General turned and walked towards the next ship in line. Hobbs, Walker and Jim stood there with their eyes fixed on the General's back. It was then Jim saw Hunter happily cooking away with what he knew had to be a C-4 ball. It was a very common practice. The C-4 plastic explosive came in sticks, and almost every chopper had part of a stick stuck in a corner of the storage compartment. It reminded Jim of Play

---

*RA - Indicates a person who has enlisted, as opposed to a U.S. for draftees.

**E-1 - Lowest rank in the Army.

Doh. The stuff would stick to anything. Then, when one had enough time to heat his C's, he just pulled a little loose, rolled it into a ball about the size of a marble, put it between some stones on the ground and set it on fire. The stuff was truly wonderful. It would burn extremely hot, but never explode. It took a blasting cap to make C-4 explode, which made it totally safe to cook with. The only problem was some officers didn't like the idea. Jim knew it was going to cost Hunter one hundred dollars, which made Jim realize the General hadn't told him the amount of his fine.

It was at this point, Major Hobbs spoke. "There goes a truly sorry son of a bitch."

It was Wright seated inside the aircraft who let out a loud, hard laugh that made the other three turn and give him the evil eye. Wright's laughter stopped instantly and he said, "Major, it just reminded me of how I feel about washing and waxing Hueys!"

Jim said, "You know, Major, our wonderful Commander didn't even tell me how much he's going to stick me for."

The Major turned and looked surprised as he said, "You lucky bastard! I'd swear you could fall in a shit pile and come out smelling like a rose!"

Startled, Jim asked, "How do you figure that?"

"If the man didn't tell you how much that Article 15 was going to cost you, then you're not getting one."

"Why not?"

"Because! It's a matter of pride for someone like him. If he didn't tell you how much, then you won't get one. He didn't take your name either, did he?"

"No, Sir, just my serial number. Sir, do you think he forgot, or did I talk him out of it?"

"Mac, it's hard to say, it could be either, or the fact that you knew who he was."

"Sir, he could always stick a figure in later."

"He could, but I'd bet money he won't."

Major Hobbs was right. In two weeks there was a company formation for all flight crews, during which the CO called off the names of all the men who had an Article 15 waiting in his office courtesy of General Anber. Jim's name was not on the list. He often wondered why not, but never knew for sure. All the officers caught smoking in the Hueys paid one hundred dollars for the education they received that day. The enlisted men's education wasn't quite as expensive, but at fifty dollars each, it still hurt.

It was Mr. Walker who turned to Major Hobbs and asked, "Major, you going to warn the rest of the flight?"

The Major watched General Anber move on to the next ship up the line. After watching his lieutenant start to write down more names, Hobbs turned to Wright, who spoke before the Major had a chance. "Major, if you really don't mind, the General told me to sit here and be a good little boy and that's just what I'd like to do. Unless of course, you order me to walk past that man. I'm sure he wouldn't hold me responsible for obeying a direct order."

Major Hobbs said, "Yeah, I can't blame you for that. You know I could call Lead on the radio, he probably has someone monitoring company frequency in case six tries to contact us. But what the hell, misery loves company. Mac, any of the C's still hot?"

Jim gave a 'how should I know' look at Hobbs and then picked up the four still warm C-ration cans. He placed each can beside its box, but held on to the beans and frankfurters. In the box was a can of crackers and cheese and a pound cake.

He watched with interest who took what meals, as he tore open the accessory packs. Major Hobbs took spaghetti with beef chunks. Mr. Walker took beans with meatballs in a tomato sauce, leaving Wright with the chopped ham and eggs.

Every time Jim opened an accessory pack he had to laugh at the Army. They just couldn't bring themselves to allow anything to keep its common name and the accessory packet was an excellent example. On the pack was a listing of everything inside: matches, chewing gum, toilet paper, instant coffee, cream substitute, sugar, salt and a stimulater interdental. Whoever heard of a stimulater interdental? Who even knew what a stimulater interdental was? It was only through the process of elimination that he'd found it was a toothpick.

They were just about finished eating when Lead's crew chief walked up and told them all the officers were wanted at Lead ship.

Once the pilots left, Jim stretched out on the ship's passenger seats for a nap, using his chicken plate as a pillow. Wright started to play with some local kids who'd come out from nowhere. There was something about Wright that just seemed to attract them. For the life of him, Jim couldn't understand why. All Wright ever did was torment the poor kids. There were five of them ranging in age from about four to seven, each with the same sad little cutoffs as shorts. Two of the kids had shirts on, one still had two buttons but no sleeves and the other had sleeves but only one button. All five were barefoot and their dark skin was deeply tanned. They must have all gone to the same barber who knew one type of haircut, a butch. The biggest one had only a stump where once had been a right hand. No doubt one of the saddest by-products of war.

The saddest thing about the whole group was their eyes; those poor, sad, deep, dark little eyes. Yet, these same little sad eyes could instantly turn to life and sparkle with all the alertness of a normal, healthy child whenever Wright pulled out some little trinket. It didn't take much, something like a roll of toilet paper or a packet of creamer and Wright would have those kids doing all kinds of tricks. Just like training a puppy, you show him his treat, then have him do a trick and you give him his reward. The better the trick, the greater the reward and the same for those kids. Wright's fame in the company came from once getting a group of kids to make a human pyramid for a can of beans and weenies.

Jim awoke to a terrible racket which caused him to sit up. There were three South Vietnamese CH 34's taxiing down the runway. Wright stopped playing with the kids long enough to tell Jim they'd landed for fuel while he'd been asleep. Both GI's watched what were commonly called, 'flying death traps', lumber down the runway. The CH 34's had picked up that nickname because the crew chief's seat was located directly under the transmission, which had the tendency to break loose during a hard landing and fall on him. When the CH 34's had been given to the South Vietnamese, their pilots were so short the foot pedals had to be extended for their shorter legs, and the seats raised so they could see out the window.

By this time almost everyone in the area was watching the South Vietnamese pilots roll their helicopters towards the end of the runway. Jim, like most of the other Blackhawks, began to wonder when they were going to pull pitch and become airborne. Like a magnet, all eyes were drawn to the first of the three CH 34's as it reached the end of the runway and rolled down the hillside without ever leaving the ground. The second chopper followed the first in perfect formation right down the side of the hill, being preceded in death by the explosion of the first chopper. Not wishing to be outdone, it also exploded like the first into a giant fireball. The third pilot in line, having seen the fate of the first two, pulled pitch for all he was worth and managed to get his 34 off the ground at the last second. He was obviously unable to maintain flight as he dipped his nose down and disappeared below the trees. Yet, there was no explosion, and everyone who wasn't running in that direction stood with their mouths open, not really believing what they had just seen. Then, as though resurrected from the dead, the third chopper suddenly reappeared above the trees and headed south.

Wright returned to playing with the kids, a group that had expanded to twelve. Jim moved up into his seat behind the M60 and picked up his camera. These were the type pictures he liked to take. Kids doing their thing, local people in their daily lives, and general aerial photographs of the countryside were what he wanted to record on film. Unlike some guys, he'd never taken that first photo of a dead or wounded GI; it wasn't what he wanted to remember. There were guys who took pictures of every dead or wounded person they came across. It was almost as though they needed to prove to themselves or to others they'd been where the action was.

Jim had just finished taking a photo of Wright holding a C-ration can above his head and the kids trying to get it, when one of them grabbed the obvious leader of the group. It was almost like instant panic set in, the Vietnamese kids' normal fast chatter and smiles turned to shouts at machinegun speed, and their smiles were gone. In seconds the whole bunch had left with the smallest one quickly running back the ten feet he'd already traversed to make one final gesture for Wright to give him the can of C-rations.

Wright handed him the can and turned to Jim. "Hey, Mac, what the hell scared them off? You'd have thought Ho Chi Minh himself just popped up."

"I don't know, Wright. Something sure scared them off quick. It kind of looked like they were afraid of those other kids coming, but there are only five of them, even if they are a little older. Besides, kids usually work their way up the line of choppers. Those little guys just split. I don't understand."

"Ya know, Mac, I had the impression that little guy who came back was trying to tell me something. He kept saying, 'Number ten, number ten,' but I thought he was talking about me making them beg. Mac, hop out, I'm going to shut this cargo door."

Jim put his camera back in the corner and helped Wright slide the door shut. Jim thought about walking on up the line to Athia's ship, but decided it might not be a good idea to leave the ship since they couldn't shut the left door. So he opened the peter pilot's door, climbed in and sat down to watch the ship and Wright until those kids left. Besides, it was so hot his shirt back was soaked with sweat and he wanted to stay in the shade.

There were five kids in this group. All were older than any of the first group, most were in the eleven to fourteen age bracket. Wright started right in on them, just like every other group, by holding a can of C-rations as though he didn't know what to do with it. Both GI's relaxed as this group of kids responded just like every other. Shortly Wright was doing his routine.

Jim turned on AM Saigon. Turning all the other radios off and the volume up on Hobbs' helmet, he could easily hear the DJ in Saigon giving the time and temperature. No wonder his shirt was all wet down the back, 106 degrees in the shade and like the DJ said, "I know all you GI's out there in the bush are in the shade and if you aren't, you really don't want to know how hot it is in the sunshine."

Jim almost jumped through the windshield as a single 38 caliber pistol shot rang out right next to him. Turning, he saw Major Hobbs standing there with smoking pistol in hand.

All the officers had collected at Lead's ship while the flight waited for instructions. It hadn't been long when the pilot monitoring the radios broke up their chatter. He'd just received word the South Vietnamese were sending up an elite ranger unit to help move their infantry unit forward. It didn't take a genius to know how that would work. The rangers would land behind the ARVN unit and simply tell them to move out or be shot. They'd move.

It was almost an hour later when the ARVN choppers landed to put on fuel. As they touched down all kinds of fun was poked at them by their American counterparts. The general lack of respect by the Americans was even more evident as the ARVN aircraft started to roll down the runway. They laughed and joked about how it wouldn't be surprising if the gooks flew those 34's down the hillside instead of into the air. Yet all stood with their mouths open in a shocked state of disbelief as each CH 34 went down the hill. No one moved, the laughter stopped and the American eyes slowly dropped to the ground.

There was a steady stream from the end of the runway of people running towards the downed choppers. It was Major Hobbs who finally turned to the American pilot monitoring the radio and said, "You better call C & C and tell them what happened to their elite ranger unit."

It was over an hour before they received word from Blackhawk Six. The American officer in charge of the GI's on the ground had decided he wasn't sending American boys in to fight North Vietnamese when South Vietnamese refused. The order came down to pull out the American troops they'd just put in. The South Vietnamese troops were to provide cover for the extraction, and then walk out.

Major Hobbs and Mr. Walker had headed for their ship together, talking as they walked. At the helicopter before theirs, Mr. Walker cut between ships to speak to another pilot. It was then that Major Hobbs first looked ahead at the kids beside his ship. There was Wright teasing a group of kids with a can of C-rations, yet something was wrong. As Major Hobbs slowed his pace, he couldn't understand why one of the smaller kids was standing back towards the storage compartment by himself. Each step for the Major was slower than the preceding one. His eyes were glued to the little kid standing alone. He was barefoot, with ragged cutoffs and a short sleeve shirt about two sizes too large. The child's haircut was the standard Vietnamese boys cut, a butch, but it was his left hand that held the Major's attention. His left hand was holding something inside his partly unbuttoned shirt. Major Hobbs had stopped walking beside the preceding ship's tail rotor. He didn't yet know what was going on but figured, what the hell, they'd be in the air in a couple of minutes.

It was at the same moment, he saw the kid's right hand reach up and open the fuel cap. Major Hobbs shouted, "Hey kid, what the hell you doing?"

With that, the other kids started to run. Wright turned to look at the Major as the kid pulled the pin on the now exposed hand grenade. Only a fraction of a second passed, but Major Hobbs knew he was too far away to stop him physically. In that same fraction of a second, Major Hobbs knew what he had to do and he did it. The snubnose .38 came out of his shoulder holster in a flash, and one round was fired just as the kid raised the grenade to stick it in the fuel tank.

No one said a word as the Major ran up to the prone kid. He was dead, a bullet hole in the right side of his head just above and in front of the ear. Major Hobbs picked up the hand grenade and without speaking, held it out to show the large rubberband holding the handle in place. There were several GI's from the next couple of ships up the line who stood there gaping.

It was Wright who finally broke the silence. "My God, Major, he was just a kid!"

"Yes! A kid who would have blown this helicopter and everyone on it, including your young ass, into a thousand pieces! Mr. Walker, get on the radio and see if you can get some MP's out here to pick him up! The rest of you, get back to your ships. Now!"

Jim and Wright remained standing beside each other after the others had started to leave. Major Hobbs picked up the pin and placed it back in the grenade's handle. Looking up at Jim and Wright, he spoke somewhat curtly. "What are you two looking at?"

Without hesitation, Jim spoke, "You, Sir."

"What's the matter with you, MacLaughlin? He was VC. He just tried to stick a grenade in your fuel tank." Hobbs could see the look of disgust in Jim eyes.

"All right, MacLaughlin, what would you have done? I was clear up to the next ship. There was no way I could have reached him before he dropped that grenade inside your fuel tank. Let me ask you something, Mac. You going to fly in this thing knowing there's a grenade with only a rubberband around its handle in the fuel tank?"

Jim slowly shook his head. "Okay, so if you're not going to fly in it, are you going to help pull the fuel cell out, knowing that every second that passes, the JP-4 fuel has weakened the rubberband a little bit more?"

"I wouldn't be very happy about it, Sir."

"I didn't think so. Look, I'd already hollered at him. That didn't stop him, nothing short of a bullet was going to."

"Sir, it didn't have to be in the head!"

"How the hell do you know? Were you standing where I was standing? Did you see my line of fire? Look at it this way; he had a great future ahead of him as a Viet Cong. There are a lot of GI's he'll never kill! Mac, back to the first question, what would you have done?"

Jim paused and slowly said, "The same thing, Sir."

Jim turned and walked towards the fuel cap, stepping over the dead kid. It bothered him, it really did. Yet he knew deep down inside the Major was right. He had done just exactly the right thing, there was no question about it. If he'd hesitated for even a second, it would have been too late. Whoever said, 'war is hell' was right, but he should have added, 'it also makes you want to puke.'

There wasn't any of the usual chit chat as the helicopter lifted and fell in line behind everyone else in a trail right formation. The tension between the enlisted men and Major Hobbs could be felt by all aboard the ship. It was Major Hobbs who decided he had to do something to get his crew's minds off recent events.

"Hey, Mac, you back there?"

"No, Sir, I took a flying leap."

Major Hobbs decided to ignore the obvious sarcasm. "I was talking to one of your admirers at Lead, a Mr. Gail. He told me quite a story about the one time you two flew together." There was only silence for a response. "Well, Mac, come on, let's hear it."

"Major, I thought you said Mr. Gail already told you."

"He did, but I wanted to hear it from you. There are two sides to every story and I don't care what you called him, it's water over the dam. I'm not going to do anything about it now. But I will nail your balls to the wall if it happens again. So, tell me the story."

"Major, I really don't remember what you're talking about."

"MacLaughlin, I've got hammer and nails back at Tay Ninh. I could start nailing tonight unless you want to tell me a story now! I mean, everybody loves a good story. Wright, you'd like to hear Mac's story, wouldn't you!"

"No, Sir."

Jim laughed to himself, *Good old Wright, the man does have brass.* Hobbs' anger was clear in the tone of his voice, "Alright dammit, I've tried to be nice about it; now tell me the damn story and that's an order!"

"Okay, Major, I'll tell you what happened. Polaski was the gunner, Mr. Gail and another pilot from the other platoon drove, and I was the crew chief. Mr. Gail, by the way, is in the other platoon also. That's why I've only flown with him once. I didn't refuse to fly with him or anything like that. I can't remember the peter pilot's name or, for that matter, why we didn't have pilots from our own platoon. You have to remember, Major, that was back before they made us an all C.A.* company. We'd fly maybe one or two C.A.'s per week and the rest were all single ship missions. We called them ash and trash, or milk runs. Basically, you name it and we hauled it, and very seldom were any of them dangerous. I remember one time, just as an example, I spent the whole day flying sampans from Saigon to some little hamlet way down in the Delta. I knew I got picked for that job because I had one of the few helicopters in the company that still had a cargo hook in the hell hole. Most guys take the hooks out because they are hardly ever used and they make it really tough to crawl up into that hell hole. Anyway, this fishing hamlet had been hit by VC the night before and Chuck had, as a parting gesture, burned all the sampans. So our Uncle bought 'em all new ones, and we hauled them down there."

Major Hobbs broke in, "Mac, what's that got to do with you and Mr. Gail?"

"Nothing, Sir. I just thought if I talked long enough, I could stray far enough off the subject that you'd forget what I was supposed to be talking about."

"And you're still trying it."

"No, Sir, I'm getting to it, it just takes a while." Jim took a deep breath and said, "Anyway, we'd spent the morning hauling around a light Colonel and a Captain from Psychological Operations. Mostly we'd been down in the Delta. We'd take them to this place or that place, and they'd get out and talk to somebody for a little while, then

---

*C.A. - Combat Assault.

we'd take them someplace else. I remember at one point, we came across an old outdoor oven that had some old pots sitting around it, some were broken, some weren't. That Colonel wanted me to break the rest of the pots. So while Mr. Gail circled the oven, I shot up the unbroken pots and then started on the oven. I'll bet I wasted eight hundred rounds on that stupid oven before the Colonel decided it wasn't going to shoot back at us. We'd also spent some time over in the Plain of Reeds area dropping leaflets asking Chuck if he wouldn't like to give up, with instructions on how to go about it."

"Mac, would you get on with it!"

"Okay, okay, I'm getting to it. Anyway, when it came time for lunch we took our passengers back to Bien Hoa. They told us we could have an hour and a half lunch. So Mr. Gail got all excited and started hopping up and down in his seat. He was going to the officers' club in Saigon for lunch. Well, we flew on over to Saigon and the two officers hopped out almost before the main rotor blades had quit turning. So I hollered at Mr. Gail as he hot footed it off, 'Hey, how about us?' You see, Major, they didn't give us C-rations except when we were flying C.A.'s. Otherwise, we were supposed to eat in somebody's mess hall. Well, Mr. Gail said he didn't care what we did, just so we were back and on the ship by 1345. That way we'd have plenty of time to fly over to Bien Hoa by two o'clock. He even suggested we go to the enlisted men's club and eat. Well, I'd been there before and it takes over a half hour to walk one way. There was no way we could have walked there and back, plus eat and be on the ship by 1345. So I asked if we could go to the PX; it was only about a fifteen minute walk one way and we could get something to eat there. Mr. Gail told us, 'Sure, go ahead, and to pick him up a can of shaving cream while we were there.' So Polaski and I headed for the PX. We ate at the snack bar and still had plenty of time, so we decided to walk around the PX for a while. Man, oh man, is that place something. I'd never been in a place like that before, it's enormous. Plus it had everything under the sun for sale: cameras, and lenses the likes of which I'd never seen, diamonds and all kinds of rings and jewelry with rubies and sapphires. You can buy all kinds of clothes, even have a complete suit hand made. There's even one desk there where you can order a brand new car, any make you like, made to your specifications and delivered to the dealer closest to your home or next duty station. Anyway, we both got some things we needed along with Mr. Gail's shaving cream, and got in line to check out. There were only two people in front of us and I remember looking at my watch and thinking we still had about nine minutes to spare. The next thing I knew, three officers walked up and got in line in front of the two guys in front of us. Now we were five people back. The check out guy was working on the last officer when up walks two captains, and they pull the same trick. I'm beginning to think I'll spend the rest of my tour over here just trying to get checked out. Of course, by this time the line behind us had gotten long enough, you couldn't see the end. The thing that finally got things moving again was when some Air Force Full Bird walked up and wanted to know why the line was getting longer instead of shorter, just as a group of four army warrants jumped the line. Man, did that Air Force Colonel get mad. He'd been waiting in line and so could they. When he got done with 'em, they went to the end of the line. I remember he sat his stuff down on the checkout counter and asked where he could find the officer in charge. He was going to put a stop to this crap.

"By this time it was, of course, way past time for Polaski and I to leave. So we sat the stuff we were going to buy down and left. I'm telling you the truth, Sir; we ran all the way back to the chopper.We still got there five minutes late. But from where we were parked it only takes five minutes by air to get back over to Bien Hoa.

"Mr. Gail saw us coming and by the time we got to the ship, he'd untied it and had it running. The last thing Polaski said before we reached the chopper was, 'Mac, what's this guy's problem? We've still got ten minutes to get to Bien Hoa and that's plenty of time.' I told him I didn't know. But if he's in such a hurry that he's got it running already, we can expect to catch hell for being late. Anyway, when I climbed in, lo and behold, there in the passenger's seat sat another warrant officer whom I'd never laid eyes on before.

"We were in the air before I had my helmet or seatbelt on. In fact, I'd climbed in, sat down, and started to put on my flight gloves when he pulled pitch and took it up. Needless to say, I took my own sweet time putting my helmet on and hooking it up. Less than a second after I'd plugged it in, Mr. Gail said, 'MacLaughlin, you plugged in yet?' I told him I was and the first thing he asked me was, did I get his shaving cream? So I told him what had happened to us at the PX and he never said a word. I asked who our passenger was and Mr. Gail said he was an old friend of his from flight school. That was the last thing said until we got back to Bien Hoa. In the meantime, he'd redlined it all the way up to Cu Chi where he dropped our passenger off, and then redlined it all the way back to Bien Hoa. Needless to say, by the time we got back to Bien Hoa we were almost thirty five minutes late, and there, standing on the heliopad at parade rest was our Captain. So Mr. Gail says, 'Oh, shit, that man is pissed! MacLaughlin, if I catch hell for being late, I'll nail your balls to the wall.' Well I don't mind telling you, Major, his telling me that really jerked my chain. I told him, 'Hey, look, we'd a been on time if you hadn't taken that joker all the way up to Cu Chi, so you don't need to go sticking the blame on me. Besides, a man admits to his mistakes and you made one, not Polaski or me.' Needless to say, that jerked Mr. Gail's chain completely out of its socket. The only thing that kept me from catching it right then was that we were on the ground and the Captain had Mr. Gail standing at attention, chewing him up one side and down the other. To say he was upset would be a major understatement. The funniest part was when the Captain had just finished with him, out walked the Colonel, and he started in on him, too. Finally, it was Mr. Gail's turn and you could see the little worm passing the buck to Polaski and me. Once he got back in the chopper, nobody said poop to anyone.

"The first place we landed was just outside the Hobo Woods. The infantry had found a VC tunnel and the Colonel wanted to talk to the tunnel rat* when he came out, if he came out. Anyway, once we'd landed, the Colonel told us to shut it off, we'd be there awhile. So, while I was back there tying the main rotor blade down, Mr. Gail walked up and said, 'MacLaughlin, come here, I want to talk to you.' We walked another twenty feet away from the chopper where it was just him and me. He started in by giving me this line that one of his goals when he'd entered the Army was to spend his time without handing out any military discipline, but it looked like I'd just made that

---

*Tunnel Rat - Small G.I. sent in V.C. tunnels.

goal unobtainable. So I asked him why, and he said, 'Two reasons: one I was late reporting for duty after lunch and two, my smart mouth in front of others. As an enlisted man I had no right to question his decisions and I didn't have the right to make smart ass comments or give him any kind of back talk. Did I understand that?' Well, to make a long story short, I told him I understood and he wouldn't have any more problems from me."

Major Hobbs interrupted, "Mac, you just skipped the part I've been sitting here listening to all your rambling for. You've made this story as long as you possibly could. Now, Mr. Gail remembers very well what was said next." There was a long silence before the Major continued, "Mac, I'm waiting."

"Major, I'd just as soon forget about it if you really don't mind."

"Let's put it this way, I mind."

Again there was silence before Jim finally said, "Sir, isn't there a law against self incrimination?"

Major Hobbs practically shouted, "MacLaughlin!"

"All right, Major. I asked him if he'd passed the buck about our being late to me. He told me, 'that was irrelevant.' I knew it was just the two of us and that nobody would be able to prove later what either of us had said. So I told him, 'Like hell it was. I knew good and well he'd been too big of a coward to take the rap himself for his own mistake, and that if he hadn't taken that joker to Cu Chi, we would have been on time and he knew it. Besides, we were out here having this little chat probably because the Colonel had told him to. Further, that I personally thought he was lower than a toothless, yellow-bellied swamp snake with the bite of a sabertooth crotch cricket, that not only had a yellow belly, but had a yellow streak running down the center of his back going from one shoulder to the next. And as far as his goals were concerned, there wasn't going to be any military punishment and we both knew it. In the first place, it wouldn't be too hard to find that Air Force Colonel from the PX. In the second place, I wouldn't have been in that line if he hadn't asked me to buy him shaving cream, and finally, even if I'd been on time, we still wouldn't have made it to Cu Chi and back to Bien Hoa on time. Anybody with the brains of a stick knows that, including him when he was offering that warrant officer a ride.' Well, he started jumping up and down claiming he'd break me to E-1 for talking to him like that. I just told him, 'Look, I won't give you any more trouble on the ship, but I'll deny ever having had this conversation. So it'll be your word against mine, and without a witness, you haven't got any more chance than an ice cube in hell,' which was about how mad he was when he turned and walked away. That's the last I've heard about it until today. Is that what you wanted to hear, Major?"

"Yep."

"Well, Major, how much difference was there between Mr. Gail's version and mine?"

"They were almost word for word at the important parts."

"So what happens now, Sir?"

"I told you, nothing, before you started and I meant it then just as I do now, nothing."

The Major was pleased with himself. MacLaughlin wouldn't be thinking about that kid for a while.

Lift after lift was made without incident and the Blackhawks had quickly settled into the boring routine of extracting troops from point A and putting them in at point B. The day had been long and everyone was tired. It also had been hot, very hot and humid. As a result, the engines weren't putting out as much power as they should have and the men alternated between sweating on the ground during pickups and being chilled when that sweat hit the cooler air at eighteen hundred feet. Thoughts of a cold beer, a warm shower and bed, even if it was an Army fold up cot, began to creep into everyone's mind. One more extraction and they could head home.

Everyone on board Jim's ship had been laughing about how this had been such a bad day, starting right off with that duck and going straight down hill from there. It was agreed by all, they'd feel a whole lot safer back at Tay Ninh on the ground for the night. After all, there were only two worse things that could have happened to them, to go down in the trees, or for someone to take a hit.

One of the unwritten rules on board a helicopter was never to suggest the possibility that one of the four crew members could be killed, wounded yes, but never, never killed.

The flight was on short final when Lead came over the radio, "Flight, this is Lead, this is the last extraction for the day. The ARVN troops will be providing ground cover on this lift and then walking out. There are some things your crew chiefs and gunners should remember. First, if we start receiving fire it will probably be on the way in, unfortunately, you won't be able to return it because of the ARVN troops. However, I want you to keep your eyes on those troops. If you see one of 'em turn and open up on us, blow the bastard away. Just be damn sure it's us he's shooting at. Lead out."

Mr. Walker spoke as soon as Lead quit, "Okay, Wright, just for your information, it's on this kind of lift that we usually find a real hot LZ. ARVN will turn tail and run and Charlie knows it, so he won't hesitate a second about trying to put us on the ground with a few grunts. Just to make you feel better, it's usually Trail who gets it the worst. In other words, if you're sitting there looking at muzzle flashes, don't ask permission to return fire, just blow 'em away as Lead says. Any questions?"

"No, Sir."

They were only a few seconds from touch down when the left tree line erupted like the Fourth of July, with sustained bursts of light. The American troops were on board even before the chopper touched down, and in less than two seconds they were up.

"Flight, this is Lead, open fire on that left tree line."

Instantly, every one of the Flights' ten door gunners opened fire. Jim, being on the right side of the chopper, could only sit and listen as the door gunners opened fire.

The radio cracked with background noise, as first one, and then a second ship reported taking hits. The first ship continued to fly and reported no apparent substantial damage. It was the second one that got everyone's attention; one of the grunts on board had taken a hit as they passed over the tree line.

Mr. Walker had been busy. He hadn't anymore than finished giving Wright instructions than they were in the LZ. The grunts started to jump on before he was on the ground, which he always hated. It's hard enough to land a Huey without four or five guys jumping on the skids rocking it. The temptation was always to just drop it straight down, but if he caught a foot or leg, it'd be crushed. All he could do was try to hold it steady and work it on down. They were all loading from the same side, which made it only slightly easier. Just as he'd gotten it down, Wright had said, "You're loaded, GO!"

He called Lead and said, "Trail to Lead, we're loaded, Sir."

As though lifted by puppet strings from an unseen hand, the Flight lifted as one and moved forward.

Walker had heard the first two reports of ships hit and knew it would be a wonder if his didn't take damage, too. That was the worst thing about flying trail, you were the last in and the last out, and you caught the most lead. At times he could just about feel Charlie's frustration. As each ship escaped, the VC turned their attention to the one chopper they could have their guns on the longest, Trail.

Time always seemed to move so terribly slow for Walker as he raced his ship towards the safety of the sky. It just seemed at times like this he'd twist the throttle grip off, his hand would actually ache from the twisting grip he held on that throttle. He even found himself rocking back and forth in a futile effort to gain airspeed and a quicker escape. It was now their turn to cross the tree line where the others had taken fire. Their airspeed indicator read seventy-two knots, which meant Charlie wouldn't have much of a shot at them. Both door guns were raking the tree line with lead and all on board thought they'd made it by safely.

Wright was still firing and Jim had just quit when Major Hobbs' foot pedal bubble exploded, and Mr. Walker saw Hobbs jump like he'd been hit with an electric prod. It was Major Hobbs' voice that the other three crew members heard screaming in their earphones. "I'M HIT, MY GOD, I'M HIT!"

Jim's head jerked to the left in time to see Major Hobbs slump into a fainted position.

Walker yelled, "Mac!", and was interrupted by Jim's , "I'm already on my way," and indeed he was.

The monkey belt had been unhooked and a grunt pushed out of the way. The grunts, unaware of what had happened, watched dumbfounded as Jim climbed into the cargo area and half motioned for the grunts behind Hobbs' seat to move as he shouted, "Move! Move!" Dropping to his knees, Jim grabbed both red handles at the bottom of Hobbs' seat. In one big yank, he broke the small safety wires and pulled the seat retaining handles down. With his right hand, Jim reached up to the handle on top of the seat and gently pulled the back down. The grunts, now aware of what was happening, started to help by removing Hobbs' helmet as Jim released the Major's seatbelt. This done, they pulled him back into the cargo area. There was so little blood it took Jim a minute to locate the wound. Once located, his switch blade quickly cut away the left pant leg, exposing a nice neat .30 caliber sized hole. Jim went to work bandaging Major Hobbs' leg and almost cried with envy. The man had the perfect wound. It was small caliber and had entered and exited his calf muscle without doing any major damage. It hadn't hit the bone, and from the small amount of blood it was obvious there wasn't any damage to the major blood sources.

Jim had been aware of the grunts' activities over Hobbs. Now, however, for the first time he looked up. To his great surprise he saw a black PFC giving mouth to mouth and another man pounding on Hobbs' chest. Jim sat there stunned, the implication was obvious. The mean, super tough, 'I eat nails for breakfast,' Major Hobbs had gone into shock and had heart failure, all from a wound that wouldn't even have gotten him out of the country. He'd have spent a week or ten days in a Saigon hospital, followed by another two or three weeks back in the company area on restricted duty. Instead, he lay on the Huey's aluminum floor whiter than snow. The grunt giving mouth to mouth stopped long enough to feel Hobbs' neck for a pulse. He slowly shook his head and stopped his buddy still pushing on the Major's chest. "He's gone," was shouted over the roar of the Huey.

Jim's response was rage, not only at the grunts because they were quitting, but even more so at Hobbs for dying. Jim's shouts could be heard by all the grunts as he jumped on Hobbs' chest. "Live, you stupid son of a bitch, live, damn you, live!" Grabbing the Major's shirt, he shook and shouted at the same time. "Damn you, don't die on me, you son of a bitch, you're so fucking tough, wake up." The tears were gently rolling down the side of Jim's face when the first grunt pulled Jim back and slowly shook his head.

"He's dead, man, he's dead." Then pulling an olive drab handkerchief from his pocket, he handed it to Jim who wiped his eyes and blew his nose.

They were almost on the hospital pad before Jim plugged in his helmet, which had come unhooked as he climbed forward to pull

Hobbs out of his seat. Neither Wright nor Mr. Walker could believe what Jim told them.

The ride home was in silence and seemed to take forever.

14

"We played the flute for you, and you did not dance; we sang a dirge and you did not mourn." Matthew 11:17 NIV

Is This Really What We Fight For?

When Gillett found Jim, he was alone at a corner table writing a letter; there was a bottle of Jack Daniels Black, a can of Coke and a coffee cup to keep him company. Gillett got a Coke from the bar before walking to Jim's table.

"Hi, Mac!"

"Hi, Gillett, have a seat. Help yourself to the bottle."

Gillett took a big gulp of Coke, poured a healthy amount into the can from Jim's bottle and slowly swished it. "I hear you had quite a day. It should make interesting reading for your folks."

"If I was writing about it, it probably would, but I'm writing about the weather and Hobbs making us police the flight line. I haven't gotten to it yet, but I'll add the duck flying through our windshield and that's about it."

"What do you think you're doing, protecting them?"

"You're damn right! At least my parents know I'm here and flying combat missions; that way if I get it they won't be too surprised, but they don't need to know any more. It wouldn't do any good for them to know more." There was a pause before Jim continued, "You know,

Gillett, for the life of me I don't know how those guys who tell their folks they're in Alaska get away with it. I mean what in the world would you write about?"

"I don't know, but there are guys who do it and, of course, with only an APO number for an address, they get away with it."

"Yeah, and if they get their brains blown out, their parents go into as deep a state of shock as Hobbs did. I take it you've heard about Hobbs?"

"Yeah, I talked to Wright a little while ago. He also told me about the kid with the frag. Just between you and me, I'm not all that unhappy about Hobbs. I don't like to see anybody killed, but I'm real glad he's not going to be in the company any more."

"Gillett, he'd have been all right!"

"I don't think so, Mac. He'd a had us playing all kinds of stupid games."

"Only until he made CO, then they would have stopped."

"Well, Mac, we'll never know whether you're right or not, and personally, I'm glad. Speaking of good news, I've got some that should cheer you up. They let the KP's back on post today. So I asked one of them who had done some things for me before if he wanted a monkey. That guy got a long stick, stuck an orange on it and got the monkey out of the rafters with it. Then when the monkey was on the floor eating its orange, the gook clubbed the hell out of it with his stick. Then he tied the monkey to the same stick, I never saw one stick get so many uses."

Both men laughed as Jim asked, "Where was Kenny during all this?"

"Remember, I put him on a convoy going to Saigon this morning."

Jim looked surprised, "Gillett, he was on the EM's side of the club when I came in a little while ago."

"Well, I know he was in the convoy when it left post this morning. I checked. Which reminds me, how'd you get your daily inspection done so fast?"

"I didn't do it, that's how."

Gillett looked disapprovingly at his friend and said, "You'd refuse to fly with anyone who pulled that kind of trick."

"Yeah, I know."

"Mac, you look beat, why don't you finish that letter and go to bed?"

Jim drained the cup as he watched a tall, over six foot, skinny bean pole Spec-Four rank approach.

"Sergeant Gillett?"

"That's me."

"Sergeant, Operations sent me to tell you they need a crew and a ship for a night mission."

Jim responded instantly, "I'll take it, Gillett."

"Just a minute, Mac. Okay, Specialist, tell 'em I'll get a crew and then report personally to Operations. By the way, did that convoy that left this morning come back?"

"Yeah, it got back about an hour, hour and a half ago. The NVA had knocked out one of the bridges between here and Dau Tieng that the engineers had just replaced yesterday, so they just turned around and came home. Will that be all, Sergeant?"

"Yes, thank you."

The walking bean pole hadn't gone out the door yet when Gillett turned to Jim, "Mac, I can get somebody else. Go to bed."

"Oh, I'm okay, besides, I'd rather fly than sit around here bored to death getting hit with 122MM rockets."

Gillett looked Jim over good. He didn't have to let him go. He could send someone else and order Mac to bed. His eyes were puffy with dark circles and the left one was a little blood shot. He needed a shave and his face was still splotchy with mosquito bite welts from walking in the jungle. Yet, the fatigue that had been so very obvious just moments ago had already begun to disappear with the prospect of flying.

"Okay, Mac, go ahead, I'll get Wright."

Jim had just locked his wall locker after putting his writing paper away when he heard Meyers let out a loud, long profanity.

"Hey, Meyers, what's wrong with you?"

"Oh, Mac, that damn mother of mine screwed me over good."

"What?"

"A couple of weeks ago I wrote home and told my Mom to send me five hundred dollars from the money I've been sending home. I'm supposed to go on R&R next week if they get it opened up again. Anyway, I've been sending all my extra money home and having my Mom put it in a savings account for me. She knew it was my money and she knew what I was saving it for. Tonight I get a letter saying she's very sorry but she's emptied my savings and bought my sister a new car. The little bitch just turned sixteen a month ago. You know, Mac, it's at times like these I can understand why my dad used to beat the hell out of that stupid woman. I've wondered for a long time why he ever married her, but I'll tell you, I KNOW why he divorced her."

Jim looked down at the boyish-looking nineteen-year-old Spec-Four from Texas.

"Hey, Meyers, it'll work out; some of us can go together and loan you enough so you can still go. Plus, you might get another pay day in there first, which would help. Just one more thing, you may know why he beat her, but it still wasn't right. It's never right!"

"I know, Mac, and thanks for the offer of money, I really appreciate it."

When Jim got to his ship, Mr. Walker and Mr. O'Neal were already there. Greetings and small talk were exchanged as Jim untied the rotor blades and prepared for flight.

It was Green who walked up and threw his gear on the ship instead of Wright. He explained that Gillett couldn't find Wright, so he'd volunteered. Once in the air, Mr. Walker explained they were going to Saigon to pick up an entertainment group.

At Hotel Three, the group of entertainers loaded their gear quickly and climbed in.

Three women with bags, rabbit fur coats, spike heels and speakers sat awkwardly through the ride back to Tay Ninh. They looked as much out of place as they had to feel. It was the contrast that struck Jim. Only a few hours ago a dead Major and infantrymen covered with sweat and mud had sat in the cargo area now occupied by these three women. The fur on the rabbit coats whipped back and forth and each woman tried unsuccessfully to hold her hair in place.

Steadily the craft flew northwestward, going over artillery fire where it could and around it where it couldn't. The women didn't see or know of the F-4 Phantom that shot by on their left, or the B-52 strike they flew around just south of Cu Chi, nor would they ever know of the small arms fire directed their way on short final approach into Tay Ninh. No return fire was given since no hits had been taken and to keep the women from knowing just how far away from the civilized world they really were.

Once on the ground, the three struggled to walk in their spikes. Besides, those rabbits which probably felt good in the air, had to be terribly hot now.

They were met by a jeep and a three quarter-ton pick up. The girls were quickly loaded into the jeep, but not without exposing more than their legs. Once the jeep had departed, the enlisted men loaded the pickup and made numerous comments about the girls, not all of which were nice. Jim rode back to the company area in the pickup and then headed straight for the hooch.

He quickly stored his gear and went to the club. The partitions between the NCO side and the EM side had been removed to allow for greater viewing area. GI's were busy on the stage setting up mikes and other sound equipment; all the tables had been removed and chairs were stacked along the walls. Jim headed for the bar thinking a beer would taste good, but it had been closed until after the show.

It was another twenty minutes before the CO climbed on the stage and asked for everyone's attention. "Men, we're very lucky tonight that our company clerk was able to bring in this entertainment on such short notice. They were supposed to go down to Tan An tonight, but Tan An is under siege, so they're here instead. I just want you men to know I'm damn proud of you, you're the best assault helicopter company in the world. You deserve the best and, believe me, I know you won't be disappointed."

There was a big applause with cheers as the CO held up both hands to regain control. With a big smile the CO continued, "Besides, I explained that I have the only transportation off this island, so you damn well better not be disappointed. Without any further ado, I give you the Australian Pussy Cat and her Two Kittens."

With that the three girls stepped through the door behind the stage. They were jumping, shaking and singing.

By now the club was so jammed with GI's shouting and cheering, it was not possible to move. They were one solid mass of humanity standing and stomping on each others' toes watching the three women singing and wiggling. Their singing wasn't that great, but they did know how to wiggle and that's all most of the GI's really cared about.

The Pussy Cat was dressed in typical show girl attire. Bright blue spike heels and a very loosely flowing full length dress that was split up the left side to just above her knee. There was a long white feather shawl wrapped around her shoulders to partially hide the low cut front of her dress. As the shawl moved and was finally discarded during one of the songs, it left her exposed down to the nipples. She was dark complected with dark hair and slightly overweight, with hardly enough makeup to hide the fifty some odd years she'd been around. The two back up girls, one light black and one blond, played guitars and wore matching outfits, bright red with high neck lines but backless and a hemline about eight inches above their knees.

They told bad jokes, sang poorly and stripped. By the end of the show, the two kittens wore only their shoes and had swung their breasts around enough to have made a man sore, let alone two women. Yet it truly was the Pussy Cat who was the show's star. She, too, had stripped during the course of the show, leaving her with only a G-string and her shoes. It was, however, the muscle control she had in her chest that stole the show. Able to move one breast independently of the other, or together, she had the group of GI's not believing their eyes and shouting for more by the show's end.

Within a few minutes of the show's completion, all the officers and most of the enlisted men had left the club. Jim moved over to the NCO side and ordered a Coke and his bottle of Jack. Hunter, already seated at a table, waved for Jim to join him. It was only minutes later when Athia, with beer in hand made it a threesome. There was a lot of joking, laughing and discussion of what they'd just seen.

Twenty minutes later Gillett walked up, "Mac, where the hell you been?"

Jim looked up with a bewildered look, "Right here. Why?"

"Because everybody's sitting on your ship waiting for you. You're supposed to take those girls back to Saigon."

"Gillett, you've been telling me I should quit flying all these night missions, so I think I'll just sit this one out. Besides, nobody told me I was supposed to fly 'em back. And I really wouldn't call them girls."

"You what? Get your ass out there!"

"Hey, Gillett, stay cool, man. I'm telling you, I'm not flying them back. Get somebody else or let 'em walk for all I care."

"What the hell is eating you, Mac? Didn't you like the show?"

"Sure, I enjoyed it at the time, but the more I think about it the less I think of it, and I'm not going to waste my time flying them back to Saigon."

Athia spoke up, "Hey, Gillett, I thought it was a great show, I'll fly 'em back."

Jim looked over at his friend, "Athia, you're a jerk, you know that?"

"Oh, Mac, get off your self righteous kick. You enjoyed what you saw as much as the next guy and, in fact, you were probably breathing heavier than most."

"Athia, you're so damn stupid, you can't even see that's the point! What good did it do any of us? Furthermore, the only reason those broads were here in the first place is they can't sing or dance well enough to get a legit job anyplace else. And the only reason they take off their clothes is they couldn't get anybody to pay them to do anything else. Besides, that Pussy Cat is so damn old, the only place she could get anybody to watch her take off her clothes is where there are a bunch of GI's shut off from the world."

Athia, who had risen to leave, turned back towards Jim, "MacLaughlin, you sure know how to ruin a perfectly good evening, you know that? But what do I care, I get to fly 'em back to Saigon. See you later, Sucker."

The alcohol was working on Jim by now and it heightened his anger. "Athia, you're an asshole. What do you think you're going to do, fly 'em home and have one of 'em suck you off on the way? You know that's never going to happen just like I do. In fact, I'll bet you fifty bucks you don't even get a peck on the cheek. They've got their thirty pieces of silver and to hell with you and me and how we feel, or our emotions."

Athia looked down at his friend and said half out of anger and half from a feeling of comradeship, "Fuck you, Mac."

Several days later, Athia and Jim were in the club having a drink. Athia brought it up by saying Jim had been right and he had known it even before he'd left the club that night. Jim laughed and bought the next round.

After Athia left the club, Gillett sat down with Jim. "Mac, you and

I are the old soldiers in this outfit."

Jim interrupted, "Yeah, and I just turned twenty years old. Now, ain't that a gas?"

"You know what I mean. You've only got about two months left before your year's up and you go home. I'm the only one in the platoon who's been here longer than you, and that's only because I extended for six months so I could get out of this crummy Army early. The point is, you know I'm not going to pull rank on you unless you back me into a corner, so don't pull that kind of trick on me in front of somebody again. Most of these guys already know you and I are old and close friends. They also suspect I don't treat you quite the same, even though you and I both know better.

"Look, you've had too much to drink, you're tired, and you've had a stressful, trauma-filled day. Besides, you look like you're physically exhausted. Go to bed!"

"Okay, Gillett, just as soon as I finish my drink."

"You hear about Willard and Mr. Tracy?"

"No, what happened to them?"

"Well, you know we've been flushing some of the older engines the last couple of weeks, and Willard's ship had one that should have been replaced a hundred hours ago, but we can't get any new engines. You remember the proper flush procedures?"

"Sure, I've done it enough. Have somebody turn the engine over without starting it while you throw a quart of solvent in the intake. Let it set for half an hour then run it up and throw about five gallons of water through it."

"Right. Well you know how Mr. Tracy is such a know-it-all and us poor crew chiefs are all stupid as hell?"

"That's the one allright."

"Well, Mac, he really stepped on himself tonight. He was mad because he had to help Willard flush his ship, so when Willard told him how it's supposed to be done, Mr. Tracy told him just throw in the solvent while he was running it. Willard told him he was crazy, that he'd just end up ruining the engine. Well, Mr. Tracy gave Willard a direct order to throw the solvent in while it was running. You care to guess what happened?"

Jim was laughing as he answered, "Willard did it, and that would be about like throwing gasoline into a burning pot belly stove, so I'd say he probably blew it up?"

"You got it. The sucker threw about a fourth of its turbine blades out."

Both men were laughing hard enough that others began to look their direction.

"I'll tell you the best part, Mac. Captain Wolf told me just before the show started that the Colonel is making Tracy pay for the engine. He has a nice little sum taken out of his paycheck every month, and he also loses his AC status. Don't you know that'll just kill our Mr. Know-It-All."

"You know, Gillett, we had a pilot like Mr. Tracy in the company I came over with, a Second Lieutenant Point. He was the maintenance officer until he got sent to another company. The man had no more idea of how a Huey works than a nurse does. He didn't even know the difference between an open-end and a box-end wrench. Anyway, he was always trying to tell us guys in maintenance how to do things and he was always wrong. So we'd just say, 'Yes, Sir,' and as soon as he left we'd do it the right way. Well, one night he showed up to test fly a ship we'd just put a new engine in, but he was drunk as a skunk. The guy in charge of our maintenance crew told him he was too drunk to fly and refused to get into the aircraft with him. As you well know, you don't do that. In fact, if anybody on a crew refused to fly on the test flight, you had to pull it back in and do it all over again. But for some reason, our crew leader was able to convince the lieutenant the only reason we wouldn't fly with him was because he was drunk.

Needless to say, Lieutenant Point was mad as hell. He started it up and began to taxi to the runway. He was doing just fine until he started to turn to take off and turned the tail boom into another ship parked, ready to come into maintenance that night. Talk about an instant change in a man's attitude. The good lieutenant hadn't anymore than crawled out of the aircraft, than he was trying to buddy up to us. He kept talking about how he'd lost tail rotor control and how glad he'd been that none of us were on board. The man didn't have a chance. He'd totaled it, but it hadn't burned, so we checked out the tail rotor controls that same night. They were fine. The next morning, the CO called our whole crew in, one at a time, and asked what had happened. Everyone of us told him the lieutenant was drunk and unfit to drive, that was why we hadn't flown with him and why he'd crashed. So, to make a long story short, the CO pulled Point's AC status, put him into the flight platoon as a peter pilot and fined him enough so that he'll get about fifty dollars per month for the rest of his time in service. With that on his record, you know he'll never make captain."

Gillett watched Jim finish his drink and said, "Mac, go to bed."

"Okay, I'm on my way."

15

From The Depths Of Terror To Euphoria

The sharp pain that struck Jim between the eyes drove itself deep into his brain. Pulling the covers over his head protected his eyes from the overhead lights that Gillett had turned on, but not from the platoon sergeant's mouth.

"Okay! Everybody up! It's another bright and beautiful day! Let's go. Let's go. Out of your rack!"

As Gillett moved on down the row of bunks still shouting and clapping his hands, Jim pulled the covers off his head. He had one terrible headache. For some reason life didn't seem so wonderful, even if it was a "bright and beautiful day". Not only was his headache getting worse, but the rest of his body's sensor controls were beginning to function and report to his slowly operating brain.

His mouth was full of cotton, his eyes wouldn't focus, his tongue was twice as large as it should be, his nose reported a foul bitter smell and as he slowly stood, his back and shoulder muscles reported they were all still very sore and stiff from carrying Mr. Mace through the jungle.

Jim stood partly bent over with his head resting against his wall locker. One eye was only slightly open as he worked the combination lock, first one direction and then the other, until, with a metal thunk, it fell open. It was Gillett's hand that rested on Jim's left shoulder and Gillett's voice almost in a whisper, "Mac, you'd feel a lot better after a shower. The only problem is the officers' shower is the only one with water."

"What time is it, Gillett?"

"Four thirty-eight."

"I think I'll go take a shower. I feel terrible."

"Don't get caught or your butt will be sore from getting your ass kicked out."

Jim smiled as he headed out into the all consuming darkness.

The officers' showers were constructed basically the same as the enlisted men's. There weren't any lights and it had a gravity fed water system. It also wasn't quite as busy since there were about fifty less officers than enlisted men. Still, of the two hundred fifty men in the company, one hundred were pilots and officers, so it wasn't like the place was never used.

Jim knew the officers didn't like it one bit when an enlisted man used their showers or anything else that belonged to them. But as long as he didn't say anything, no one would be able to recognize him in the darkness. Still he was a bit uncomfortable as he entered since the water from one of the faucets was running. Jim acted like he belonged there and his attire (flip flops and towel wrapped around him) was the same as any officer coming in for a shower. He headed for the faucet farthest from the naked body being rinsed off. Jim had just turned on the water and stepped under its ice cold flow when he heard the all too familiar voice of Mr. Halsey.

"Good morning."

Jim's first thought was, Oh, shit! His second thought was, What do I do now?

Again Halsey spoke, this time a little louder, "Good morning!"

This time Jim stuck a hand out and waved hello.

"Hey, who is that down there?"

By now Jim had quickly soaped and was rinsing off. In a jolly voice

Jim answered, "Good morning, Mr. Halsey!"

"MacLaughlin, what are you doing in here?"

"There isn't any water in our shower, Sir."

"Life can be a bitch can't it, Mac?"

"Yes, Sir, especially over here."

"Okay, you've had your shower, now get your smart ass out of here!"

Jim finished drying and wrapped the towel around his waist. "Mr. Halsey, you know, Sir, the two of us are standing here naked and I just can't see any bars tattooed on your shoulders."

"Are you disobeying me?"

"No, Sir, I'm leaving but I do want to know something." Leaning closer he almost whispered, "How old are you?"

"Twenty, why?"

"I was just thinking that if you have any desire to be twenty-one, grow up and start being an officer instead of a jerk. In case you're thinking about it, I'll deny ever being in this shower, let alone talking to you." With that he walked out.

Dawn was beginning to break over South Vietnam, and it was already hot and humid. Moisture dripped down Jim's back, wetting his clean shirt. With each step, miniature dust clouds puffed up, masking the polish on his boots and the air already reeked with the stench from the burning of human waste.

As he climbed the two steps going into the mess hall, Jim stomped his feet and brushed off his clothes in a futile effort to separate himself from the world in which he lived.

Gillett and Athia were almost finished eating as he sat down. As always, Jim forced down the malaria pill with the heated black water. It was Athia who spoke first, "Mac, you look exhausted!"

Jim looked up from his plate of over easy eggs, smiled and said, "Athia, you looked in a mirror lately?"

All three men laughed. Gillett finished the last bite of toast and asked, "Mac, did you get caught in the shower?"

"No, nobody there but me."

"Good, I was sure with your luck Halsey would decide to take a shower at the same time!"

Gillett hadn't finished speaking when Kenny walked up and said in a very angry voice, "Gillett, you gave my monkey to the gooks!

Didn't you?"

Gillett looked up, unsmiling at the still standing Kenny, "Yes, I did. I..."

Kenny curtly interrupted, "I don't give a shit what you think, you son of a bitch, you had no right! It was my monkey. I fed him, took care of him. He was mine!"

Gillett and Jim glanced into each others eyes when Kenny made the reference to Gillett's mother, neither man could believe what they'd just heard. Gillett, trying to control his anger, fingered the staff sergeant insignia, looked up and spoke sharply, "Kenny, what's this?"

"So you're an E-6, big deal. You still had no right..."

Gillett, who had risen to his feet, leaned with both hands on the table in Kenny's direction. His voice now slightly raised, clearly showing the anger he felt as he interrupted Spec-Four Kenny, "Shut up, you stupid asshole, and come to attention! Just who the hell do you think you are anyway?" Kenny had halfway straightened up. "I said, come to attention! Now! Lock those heels!" Gillett then lowered his voice to a more normal tone, "I want to tell you something. First of all, I'm your platoon sergeant and I don't have to justify a damn thing to you, Specialist. Secondly, you're dead weight around here. You don't fly because nobody will fly with you and, if I felt like it, your stupid big mouth would get you a trip to LBJ. Instead, you just got yourself a week's KP, so be good at it or I'll take a stripe just for the hell of it. Finally, I gave you a direct order to get rid of that monkey and you didn't do it. The Captain told you to get rid of it and you didn't do it. So you got any more smart ass questions?"

"No."

"No, WHAT!?"

"No, Sergeant!"

"Okay, you're dismissed, and do yourself a favor, Kenny, don't let me see your face for the rest of the day starting right now! You got it?"

"Yes, Sergeant." Kenny turned and left.

The season's first monsoon had started sweeping across the company area. Rain beat viciously against the mess hall's tin roof making it impossible to talk without shouting. As a result, each man sat quietly looking out at the force of nature as it swept by. Someone turned on the lights and Jim realized how dark it had gotten, yet it was more than just dark, it was a deep, opaque blackness that worked its way into every crevice. Wind rocked the mess hall roof, walls and floor and Jim felt his smallness in the hands of God.

Suddenly, as though a mystical hand had turned off a valve, the rain stopped. The wind quit blowing and light once again showed itself on Blackhawk land.

Gillett stood and turned towards the guys behind him. In a louder voice than necessary, he said, "Okay, you guys. It's over. Let's go to work. And for you men who just went through your first monsoon rain, get used to it. The one that just went through was a baby. During the peak season, we'll have two or three a day and they'll all be bigger, meaner and longer than that one. Okay, let's go." Gillett gave two quick claps with his hands and watched as the place cleared out. Gillett turned back to look at the still seated MacLaughlin, "Mac, what are you waiting on?"

Jim looked up and smiled as he said, "The applause."

"I'll swear, Mac, you're hard! You know that?"

Jim gave a look of half-surprise and half-amusement that caused Gillett to chuckle. Jim stood, picked up his tray and with Gillett at his side, headed for the trash barrel.

"You know, Mac, this war will go down in history as the one that destroyed military discipline. I mean really, just look at the way enlisted men talk to their NCO's. In the Second World War, you'd have gotten an Article 15 for a smart ass remark like that. And Kenny, he'd have gone to jail for that little outbreak of his."

"Well, Gillett, look at the way we talk to our officers. I know I'm probably worse about it than a lot of guys. But almost anybody who's been here for a few months says whatever he damn well pleases to any of these warrant officers. For that matter, there aren't many of the hard bars who get a lot of respect."

"That's true, but then we don't have to put up with a lot of the bullshit from officers that our fathers did."

"Hell, no! Gillett, there isn't an officer in country* today who doesn't have some of his actions controlled by the fear of being fragged."

"Or having his knees shot off."

*In Country - In Viet Nam.

"True, but you know, Gillett, a lot of us EM are just as smart or smarter than some of our officers. I mean, we're high school grads and that's all most of them are. You have to wonder how some of 'em got through high school."

"There are some good ones though."

"No question about it. There are some who are very smart and are very good officers, plus being nice guys. The trouble is there are too many like Halsey who cause a loss of respect for all officers, not just the bad ones."

"It's called guilt by association. But you're right. If a man doesn't respect his officers, how can you expect him to show any respect for his NCO?"

When the two men walked out the mess hall door, they stopped at the bottom step and looked at the giant mud puddle that had been ankle deep dust when they went in. There was no way around it, so each man resigned himself to having wasted his time and effort putting Kiwi on his boots.

By the time Jim got to his ship, his boots were covered with the reddish brown mud that had replaced the dust. The first thing he noticed was the left cargo door was shut, which meant maintenance had been out during the night and fixed the track. He stowed his gear and checked the log book. Just as he'd suspected, his old friend, J.B., had taken care of him once again.

J.B. and Jim had first met shortly after the 191st had arrived in country. Both were in maintenance and ended up living in the same hooch. Although they weren't in the same work crew, they did occasionally work together when two crews would work on one ship. As a result of working and living together, they had become friends. After all the recovery crew except Jim had been killed, he asked to join the same work crew as J.B. Then they both were infused up to Tay Ninh. At Tay Ninh, everyone dragged their duffel bags off the Chinook and fell into formation. The officers were called out by their new platoon leader first, then a staff sergeant stepped forward and called out his crew chiefs and door gunners. When he had all his people, he left with them and the next staff sergeant stepped forward and started reading off the names of his crew chiefs.

J.B.'s name was the last crew chief he called out. There was only one problem, J.B. wasn't a crew chief and didn't want to become one. His response was a surprised, "But, Sergeant, I'm not a crew chief, I'm in maintenance."

"Well, Specialist, you're in the flight platoon now!" There was such a look of surprise and disbelief on J.B.'s face that the sergeant looked down at the orders he held in his left hand. After reading aloud J.B.'s full name, rank and serial number, he looked up and asked, "Is that you?"

"Yes, Sergeant, but I don't fly! You can ask any of these guys I was in maintenance with. I didn't even fly on test flights, which caused me a lot of problems until our maintenance officer realized I wasn't just trying to get away with something."

"Look, Specialist, I don't care what you did in the other company. These orders say you're in my flight platoon and that means you're a crew chief, so fall out with the rest of my group."

J.B. didn't move. "Sergeant, look, I promised my mother when I joined the Army I wouldn't fly anymore than absolutely necessary and I'm not going to break that promise!"

In a very sarcastic tone of voice, the sergeant replied, "Well, mommy's boy, I don't care what you promised your mommy. You're either going to fly or go to jail!"

After a short pause J.B. said, "Sergeant, I don't want to go to jail. But I'm not going to fly."

The two men stood looking each other in the eye when Jim spoke, "Sergeant, if I may, I think I can solve this problem."

"Good, how?"

"I'll fly in J.B.'s place."

The sergeant looked at Jim's name tag and then down at his papers. He found Jim's name and read it aloud, along with his rank and serial number. Then he asked, "Is that you?"

"Yes, Sergeant."

"Okay, you're the same rank with the same M.O.S.*, I can do that. It'll be less paperwork than sending your buddy to jail."

That was how Jim became a crew chief. J.B. never directly said thanks, but his signature or initials signed off a great deal of work

*M.O.S. - (Job title) - Military Occupational Specialty.

on Jim's ships. Plus J.B. got him parts other crew chiefs couldn't get. A good example was the fire extinguisher.

It had been about three months ago when Mr. Halsey had been flying as the peter pilot. He'd decided to give Jim's ship a super close pre-flight inspection. Not finding anything wrong that wasn't already written up in the log book, Halsey opened the peter pilot's door. The fire extinguisher in a Huey is held by a quick release clamp on the floor beside the right hand pilot's seat. For some reason, about a third of the company's fire extinguishers were missing or empty. So when Halsey saw this one he removed it from the clamp and looking at Jim asked, "Does this thing have anything in it?"

"Yes, Sir."

"You checked it lately?"

"Yes, Sir." Jim turned and leaned inside the cargo area to remove the log book with the intention of showing Halsey the page where he'd recorded the date of inspection and weight of the extinguisher. He turned back just as Halsey pulled the pin. Jim, in a slightly raised voice said, "Hey, what are you doing?"

Halsey spoke and squeezed the handle at the same time. "Checking to see if it really works."

A spray of foam shot onto the ground as Jim shouted, "Don't!" With a look of exasperation, Jim spoke, "You stupid jerk! Thanks to you, now I don't have a fire extinguisher either!"

Lieutenant Buton walked around the aircraft's nose just as Halsey had pulled the pin. He looked at Jim, "Hold it right there, Mac. That man is an officer you're talking to." Lieutenant Buton was an ROTC man who had the respect of all the enlisted men.

"Well, Lieutenant, it's the truth. I HAD one of the few fire extinguishers in the company! Because I took care of it, even to the point I hid it in the ship at night. Then Mr. Halsey comes along and because he doesn't know what the hell he's doing, I now have to fly without a fire extinguisher and if this aircraft has a fire, it's my butt that burns up because of him!"

Halsey, realizing he'd made a mistake, tried to replace the pin as the extinguisher made a soft, almost silent hiss.

"Oh, come on, Mac. All I've got to do is replace the pin and it'll be okay. I didn't waste that much."

"Mr. Halsey, once you pull the pin you can't put it back without first fully recharging the extinguisher, and once you squeeze the handle it'll just keep on leaking until it's empty. And finally, Sir, so you don't decide to do a stupid trick like that again, you check an extinguisher by its weight. When fully charged its weight is at least as great as specified on the tag. By the way, Sir, you can check the log book to see when it was weighed last."

That exchange had taken place what seemed to Jim a long, long time ago.

The pilots were beginning to arrive at their respective helicopters. Mr. Lucas and Mr. Euclid were laughing as they simultaneously threw their gear onto the aircraft's passengers seats.

Jim came to attention and saluted. "Good morning, Mr. Lucas, Mr. Euclid."

Each officer returned Jim's salute as Mr. Lucas said, "Morning, Mac! How are you this morning?"

"I'm fine, Sir. Where's Mr. Walker?"

"He's got a toothache this morning." Still laughing, Mr. Euclid added, "He's the butt of all the jokes this morning. The poor guy was hurting so badly he tried to get the dentist during the night. We tried to tell him, "Army dentists don't make house calls, and the club was closed so he couldn't get any liquid pain killer. Finally, somebody found some aspirin but I don't think it helped a whole lot."

"Well, Sir, at least he has a dentist here on post. Think of all the guys who wake up like that and then have to get a chopper to take 'em to a dentist."

"This thing ready to fly, Mac?"

"Yes, Sir!"

"Okay. Let's you and I preflight it."

It was sometime later the flight picked up troops to start another day of search and destroy missions. There hadn't been any activity out of Charlie as lift after lift was made. On the last lift before lunch, the flight was diverted to a new LZ and still there was no activity.

Once on the ground, the C-rations were quickly distributed and the officers headed for Lead's ship. Jim ate and took the opportunity to get some badly needed sleep. When Wright awakened him, he was soaked from perspiration.

In later years he'd find it somewhat ironic that he often awoke 'in country' saturated from the heat, having never had the first nightmare while there. Back in the States, he'd often awake in the comfort of his own bed, saturated from perspiration simply due to his dreams.

"Mac, get up! Here come the pilots on a run."

"What's happened?"

"I don't know. I'll untie it."

Jim sat up and put on his chicken plate just as Mr. Lucas came running around the ship's nose. He was very excited, and with a burst of nervous energy, leaped into the cargo area and from there to his seat. As he moved quickly past Jim, he shouted, "Come on, Mac, move it! One of our gunships is down!"

Jim closed the door behind Mr. Euclid, who had entered through the pilot's door and taken his seat. Jim hadn't yet given the all clear signal when Mr. Lucas started to crank the engine.

Putting his helmet on Jim asked, "Sir, what happened to the gun?"

"Shut up, Mac. I'm listening to Six now."

Jim climbed into the ship and turned on all his radios so he'd be sure to get Six's transmission, but it was over. It seemed to take forever to get troops onboard. Then they sat on the ground at idle speed for several more minutes before Six told Lead to bring 'em airborne. Once in the air and over the crash sight area, Six couldn't decide where to have the flight land.

The other gunship had made several passes over the downed ship and had seen no signs of life. There was a clearing within a hundred meters that was large enough for a single ship to land in. The gunship's AC had asked permission of Six to land and send his crew chief and gunner to check out the downed ship. Six had refused permission since he was the only gunship on station. Almost everyone in the flight disagreed with that decision but no one spoke. Still time slipped by and the flight continued to circle.

Jim had already once advised Mr. Lucas about the chopper on his right being too close; now they were slowly getting closer and closer. "Mr. Lucas, do you have this ship on the right?" Jim could see Lucas turn his head right, followed by the helicopter moving a few feet to the left. It wasn't more than a couple of minutes when Jim once again felt Mr. Lucas had drifted far enough right to be at an unsafe distance.

"Mr. Lucas, could you take it left please, Sir?"

In a slightly irritated voice, Mr. Lucas responded, "I've got it, Mac! Okay?"

Jim didn't respond, but the aircraft didn't move left. He sat and wondered what to do and finally decided it would be better to try once more than to die in a crash, all because of some hotshot pilot who lost his cool. So, in a normal voice, Jim said, "Mr. Lucas, you're still flying too close, please take it left to a safe distance."

Mr. Lucas's voice reflected the nervous state he was in. "MacLaughlin, I've told you before and I'm not going to tell you again! I've got him, I see him and I'm getting sick and tired of your mouth! So just sit there and keep your mouth shut until we land! I don't want to hear about the chopper on my right again. I'm beginning to see why you have so much trouble with some of the pilots. You got it, MacLaughlin?"

Jim didn't hesitate, "Sir, you better get something straight! I'm the crew chief on this aircraft and as such I have several jobs besides the overall maintenance of the aircraft. One of those jobs, Sir, is to advise you when you're flying at an unsafe distance to another aircraft! And that, Sir, is exactly what I've been doing, and I'm going to keep on doing until you move it left far enough to be safe and keep it there! Furthermore, if you can't keep it at a safe distance then you should turn it over to Mr. Euclid, which you ought to do anyway because you've blown your cool and shouldn't be driving until you get your act back together! Finally, for you to give your crew chief an order to sit there with his mouth shut is in direct violation of Army General Aviation orders! Not to mention common sense, and it puts his life, your life and the lives of everyone on board this aircraft in danger. Believe me, Mr. Lucas, I don't like telling you to move left more than once anymore than you like hearing it. But you wouldn't look good with this guy on your right's rotor blade stuck in your windshield!"

There was no response from Mr. Lucas or anyone else, and Jim didn't have to tell him to move it left again. The troops were finally put in about a half mile from the crash sight. The flight then returned to Tay Ninh to sit and wait for the troops to find and secure the crash site.

Once on the ground, Jim sat in his seat for a few seconds looking empty faced at the clay colored soil. Here or there a weed or bunch of grass made a valiant effort to survive. And behind the row after row of black, L shaped revetments, stood the dirty brown buildings the Blackhawks called home. Slowly, as though resigning himself to the futility of trying to hide, Jim climbed out of his seat. He stepped up on the skid after opening Mr. Euclid's door and watched the gauges as Mr. Lucas shut it down.

Hearing Lucas's voice, Jim looked the pilot in the eyes as Lucas spoke, "Mr. Euclid, you can finish shutting her down."

Jim watched Mr. Lucas's eyes lead a path to the radio control switch where the pilot's right hand rested. The hand made only a small movement as it turned the control knob and Mr. Lucas's head and eyes moved in a manner to direct Jim to his own radio control switch. Nodding his head in recognition, Jim climbed up into the cargo area, turned his control switch to private and sat down on the passenger's seat. Expecting a first class chewing out, Jim looked up and slightly to his left.

Mr. Lucas had turned in his seat to the right so he could face Jim when he spoke. "You there, Mac?"

Jim knew perfectly good and well Mr. Lucas knew he was there. He watched him turn his control switch to private, and he could hear Jim's breathing just as Jim could now hear the pilot's breathing due to the 'hot' or live mike situation between the two men. "Yes, Sir."

There was no expression on either man's face as their eyes locked. "Mac, I want you to know I'm sorry for climbing on your back there."

"Forget it."

"No, it's important for me to say. You were right, I lost my cool and I was using my rank to cover it up. You had every right to tell me to keep it at a safe distance. That's your job and that's all you were trying to do. I know that. I'm sorry I lost my cool and I'm sorry I got on you because of it. Thank you for valuing your life and mine enough to stand up to me."

His facial expression told Jim he was finished. "Forget it, Sir. It's over. It's done and who knows, maybe you'll be a better pilot and officer because of it." First there was a big smile, then Jim could see Mr. Lucas's face fight back the tears. "Mr. Lucas, forget it! It's okay, really. Hey look, anybody who's been in combat every day for several months has lost his cool at some point."

"Somehow I can't picture you ever losing yours."

Jim slowly nodded his head and said, "I did."

"How? Why?"

"When I first came over, I was stationed at Bear Cat. We got hit with a few mortars which I never thought were much more than big cherry bombs. After we were there a few weeks, they quit, and we had things pretty easy. Then I got sent up here. I hadn't been here a week when all hell broke loose one night. The CO said later that we had averaged one 122MM rocket hit in our company area every second. I don't remember how long this went on, but it was something like one or two hours. I was in the bunker beside my hooch and I was scared. I mean, I had never been so terrified in all my life. The grating sound those rockets make just before they hit, which you only hear if you're within thirty meters of ground zero, had me totally terrified. Then these sirens started blowing just as the rockets quit. Our platoon sergeant at the time was in the bunker with us and somebody said, 'Hey, Willie, what's that siren mean?' Just then, the rockets started to fall again but not quite as bad. The sergeant shouted, 'It means the post is being over run!' I had goose pimples all over my body. I could just see some gook throwing a frag into that bunker and all of us being killed. Just as I had that thought, I could see, because of a flashlight someone had on, this guy crawl into the bunker. He looked just like a gook to me. He even had on one of those round pointed hats they wear. He squatted down right by the door just like they squat. Mr. Lucas, the Lord Jesus Christ knows every man's heart, and believe me, He and I both knew if I'd had my M16, I'd have killed him. I even looked around trying to find one I could get hold of, and then move real slow so he wouldn't see me pointing it at him. Believe me, I give thanks to God every day that I'd left mine in the wall locker and I couldn't find another. I kept thinking why doesn't he just drop his frag and run? But then I figured he didn't want to get killed by his own rockets and as soon as they quit again, he'd drop it and move out the door. Finally, I got control of myself enough to poke Gillett, who was sitting beside me, and said, 'Hey, look at that guy by the door!' Gillett picked up the M16 he had on the other side of him and, pointing it at the guy, said, 'Hey you in the gook hat, you better speak English and identify yourself, or you're dead!' The guy raised his head and said, 'Who me?' Gillett said, 'Yeah, you! What's your name?' 'Zettler, and what are you pointing that thing at me for?' I knew at that moment I'd lost my cool totally and would have killed a man because of it. It was by the grace of God I didn't have a gun handy. I promised myself then I'd never ever lose my composure again, no matter how bad things got. And I haven't. I later learned the guy was one of the pot heads in the other flight platoon who thought it was cool to wear one of those stupid hats. By the way, Mr. Lucas, you're the only person I've ever told this story. Zettler never knew how close he came to being killed that night because of that stupid hat and my fears.

"That's my story, Sir. Now you have yours."

Mr. Lucas smiled slightly, "Mac, you probably know you're quite the point of controversy in the officer's corner. But I want you to know I now understand why Walker and some of the others think you're the best. And I'd consider it an honor, if anything ever happens to Walker, if you'd ask for me as your AC. I really am a good pilot and officer, and after today, I'll never loose my cool again, no matter what."

Jim's face had a great big smile on it as he responded, "Thank you very much, Sir. That's very kind of you. I hope nothing ever happens to Mr. Walker, but if it does, I'll keep you in mind."

Mr. Lucas reached down and turned his switch back to internal.

The flight sat there for about an hour before one of the ships was sent to pick up the remains that had been secured by the grunts. The always present black rubber body bags had somehow not landed on Jim's ship, for which he was thankful. Several minutes after the chopper had left to pick up its cargo, Jim decided to listen in on the company frequency to hear whatever was said about the crash. It was several minutes more before Chalk Seven's pilot came on the radio, "Lead, this is Chalk Seven, do you copy? Over."

"This is Lead, go!"

"Lead, we have all four remains on board and are headed for Saigon. Be advised also my crew chief swears up and down that the mask was cut off by the rotorhead. I will have to agree the rotorhead is quite a ways from the crash site and both the mask and head have some strange marks on 'em."

Suddenly another voice broke in. "Chalk Seven, this is Six! Discontinue this conversation right now! Do you copy, Mr.?"

"This is Chalk Seven. Yes, I copy."

"Very good, Chalk Seven. Now I want to see you and your entire crew at my ship after we're discharged for the night! Understood?"

"Yes, Sir."

"Lead, this is Six, you're to crank the flight at once and go pick up those troops. We're not going far with them, just a few kilometers and I'll mark your LZ once they're on board. Let me know when the flight's up! Six out."

"Roger, Six."

Jim could see the pilots moving quickly back to their ships as he stepped out. He untied the main rotor blade, put on his chicken plate and helmet. Mr. Lucas had started to crank the engine as Jim plugged in his helmet.

"Mac, you there?"

"Yes, Sir. What do you need, Mr. Lucas?"

"I don't get any engine oil pressure!"

Jim knew exactly where to look for the gauge. It was the second one down on the left just below fuel pressure. Mr. Lucas was right, the gauge that measured engine oil PSI read zero.

"Sir, shut it down, right now!"

Jim heard the reduced pitch in the engine and at the same time heard Mr. Lucas say, "You got it, what's the problem?"

"Probably just a bad sensing unit or gauge but I'm not flying in it 'til I find out."

"Okay, Mac, check it out. I'll call Lead."

Jim finished and walked around to Mr. Lucas, who was just climbing out of his seat, "Sir, I can't find anything, we'll have to call maintenance and have them do a more complete run down."

Mr. Lucas put on a big smile and tapped Jim playfully on the chest with his finger. "I'm already ahead of you, Mac. I called Operations and they said there was a ship just out of maintenance that was being test flown now. We're going to trade. I'll bet this is it now."

The dust being kicked up by the landing Huey caused both men to turn their backs and pull up their collars. Sand and dirt went into their ears, hair and down their backs. It was almost as though the maintenance officer who was driving got a sadistic joy out of dusting them off and held pitch in the rotor blades just a little longer than necessary. Finally, he rolled back the RPM and leveled out the rotor blades' pitch. Mr. Lucas ducked under the rotor blades and opened the pilot's door to talk to the maintenance officer.

Every time Jim saw someone walk under the still turning rotor blades, he cringed and a rapid shiver went down his spine. He remembered well back at Bear Cat, standing and talking to another fellow as a Huey landed on the maintenance pad. The pilot had shut it down and climbed out. With the main rotor on its last cycle, the tall slender pilot removed his helmet and started to walk. He would have been okay if the helicopter had been running, as it wasn't possible for the blades to tip while at speed.

Once the helicopter had been shut off and the rotor blades slowed down to the last couple rotations, the weight of the blades and the slow speed allowed the pilot's controls to be pulled forward. This, in turn, allowed the rotor blades to dip down low enough to strike the pilot squarely in the head. His head exploded like a ripe, slightly rotten pumpkin, sending pieces of hair, bone, brain, skin, teeth, tongue and eyes flying to the left of the slowly falling torso. Jim still, all too clearly, remembered having to pick up every last bone chip, tooth, glob of brain or flesh and putting it in a bucket. When someone from the hospital arrived with the black rubber bag, they placed the torso inside and poured the bucket's grotesque contents into a pile where there should have been a head. They then zipped the black rubber bag shut and left.

As the maintenance officer signed off the log book clearing the helicopter for flight, everyone else moved guns and ammo to the other ship. Jim was pretty upset with himself for forgetting to take his tools, water jug and some of his personal gear. He still had his camera around his neck as he read the log book's last few entries. As he moved back into his seat, Mr. Lucas asked, "Log book okay, Mac?"

"Yes, Sir. It was in for an electrical short but I'm not sure from the way it was signed off that they're sure they found the problem. So it might be a good idea to keep a closer eye on the gauges than usual."

"Anything you say, Mac."

They had just cleared Tay Ninh Village and were about a thousand feet up when Mr. Euclid said, "Hey! We've got circuit breakers going off like popcorn!"

Then it was Mr. Lucas's voice that broke in with control, but still betraying his concern, "Mac! I've got a light on that says engine fire!"

Jim looked out and back at the engine compartment and knew the light was correct. Almost shouting, Jim commanded, "We're on fire, put it on the ground! QUICK!"

Mr. Lucas didn't hesitate. He jerked the controls into a maneuver he'd never practiced but had heard others talk about.

There was only one way to get a burning Huey on the ground from that altitude fast enough. It required laying the aircraft on its left side so it would fall like a rock, unobstructed by the rotor blades. The hard part was to pull it out before you crashed, but not too early.

Jim, still strapped in his seat, looked out his door and suddenly found himself looking straight up at a clear blue sky. Speaking to himself and his God he thought, *Oh, God, help us, we're going to die.* Able to see nothing but the sky as it went rushing by him almost as though he was falling backwards through a tunnel, Jim grabbed the metal support post on his left and waited for the impact. Suddenly he heard a terrible metallic scream. It was almost as though the helicopter was fighting the giving up of its soul as Mr. Lucas pulled it out of its dive and righted it to land.

It wasn't a perfect landing and as a result, the skids were about half-way flattened out. Nobody cared since they were all alive and on the ground, though still in a burning Huey.

Once Jim felt the sudden jerk of the ship being righted, his mind went to work deciding what to do first. By the time they hit the ground he had his M16 in his right hand and his left on the seatbelt buckle. Only a fraction of a second passed between impact and the time Jim had his seatbelt off. He was out of the now rapidly burning aircraft in less than a second and moved in one leap to Mr. Euclid's door. It was jammed shut from the hard impact. Jim could see Mr. Lucas climbing out the other side as he jerked on the still jammed copilot's door. Realizing it wasn't going to open, he grabbed the safety pin on the bottom and gave a big jerk. It came out, and in the same movement Jim threw it, he grabbed the top pin and pulled it out. Before he could get out of the way, Mr. Euclid kicked the door open and jumped out, landing beside Jim. The two helped pick each other up as they tried to run and stand erect at the same time but found themselves stumbling more than running. Finally at a safe distance, they turned to watch the flames leap from the aircraft.

It was Mr. Euclid who broke the silence, "Somebody in maintenance should have their ass kicked."

Jim didn't know why it struck him so funny but he stood there and laughed and laughed. Mr. Euclid started to laugh also, and the two had to hold their stomachs, they were laughing so hard. By the time Wright and Mr. Lucas arrived, they had just about gotten control of themselves.

Mr. Lucas spoke first with hands on hips and head slightly back, "I don't see what you two stupid fools find so damn funny!"

All that did was make the two laughers start all over and laugh that much harder. It was a good five minutes before they finally got enough control of themselves to quit causing each other to laugh by just looking at each other.

After regaining control, Jim sat for a few minutes more in an effort to catch his breath as he looked at his surroundings for the first time. They'd landed in a clearing that separated the jungle from the rice paddies. Another twenty meters one way and Mr. Lucas would have put it in the trees. Fifty meters the other way would have put them on the rice paddy dike where they all now sat. Looking behind him, he could see several villagers heading their way, walking on top of the dikes, past the almost ripe rice that ever so softly waved in the breeze like an endless golden flag.

Rising, Jim walked over to where Mr. Lucas was seated. Sitting down between Lucas and Wright, Jim said, "Sir, you're right. You're a damn good pilot. You did one hell of a good job!"

Looking over at Jim, Mr. Lucas smiled and responded, "I didn't lose my cool either, did I?"

"No, Sir, you didn't. You did a very good job. This is something you can tell your grandchildren about. After all, there will only be a handful of men who will ever do that maneuver and live to tell about it, and you're one of them. Congratulations!"

"Thank you, Mac. Just out of curiosity, how much time do you think we had to spare?"

"Not more than two or three seconds. It was already uncomfortably hot by the time Mr. Euclid got out."

Mr. Euclid looked their way and said, "By the way, thanks Mac, for sticking around and getting my door open."

"You're welcome."

"And I don't think we had three seconds. When my door wouldn't open the first time, I looked around back thinking I'd go between the seats and out the cargo door, but the floor was already on fire."

Wright spoke for the first time, "Do you suppose anyone besides the villagers know we're here?"

Mr. Euclid responded, "I hope so but I only got out one May Day before we hit the ground."

Mr. Lucas kiddingly interrupted, "What do you mean hit the ground? That was a precision, controlled landing!"

"Yeah, that's why the skids were flat and my door wouldn't open. But don't misunderstand me, I agree with Mac. You did a wonderful job. I think I'll even put you in for a D.F.C.*"

The villagers who came scurrying across the rice paddy dikes were all old men or young children. As three of the old men shouted in Vietnamese and made gestures at the four Americans, the children looked over the charred remains in the background. Mr. Lucas tried without much success to converse using sign language, but the constant chatter from the farmers just kept on coming.

Standing and watching, Jim was impressed by the difference in the two groups. The Americans were all taller, more muscular, in uniforms with boots and each had a mouth full of normal healthy teeth. The locals all stood between five foot or five foot five, but were wiry looking men with an obvious strength beyond their sizes. They wore thin black shirts with four buttons, and pants that ended just above the ankle made from the same material. Each wore homemade sandals constructed from old rubber tires that were probably better for the feet than the jungle boots the GI's wore. Like most locals, their teeth were a mess. Some teeth were missing but the ones that were there

---

*D.F.C. - Distinguished Flying Cross.

made a person half sick to look at them. They were green and black stubs with only the smallest flakes of gray enamel still visible. Some teeth had half moon shapes missing from the sides, others looked like an upside down T, while others were simply points sticking out through the gums.

All the Americans were happy to first hear the whopp-whopp of approaching Huey blades, and then see the familiar silhouette headed their way. None were as happy as Mr. Lucas, who had thrown up his hands in frustration.

Once back in the company area, they learned that Operations had heard their May Day. Operations then contacted the courier ship that was due into Tay Ninh about that time and asked them to pick up the downed Blackhawks.

By the time the courier ship dropped off its passengers and they reported in at Operations, maintenance had also reported Jim's ship as fixed and flyable. Wright and Mr. Euclid went to supply to pick up two new M60 door guns while Jim and Mr. Lucas checked on his ship. It had been test flown from the spot they'd left it back into its revetment, so it took them longer than it should have to find it. The first thing Jim did was check the log book. Mr. Lucas stood watching Jim's face as he read the signed off form.

"Well, Mac, what did they find?"

"All that was wrong was a bad engine oil pressure gauge. They replaced the gauge, test flew it and signed it off as okay."

"You mean to tell me the four of us almost burned to death because of a bad gauge?"

"That and some dumb ass in maintenance who let that other crate out before it was fixed."

It was several minutes before Mr. Euclid and Wright walked up, each carrying an M60. Jim, in the meantime, had checked his gear and was pleased to find everything he'd left on board still there. From the revetment, they hovered over to the ammo bunker and put on ammo. Jim also picked up two frags and hid them in the storage compartment.

They were told by Blackhawk Six to rejoin the flight at Duc Hoa, picking up ARVN troops for transport over to the Plain of Reeds. It would take almost an hour to get down to Duc Hoa, so Jim dropped the dark sun visor on his helmet and pulled his seatbelt up tight.

He'd just settled in for a nice nap during the long, boring flight, when Wright's voice came over the intercom, "Hey, can anybody see those fixed wing jobs flying formation at about 10 o'clock and low?"

Mr. Lucas was the next voice Mac heard, "Yeah, I've got 'em. Those are C-130's. Wouldn't that be something, flying at tree top level in a V formation with three C-130's?"

Wright asked, "What are they doing?"

"Spraying a defoliant," answered Mr. Lucas. "I can't remember what it's called."

Jim said, "Agent Orange."

"Yeah, that's right. I remember now, they got the name from the orange stripes of the drums the stuff comes in. The whole idea, of course, is to kill all the vegetation so Charlie won't have anyplace to hide. Or course, he'll see us coming better, but we're not supposed to worry about that."

Wright said, "If they put enough of that stuff on to kill all the vegetation, what's it do to people?"

Lucas spoke, "Nothing. The only things it hurts are plants."

Jim interrupted, "Not according to some of the Special Forces guys I've talked to."

Lucas said, "Mac, I've seen the poop sheet on the stuff. It's totally harmless to everything but plants. Besides, you know the Army, or for that matter the government, would never use a chemical that could harm people. All that stuff has been thoroughly tested for years before it's used."

"Yes, Sir, I know. But I also know I was on a single ship night mission about a month ago. We picked up a group of Green Berets and, while the pilots were being briefed on where we were going, I got a conversation started with a staff sergeant in the group. I'll tell you what, he was most unhappy about where they were going. He kept calling it Death Valley. I finally said, 'I don't know where that's at. I'd never heard of the place and I'd been almost everywhere in the Third Corp area.' So he said it was just a little ways outside Tay Ninh, that Death Valley was slang for almost anyplace that had been sprayed with Agent Orange. He couldn't understand why they were being sent in there. They never found any signs of Charlie. He was smart enough to stay out of there. The thing I found most interesting was when he told about finding dead birds and animals. He claimed there was nothing alive in Death Valley, not even insects. I remember him saying it was so quiet in there that at night it was really eerie. He claimed it was so dead, even the ant hills were dead. Not to mention the fact there wasn't any plant life—no trees, no bushes, no grass—nothing, and if he had his way he wouldn't ever go in it again.

Mr. Lucas said, "Mac, I can't believe you're so gullible you fell for that story. That man was pulling your leg. He saw someone he could tell a tale to and be stupid enough to believe it."

"If that's so, Sir, then everyone in his group was in on it because they all agreed with him. There is nothing alive in those sprayed areas and anyone that goes into 'em is stupid."

"Mac, look, I don't care what they said. You know the government wouldn't use something that strong. I mean, if it's going to kill animals, it'll kill us and they don't want us dead."

Jim said very sarcastically, "Whatever you say, Sir."

16

"These men lie in wait for their own blood." Proverbs 1:18 NIV

"But I Don't Want To!"

Duc Hoa was just like every other Vietnamese village with its wood shacks, dirty ragged kids and dirt roads. The ARVN camp was undoubtedly the saddest part of all. Whole families lived in ten foot square cubicles, sectioned off inside one long wooden rectangular building with a plywood divider to separate their living quarters. The tin roof was coming loose in several places and was completely gone from one section. It was hard to imagine as many as three generations living in one cubicle.

The ARVN troops were all lined up and waiting. Their uniforms were almost identical to the Americans with the only real difference being the rank insignia. The NCO's stripes were upside down and the officers wore funny little things that Jim seldom could figure out. There was pride in those uniforms, though, as they were clean and most all had been tailored. It was their faces and mannerisms that struck Jim as being the most out of place. Whenever they picked up Americans for a lift they were always quiet, reserved, sometimes openly afraid of where they were going, yet never lacking the courage to climb on the helicopter, even if they were a bit hesitant. Yet here stood

ARVN troops, slapping hands, obviously making jokes with their M16's. It was almost as though they couldn't wait to get into combat like green troops who still thought combat would be a lot of fun; a great adventure, a chance to prove their manhood, a place to find fame and glory, and totally believing in their invincibility. Was it possible they didn't yet realize there would be no music, no stirring drum beat in the background, and no trumpet blowing, only the extreme loneliness of their own thoughts and fears?

Climbing on the choppers, they continued to laugh and make brave gestures with their M16's. Maybe they would be lucky and not have any contact with the enemy and could live another day in their illusion of grandeur.

The air blew cold over their charged bodies as it rushed in through the open cargo door. At two thousand feet it hit their sweat soaked shirts causing each man to move a little closer to his buddy.

The Plain of Reeds was appropriately named. It was a large flat lowland marsh type area. Grass and various reeds grew to heights taller than the helicopters that would be landing shortly on another dirt road.

From one dirt road to another they had flow. Unlike the first one, this dirt road had been built up several feet to help maintain a dry base and there were no friendly, happy and excited troops awaiting their arrival.

"Flight, this is Lead. Six advises there is pretty good reason to believe we'll be landing very close to a VC command center. Everybody stay sharp, there are no friendlies down there and all guns can open fire at will." With a sudden increase in tempo and pitch the same voice said, "I'm receiving fire from the right! My God we're going to land right on top of it!"

Jim could already see the muzzle flashes and like everyone else opened fire. He'd only seen this type of fire a couple of times before. It came up at them directly from the ground itself, which meant only one thing, bunkers. They were right along the road and so well camouflaged one could have walked by and never seen that first one. Jim aimed his fire at the flashes directly across from where he would be landing shortly. Every fifth round the door gunners fired was a tracer, allowing Mr. Euclid to follow Jim's tracer rounds as they went in on the opposing machine guns. Each machine gunner knew what he had to do to live, and like the duelist of old, was putting all his skill into that one objective. Jim could now see the gun barrel as it continued to fire on his aircraft and moved ever so slowly to gain a better shot. For a full second more the two machine guns threw lead at each other with all the fury of the machines of death that each gun was. Then suddenly the still firing machine gun barrel protruding from the ground jerked straight upward and fell silent.

Mr. Euclid, with joy and excitement unrestrained in his voice said, "MacLaughlin, that was beautiful! You must have held your fire on him for a full four seconds! I kept wanting to shout, get him, Mac! Get him! I could see those tracers going right down his hole and wanted to shout, 'You got him, Mac! Get him! You got him just hold it on him!' But man I wasn't saying shit, except to myself! Because I didn't want to do anything to distract you! You were doing a fine job and we're one hell of a lot bigger target than he was and not more than fifteen feet away!"

Jim's gun stopped firing, the ARVN troops had started to jump off. As Mr. Euclid stopped speaking Mr. Lucas pulled pitch and started to leave. As he finished the last few words of his sentence, Mr. Euclid turned to look at Jim. Much to his surprise, there in the center of the bench seat, with his back pressed tightly against the soundproofing, sat an ARVN soldier. Without ever breaking off his sentence Mr. Euclid said, "Hey, there's still an ARVN soldier on board!"

Mr. Lucas, who had only moved it about forty feet immediately put it back down and said, "Mac, get him out of there!"

Jim unhooked his radio and seatbelt. Stepping around the seat he could see the fear in the ARVN's face. Jim felt no emotions, he was simply following orders, and not wanting to waste any more time in a hot LZ, he grabbed the fear struck soldier by one arm and tried to rip his clamped fingers loose from the seat. With the second jerk the ARVN's right hand ripped loose, but not the left. The two allied soldiers shoved and pulled at each other for a full five seconds before Jim looked around in frustration at Mr. Lucas who was looking back in his direction.

With one quick movement of his hand and facial expression, Mr. Lucas made his meaning clear, "Get him off, and get him off, now!"

Jim's movement was quick and without hesitation. The right fist came crashing in hard against the ARVN's left cheek, sending his head backwards and bouncing off the soundproofing behind. Jim grabbed the stunned soldier by the shirt and, in one motion, threw the crying ARVN soldier off the helicopter. As Mr. Lucas pulled pitch to leave, Jim threw the ARVN's M16 off.

Swinging around the bench seats to get back into his own seat, Jim could see the same ARVN soldier running after them down the road with M16 in hand. Suddenly the ARVN stopped in mid-stride. His head jerked backward as both arms flew outward, releasing the M16 into midair. His body leaped forwards and landed several feet ahead of his original position.

Jim sat down and hooked up his seat belt. It took him longer than usual to reconnect the helmet's radio wires, "Mr. Lucas, I just killed that man."

"For crying out loud, Mac, you didn't hit him that hard!"

"No, Sir, but he got up and started to run. He took a machine gun burst square in the chest."

"Well, we can't go back and get him. We have to join the flight and take in more troops, so we can bring him out then. Besides, it's hard to believe we didn't take any hits back there as it was."

Mr. Euclid said, "You're telling me. I thought sure that bunker would get us but Mac quieted him and then we sat on the ground for a full fifteen seconds trying to get that stupid ARVN off."

Lucas interrupted, "They probably figured we were shot down, unable to fly. So why waste time and ammo on a dead bird, you can always cut his head off later. Besides, Mac, you did what you had to do. If that stupid gook won't fight for his own country, how can he expect us to?"

Jim lowered his head into both hands and wept. No one but the wind could hear him crying as it rushed by his face and melted his sobs into the roar of the engine and the scream of the transmission. Locked in the subconscious of his mind he would remember the ARVN soldier's eyes only in his dreams.

There were two more lifts made into the same area. On the last lift Jim's ship had an American TV man on board. The batteries and camera had to be a real pain to carry around. It was the antenna sticking up that Jim figured would make him no one's friend. Even the greenest of troops knew an antenna would draw fire like bees to honey. After all an antenna usually meant a radio, which meant an officer, and it was always important to remove an officer no matter what side you were on. After the drop Jim watched as long as he could and wasn't surprised to see the ARVN soldiers move quickly away from the cameraman. He tried to stay with them but nobody wanted him around.

After the last lift the flight was sent to Saigon to pick up as much food as they could transport back to Tay Ninh. From the unloading platform the ships refueled and then parked for the night.

Jim had to pull an intermediate fifty hour inspection. It was already dark when he got started and, by the time he finshed, it was almost ten-thirty. There wasn't any question about what he'd do first—shower. The water was cold but felt better than the grease and oil he was washing off.

Once back in the hooch Jim sat down on his foot locker to put a little Kiwi on his boots. He'd just started the first boot when the screen door flew open and in walked Gillett. The giant steps and hunchback stance indicated Gillett was all business.

Using his voice of command, Gillett barked out, "Schott! You got that letter written yet?"

"Yes, Sergeant, right here."

Rick Schott was your basic, good ole Southern boy, complete with Mississippi accent, wiry frame, about an inch shorter than Jim and an easy going, happy go lucky disposition. However, in an irritated manner, Rick walked up and slapped an envelope into Gillett's outstretched hand.

Gillett said simply, "Thank you."

Then turning to Jim, "You just get in?"

"Yeah, I had an intermediate to pull."

"Find anything?"

"The only thing was a little metal on the internal transmission oil filter, but nothing I thought was unusual."

"Good. Come on, Mac, put something on besides your shorts and I'll share my bottle of Jack."

"Thanks anyway, Gillett, but I'm exhausted. I'm going to bed as soon as I brush off this polish."

"Okay, see you in the morning."

Jim finished his boots and walked down the aisle to Schott's bunk. Sitting down on the next bed's foot locker so he could look Rick in the face he asked, "Rick, what was that all about?"

Rick sat up on the side of his Army cot and answered, "Mac, this Army is so screwed up I can't believe it, but my sorry ass mother is worse."

Jim half laughed as he asked, "What are you talking about?"

"My mother, God bless her, called the Red Cross, asked them to find out why her little boy Rickie hadn't sent her a letter for almost a month. So the Red Cross at home called the Red Cross in Saigon. They called the CO who asked the First Sergeant to look into it. The First Sergeant told Gillett he'd like to meet the asshole who was responsible for the CO having to spend ten minutes on the phone with the Red Cross in Saigon. I'm telling you, Mac, when the man got done with me, I had to check to see if I had any ass left or if he'd chewed it all off."

"So why haven't you written home?"

"I did! I try to get a letter out every week or ten days. Well, you know there hasn't been any mail leave here since Tet opened up until today. So, of course there's a letter in there, but since it's gone, the First Sergeant can't check to see that I'd put a letter in the mail drop the night Tet started. And, I had a letter on board that plane that went down a couple of weeks ago. To say nothing about the fact we've been kind of busy lately. I mean, she must think I have nothing to do but write her letters. Anyway, my letter must be laying out there in the jungle rotting, courtesy of the US Air Force. So you'll never guess what I get to do now, Mac. I get to sit down each and every night and write my dear sweet mother a letter. For two full weeks, it doesn't make any difference how late we land, how bad a day I've had, or if I even have anything to write about. Then I have to put it, unsealed, in Gillett's hand each night, who then has to put it on the First Jerk's desk the next morning, who will not read my letter, but check to make sure I wrote a full page worth, before sealing it and mailing it. So I wrote her a real nice letter telling her what she did, and how much trouble she got me into, and that she'll get her fourteen letters and not another single one for the rest of my nine months over here."

The two men just looked each other in the eye before Jim said, "Rick, don't punish your mother for loving you. When she gets your letter she'll realize she made a mistake and did a stupid thing, but she still loves you and that's why she did it. Besides, if you think about it, it's probably easier for us over here than it is for them at home. They know we're in an all combat assault company and where we're stationed. They watch the six o'clock news every night and know we're right in the middle of the biggest battle of this war. My man, we're right smack in the middle of this thing and they know it. This is just like the Battle of the Bulge in WWII with better news coverage. As a result, those letters are the only thing that they can touch and hold and say 'Hey, at least I know he was still alive and okay when he wrote this letter, dated whenever.'

"Besides, what happened to you that was so terrible? You got a good chewing by Top, and right now you're a little embarrassed. Big deal! That doesn't give you the right to punish her like that, just because she loves her son, does it?"

Somewhat dejected Rick replied, "No." There was a pause before he continued, "Mac, how'd you get so damn smart so young and only a Spec-Five?"

"Hey, when I get home I'm going to college to get my book learning, because I've already had my education."

Epilogue

Many call the Tet Offensive of 1968 America's biggest defeat of the Vietnam War. In fact, it was America's greatest victory of the war. If the North Vietnamese could have held their offensive for another two or three days they would have kicked us out, just like they did the French. The North's only hope was that American forces would run out of fuel. That, in fact, happened and for two days the only JP-4 fuel available in the III Corp area was at Saigon and Vung Tau.

Yet American Forces survived because it truly was an Air Mobile Army. We lived and died by the helicopter. Because of that we were able to pull troops that were in the bush back to base camps and regroup. Army and Air Force units brought in fuel bladders* and we struck back with the finest Army ever assembled on the face of the earth. When Tet was over we had won, the war was over. All that remained was to go in and finish it. What came very close to being America's final defeat turned out to be her greatest victory of the war. There was only one problem. Anti-war activists at home, both in and out of Congress, had forced President Johnson to decide we would fight to lose. One needs to understand that by definition a country either fights to win a war, or it loses. So Jim MacLaughlin, like the thousands who would follow him, would continue to fight the war to lose.

Jim was eligible to quit flying May 5, 1968, but by his own request continued past that date. After Tet, there wasn't that much activity so he didn't feel too concerned about it. The only thing that bothered him was that there were no more VC. When contact was made it was always against NVA who were better trained and better armed. The Viet Cong had all been killed during Tet. On May 14th, Jim flew his

---

*Fuel bladder - A rubber, collapsible fuel drum that held between 2,000 and 50,000 gallons.

last mission. Mr. Walker and Wright had threatened to break his arm that night if he didn't tell Gillett that was the last one. He left Tay Ninh for the last time along with several others on the 17th. He spent that night at Cu Chi jumping in and out of a bunker, as Cu Chi was under mortar and rocket attack all night.

On May 20, 1968, after countless inspections for contraban, Jim stepped on board the TWA freedom bird that would take him home. He saw several of the guys he'd come over with and wondered if he looked as much older to them as they did to him. His last memory of Viet Nam is of waiting on the concrete under a tent to board the plane home and watching the big round thermometer slowly climb as the hours passed. He walked by it as he stood in line to board, one hundred nineteen degrees in the shade.

The first stop was Guam, then Alaska. It was in Alaska the pilot came over the speaker just after touchdown and said, "Gentlemen, we just touched down in Alaska, I want to congratulate you on your completion of a tour in Viet Nam and I want to be the first to say, WELCOME HOME! You're in America now!"

A great cheer went up and the stewardess laughed and applauded and then cried.

Their next stop was McGuire Air Force Base, Maryland. Fifty-two hours after his last look at the thermometer in Viet Nam, Jim kissed his mother and father "hello" and gave his sister a hug.

As he walked in the back door of their home, he turned and looked at the land around him and said to his father, who was the only one in hearing distance, "You know, there was more than once I thought I'd never live to see this place again." They both wiped away their tears and entered the house.

He had thirty days leave during which he went to parties, worked the farm, had several dates, and did a lot of sleeping. It wasn't until sometime later that he realized his introduction to women during R & R was an unrealistic and a bad experience and certainly one he'd have been better off without.

After thirty days leave Jim reported to Fort Rucker, Alabama, to spend the remaining fourteen months time in service. During that time he was trained to teach school. It was during this training he received the first of four sets of orders which would have sent him back to Viet Nam. Jim got out of that first set of orders because he was still in Army schooling. It was then he made up his mind he would not go back. He would not desert, but they'd have to put him in chains and carry him onto the plane. He figured Christ had kept him alive during one tour and Jim wasn't about to put Him to the test twice. Jim also knew that if he'd been back only sixty days and received one set or orders it wouldn't be his last. Yet deep inside he never doubted that Jesus would not allow him to be sent back. His parents wrote their congressmen and senators. They received very nice letters in response saying basically how sorry they were, but Jim had a critical job that was in high demand, and there was nothing they could do to prevent his return.

Jim's second set of orders sending him back came down about sixty days later. His CO brought them to him one day at work (he was teaching aircraft engines) and said, "'Mac, I've got a set of orders here sending you back to Viet Nam. You want to go?"

"No, Sir, I do not!"

"Are you happy here? What I'm thinking is if you'd like to stay here and teach, I'll try to get you out of 'em."

"Thank you, Captain, I'd really appreciate it if you would. I don't want to go back! Besides, I do like it here, this is a wonderful place!"

The Captain laughed and said, "You don't have to be quite so sarcastic. Mac, understand two things. One, I'm going to try. Because you put out one hundred percent, you're very good at your job and have never given me any trouble. Two, I don't know if I can do it, but I play golf once a week with the major in charge of personnel and he owes me a couple. So let me hang on to these orders for a few days and we'll see."

"Thank you, Sir, I really do appreciate it."

The third set of orders came down while Jim was TDY (temporary duty) at Edgewood Arsenal. Military regulations prevent a person from receiving orders for a new duty station while on TDY. The final set of orders came down and he had a new CO who wouldn't help him out. So he figured he might as well spend the time processing out, thus giving Christ the time to once again work a miracle. When he reported to personnel, there was a room full of people who were starting to fill out the paperwork. The NCO running things asked if there was anyone in the group with less than ninety days left in service, Jim's hand went up.

"When is your ETS date, Sergeant?"

"One September '69, Sergeant."

"You're right, you've got eighty-nine days left. You can go back to work, unless you want to go back to Nam. If you do, I can get you a waiver to sign, otherwise, we can't send you back unless you have ninety days or more left."

Jim stood and walked toward the NCO, dropped the orders on his desk and said, "I don't!"

While teaching at Fort Rucker, Jim came in on break between classes one day and found one of the men (the last of three) represented by Mr. Walker waiting for him. That night they went for a drink and talked over old times and people.

The character Mr. Walker, in this book was in reality three different permanent pilots and several temporary AC's. The first of the three was shot in the shoulder, operated on in Nam, and had a good start toward recovery when put on a hospital aircraft for home. The second one developed a personality conflict with Jim after they had flown together for several months. Finally, Jim refused to fly with him again. About a month before Jim rotated home, he flew a single ship night mission where the second Mr. Walker was the AC. The only reason he'd flown it after recognizing the AC, was as a personal favor to the platoon officer. He has always been glad he did. The mission was dangerous and required a high level of skill by both AC and crew chief. Everything went smoothly because Mr. Walker number two was good, very good, in fact the best. After they landed back at Tay Ninh and Jim was left alone on the mike with Mr. Walker, Jim said, "Sir, I just want you to know there is no one I would rather have had in the left seat tonight than you."

"Mac, I've been trying for the last half hour to think of a way to tell you there isn't anyone I'd rather have had in the back seat than you. And I'm not just saying that because you did."

"I know, Sir."

"You know I'm sorry we had to go our own ways. It was really great being a team again, and Mac, I wish you the best and hope you make it back okay."

"Thank you, Sir. That means a lot to me and I wish you the best, and I truly do hope you make it back also. You know, if I didn't already have an AC I'd ask for you back."

"I'd accept, if I didn't already have a ship and crew chief."

It was the third Mr. Walker who told Jim the second one had made it okay, and that Mr. Halsey was still playing his stupid games and had less respect from the men than when Jim had left. Mr. Lucas had become one of the best pilots in the company and had been made platoon maintenance officer. As a result, he'd become the EM's best friend in the company and was always trying to help them out in any way he could, even going to bat for some of them when they'd gotten into trouble. Needless to say, he'd become one of the nicest and best liked officers in the company.

Schott, Wright, Green and Meyers were all okay and Meyers was due to join them at Rucker in a couple weeks. Athia, Gillett and Kenny all made it home. Mr. Euclid had been shot in the butt, and got a free ride home out of it. Hunter was killed in action.

It was at Fort Rucker the nightmares started for Jim and would last off and on for the next nine years.